Digital Currencies and the Green Economy

Ranjan Aneja · Robert Dygas
Editors

Digital Currencies and the Green Economy

Opportunities and Challenges in Achieving Sustainable Development Goals (SDGs)

palgrave
macmillan

Editors
Ranjan Aneja
Department of Economics
Central University of Haryana
Mahendragarh, Haryana, India

Robert Dygas
East Asian Economic Studies
SGH Warsaw School of Economics
Warsaw, Poland

ISBN 978-981-95-2281-1 ISBN 978-981-95-2282-8 (eBook)
https://doi.org/10.1007/978-981-95-2282-8

This Palgrave Macmillan imprint is published by the registered company Springer Nature Singapore Pte Ltd.
The registered company address is: 152 Beach Road, #21-01/04 Gateway East, Singapore 189721, Singapore

Preface

In an era defined by rapid technological advancements and an increasingly interconnected global economy, digital currencies have emerged as a transformative force with the potential to redefine the foundations of achieving Sustainable Development Goals (SDGs). This book gives a broad spectrum of the problem raised by the authors especially from India, Poland, Uzbekistan, and Iceland. It is a joint effort of Indian, Polish, and Icelandic academic scientists to make this book up-to-date with the problem analysis. **The main research question of the book is how digital currencies impact the development of the Green Economy**. There are also other questions which relate to the main challenges and opportunities. The book consists of 19 chapters. Chapter 1 analyses the technological innovations that support sustained long-term economic growth. The chapter reviews the literature on the effects of CBDC on economic growth and inflation, and based on its impact on economic growth, assesses its potential contribution to achieving the SDGs. Chapter 2 highlights the approaches potential to accelerate progress in sustainability-related aspects by integrating with the SDGs and Agenda 2030 of the United Nations. It was achieved through the analysis of the worldwide adoption of cutting-edge carbon offsetting and emission reduction strategies using reports from ongoing projects and practical applications. Chapter 3 identified the questions of how Central Bank Digital Currencies (CBDCs) can help achieve social justice, equalize wealth, and promote economic development in Indian society. Chapter 4 examines the role of digital currency and blockchain in affecting the financial stability. It gives particular emphasis to an industry-based investigation and opportunities given by digital currencies towards financial stability. Chapter 5 highlighted the expected reach of the Digital Currency (DC) as compared to the population of the country along with its positive and negative effects on the environment as well as costs and management. There have also been case studies of countries doing CBDCs covered in the chapter. This study has focused on the significance of DC and its impact on environment with respect to India, The Bahamas The Bahamas, Jamaica Jamaica, and Nigeria Nigeria. Chapter 6 explores a unique opportunity of CBDCs offer to align with long-term viability goals and support the Green Economy. CBDCs can contribute to sustainable development goals (SDGs) by fostering low-carbon financial infrastructure and leveraging energy-efficient blockchain technologies. This chapter gives the examples of the Scandinavian countries. Chapter 7 focuses on the fundamental relationship between monetary policy and environmental protection. It analyses potential environmental impacts in the economy from an economic perspective, as well as the obstacles and conflicts that arise in this context, with a view to the German economy and the international context and a special focus on digital innovations. Chapter 8 develops the crucial significance of community involvement and stakeholder cooperation in attaining sustainable development objectives. This chapter argues for a comprehensive strategy that utilizes community expertise and establishes collaborations, guaranteeing that sustainable development projects are efficient and fair. Chapter 9 looks at how new types of money, like cryptocurrencies and digital currencies from central banks, affect economic growth and fit with global goals for a better world by 2030. The main objective is to understand both the positive impacts and the difficulties these digital currencies bring to achieving important global goal, such as reducing poverty, promoting financial fairness, and supporting a healthier planet. Chapter 10 provides in-depth review of the environmental impacts of Proof-of-Work (PoW) mining in the cryptocurrency sector. By integrating data from both traditional databases, it highlights the substantial energy consumption and carbon emissions linked to Bitcoin Bitcoin mining. Chapter 11 analyses the potential for achieving sustainable development goals and an analysis of examples of projects that realize Green Economy potential in reality. Chapter 12 examines the transition to a Green Economy in Poland indicating numerous challenges, and the adoption of digital currencies adds complexity to this process. Chapter 13 seeks to contribute to the scholarship over the comparative analysis of global practices dealing with the digital currencies' induction within their monetary system and its interplay with models of sustainability, essentially the green economy, doughnut economy, and circular economy. For this, it would entail case studies from Asia and Europe over the efficiency of the said models. Chapter 14 presents a green finance development index (GFDi) that could assist policymakers and investors in making more informed decisions regarding the advancement of green finance. South Asia South Asia should prioritize the implementation of the green shift strategy to attain sustainable economic growth. The present study created a summary index of green financial development for 8 emerging South Asian countries namely Afghanistan, Bangladesh, Bhutan Bhutan, India, Nepal, Maldives, Pakistan, and Sri Lanka. This study has utilized panel annual data for a time frame of 20 years from 2002 to 2022. Chapter 15 made an attempt to dissertate on the social and economic implications associated with the practical application of the digital currencies in solving the real-world problems while achieving the goal towards a Doughnut Economy. Simultaneously, the decentralized nature of cryptocurrencies, exemplified by the pioneering Bitcoin and the multitude of alternative coins, has garnered considerable attention in the Green Economy. In this exploration of the impact of digital currencies on Green Economy, it is crucial to examine the multifaceted aspects of this technological shift. Beyond the financial benefits, the integration of digital currencies necessitates a comprehensive understanding of regulatory frameworks, cybersecurity considerations, and the potential social and economic ramifications. As the world moves towards a more digitized and interconnected future, stakeholders, including governments, financial institutions, businesses, and consumers, must navigate the evolving landscape of digital currencies to harness their benefits while addressing challenges and ensuring the stability of the international financial system. This comprehensive analysis aims to provide insights into the intricate dynamics that shape the future of Green Economy in the digital age. Chapter 16 explores the Urban air mobility (UAM) services provided by electric-powered aerial vehicles which will lead to a reduction in energy consumption and carbon emissions in the urban transport sector. Urban air transport based on autonomous aerial vehicles will increase the capacity of the coordinated passenger transport network, replacing ground-based single-passenger travel with air travel with shared seating. UAM services, based on advanced electric-powered aircrafts, are part of the trend towards a Green Economy. This paper discusses the legal aspects related to the use of UAM services. In this context, the reasons for the development of UAM services are analysed. Furthermore, this chapter discusses the various definitions of the term "Urban Air Mobility" as well as the definitions of aircraft suitable for the provision of UAM services. Furthermore, this paper analyses the development of the regulatory framework for UAM services in Europe, in particular the new regulatory package 2024. This chapter also discusses the legal aspects of the possible replacement of a human pilot by an artificial agent, as well as the privacy issues related to the provision of UAM services. Chapter 17 analyses the nexus between sustainable economic growth and digital currencies, particularly looking at the current adoption of these in economic frameworks is underlined while exploring emerging trends such as Decentralized Finance (DeFi). Chapter 18 answers the question how sustainable practices and technological advancements can reduce the carbon footprint associated with these systems. Through case studies from various countries, the chapter highlights how governmental and institutional actions can accelerate the adoption of eco-friendly practices in the financial sector. The analysis has shown that green digital payment digital payment is thus important to contribute to economic development, particularly in developing economies, where such an innovation may lead to both financial inclusion and environmental sustainability. This chapter concludes by calling for a multi-stakeholder approach wherein governments, financial institutions, technology providers, and consumers work in concert to ensure that digital payments help create a low-carbon future. In this way, by promoting green innovation, the financial sector can reduce its carbon footprint and contribute to broader sustainable development goals. Chapter 19 examines the multifaceted environmental impacts of cryptocurrency mining, especially Bitcoin, focusing on its energy consumption, greenhouse gas emissions, water and land footprints, e-waste generation, and impacts on local communities. Initially, we contextualize the blockchain fundamentals and consensus mechanisms of currency mining detailing how mining operates through computational puzzles and decentralization validation. Further, we analysed the staggering energy demand of proof of work mechanisms including its carbon intensity and greenhouse gas emissions of Bitcoin. Drawing on the empirical data, the study highlights how Bitcoin mining contributes to the rising carbon, land, and water footprints across the globe. Additionally, the chapter explores the growing problem of e-waste generated from obsolete hardware. Finally, the study discussed how digital currency mining has serious impacts on quality-of-life impacts of local communities. By synthesizing the impacts, this chapter advocates for the urgent sustainable alternatives to mitigate the ecological harm of cryptocurrency mining while balancing technological innovation.

Simultaneously, the decentralized nature of cryptocurrencies, exemplified by the pioneering BitcoinBitcoin and the multitude of alternative coins, has garnered considerable attention in the Green Economy. In this exploration of the impact of digital currencies on Green Economy, it is crucial to examine the multifaceted aspects of this technological shift. Beyond the financial benefits, the integration of digital currencies necessitates a comprehensive understanding of regulatory frameworks, cybersecurity considerations, and the potential social and economic ramifications. As the world moves towards a more digitized and interconnected future, stakeholders, including governments, financial institutions, businesses, and consumers, must navigate the evolving landscape of digital currencies to harness their benefits while addressing challenges and ensuring the stability of the international financial system. This comprehensive analysis aims to provide insights into the intricate dynamics that shape the future of Green Economy in the digital age. We hope that this book will help professionals and academic researchers to better understand digital currencies in the aspects of environmental protections and green concepts.

Mahendragarh, India
Warsaw, Poland

Ranjan Aneja
Robert Dygas

Contents

Editors and Contributors

About the Editors

Prof. Ranjan Aneja is a distinguished economist currently serving as a professor in the Department of Economics and Dean of the School of Business Management Studies at the Central University of Haryana, India. With over 20 years of teaching and research experience, he specializes in areas such as economic modelling & analysis, and energy economics. He earned his Ph.D. from Guru Jambheshwar University of Science and Technology and his master's degree from Kurukshetra University, India. Prof. Aneja has made significant contributions to the field of economics, publishing numerous research papers in reputed journals indexed in Scopus, Web of Science, ABDC, and SSCI. His work often explores the intersections of economic growth, inequality, and sustainable development, particularly within the Indian context. He has edited notable books, including "Digital Currencies and the New Global Financial System," published by

Routledge, which focuses on Central Bank Digital Currencies and their global financial implications. Another of his works, "Digital Currencies in the New Global World Order," published by Palgrave Macmillan, examines the transformative roles of digital currencies in trade and finance, with a focus on economies such as India, China, and the U.S. Prof. Aneja also served/serving on the editorial board of several journals such as the Journal of Public Affairs, Wiley, SN Business and Economics, Springer-Nature, Social Sciences & Humanities Open, Elsevier, Cognet Economics and Finance, Taylor and Francis, etc. Beyond academia, he has been involved in applied research projects, including studies on the socioeconomic impacts of government policies such as the Pradhan Mantri Mudra Yojana and the Parivartan Scheme in Haryana. He has presented his research at over 60 national and international conferences and is widely recognized for his expertise in economic strategies for regional and national development.

Robert Dygas, Ph.D., is an assistant professor at SGH Warsaw School of Economics at the East Asian Economic Studies Department of the World Economy Research Institute. He completed his master's studies at the Warsaw School of Economics majoring in Finance and Banking and at the University of Aarhus in Denmark majoring in Management. He received his Ph.D. in Economics from the Warsaw School of Economics in 2003 (dissertation: "Strategic Management in the Mobile Telephony Industry in Poland in 1995–2001"). In 2011 he was awarded the Executive Master of Business Administration degree by the Warsaw University of Technology Business School. He has 23 years of professional experience in multinational corporations in IT telecommunications and the public sector. From 2015 to 2020 he worked also as the external expert for the evaluation of Horizon2020-ECI-FTI proposals (Research Executive Agency EASME under the power delegated by the European Commission).

Academic interests: geo-economics, economies of Asian countries.

Contributors

Ranjan Aneja Department of Economics, Central University of Haryana, Mahendergarh, India

Ananya Bhardwaj Department of Economics, Manipal University Jaipur, Jaipur, India

Sanjay Bhayana Food Business Management and Entrepreneurship Development, National Institute of Food Technology Entrepreneurship and Management, Kundli, Haryana, India

Andreas Bielig SGH Warsaw School of Economics, Department of German Economy Research, World Economy Research Institute, Warsaw, Poland

Suman Dahiya Department of Commerce, Central University of Haryana, Mahendergarh, Haryana, India

Narendra N. Dalei Department of Economic Studies, Central University of Punjab, Bathinda, India

Satyanarayana Murthy Dogga Department of Economics, Central University of Rajasthan, Ajmer, India

Robert Dygas SGH Warsaw School of Economics, Warsaw, Poland

Naived George Eapen Department of Computer Science, Christ University, Bengaluru, India

Mohit Fogaat Department of Commerce, Central University of Haryana, Mahendragarh, India

Pushp Gautam National Institute of Food Technology Entrepreneurship and Management, Kundli, Haryana, India

Rajender S. Godara Department of Economics, Mittal School of Business, Lovely Professional University, Phagwara, India

Stefan Bjarni Gunnlaugsson Faculty of Business Administration, University of Akureyri, Akureyri, Iceland

Jaishree Department of Economics, Central University of Rajasthan, Ajmer, India

Shine Raju Kappil School of Business and Management, Christ University, Bengaluru, India

Ravinder Kaur Department of Commerce, Central University of Haryana, Mahendergarh, India

Marta Kotlarska Revolut Ltd, Kraków, Poland

Andrzej Krasuski Academic Department of Social Sciences, European Humanities University, Vilnius, Lithuania

Helga Kristjansdottir Faculty of Business Administration, University of Akureyri, Akureyri, Iceland

Ashok Kumar Chauhan Department of Economics, Kurukshetra University, Kurukshetra, India

Pankaj Kumar Department of Economics, Pondicherry University, Puducherry, India

Sunil Kumar Department of Economics, Mittal School of Business, Lovely Professional University, Phagwara, India

Vinay Kumar Department of Economics, Kurukshetra University, Kurukshetra, India

Madan Lal Department of Commerce, Delhi School of Economics, University of Delhi, Delhi, India

Suzanee Malhotra Department of Commerce, Maitreyi College, University of Delhi, Delhi, India

Rajendra Prasad Meena Department of Commerce, Central University of Haryana, Mahendragarh, India

Suyash Mishra Retail and Logistics Management, Department of Vocational Studies and Skill Development, Central University of Haryana, Mahendergarh, India

Gabriel A. Ogunmola Department of Economic Theory, Tashkent State University of Economics, Tashkent, Uzbekistan

Yash Pal Department of Economics, Central University of Himachal Pradesh, Kangra, India

Jesty Mariam Philip School of Business and Management, Christ University, Bengaluru, India

Manas Roy Department of Economics, Faculty of Management Studies, Marwadi University Rajkot, Rajkot, India

Amisha Sherawat Department of Economics, Central University of Haryana, Mahendergarh, India

Kjartan Sigurdsson Faculty of Business Administration, University of Akureyri, Akureyri, Iceland

Arun Kumar Singh Department of Law, North-Eastern Hill University, Shillong, India

Bhushan Singh Department of Commerce, Central University of Haryana, Mahendergarh, Haryana, India

Grzegorz Sobiecki Department of Financial System, SGH Warsaw School of Economics, Warsaw, Poland

Sushila Kumari Soriya Department of Commerce, Central University of Haryana, Mahendergarh, Haryana, India

Wagisha Department of Law, North-Eastern Hill University, Shillong, India

List of Figures

List of Tables

CHAPTER 1

Central Bank Digital Currency: Implications for Economic Growth, Inflation, and the Path to SDG Achievement

Vinay Kumar and Ashok Kumar Chauhan

1.1 Introduction

The Central Bank Digital Currency (CBDC) functions as a digital counterpart to the traditional paper currency issued by a nation's central bank, representing a direct liability of the issuing monetary authority. The interest in Central Bank Digital Currencies (CBDCs) has significantly increased in recent years, with 134 countries actively exploring their potential implementation. A few nations, such as The Bahamas, Nigeria, and Jamaica, have successfully launched their CBDCs, integrating them into their financial ecosystems. Additionally, over 30 countries, including India, are currently engaged in pilot programs to assess feasibility and impact. However, some nations, including Denmark and Ecuador, have opted against CBDC adoption due to concerns regarding financial stability and security (Di Maggio et al., 2024).

V. Kumar (✉) · A. Kumar Chauhan
Department of Economics, Kurukshetra University, Kurukshetra, India

R. Aneja and R. Dygas (eds.), *Digital Currencies and the Green Economy*, https://doi.org/10.1007/978-981-95-2282-8_1

The digitalization of money carries significant implications for economic systems, influencing both efficiency and macroeconomic stability. Economic growth and inflation are fundamental macroeconomic indicators that shape the stability of an economy. Central banks employ monetary policy as a primary tool to regulate these variables, ensuring economic equilibrium. The introduction of CBDCs presents a novel mechanism for managing these indicators, potentially enhancing economic growth and stabilizing inflation. Notably, a fully centralized monetary system operating with 100% CBDC issuance could improve price stability and facilitate more effective allocation of funds towards productive investments, thereby fostering long-term economic resilience (van Egmond & de Vries 2024).

Technological innovation plays a crucial role in driving sustained economic growth in developed economies (Verspagen, 2006). As a form of technological innovation, Central Bank Digital Currency (CBDC) has the potential to influence economic growth and overall macroeconomic stability. Given this significance, it is essential to assess the impact of CBDC adoption on these economic factors.

Nigeria introduced its CBDC in October 2021, marking a significant step in digital financial transformation. Ozili (2024) found that the introduction of CBDC had a positive effect on economic growth while simultaneously contributing to increased inflation. The study observed a rise in both economic growth and inflation following the launch of CBDC in Nigeria. Similarly, Hermawan et al. (2024) examined the influence of CBDC on money velocity and inflation, concluding that its integration within a broader monetary policy framework can contribute to inflation stabilization.

The Sustainable Development Goals (SDGs), introduced in 2015, aim to be achieved by 2030 and consist of 17 goals. Among them, SDG 8, which focuses on economic growth and productive employment, is particularly relevant to CBDC implementation. SDG 8 comprises 10 targets, including Target 8.1, which emphasizes sustained economic growth, and Target 8.2, which highlights the importance of higher economic productivity and innovation. If CBDC contributes to enhanced economic growth, it can serve as a valuable instrument in advancing the achievement of SDG 8.

This chapter presents a review of the existing literature examining the impact of Central Bank Digital Currency (CBDC) on economic growth and inflation, as well as its potential role in advancing the Sustainable

Development Goals (SDGs). The discussion will explore how CBDC influences macroeconomic indicators, particularly economic expansion and price stability, and assess its contribution to achieving SDG 8, which emphasizes sustained economic growth, higher productivity, and innovation.

1.2 Conceptual Background

1.2.1 Origin of CBDC

Bitcoin, introduced in 2009, was the first digital currency, paving the way for the emergence of numerous private cryptocurrencies based on blockchain technology. Unlike government-backed currencies, these cryptocurrencies operate as private digital assets without official regulatory approval.

In 2017, the Swedish central bank introduced its digital currency to reduce the reliance on cash transactions, aiming to address the declining use of physical currency. Subsequently, in 2020, The Bahamas launched the "Sand Dollar," marking the introduction of a state-backed digital currency designed to enhance financial stability, promote a secure digital payment system, and modernize the financial infrastructure.

Additionally, Ecuador conducted an experiment with CBDC from 2014 to 2018; however, the initiative was eventually discontinued due to various economic and structural challenges.

Figure 1.1 illustrates that over 90 countries are currently engaged in CBDC research. However, only three countries have fully implemented a CBDC, while more than 20 nations are conducting pilot projects. This highlights the growing global interest in Central Bank Digital Currencies (CBDCs), as an increasing number of countries explore their potential.

Figure 1.2 presents a global map illustrating the various stages of Central Bank Digital Currency (CBDC) adoption across different countries. It categorizes nations based on their progress, indicating those that are currently in the research phase, conducting pilot programs, have officially launched a CBDC, or have discontinued their initiatives. This visual representation provides a comprehensive overview of the global landscape of CBDC development.

Table 1.1 provides a detailed list of countries at various stages of Central Bank Digital Currency (CBDC) adoption. It includes the name of each country, its respective central bank, and the year of adoption.

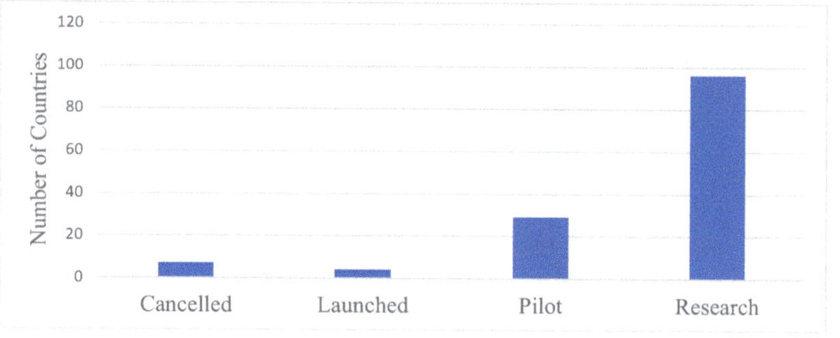

Fig. 1.1 CBDC Status Around the World. *Source* https://cbdctracker.org

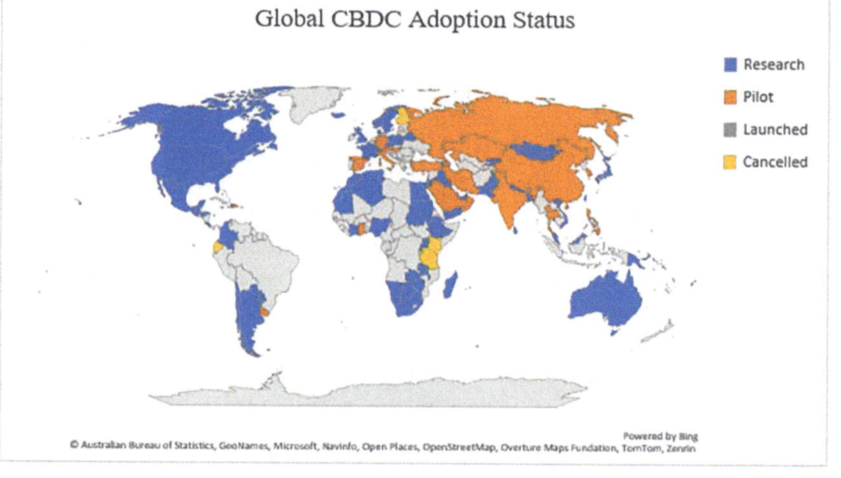

Fig. 1.2 Current Global Scenario of Central Bank Digital Currency. *Source* Author's Own

The final column outlines the current status of CBDC development, categorizing it as being in the research phase, undergoing pilot testing, officially launched, or discontinued. This table serves as a structured reference for understanding the global progression of CBDC implementation. According to the table, Finland was the first country to introduce and later discontinue its digital currency, "*Avant*," in 1992.

Table 1.1 Central Bank Digital Currency (CBDC) Status Around the World

Country/Region	*Central Bank*	*Digital Currency*	*Announcement Year*	*Status*
Ethiopia	National bank of Ethiopia	Ethiopia CBDC	2024	Research
Germany	Deutsche Bundesbank	Trigger solution	2024	Pilot
Italy	Banca D'Italia	TIPS hash-link	2024	Pilot
Papua New Guinea	Central Bank of Papua new Guinea	Papua New Guinea CBDC	2024	Research
Kyrgyzstan	National bank of the Kyrgyz Republic	Digital Som	2024	Research
Malawi	Reserve bank of Malawi	Malawi CBDC	2024	Research
Aruba	Central Bank van Aruba	Digital florin	2024	Research
Hong Kong	Hong Kong monetary authority	Cross-border projects	2024	Research
Montenegro	Central Bank of Montenegro	Montenegro CBDC	2023	Research
United States of America	US Federal Reserve	Wholesale digital Dollar	2023	Research
Mauritius	The Bank of Mauritius	Mauritius CBDC	2023	Research
Israel	Bank of Israel	Sela	2023	Research
Maldives	Maldives monetary authority	Maldives CBDC	2023	Research
Armenia	Central Bank of Armenia	Armenia CBDC	2023	Research
Belarus	Central Bank of Belarus	Digital Ruble	2023	Research
Mauritania	Central Bank of Mauritania	Mauritania CBDC	2023	Research
Colombia	Banco de la República	Colombia CBDC	2023	Research
Jamaica	Bank of Jamaica	JAM-DEX	2023	Launched
South Korea	Bank of Korea	South Korea wholesale	2023	Pilot
Solomon Islands	Central Bank of Solomon Islands	Solomon Islands CBDC	2022	Research

(continued)

Table 1.1 (continued)

Country/Region	*Central Bank*	*Digital Currency*	*Announcement Year*	*Status*
Jordan	Central Bank of Jordan	Jordan CBDC	2022	Research
Denmark	Nationalbanken	Denmark CBDC	2022	Research
Iraq	Central Bank of Iraq	Iraq CBDC	2022	Research
Qatar	Qatar central bank	Qatar CBDC	2022	Research
Uganda	Bank of Uganda	Uganda CBDC	2022	Research
Yemen	Central Bank of Yemen	Yemen CBDC	2022	Research
Zambia	The Bank of Zambia (BoZ)	Zambia CBDC	2022	Research
Malaysia	Bank negara Malaysia	Malaysia CBDC	2022	Research
Sudan	Central Bank of Sudan	Sudan CBDC	2022	Research
Botswana	Bank of Botswana	Botswana CBDC	2022	Research
Fiji	Reserve bank of Fiji	Fiji CBDC	2022	Research
Bangladesh	Bangladesh bank	Bangladesh CBDC	2022	Research
Central Africa (EMCCA)	Banque des états de l'Afrique Centrale	EMCCA CBDC	2022	Research
Cote d'Ivoire	Cote d'Ivoire	Cote d'Ivoire CBDC	2022	Research
Israel	Bank of Israel	Project icebreaker (Israel)	2022	Research
Nepal	The Nepal Rastra Bank	Nepal CBDC	2022	Research
Norway	Norges Bank	Project icebreaker (Norway)	2022	Research
Sweden	Sveriges Riksbank	Project icebreaker (Sweden)	2022	Research
Oman	Central Bank of Oman	Oman CBDC	2022	Pilot
Singapore	Monetary Authority of Singapore	Project Ubin+	2022	Research
Mongolia	Bank of Mongolia	Mongolia CBDC	2022	Research
Algeria	Banque d'Algérie	Algerian digital dinar	2022	Research

(continued)

Table 1.1 (continued)

Country/Region	*Central Bank*	*Digital Currency*	*Announcement Year*	*Status*
Singapore	Monetary Authority of Singapore	Project cedar phase I	2022	Research
France	Banque de France	Project Mariana (France)	2022	Research
Hong Kong	Hong Kong monetary authority	Sela (Hong Kong)	2022	Research
Singapore	Monetary Authority of Singapore	Project Mariana (Singapore)	2022	Research
Switzerland	Swiss national bank	Project Mariana (Switzerland)	2022	Research
Argentina	Banco central de la República Argentina	Digital peso	2022	Research
Sri Lanka	Central Bank of Sri Lanka	Sri Lanka CBDC	2022	Research
Hong Kong	Hong Kong monetary authority	Project Aurum	2022	Pilot
Spain	Banco de España	Spanish wholesale CBDC	2022	Pilot
France	Banque de France	Project Venus (France)	2022	Research
Luxembourg	Banque Centrale du Luxembourg	Project Venus (Luxembourg)	2022	Research
Azerbaijan	Central Bank of Azerbaijan	Azerbaijan CBDC	2022	Pilot
Dominican Republic	Banco central de la República Dominicana	Dominican Republic CBDC	2022	Pilot
Euro area	European Central Bank	Wholesale digital euro	2022	Pilot
China	People's Bank of China	mBridge (China)	2022	Pilot
Hong Kong	Hong Kong monetary authority	mBridge (Hong Kong)	2022	Pilot

(continued)

Table 1.1 (continued)

Country/Region	*Central Bank*	*Digital Currency*	*Announcement Year*	*Status*
Saudi Arabia	Saudi Arabian monetary authority	mBridge (Saudi Arabia)	2022	Pilot
Thailand	Bank of Thailand	mBridge (Thailand)	2022	Pilot
United Arab Emirates	United Arab Emirates central Bank	mBridge (UAE)	2022	Research
Czech Republic	Czech national bank	Czech Republic CBDC	2021	Research
Morocco	Bank-Al-maghrib	Morocco CBDC	2021	Research
Macau	Macau government	Macau CBDC	2021	Research
Austria	Oesterreichische Nationalbank	DELPHI	2021	Pilot
France	Banque de France	Project Prosperus (France)	2021	Research
Tonga	National reserve bank of Tonga (NRBT)	Tonga CBDC	2021	Pilot
Tunisia	Central Bank of Tunisia	Project Prosperus (Tunisia)	2021	Research
Vanuatu	Reserve bank of Vanuatu	Vanuatu CBDC	2021	Research
Costa Rica	Banco central de Costa Rica	Costa Rica CBDC	2021	Research
Madagascar	Banky Foiben'i Madagasikara	e-ariary	2021	Research
Guatemala	Bank of Guatemala	iQuetzal	2021	Research
France	Banque de France	Jura (France)	2021	Research
Paraguay	Central Bank of Paraguay	Paraguay CBDC	2021	Research
Switzerland	Swiss national bank	Jura (Switzerland)	2021	Cancelled
Singapore	Monetary Authority of Singapore	Project orchid	2021	Research
Trinidad and Tobago	Central Bank of Trinidad and Tobago	Trinidad and Tobago CBDC	2021	Research

(continued)

Table 1.1 (continued)

Country/Region	*Central Bank*	*Digital Currency*	*Announcement Year*	*Status*
Zimbabwe	Reserve bank of Zimbabwe	Zimbabwe CBDC	2021	Research
Namibia	Bank of Namibia	Namibia CBDC	2021	Research
Mexico	Bank of Mexico (Banxico)	Moneda digital del banco de Mexico	2021	Research
Tanzania	Bank of Tanzania	Tanzania CBDC	2021	Cancelled
Philippines	The Bangko Sentral ng Pilipinas	Philippines CBDC	2021	Pilot
France	Banque de France	French wholesale CBDC	2021	Launched
Nigeria	Central Bank of Nigeria	e-naira	2021	Research
Honduras	Central Bank of Honduras	Honduras CBDC	2021	Research
Bhutan	Royal monetary authority	Digital ngultrum	2020	Launched
Haiti	La Banque de la Republique D'haiti	Gourde Digitale	2020	Research
Hungary	Central Bank of Hungary (MNB)	Hungary CBDC	2020	Pilot
South Korea	Bank of Korea	Digital won	2020	Pilot
Taiwan	The central Bank of Taiwan	Taiwan CBDC	2020	Research
Switzerland	Swiss national bank	Helvetia	2020	Pilot
India	RBI	Digital rupee	2020	Pilot
United States of America	US Federal Reserve	Digital Dollar	2020	Research
Australia	Reserve bank of Australia	eAUD (retail)	2020	Research
Australia	Reserve bank of Australia	Acaia	2020	Research
Kazakhstan	National bank of Kazakhstan	Digital tenge	2020	Pilot
Hong Kong	Hong Kong monetary authority	LionRock	2019	Research
Tunisia	Central Bank of Tunisia	e-dinar	2019	Research

(continued)

Table 1.1 (continued)

Country/Region	*Central Bank*	*Digital Currency*	*Announcement Year*	*Status*
Switzerland	Swiss national bank	e-franc	2019	Research
Saudi Arabia	Saudi Arabian monetary authority	Aber (Saudi Arabia)	2019	Pilot
United Arab Emirates	United Arab Emirates central Bank	Aber (UAE)	2019	Pilot
Saudi Arabia	Saudi Arabian monetary authority	Saudi Arabia retail CBDC	2019	Research
South Africa	South African reserve Bank	Khokha	2019	Research
Kuwait	Central Bank of Kuwait	Kuwait CBDC	2019	Research
Pakistan	State Bank of Pakistan	Pakistan CBDC	2019	Research
Saudi Arabia	Saudi Arabian monetary authority	Saudi Arabia wholesale	2019	Research
Chile	Central Bank of Chile	Chile CBDC	2019	Research
South Africa	South African reserve Bank	South Africa CBDC	2019	Research
Rwanda	The National Bank of Rwanda	Rwanda CBDC	2019	Research
Hong Kong	Hong Kong monetary authority	Project ensemble	2019	Research
Eswatini	Central Bank of Eswatini	Digital lilangeni	2019	Research
Russian Federation	Bank of Russia	Digital Ruble	2019	Pilot
Iceland	Central Bank of Iceland	Rafkrona	2018	Research
Bahrain	Central Bank of Bahrain (CBB)	Digital dinar	2018	Research
Curacao	Central Bank of Curacao and Sint Maarten	Curacao CBDC	2018	Cancelled

(continued)

Table 1.1 (continued)

Country/Region	*Central Bank*	*Digital Currency*	*Announcement Year*	*Status*
Kenya	Central Bank of Kenya	Kenya CBDC	2018	Cancelled
Egypt	Central Bank of Egypt (CBE)	Egypt CBDC	2018	Research
Turkey	Central Bank of the Republic of Turkey	Digital lira	2018	Pilot
Iran	Central Bank of Iran	Digital rial	2018	Pilot
Ghana	The Bank of Ghana	E-cedi	2018	Pilot
United kingdom	Bank of England	Digital pound	2018	Research
Ecuador	Central Bank of Ecuador	Dinero electronico	2017	Cancelled
Poland	Narodowy Bank Polski (NBP)	Digital zloty	2017	Research
Palestine	Palestine monetary authority	Palestine CBDC	2017	Research
Denmark	Nationalbanken	E-kroner	2017	Cancelled
Eastern Caribbean economic and currency union	Eastern Caribbean central Bank (ECCB)	DCash	2017	Research
Bahamas	Central Bank of Bahamas	Sand Dollar	2017	Launched
Canada	Bank of Canada	Digital Loonie	2017	Research
Malaysia	Bank negara Malaysia	E-ringgit	2017	Research
Euro area	European Central Bank	Stella (euro area)	2016	Research
Japan	Bank of Japan	Stella (Japan)	2016	Research
United kingdom	Bank of England	RScoin	2015	Research
Uruguay	Central Bank of Uruguay	e-peso	2014	Pilot
China	People's Bank of China	e-CNY	2014	Pilot
Finland	Bank of Finland	Avant	1992	Cancelled
Vietnam	State Bank of Vietnam	Vietnam CBDC	2017	Research

Source https://cbdctracker.org

1.3 Literature Review

1.3.1 CBDC and Economic Growth

As of now, only three countries—Nigeria, The Bahamas, and Jamaica—have officially launched Central Bank Digital Currencies (CBDCs) in 2021, 2020, and 2021, respectively. Due to the relatively recent adoption of CBDCs, empirical evidence on their impact on economic growth and inflation remains limited. Few studies have utilized actual data from these nations to assess the macroeconomic implications of CBDC implementation.

In the case of Nigeria, Ozili (2024) examined the effects of the eNaira, finding significant growth in the agriculture, finance, and manufacturing sectors following its introduction. His study utilized data from 2019 to 2022, segmenting the period into pre-CBDC and post-CBDC phases. The results indicated a notable increase in economic growth after the launch of the eNaira. Hermawan et al. (2024) found that the issuance of CBDC in Indonesia, amounting to 5% of the nominal GDP, would result in a permanent increase of 1% in real GDP. This suggests that CBDC implementation can have a lasting positive impact on economic growth, potentially enhancing monetary efficiency, financial inclusion, and economic stability in the long run. Tong & Jiayou (2021) conducted a quantitative study on the economic effects of digital currency issuance in China, where a digital currency trial was launched in 2020. Their analysis revealed that the substitution effect of digital currency is minimal, while a unit increase in digital currency usage can lead to a 0.15% increase in economic growth. Overall, their findings suggest that the introduction of digital currency has a positive impact on economic growth.

Similarly, Auer et al. (2022) highlighted that CBDCs could contribute to economic growth by facilitating faster and more cost-effective cross-border transactions, thereby enhancing financial inclusion and economic efficiency. CBDCs have the potential to boost economic growth by enhancing payment system efficiency, promoting economic digitalization, and reducing reliance on foreign payment service providers (Clemens et al., 2021). A well-structured digital payment system can improve financial inclusion, streamline transactions, and strengthen the financial sector. Baltgailis (2023) while analysing role of digital currencies and FinTech innovation in economic growth argues that inflation negatively impacts GDP, while digital currency adoption could foster financial inclusion and reduce the shadow economy.

Additionally, Ozili (2022) identified three ways in which CBDCs can support the growth of a circular economy: (1) Ensuring accessibility for all merchants, allowing businesses to seamlessly accept CBDC transactions, (2) Offering an improved payment solution that enhances financial transactions and lowers costs, (3) Incorporating features within CBDC design that specifically support circular economy principles, such as resource efficiency and economic sustainability.

Chiu & Davoodalhosseini (2021) analysed the design of a central bank digital currency (CBDC) and suggested that a cash-like CBDC, which can be used both offline and for general transactions, may be more effective than a deposit-like CBDC limited to digital payments. They further contend that a cash-like CBDC enhances payment efficiency, stimulates consumption, and strengthens banking intermediation. Their model indicates that, rather than displacing traditional banking, a well-designed CBDC has the potential to integrate and support the banking sector.

Zhang et al. (2024) analysed city-level data from 2013 to 2020, a period during which China conducted pilot testing of digital currency. Using the Difference-in-Difference model, their findings indicate that regions actively promoting digital currency were more likely to attract businesses and encourage investment in fixed assets. This increased business activity and investment is expected to contribute to economic growth.

Cukierman (2019) argued that CBDCs can contribute to economic growth by enabling central banks to play a more active role in credit allocation. However, he also cautioned that credit allocation should remain the responsibility of private banks, as they possess greater expertise in assessing credit risk and directing funds efficiently. He suggested that central banks should focus on areas where they have a comparative advantage, rather than directly providing credit, as private financial institutions are better equipped to manage lending risks and stimulate economic growth.

Similarly, Pratiwi (2024) raised concerns regarding the volatility of the CBDC framework compared to traditional financial systems. She emphasized the need for a well-defined regulatory framework to ensure stability and predictability in CBDC operations. Without proper oversight, the inherent volatility of CBDC could disrupt cross-border transactions, potentially affecting international trade. However, if CBDC volatility is effectively managed, it has the potential to support economic growth by enhancing financial stability and transactional efficiency.

1.3.2 CBDC and Inflation

Central Bank Digital Currency (CBDC) is a digital representation of traditional fiat currency, issued and regulated by the central bank. One of the key functions of a central bank is to control inflation by managing the money supply through monetary policy adjustments, including interest rate changes. As a digital currency, CBDC has the potential to enhance the central bank's ability to regulate money supply within the economy. CBDC could strengthen financial stability by offering state-backed digital currency against private cryptocurrencies (Kumar & Godara, 2024).

Nigeria introduced eNaira as its official CBDC, which operates as a non-interest-bearing digital currency. Ozili (2024) conducted an analysis using data from 2019 to 2022 to evaluate the impact of eNaira on inflation. The study found that inflation increased during the post-CBDC period, indicating potential macroeconomic effects following the introduction of eNaira in Nigeria.

Hermawan et al. (2024) examined how transaction cost-induced variations in money velocity impact inflation in Indonesia. The study found that a 10% reduction in money velocity, potentially resulting from the introduction of CBDC, could lead to a decrease in inflation ranging between 0.6% and 1.7%. Additionally, the research suggests that following CBDC issuance, both nominal and real interest rates are expected to decline.

Marsh (2022) highlighted that CBDCs could effectively control inflation if they are interest-bearing, as this would encourage savings and discourage excessive spending. By offering tiered interest rates, CBDC accounts could specifically target individuals with a higher marginal propensity to consume (MPC), thereby regulating demand without hampering economic growth. Similarly, Minesso et al. (2022) also emphasized that CBDC could serve as a useful monetary policy tool for inflation control when it carries an interest rate. Egbuna (2022) & Infante et al. (2022) assert that CBDCs have the potential to enhance the effectiveness of monetary policy. However, they also pose challenges, including cybersecurity risks, regulatory uncertainties, market volatility, and potential threats to financial stability.

The case of Nigeria's eNaira, which is a non-interest-bearing CBDC, was analysed by Ozili (2024). His study found that economic growth and inflation both increased following its launch. This suggests that had eNaira been interest-bearing, the results might have been different, aligning with the arguments of other researchers advocating for interest-bearing CBDCs as a mechanism to control inflation.

Further supporting this view, Bhowmik (2022) and Keister & Sanches (2023) asserted that an interest-bearing CBDC could absorb excess liquidity from the economy, thereby reducing both money supply and inflation. However, Beniak (2019) argued that if both cash and CBDC are available in the economy, monetary policy may become less effective in controlling inflation and money supply. He further suggested that the most effective way to manage inflation would be to make CBDC the sole legal tender and ensure it remains interest-bearing.

Conversely, Chen and Siklos (2022) contended that the introduction of CBDC alone would not necessarily help control inflation, unless it is accompanied by the elimination of large-denomination currency notes, which are often used for high-value transactions and cash hoarding.

Overall, the literature suggests that CBDC can serve as an effective tool for inflation control, provided it is interest-bearing. By influencing liquidity absorption, monetary policy effectiveness, and savings behaviour, interest-bearing CBDCs could help stabilize inflation without suppressing economic growth.

1.3.3 CBDC and Sustainable Development Goals

The Sustainable Development Goals (SDGs) were introduced by the United Nations in 2015 as part of the 2030 Agenda for Sustainable Development. The 17 SDGs encompass social, economic, and environmental dimensions, with each goal comprising specific targets and indicators to track progress.

Among these, SDG 8 (Decent Work and Economic Growth) is particularly relevant to Central Bank Digital Currency (CBDC). This goal focuses on fostering sustained, inclusive, and sustainable economic growth while ensuring decent employment opportunities for all. It includes 12 targets and 16 indicators to measure advancements.

Two key targets—Target 8.1 ("Sustained Per Capita Economic Growth") and Target 8.2 ("Enhancing Economic Productivity through Technology and Innovation")—can potentially be realized through CBDC adoption, provided that it successfully stimulates economic expansion and technological innovation.

Ozili (2023) asserts that CBDCs have the potential to facilitate financing for sustainable projects, enhance payment efficiency, and broaden access to capital, especially in developing nations. By improving financial inclusion and optimizing fund allocation for healthcare, education, and climate initiatives, CBDCs could play a crucial role in advancing the Sustainable Development Goals (SDGs).

Since most studies suggest a positive relationship between CBDC implementation and economic growth, it can be inferred that CBDCs have the potential to support nations in achieving their SDG commitments.

1.4 Conclusion

This chapter reviewed existing literature on the potential effects of Central Bank Digital Currency (CBDC) on economic growth and inflation. Given that CBDCs have only been fully implemented in three countries, there remains a limited body of empirical research utilizing actual economic data. The scarcity of studies stems from the novelty of CBDC adoption and the lack of long-term data for analysis.

Empirical research on Nigeria's CBDC, eNaira, suggests a positive correlation between CBDC introduction and economic growth. Specifically, studies indicate that economic growth has increased during the period following the implementation of CBDC. However, a simultaneous rise in inflation has also been observed post-launch. It is important to note that eNaira is a non-interest-bearing digital currency. Many researchers contend that interest-bearing CBDCs could yield both higher economic growth and lower inflation, as they can absorb excess liquidity and influence monetary policy more effectively. The case of Nigeria supports this perspective, as the observed increase in economic growth aligns with theoretical expectations, while inflation remains a challenge due to the non-interest-bearing nature of eNaira.

From the review of literature, it can be inferred that the introduction of CBDCs, particularly those with interest-bearing features, may contribute to higher economic growth and more stable inflation levels. The positive impact on economic growth is particularly relevant in the context of the Sustainable Development Goals (SDGs). Higher economic expansion aligns with SDG Targets 8.1 and 8.2, which are assessed through the "Annual Growth Rate of Real GDP Per Capita" and the "Annual Growth Rate of Real GDP Per Employed Person," respectively. Consequently, CBDC adoption could play a significant role in supporting sustainable and inclusive economic development.

References

Auer, R., Frost, J., Gambacorta, L., Monnet, C., Rice, T., & Shin, H. S. (2022). Central bank digital currencies: Motives, economic implications, and the research frontier. *Annual Review of Economics, 14*(1), 697–721.

Baltgailis, A. (2023). Digital currencies and financial innovations: Insights from European economies. *Marketing and Management of Innovations, 3*, 15–28.

Beniak, P. (2019). Central bank digital currency and monetary policy: A literature review. *2019 Shanghai Forum as well as High-Level Conference on Successes and Challenges in the CEE Region.*

Bhowmik, D. (2022). Monetary policy implications of central bank digital currency with special reference to India. *Asia-Pacific Journal of Management and Technology, 2*(3), 1–8.

Chen, H., & Siklos, P. L. (2022). Central bank digital currency: A review and some macro-financial implications. *Journal of Financial Stability, 60*, 100985.

Chiu, J., & Davoodalhosseini, S. M. (2021). Central bank digital currency and banking: Macroeconomic benefits of a cash-like design. *Bank of Canada Staff Working Paper, No. 2021-63.*

Clemens, U., Cousin, G., Feller, J. B., Monteiro, D., & Salto, M. (2021). The economic consequences of central bank digital currencies. *Quarterly Report on the Euro Area, 20*(3), 37–48.

Cukierman, A. (2019). Welfare and political economy aspects of a central bank digital currency. *CEPR Discussion Paper Series No. 13728.*

Di Maggio, M., Ghosh, P., Ghosh, S. K., & Wu, A. (2024). Impact of retail CBDC on digital payments, and bank deposits: Evidence from India. *(NBER Working Paper No. 32457)*. National Bureau of Economic Research.

Egbuna, N. E. (2022). Digital currencies: Emerging trends, challenges, and the future of the monetary system. *Central Bank of Nigeria Economic and Financial Review, 60*(4), 97–119.

van Egmond, N. D., & de Vries, B. J. M. (2024). Reforming the eurozone financial system: A system-dynamics approach. *International Review of Financial Analysis.*

Hermawan, D., Lie, D., Sasongko, A., & Yusan, I. (2024). Money velocity, digital currency and inflation dynamics in Indonesia. *Bulletin of Indonesian Economic Studies., 60*(3), 305–3045.

Infante, S., Kim, K., Orlik, A., Silva, A. F., & Tetlow, R. J. (2022). The macroeconomic implications of CBDC: A review of the literature. In *Finance and economics discussion series 2022–076*. Federal Reserve Board.

Keister, T., & Sanches, D. R. (2023). Should central banks issue digital currency? *Review of Economic Studies, 90*(1), 404–431.

Kumar, S., Godara, R.S. (2024). RBI's digital currency and its significance in global trade. *In:* Aneja, R., Dygas, R. *(eds)* Digital currencies in the new global world order. Palgrave Macmillan, Singapore.

Marsh, L. C. (2022). *New digital currency (CBDC) monetary policy tool to stop inflation without causing a recession*. University of Notre Dame.

Minesso, M. F., Mehl, A., & Stracca, L. (2022). Central bank digital currency in an open economy. *Journal of Monetary Economics, 127*, 54–68.

Ozili, P. K. (2022). Circular economy and central Bank digital currency. *Circular Economy and Sustainability, 2*(4), 1501–1516.

Ozili, P. K. (2023). Using Central bank digital currency to achieve the sustainable development goals. *MPRA Paper No. 118806. Munich Personal RePEc Archive.*

Ozili, P. K. (2024). Central bank digital currency, economic growth, and inflation. *Journal of Money and Business. Emerald Publishing Limited, e-ISSN*, 2634–260X.

Pratiwi, E. (2024). The impact of central Bank digital currency (Cbdc) volatility on monetary policy efficiency in financial inclusion and investment. *Journal of Social and Economics Research, 6*(2).

Tong W. & Jiayou C. (2021). A study of the economic impact of central bank digital currency under global competition. China Economic Journal. 2021, Vol. 14, No. 1, 78–101.

Verspagen, B. (2006). Innovation and economic growth. In *The Oxford handbook of innovation* (pp. 487–513). Oxford University Press.

CHAPTER 2

Carbon Offsetting and Emission Reduction Strategies with Digital Currencies and Renewable Energy: Pathways to Sustainable Development

Yash Pal, Pankaj Kumar, and Narendra N. Dalei

N. N. Dalei (✉)
Department of Economic Studies, Central University of Punjab, Bathinda, India

e-mail: nndalei@cup.edu.in; nndalei@gmail.com

P. Kumar
Department of Economics, Pondicherry University, Puducherry, India
e-mail: jaryalpankaj7273@gmail.com

Y. Pal
Department of Economics, Central University of Himachal Pradesh, Kangra, India
e-mail: yash.shalog@gmail.com

R. Aneja and R. Dygas (eds.), *Digital Currencies and the Green Economy*, https://doi.org/10.1007/978-981-95-2282-8_2

2.1 Introduction

Climate change is a significant global environmental issue affecting all sectors and social groups (Abbass et al., 2022). However, its consequences vary significantly due to varying susceptibility levels influenced by environmental and socioeconomic factors. Socioeconomic factors, such as poverty, population density, and access to information, often affect vulnerability. These disparities in sensitivity across regional and temporal dimensions make it difficult to universally assess the implications of climate change.

2.1.1 Overview of Climate Change as a Critical Global Concern

"Climate change, a multifaceted global concern, impacts ecological, environmental, socio-political, and socio-economic disciplines. It involves increased temperatures in many regions and has been exacerbated by the industrial revolution" (Leal Filho et al., 2021). Prompt intervention and suitable actions may alleviate its devastating consequences. Nevertheless, it is unrealistic to ascertain the precise ramifications of climate change on a sectoral level. The growing acknowledgement and integration of climate uncertainty in policymaking at local and national levels demonstrate the necessity for prompt response (Hall et al., 2012; Pettorelli et al., 2021). Climate change is a global issue characterized by long-term changes in temperature, precipitation, atmospheric pressure, humidity levels, and erratic climatic patterns (Kumar et al., 2021). The Paris Agreement, established in 2015 by the UNFCCC, aims to limit global temperature increase to below 2 °C and potentially 1.5 °C. This agreement is a pivotal moment in the global battle against climate change, as it aims to enhance global response and financial support for developing countries.

2.1.2 Economic Activity, CO2 Emissions, and Climate Change

The Industrial Revolution led to economic growth, but it also exacerbated global warming and climate change. Since the 1990s, industrialized economies have increased CO2 emissions, causing environmental degradation (Mitić et al., 2023). The economic growth, energy consumption, and environmental protection postures a global challenge for policymakers.

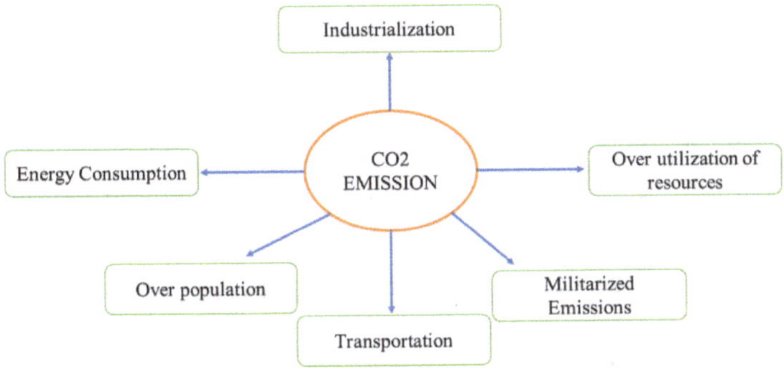

Fig. 2.1 Contributor to Co_2 emission. *Source* Author Compilation

Figure 2.1 revealed that the industrialization, energy consumption overpopulation, transportation, and war between countries are major contributors to CO2 emissions. These factors are also intercorrelated, as increasing industrialization leads to increased energy consumption and transportation; furthermore, it also leads to increased economic growth and environmental concern across the globe.

Humanity faces economic development and environmental preservation challenges, with environmental degradation causing global warming and climate change, primarily due to CO_2 emissions. Furthermore, due to rapid economic growth and commitment to climate change mitigation, such as the Paris Agreement and Kyoto Protocol, are crucial for its ongoing development. However, balancing pollution reduction with economic growth remains a challenge. A comprehensive environmental assessment could offer insights into reducing CO_2 emissions.

The increasing in energy consumption is instigating worldwide environmental problems, including droughts, sea levels, and heatwaves. Ajmi et al. 2015 linked between economic growth, non-renewable energy, and CO2 emissions. Carbon dioxide emissions have risen since 1960 due to coal, oil, gas, and fossil fuels, with the US, Europe, and China being the primary emitters.

Figure 2.2 revealed that over the course of time; the CO_2 emission increases. In the 1990s, the United States was the top emitter, followed by the European Union and China. But after 2005, China became the highest emitter of CO_2 emissions in the world. Furthermore, the CO_2 emission contributes to environmental degradation and universal

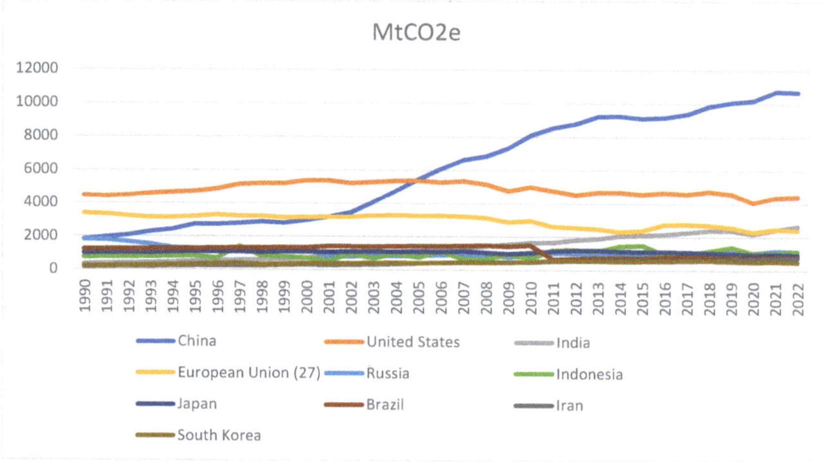

Fig. 2.2 Top emitter of CO_2 emission. *Source* Climate Watch (2025)

warming, posturing a momentous challenge for the globe and its forthcoming. Contempt a lessening in emissions in 2020 due to COVID-19, key GHG like CO_2, MH_4, and NO_2 have continued to rise, resulting in a global temperature increase exceeding 3 °C (Hao, 2022). This increase is likely to origin calamitous weather events, ozone exhaustion, and ecology dilapidation, intimidating humanoid efficiency and life.

Additionally, human activities have consistently increased greenhouse gas emissions, mostly CO_2 (76%), MH4(16%), and NO2 (2%). These gases contribute to climate change by capturing infrared radiation and reradiating it back, contributing to rising temperatures. Methane and nitrous oxide are more effective in heat retention than CO_2. Until 2019, the "US, UK, EU, Canada, Australia, Japan, and Russia" were the principal CO_2 emitters, accounting for 61% of global emissions. Currently, China accounts for the largest share of CO_2 emissions at 27%, followed by the United States at 11% and India at 6.6%. India ranks tenth on a per capita basis (Shivanna, 2022).Figure 2.3

Climate change is expected to significantly impact biodiversity, agricultural output, and food security. Rising temperatures are also affecting species' territorial boundaries, affecting reproduction and survival (Muluneh, 2021). Furthermore, climate change has momentous influences on anthropological health and well-being, creation it the

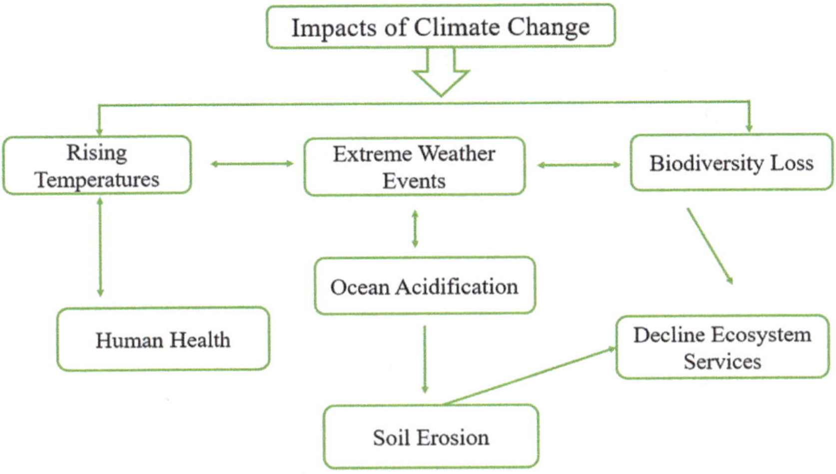

Fig. 2.3 Impacts of climate change. (*Source* Author Compilation)

furthermost noteworthy worldwide health apprehension and opportunity of the twenty-first century. Contempt its potential, many remain unaware of its health implications. Informing people about climate change's health detriments and potential solutions could boost public support for mitigation measures (Kotcher et al., 2021). Furthermore, also affect overall ecosystem services.

Furthermore, due to the increasing economic activities across the worldwide, CO_2 emissions have increased exaggeratedly over time. The impacts of climate change have been made worse by an increase's emissions carried on by expansion of industrialization, transportation, and urbanization and increase energy consumption (Rehman et al., 2021). As a result, there have been changes to ecosystems, livelihoods, melting glaciers, extreme weather, and rising global temperatures. Furthermore, developing and developed countries alike must adopt sustainable policies and shift to low-carbon economies in order to lessen the negative effects of climate change. International organizations that have been at the forefront of climate mitigation efforts include the United Nations Environment Programme (UNEP) the Intergovernmental Panel on Climate Change (IPCC) and other global institutions that recognize the urgency of taking action on climate change.

In order to encourage collaboration in depressing CO_2 emissions, several international frameworks and agreements have also been established including the Kyoto Protocol, Paris Agreement, and UNFCCC. In the worldwide a several measures have been implemented to lessen emissions and enhance sustainability such as carbon pricing mechanism, emission trading, reforestation, and developments in green infrastructure and machinery.

These are significant accords that play a crucial role in mitigating climate change. Moreover, these initiatives also affect attitudes about climate change, perceptions, and awareness among nations. These agreements are very thorough, which ensures clarity and accountability. Developed and progressive countries possess far more instructions than impoverished nations.

Over the past decade, governments have been actively deliberating on climate change issues, emphasizing the need for global collaboration to tackle the crisis. The global fight against climate change relies on collaborative efforts and mutual obligations. The UNFCCC and Kyoto Protocol have had inconsistent outcomes, with minimal efficacy (Yu & Zhu 2015). Furthermore, major power exerts the most substantial influence, with selection inducements based on group preference and size. The Kyoto Protocol's flexibility and incentive structure also influence the efficacy of collective action. When dominant powers withdraw, rising powers may advance the collective action agenda.

In November 2021, the UNFCCC, (COP 26), marking the "long-term goal of achieving net-zero emissions". The IEA convened a Net Zero Summit in March 2021 to assess commitments and emphasize actions needed to achieve these targets. The Paris Agreement mandates Parties to submitted NDCs to the UNFCCC and instrument policies to achieve their goals. The process is dynamic, requiring periodic revisions. The initial round, submitted by 191 nations, covered nearly 90% of global $CO2$ emissions from energy and industrial processes. NDCs include both unconditional and contingent objectives. The number of nations committing to net-zero GHG emissions has increased rapidly, with the Paris Agreement aiming for a balance between anthropogenic emissions and emissions from sources.

For the achieving net-zero emission targets countries took a number of individual and group initiatives.

Table 2.1 International agreements

International Agreements	*Goal and Targets*
"United Nations Framework Convention on Climate Change" (UNFCCC)	It is established in 1992 at the Earth Summit, is a global organization with 198 ratified nations, aiming to prevent harmful human influence on the climate system. Furthermore, it offers a framework for international efforts to reduce climate change through steadying of GHG absorptions in the atmosphere. Goals: – Stabilizing Greenhouse Gas Concentrations – Ensuring Climate Adaptation and promote sustainable development – Providing Economic and Hi-tech assistance
Kyoto Protocol—1997	Its directives industrialized nations and transitioning economies to reduce GHG emissions. It was effective in 2005 and currently has 192 Parties. The Protocol, based on the UNFCCC, imposes greater burdens on industrialized nations due to their significant contribution to greenhouse gas emissions. Furthermore, the Protocol directives carbon reduction goals for 37 industrialized nations, transitioning economies, and the European Union, aiming for a 5% average reduction in emissions from 2008 to 2012. – International Emissions Trading Mechanism: Allows surplus emission units trade to exceed targets. – Joint Implementation Mechanism: Enables emission reduction units from collaborative projects.

(continued)

Table 2.1 (continued)

International Agreements	*Goal and Targets*
Paris Agreement—2015	The Paris Agreement, approved in 2015, mandates significant emissions reduction obligations from all nations, including advanced and emerging nations. It includes clauses to hold governments accountable and stimulate investments in low-carbon, climate-resilient economies. The agreement is a pivotal moment towards a more secure climate trajectory and establishes an ambitious course for the future. It encourages national action and encourages increased initiatives by municipalities, governments, provinces, corporations, and financial entities. Paris Agreements Impact on Climate Change: – Mandates all nations to commit to combating climate change. – 97% of global emissions-affected countries have committed to their NDCs. – Countries to reassess commitments by 2020 and aim to increase carbon reduction objectives by 2030. – Establishes enhanced transparency and accountability, mandating reporting of greenhouse gas inventories and estimates. – Countries to continue providing climate funds to vulnerable populations. – While not fully resolving climate change, initiates a new phase of global climate efforts.

Source Author Compilation

Table 2.2 Net-zero emission targets

Country	*Target Year*	*Country*	*Target Year*
Chile	2050	Switzerland	2050
Colombia	2050	Thailand	2065
Costa Rica	2050	United States	2050
European Union	2050	Viet Nam	2050
United Kingdom	2050	Argentina	2050
Canada	2050	Australia	2050
Germany	2045	China	2060
Nepal	2045	India	2070
Nigeria	2050–2070	Japan	2050
South Korea	2050	Kazakhstan	2060
Brazil	2050	New Zealand	2050
Türkiye	2053	Russian Federation	2060
Indonesia	2060	Saudi Arabia	2060
Peru	2050	Singapore	2050
South Africa	2050	The Gambia	2050
Bhutan	2050	United Arab Emirates	2050

Source Climate Action Tracker

2.2 Carbon Offsetting

One of the important ways in which involves funding initiatives that lower or absorb CO_2 from the troposphere is a key strategy for reducing carbon emissions.

A carbon offset is a lessening in GHG releases to offset emissions from another location. It can be used in two markets: compliance and voluntary. Compliance markets involve companies adhering to emissions restrictions, while voluntary markets involve individuals or governments purchasing offsets to reduce their own emissions (Tsai, 2020). Carbon offsets often fund initiatives to mitigate GHG releases, such as non-conventional energy projects, energy efficiency programs, industrial pollutants, landfill methane removal, land use, and REDD (Fam & Fam, 2024).

2.2.1 Carbon Offset Credits

Carbon markets operate under regulatory and voluntary frameworks, with compliance markets requiring carbon reduction, and voluntary markets allowing offset credits, with pricing and utilization varying based on market conditions (**Carbon Offset Guide**). Carbon markets emerged in the 1990s as a climate change mitigation strategy, promoting offsetting through voluntary and regulated markets. These markets use actions to offset emissions in one location, reducing greenhouse gas emissions in another (Karhunmaa, 2016). Furthermore, carbon offset credits are emissions reduction measures approved by an independent authority or government, reducing one metric tonne of CO_2 or CO2e. They are sent from the entity that eliminated emissions to another entity.

2.2.2 *Compliance Carbon Market*

In compliance markets, such as national or regional emissions trading initiatives, participants respond to obligations set by a regulatory authority. The Kyoto Protocol, enacted in 1997, outlines greenhouse gas emissions reduction objectives for industrialized nations and transition economies. These objectives are divided into permissible emission levels, distributed as Assigned Amount Units (AAUs). Annex B nations must fulfil these targets through national policies. The Protocol provides three market-based methods for trading emissions permits: "International Emission Trading (IET), Clean Development Mechanism (CDM), and Joint Implementation (JI)". These procedures aim to facilitate cost-effective greenhouse gas reduction, stimulate investments, and promote sustainable development in developing nations (Ferreyra Marinucci, 2023).

2.2.3 *Voluntary Carbon Market (VCMs)*

VCMs allow carbon emitters to offset their discharges for carbon neutrality or ecological goals. Benefits are a primary reason for businesses to acquire carbon credits in VCMs. VCMs are crucial for financing climate protection initiatives and carbon reduction projects, expediting the transition to a low-carbon economy. Effective carbon offsetting can help achieve zero-emission goals in challenging industries like aviation and agriculture. VCMs stimulate investments in technology and commercial innovation. Figure 2.4

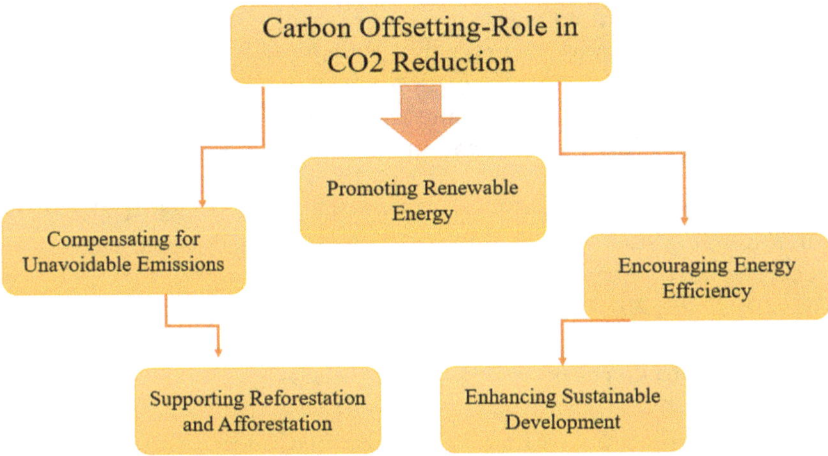

Fig. 2.4 Carban offsetting role in emission reduction. *Source* Author Compilation

2.3 Oxford's Offsetting Principles

The Paris Agreement aims to achieve net-zero carbon dioxide emissions by mid-century. This requires significantly decreasing emissions and offsetting remaining ones with removals. Many nations and non-state entities have committed to this goal, with 88% of global emissions, 92% of GDP, and over 50% of top corporations having net-zero targets. However, some sectors may struggle to achieve absolute zero emissions (Axelsson et al., 2024).

I. **Maintain the Environmental Integrity of Credits Used to Achieve Net-Zero Emissions and Update Offsetting Approach Regularly as Best Practices Progress:**

The first principle of the carbon offsetting is prioritizing emission reductions, transparency on compensation methods, and achieving carbon neutrality. Furthermore, both direct and indirect emissions must be considered, and acquired offsets must satisfy additionality criteria. Nature-based offsets can offer benefits like biodiversity preservation, social involvement, and local cash generation.

Furthermore, organizations must minimize emissions within their value chain and invest in mitigation outside their value chains. Direct reductions are essential due to the finite global capacity for removals and the need to transition from fossil fuels in energy systems. It also states that the actors must collaborate with suppliers, develop low-emissions procurement strategies, and engage with consumers to mitigate emissions (Axelsson et al., 2024).

II. **Switch to Carbon Removal Mechanisms**

Most carbon credits currently exist for initiatives preventing or diminishing emissions, but they are not a comprehensive global plan for achieving "net zero in the long term". Any leftover emissions must be offset by removals, and carbon removal objectives must be clearly defined and periodically reassessed. Investors must increase carbon removal investments to achieve net-zero emissions by 2050, following the Paris Agreement, but must carefully evaluate different options, including bioenergy carbon capture and storage.

III. **Transition to Removals Using Durable Storage to Offset Remaining Emissions by the Net-Zero Goal Date**

Adopting long-term, nature-based solutions for carbon sequestration is crucial for future equilibrium between sinks and sources. However, external factors like wildfires and sociopolitical disputes may jeopardize their long-term carbon sequestration capabilities.Figure 2.5

IV. **Promote the Development of Innovative and Cohesive Strategies to Achieve Net Zero**

It emphasizes the organizations must pledge to purchase carbon removals to offset emissions and achieve net-zero goals. Despite initial limited purchasing due to high costs, innovative initiatives can finance

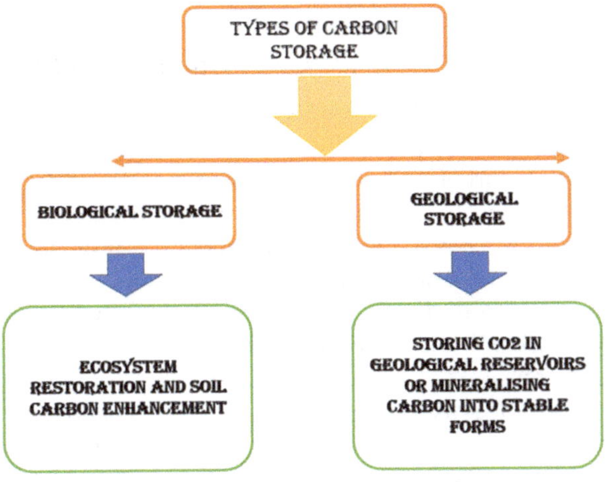

Fig. 2.5 Type of carbon storage. *Source* Author Completion

suppliers, stimulate investment, and increase sustainable carbon removal in the overtime. Furthermore, collaborating with industry organizations can establish a carbon market aligned with net zero, while enduring contracts with offset project developers ensure long-term carbon sequestration and ecosystem resilience (Allen et al., 2020).

2.4 Types of Carbon Offset Projects

See Fig. 2.6.

2.5 Carbon Offset Pricing

The cost of funding programs or projects that lower capture or prevent an equivalent amount of GHG emissions elsewhere in order to make up for carbon emissions is known as carbon offset pricing. These initiatives frequently include energy efficiency improvements carbon capture and storage reforestation and the development of renewable energy. The kind of project where it is located its certification and the state of the market all affect the cost of carbon offsets.

2.6 Role of Digital Currencies in Carbon Markets

As increased accessibility, effectiveness, and transparency of digital currencies driven by blockchain technology are becoming revolutionary instruments in carbon markets (Alzoubi & Mishra, 2023). Carbon markets which are intended to lower emissions by trading carbon credits frequently encounter issues like fraud inefficiency and low participation. By facilitating the tokenization of carbon credits and enabling each credit to be represented as a digital asset digital currencies help to address these problems. Blockchain is a decentralized, immutable digital ledger that facilitates safe, transparent transactions and data storage through interconnected blocks with distinct cryptographic codes (Laroiya et al., 2020). Blockchain technology, with its decentralized nature, ensures no one authority governs the system, preventing manipulation or illegal modifications (Werbach, 2018). Its potential to revolutionize finance, supply chain management, and healthcare is significant, improving security, transparency, and efficiency. Furthermore, it is a distributed ledger system

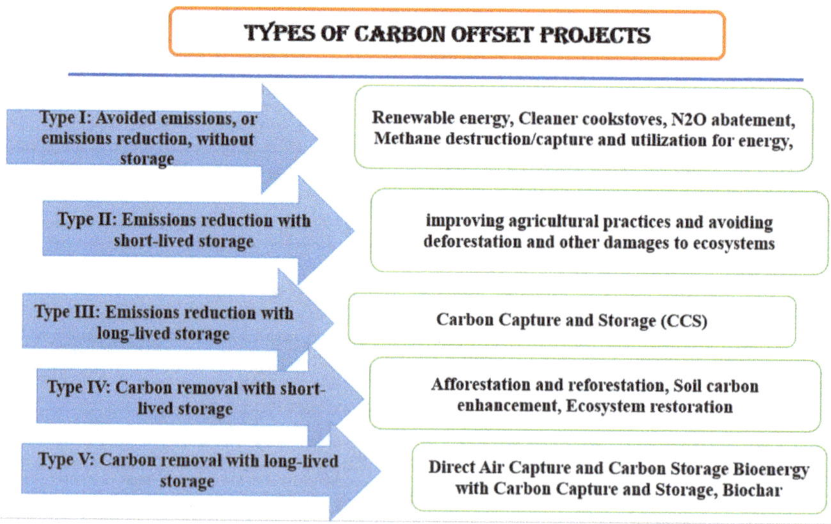

Fig. 2.6 Project types. *Source* Author Compilation

Table 2.3 Advanced approaches to reducing carbon emissions

Land Use and Forestry	
"Land Use, Land-Use Change, and Forestry (LULUCF)"	LULUCF sector is crucial for climate change mitigation, as it reduces GHG emissions and absorbs carbon. The Global Environmental Facility (GEF) supports developing nations in addressing LULUCF issues by funding initiatives to conserve, restore, enhance, and manage carbon stocks in forested and non-forested areas. Furthermore, it describes how land is used and managed, how land use has changed, and how these factors either contribute to or mitigate climate change. A significant factor in global carbon dynamics LULUCF affects both carbon emissions and sequestration. ➢ **Land Use:** utilizing land for agriculture, forest, and conservation ➢ **Land-Use Change:** Transformation of land to deforestation or afforestation. **Forestry:** managing forests for purposes like timber invention, biodiversity preservation, and carbon appropriation.
REDD+ ("Reducing Emissions from Deforestation and Forest Degradation")	REDD+ is a climate change mitigation strategy developed by UNFCCC Parties, aiming to conserve and sustainably manage forests. The Warsaw Framework, established at COP 19, provides direction for REDD+ operations. The Paris Climate Agreement recognizes REDD+'s importance, as forests help reduce deforestation and contribute to around 11% of global CO2 releases **(UNEP).**

Source Author Compilation.

that uses cryptographic techniques to link data blocks, ensuring tamper-resistance and authenticity. Additionally, consensus algorithms ensure uniformity across the network, ensuring the integrity of the data.

Table 2.4 Technological solutions

"Carbon Capture and Storage" (CCS)	CCS technologies combat climate change by sequestering CO2 releases from manufacturing processes and power plants (Anwar et al., 2018). CCS involves three primary steps: capture, conveyance, and storage. Captured CO2 is transported to a storage location via pipelines, and sequestered underground in geological formations to prevent its release into the atmosphere. Carbon capture and storage are crucial for achieving global warming goals. Furthermore, it effectively sequesters carbon emissions from industrial processes and energy production, aiding in climate change mitigation. It can permanently store carbon dioxide underground, reducing overall carbon impact. Continuous advancements in technology, cost reduction, and monitoring methodologies are needed.

Source Author Compilation

2.6.1 *Blockchain for Transparent Carbon Markets*

Blockchain-based digital currencies in particular offer an unchangeable and transparent ledger for carbon trading. By guaranteeing the traceability of each transaction this reduces the possibility of fraud and carbon credit double counting. By automating the verification transfer and settlement of carbon credits smart contracts.Figure 2.7

2.6.2 *Integration with Digital Currencies*

Blockchain technology has revolutionized carbon trading by enabling peer-to-peer verification of emissions and enhancing the effectiveness of existing systems. It guarantees "transparency, security, and accountability in carbon markets through its decentralized ledger". Smart contracts automatically implement emission reduction objectives, reducing verification and certification processes. Blockchain also allows fractional ownership of carbon credits, promoting market involvement and creating opportunities for smaller entities. The integration of blockchain in carbon trading could accelerate the transition towards a sustainable, low-carbon future.

Table 2.5 Features of blockchain technology

Increased Transparency	Blockchain Enhances Carbon Credit Transparency ➢–Blockchain technology provides secure, transparent tracking of carbon credits. –Each phase of carbon offset project's lifecycle, including emission reduction verification, credit issuing, and trading, can be documented and analysed. – Transparency boosts market confidence and ensures carbon credit authenticity.
Efficiency and Reduced Costs	Blockchain's Efficiency in Carbon Offset Trades – Removes intermediaries for automation. – Lowers expenses and accelerates settlement times. Minimizes need for repeated verification.
Enhanced confirmation and verification	Blockchain-Based Technologies for Enhanced Carbon Credit Validation – Real-time data acquisition and automatic authentication via IoT devices and sensors. – Streamlines validation process and improves carbon credit issuing precision. –Transactions involving credit trades and documentation may require validation by multiple market participants. ➢ Eliminates financial and environmental expenses associated with middlemen, ensuring market integrity.
Standardization and Interoperability	– Promotes standardization of carbon offset procedures. – Enhances interoperability among carbon markets. – Allows exchange of carbon offset units for digital currency. – Enhances liquidity in carbon market.
Programmability of Blockchain in Carbon Market	➢ Blockchain software can be used for trading carbon credits and advancing policy objectives. – Protocols can deduct a nominal fee from each transaction, used to acquire carbon credits. – The fee can also be automatically allocated to groups engaged in tree-acquiring or similar activities. – The price may be small enough to advance market utility but enough to advance policy objectives.

Source Zhang et al. (2024) Emery and Hamedani (2023) and Vilkov and Tian (2023)

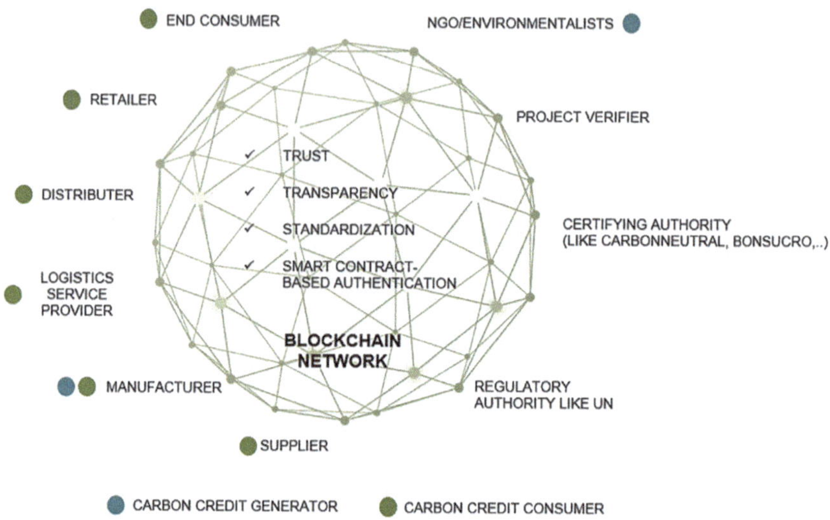

Fig. 2.7 Blockchain for transparent carbon markets. *Source* https://www.infosys.com/services/blockchain/documents/digital-carbon-credits-ecosystem.pdf

Table 2.6 Process of offsetting

STEP	*Process Description*
1	Calculate Emission (for individuals)
2	Choose a Project
3	Add Certified Emission Reductions to Cart
4	Pay
5	Receive Attestation

Source https://unfccc.int/climate-action/united-nations-carbon-offset-platform

David Chaum developed a blockchain system in 1982 using RSA encryption. The banking sector established the foundation in the 1980s, with Satoshi Nakamoto conceiving the first decentralized blockchain in 2008. Nakamoto enhanced the architecture by using a hash-like technique for time-stamping blocks without a trusted entity (Parhamfar et al., 2024).

Table 2.7 Procedure of carbon trading

Entity	*Role/Function*
Certification Authority	Makes inspection of controlled companies through a certain method
Relevant Department in Government	Sets emission baseline for the industry and allocates emission allowances based on inspections
Emission Reached Company	Can transfer surplus carbon emission to companies that have exceeded their emission limits to earn extra income

Source (Pan et al., 2019)

2.7 Future Prospects

Revolution is likely to knowingly contribute to globally decarbonization efforts, offering prospects for both private and public sectors. Recent innovations include low or non-carbon technologies, carbon capture and storage breakthroughs, and hi-tech improvements. Nevertheless, innovations recognize that tackling global challenges through innovation requires organizational, social, and economic transformations. Furthermore, the 2015 Paris Climate Change Conference has highlighted contextual factors that encourage climate change innovation, with 20 countries committing to double public investment in low-carbon technology. Additionally, the 2021 COP26 in Glasgow aims to address global warming, committing to the Paris Agreement and the UN Framework Convention on Climate Change, involving global leaders. Corporations, governments, and industries are utilizing digital technologies to achieve net-zero emission goals, offering sustainable solutions to climate change's societal concerns.

The digital discourse is a mounting extent of attention in addressing global warming, but it also climaxes the negative effects of technology on waste cohort, means feasting, and carbon dioxide emissions. Furthermore, large-scale bitcoin mining operations, with their high energy demands, highlight the contrast between rapid technological progress and the challenges of achieving net zero by 2050. While digital technologies have both optimistic and undesirable effects, there is a deficiency of inclusive aids from a broader outlook.

The recent advancements in carbon capture technology, which are revolutionizing climate change mitigation efforts, as the world faces a severe climate catastrophe and the need for innovative solutions to reduce greenhouse gas emissions.

Table 2.8 Technologies of carbon capture

Direct Air Capture (DAC)	DAC is a technology that removes CO2 from the environment using renewable or residual energy. Companies like Climeworks and Heirloom Carbon Technologies use modular facilities to sequester CO2 and deposit it in geological formations. Global Thermostat and PNNL have developed efficient and economical DAC technologies, such as Global Thermostat's residual heat-integrated technology and a carbon capture device from the Pacific Northwest National Laboratory. These technologies aim to eliminate over 1 billion tons of CO2 from the atmosphere by 2035.
Bioenergy with Carbon Capture and Storage (BECCS)	BECCS is a capable technology that uses biomass, including sustainably cultivated crops, for electricity generation. It captures CO2 emissions and sequesters them, achieving net-negative emissions, reducing atmospheric CO2 levels, and providing a sustainable energy source.
Smart Grids and Energy-Efficient Appliances	Smart grids and energy-efficient devices are reducing carbon emissions, with smart networks promoting optimal energy distribution and reducing energy waste. These technologies can be integrated with renewable energy sources to significantly decrease total carbon emissions. However, these technologies are not a solution to climate change. Continuous investment in research and collaboration among governments, enterprises, and research institutions is crucial for effective implementation. Carbon capture technology should be seen as an adjunct to alternative mitigation efforts, such as transitioning to renewable energy sources and energy efficiency measures.

Source Cole (2024, April 21)

2.8 Conclusion and Policy Implication

The Industrial Revolution led to the emission of GHG, causing climate change. The recognition of climate change began in 1979 with the inaugural international climate summit in Geneva, initiated by the WMO. The summit aimed to evaluate recent insights on climate change, estimate future consequences, and develop recommendations. In 1988, the IPCC was established to provide scientific knowledge for climate-related policies. "The UNFCCC was approved in 1992, aiming to stabilize greenhouse gas concentrations and prevent significant effects on the climate system. The treaty imposed significant responsibility on industrialized nations to enact national policies aimed at reducing anthropogenic emissions and increasing greenhouse gas sinks. The UNFCCC is ratified by 197 nations and is now ratified by 197 more. The Kyoto Protocol, established at the third UNFCCC Conference of the Parties (COP-3) in 1997, established carbon reduction obligations for wealthy nations over a five-year commitment period from 2008 to 2012".

Furthermore, the Kyoto Protocol is a global agreement aimed at reducing greenhouse gas emissions. It outlines four emission reduction units, each corresponding to one metric ton of CO2, which are tradable. These units are acquired through clean development mechanisms, collaborative implementation efforts, allotted amount units, and reforestation initiatives. The protocol also establishes an emissions trading system to exchange yearly allocated emissions saved by protocol members with those exceeding their limits. The Kyoto Protocol has established a carbon emissions market and carbon pricing, with governments establishing various schemes. Climate change mitigation involves traditional decarbonization strategies like renewable energy and nuclear energy, as well as emerging negative emissions technologies like bioenergy, biochar, and alternative techniques. Both traditional and new technologies have their advantages and risks. Additionally, also explore that by funding initiatives like carbon capture renewable energy and reforestation people and organizations can offset their carbon emissions. This procedure is completely transformed by blockchain technology which guarantees carbon credit transactions transparency traceability and fraud prevention. Its decentralized ledger system facilitates global carbon markets, tracks credit usage, and authenticates credits promoting trust and accountability. Blockchain integration makes carbon offsetting more effective, safe, and scalable enabling both individuals and companies to actively reduce emissions and advance global climate action.

Moreover, the leading global economies have need to focused more on the mitigation of climate change. To get net-zero emissions, economies must enhance their technology and reduce energy use through energy transition. Moreover, the leading economies must collaborate with certain less developed countries to bolster their technological improvement and reduce carbon dioxide emissions. Moreover, each country must operate at the grassroots level to attain sustainability goals. Governments need to focus on specific sectors to ensure their sustainability, such as promoting renewable energy, green technology, reduced energy consumption, and the use of recycled products within the industrial sector. Additionally, in the agricultural sector, deploy climate-smart agriculture, agroforestry, and organic farming. Likewise, the utilization of public transportation will contribute to the reduction of CO_2 emissions. These minor initiatives will contribute to the reduction of CO_2 emissions. Moreover, rich nations have an urgent need to finance less developed countries, as they play a significant part in emissions. Consequently, it is imperative to assign duty to developed nations to attain the objective.

Contribution and Limitations of the Study.

The study plays a crucial role in examining the implications of climate change on economies. Additionally, it emphasized the primary contributors to CO_2 emissions among countries worldwide. This study also found that governments of worldwide play a crucial role in mitigating the consequences of climate change. Over the past two to three decades, global economies have increasingly focused on reducing individual-level CO_2 emissions. Moreover, the work contributes to exploring the function of carbon offsetting and blockchain technology in reducing CO_2 emissions. The study has various limitations; it addresses multiple aspects and provides an overview of them. The future scope of study requires greater focus on specific issues, including separate research on blockchain and its implications, the function of carbon offsetting, and effective measurements of its impact on decreasing CO_2 emissions. Moreover, researchers may utilize panel data and time series analysis to assess the impacts of projects and initiatives aimed at lowering CO_2 emissions.

References

Abbass, K., Qasim, M. Z., Song, H., Murshed, M., Mahmood, H., & Younis, I. (2022). A review of the global climate change impacts, adaptation, and sustainable mitigation measures. *Environmental Science and Pollution Research, 29*(28), 42539–42559.

Ajmi, A. N., Hammoudeh, S., Nguyen, D. K., & Sato, J. R. (2015). On the relationships between CO2 emissions, energy consumption and income: the importance of time variation. *Energy Economics, 49*, 629–638.

Allen, M., Axelsson, K., Caldecott, B., Hale, T., Hepburn, C., Hickey, C., et al. (2020). *The Oxford principles for net zero aligned carbon offsetting* (p. 15). University of Oxford.

Alzoubi, Y. I., & Mishra, A. (2023). Green blockchain–A move towards sustainability. *Journal of Cleaner Production, 430*, 139541.

Anwar, M. N., Fayyaz, A., Sohail, N. F., Khokhar, M. F., Baqar, M., Khan, W. D., et al. (2018). CO2 capture and storage: a way forward for sustainable environment. *Journal of Environmental Management, 226*, 131–144.

Axelsson, K., Wagner, A., Johnstone, I., Allen, M., Caldecott, B., Eyre, N.,... & Smith, S. M. (2024). Oxford principles for net zero aligned carbon offsetting (revised 2024).

Cole, J. (2024). Technology and innovation in carbon offsetting. BlockApps.. https://blockapps.net/blog/technology-and-innovation-in-carbon-offsetting/#:~:text=Smart%20grids%20enable%20optimized%20energy.

Emery, K., & Hamedani, G. (2023, August 15). *The intersection of blockchain technology and carbon markets*. Miller Thomson. Retrieved from https://www.millerthomson.com/en/insights/esg-and-carbon-finance/intersection-blockchain-technology-carbon-markets/

Fam, A., & Fam, S. (2024). Review of the US 2050 long term strategy to reach net zero carbon emissions. *Energy Reports, 12*, 845–860.

Ferreyra Marinucci, X. (2023). *Carbon offsetting in the framework of Net Zero Carbon Buildings*. (Doctoral dissertation,. Politecnico di Torino.

Hall, J. W., Lempert, R. J., Keller, K., Hackbarth, A., Mijere, C., & McInerney, D. J. (2012). Robust climate policies under uncertainty: A comparison of robust decision making and info-gap methods. *Risk Analysis: An International Journal, 32*(10), 1657–1672.

Hao, Y. (2022). Effect of economic indicators, renewable energy consumption and human development on climate change: an empirical analysis based on panel data of selected countries. *Frontiers in Energy Research, 10*, 841497. https://unfccc.int/climate-action/united-nations-carbon-offset-platform

Karhunmaa, K. (2016). Opening up storylines of co-benefits in voluntary carbon markets: An analysis of household energy technology projects in developing countries. *Energy Research & Social Science, 14*, 71–79.

Kotcher, J., Maibach, E., Miller, J., Campbell, E., Alqodmani, L., Maiero, M., & Wyns, A. (2021). Views of health professionals on climate change and health: a multinational survey study. *The Lancet Planetary Health, 5*(5), e316–e323.

Kumar, A., Nagar, S., & Anand, S. (2021). Climate change and existential threats. In *Global climate change* (pp. 1–31). Elsevier.

Laroiya, C., Saxena, D., & Komalavalli, C. (2020). Applications of blockchain technology. In *Handbook of research on blockchain technology* (pp. 213–243). Academic press.

Leal Filho, W., Azeiteiro, U. M., Balogun, A. L., Setti, A. F. F., Mucova, S. A., Ayal, D., et al. (2021). The influence of ecosystems services depletion to climate change adaptation efforts in Africa. *Science of the Total Environment, 779*, 146414.

Mitić, P., Fedajev, A., Radulescu, M., & Rehman, A. (2023). The relationship between CO2 emissions, economic growth, available energy, and employment in SEE countries. *Environmental Science and Pollution Research, 30*(6), 16140–16155.

Muluneh, M. G. (2021). Impact of climate change on biodiversity and food security: a global perspective—a review article. *Agriculture & Food Security, 10*(1), 1–25.

Pan, Y., Zhang, X., Wang, Y., Yan, J., Zhou, S., Li, G., & Bao, J. (2019). Application of blockchain in carbon trading. *Energy Procedia, 158*, 4286–4291.

Parhamfar, M., Sadeghkhani, I., & Adeli, A. M. (2024). Towards the net zero carbon future: A review of blockchain-enabled peer-to-peer carbon trading. *Energy Science & Engineering, 12*(3), 1242–1264.

Pettorelli, N., Graham, N. A., Seddon, N., da Cunha, M., Bustamante, M., Lowton, M. J., Sutherland, W. J., et al. (2021). Time to integrate global climate change and biodiversity science-policy agendas. *Journal of Applied Ecology, 58*(11), 2384–2393.

Rehman, A., Ma, H., Chishti, M. Z., Ozturk, I., Irfan, M., & Ahmad, M. (2021). Asymmetric investigation to track the effect of urbanization, energy utilization, fossil fuel energy and CO 2 emission on economic efficiency in China: another outlook. *Environmental Science and Pollution Research, 28*, 17319–17330.

Shivanna, K. R. (2022). Climate change and its impact on biodiversity and human welfare. *Proceedings of the Indian National Science Academy, 88*(2), 160–171.

Tsai, W. H. (2020). Carbon emission reduction—Carbon tax, carbon trading, and carbon offset. *Energies, 13*(22), 6128.

Vilkov, A., & Tian, G. (2023). Blockchain's scope and purpose in carbon markets: A systematic literature review. *Sustainability, 15*(11), 8495.

Climate Watch. (2025). Historical GHG emissions. World Resources Institute. *Retrieved May 17, 2025, from https://www.climatewatchdata.org/ghg-emissions?end_year=2022&start_year=1990*

Werbach, K. (2018). Trust, but verify: Why the blockchain needs the law. *Berkeley Technology Law Journal, 33*(2), 487–550.

Yu, H. Y., & Zhu, S. L. (2015). Toward Paris: China and climate change negotiations. *Advances in Climate Change Research, 6*(1), 56–66.

Zhang, G., Chen, S. C. I., & Yue, X. (2024). Blockchain Technology in Carbon Trading Markets: Impacts, Benefits, and Challenges—A Case Study of the Shanghai Environment and Energy Exchange. *Energies, 17*(13), 3296.

CHAPTER 3

Sustainable Digital Currencies: Evaluating Social Equity and Economic Growth in India

Mohit Fogaat and Rajendra Prasad Meena

3.1 Introduction

The development of technology and the introduction of new financial solutions have widely impacted the global financial environment in what is being called globalization (Williamson, 2022). In all these changes, digital currencies can be singled out as a prominent shift, which has a great potential to change the ways of economies and the ways people think about money (Wang et al., 2022). Digital currencies are being embraced in many countries and this is not any different for India, which is on the verge of a pivotal development, the Central Bank Digital Currency (CBDC) (Boar & Wehrli, 2021). This chapter looks particularly at the sustainable digital currencies and their promising impact on the concerning subject of social justice and economic development in

M. Fogaat (✉) · R. P. Meena
Department of Commerce, Central University of Haryana, Mahendragarh, India
e-mail: Mohit201008@cuh.ac.in

R. P. Meena
e-mail: drrajendra@cuh.ac.in

R. Aneja and R. Dygas (eds.), *Digital Currencies and the Green Economy*, https://doi.org/10.1007/978-981-95-2282-8_3

the digital India economy. A Central Bank Digital Currency (CBDC) is described as a new kind of currency issued by central authorities (Chaum et al., 2021). The idea is to expand the current features of the system and at the same time harness the opportunities that the digital revolution has afforded (Barrdear & Kumhof, 2021). It should be noted that most private cryptocurrencies, such as Bitcoin and Ethereum, operate with no support of the government or other solvent organization and thus pose no value to currencies (Meaning et al., 2021). On the other hand, a Central Bank Digital Currency is created, endorsed, and aimed at becoming cashless, reliable, and safe in its use, useful, effective, and advantageous over regular cash and normal bank accounts. (Boar & Wehrli, 2021) consider Central Bank Digital Currencies as a game changer for the financial industry that still will be adopted and supported by regulatory authorities. It has also been noted by (Auer et al., 2021) that such projects require coordination between policy, technology, and social processes, which are difficult to achieve in practice. India's financial landscape has found a specific space in which a CBDC would be implemented (Williamson, 2021). Thus, as presented by the World Bank, most of the eighty percent of the Indian population are technologically competent but many of them are unbanked and thus Digital Currencies can help a lot in terms of Financial Inclusion. This is particularly true as it has been pointed out by (Chaum et al., 2021) that financial transaction costs and the functioning of payment systems can be improved by the usage of CBDCs thus enabling increased access to financial services among the lower class sections of the country. In India, where there is a high level of imbalance in income levels across society as well as in access to information and technology, using emerging technologies as a CBDC may support and help reduce this imbalance (Martin, 2021). But even as expectations are high, there are various issues pertaining to the distribution of CBDC that are still open. (Boar et al., 2020) see this as a threat to the current monetary system especially as it the benefits that commercial banks derive from providing financial intermediation are affected (Auer & Böhme, 2020). Where the banking system is critical to the stability of the economy such as in India, these risks need to be managed so as to avoid non-intended outcomes like financial exclusion or instability.

This chapter sets out to investigate the potential of social justice, reduced inequality, and economic development through the use of effective digital currencies in India, while identifying the challenges and prospects involved. In light of this, the key focus of the study will be to highlight what role does CBDCs have toward building a more vibrant and inclusive financial sector in India. The appeal of central bank digital currencies (CBDCs) in promoting economic progress and social equality can be attributed to their very essence. The alternative to the commercial banking system that the Reserve Bank of India would have, instead of the confines of the standard banking system, would be a safe and reliable, state-supported, virtual currency (Bianco, 2020). Such CBDCs would allow for greater inclusion in the economy, enabling even those who are excluded from formal services due to geography, income, or other sociodemographic variables, to use the CBDCs which such provisions would be made for (Bindseil, 2020). This may lead to the development of the economy in such a manner that all levels of society can enjoy the advantages which come with modernized banking technologies (Lee et al., 2020). Also, the research done by (Alonso et al., 2020), the implementation of a CBDC would increase the efficiency in money transfers, decrease cash management costs, and improve the speed of money flow. It is not out of place to say that the expansion of this action will enhance the economic phenomena and improve the stability of the individual's finances. Conversely, the hypothesis espoused by (Schilling et al., 2020) holds that social acceptance and integration of such digital currencies would only occur when there are adequate measures that have been planned out as well as campaigns to sensitize the public. This enables (Boar et al., 2020) to assert that regarding the successful introduction of the Indian digital rupee (CBDC), there needs to be an ability to trust and accept the currency just as much as there is a need for the technical structures and legal framework to support its introduction. In the words of (Allen et al., 2020) there is no doubt that a nation with a cash-at-heart market culture, coupled with low levels of digital skills literacy, will have a high degree of failure in trying to introduce a new form of currency. In the sphere of digital money, (Auer et al., 2020) the authors suggest policymakers should give weight to the culture and social outlook of the public while taking the clamoring for digital money. It has been said by (Bossu et al., 2020) that in order to be effective in adopting it, it will be important to have a proper process of awareness and education, a proper consultation process as well as a proper phased rollout approach.

3.2 Literature Review

The development and introduction of CBDCs is going to change the operation of the environment profoundly influencing both the economic growth and the redistribution of the economic development to citizens. When discussing about the digital economy policies for India, one should make a distinct separation from the CBDC-related interventions and try to understand what burdens such CBDCs are likely to impose with regard to bridging the gap between financial accessibility, the growth of the economy and social justice.

This literature review presents the available literature on the envisaged role of CBDC policies in shaping the economic state of India in the foreseeable future. To this end, secondary data related to the CBDC's proposal and its effects on India's economy in the coming years have been compiled from various reputable organizations such as Reserve Bank of India (RBI), International Monetary Fund (IMF), and other field experts. According to (Ferrari et al., 2020), some economically excluded groups who do not have a bank account may, however, gradually start using digital money through such CBDCs. In the report that was made public by the Reserve Bank of India (RBI) on the "E-Rupee Pilot Program," (Das, 2023) the effective utilization of CBDC rests on enabling policies, skills availability, and the willingness of the populace. The findings suggest that more intensive education efforts are needed to enhance economic engagement through digital currencies, narrow financial disparities, and foster social equity by removing barriers to inclusive socialization. In compliance with the conclusions of the Reserve Bank of India (RBI), the study of International Monetary Fund (Tan, 2023) named "Digital Currencies and Financial Inclusion" states that this might also be true in relation to the Economic State of CBDC Pioneers. "The International Monetary Fund (IMF) may be correct in their analysis that CBDCs could augment the existing remittances which are lifeline for the rural community in India, by offering the end users an appropriate, safe and easily accessible electronic currency alternative" according to the research provided on by the International Monetary Fund (IMF). One of the most pertinent papers in this discourse is what (Kiff et al., 2020). In the same line, Sarmiento's study shows that for these digital currencies to be relevant, the architecture of CBDCs should be culturally advanced in order to meet the cultural needs of particular areas (Auer & Böhme, 2020).

In a country such as India, with its diverse population and economic disparities, this is particularly crucial for achieving financial access.

Outcomes of a different study (Fernández-Villaverde et al., 2020) that examined in what ways a nation's culture impacts on the adoption of CBDC reinforced the same findings: there is a strong correlation between acceptance of a digital currency and the culture of that nation. Based on their findings, it is suggested that in countries like India which have a high level of inequality and a long-term perspective, policymakers should be cognizant of such cultural factors when formulating an integration strategy to facilitate the introduction of CBDCs. The work elaborated in (Keister & Sanches, 2019) emphasizes that (Barontini & Holden, 2019) the same is sourced from the direct capacity of CBDCs in terms of simplification of payment systems, decrease in transaction fees, and increase in inclusive access to finance thus is an enabler to create economic growth.

The Reserve Bank of India published a report titled "Payment and Settlement Systems in India: Vision 2025" (Benchmarking India's Payment System, 2022) in which they carried out an assessment of the part that CBDCs have played in stabilizing the financial system and facilitating the evolution of the digital economy. The report observes that a well-structured and well-designed CBDC can improve the existing payment systems, lower remittance costs, and secure the financial system. The report notes that a CBDC that is rightly structured and designed could simplify the payment processes, reduce the costs of remittances, and enhance the stability of the financial system. This position is further bolstered by the report of the IMF on "The Rise of Digital Money" (Tourpe et al., 2021) which suggests that CBDCs are to be central in the efforts to advance the monetary systems in most emerging economies. The role of affordability, transaction costs, and savings features as factors that are critical in adoption of CBDC. His statistics give a tell-tale sign that there is significant increased GDP growth on the country by the very fact that remittance costs could be lower and constructive economic payment through government could be more achievable through CBDC facility. Equally, (Adrian & Griffoli, 2019) explored how the international monetary order—and more specifically the hegemony of the United States dollar—could be affected by the introduction of CBDCs. None of these studies, however, answers a burning issue about how the introduction of CBDC by such major economic block such as India would nosedive the country's economy and international financial systems. It is clear that, CBDCs have their own potential upside, yet one cannot dismiss the challenges with their execution. The Reserve Bank of India's Financial Stability Report (Das, 2023) reports that introduction of CBDCs could not only endanger traditional banking systems but also pose threats such as interruption monetary policy transmission and financial intermediation. The report also advocates the evaluation of such risks and creation of adequate policies aimed at supporting the financial stability. IMF report titled Legal Aspects of Central Bank Digital Currency: Central Bank and Monetary Law Considerations (Bossu et al., 2020) sets out some of the legal and regulatory concerns that impinge on the design of CBDCs. Clear legal definitions and regulatory standards are required so as to avoid clashes when introducing to the already operational transaction system. Two economists, including (Agur et al., 2019), a monetary policy expert (Brunnermeier & Niepelt, 2019), regarded the design and implementation of a central bank digital currency in the establishment of macro-financial risk and cite such dangers as disintermediation and financial disturbances. Their studies seek to remind central banks on the need to open means of curtailing the impacts of the mentioned dangers through the endorsement of suitable monetary policies and provision of measures against systemic shocks (Brunnermeier & James, 2019). Moreover, (Khiaonarong & Humphrey, 2019) concentrated on the issue of user privacy and its relevance to CBDCs. Their findings suggest however that, fear of having important data at risk may hinder the understanding and acceptance of the virtual currencies. To assuage these fears, (Chiu et al., 2019) propose that central banks should conduct data protection and make a transparent outreach to the people on the actual usage of the consumer data.

3.3 Research Methodology and Questions

This is a study of the sustainable digital currencies in general and the Central Bank Digital Currency (CBDCs) in particular and their potential contribution toward promoting social equity, narrowing economic disparities, and fostering economic development in India. The study will specifically look at the secondary data as this will help in explaining how CBDCs can be utilized to develop an inclusive, integrated, and dynamic financial market in India. The research's methodology is of secondary data analysis where past data collected from various sources will be used in studying the effects of CBDCs toward social equity, financial inequality, and economic impact in India. Such design permits the systematic review of large databases and published documents making it possible to come up with sound and valid findings.

The research is organized around the following research questions

1. How Can Sustainable Digital Currencies Enhance Social Equity in India?
2. What Are the Potential Impacts of CBDCs on Reducing Financial Inequality?
3. How Do CBDCs Contribute to Economic Growth in the Indian Context?
4. What Are the Associated Challenges and Opportunities in Implementing CBDCs in India?
5. How Can the Adoption of CBDCs Be Optimized to Foster a More Inclusive Financial Ecosystem?

The data collection and analysis were organized based on the following sources:

1. **Government and Institutional Reports:** The analysis will lean on the government publications such as financial stability report given by the Reserve Bank of India, payment and settlement systems in India: Vision 2025 (Reserve Bank of India, 2022), and reports on the e-Rupee pilot program. Reports published by International Monetary Fund, World Bank, and other relevant international organizations will also be utilized in sourcing information about the development and use of digital currencies globally and regionally.
2. **Sources of Data and Information:** The manuscripts that will be reviewed include those that are peer-reviewed and those that are currently being worked on. This includes peer-reviewed articles in the Journal of Financial Regulation, Global Finance Journal, and Journal of Economic Policy, among others.
3. **Local and Global and Multinational Impact:** The main economic and financial indicators will be sourced from national databases including but not limited to, the National Statistical Office (NSO) of India and international databases such as the World Bank and the International Monetary Fund. There statistical information will be gathered on the Gross Domestic Product (GDP), poverty

index, financial integration, adoption of digital payments, and other indicators.

4. **Examples of Actual Cases of CBDC Implementation:** The study shall also focus on examples of real cases of the countries that have issued or are in pilot whether CBDCs such as China, Sweden, and the Bahamas. These examples will offer contrasting perspectives on the adoption of CBDCs within different social classes in different countries.

3.4 Analysis and Interpretation

The study employs descriptive approach to draw conclusions pertaining to Sustainable Digital Currencies and its impact on the socio-economic development of a developing country such as India. The analysis concentrates on the extent to which CBDC can promote social equity and justice, alleviate poverty, and catalyse growth while using reputable institutions such as the RBI, IMF, World Bank, and other works of literature. In the preparation of this interns' publication for this conference, great care was taken for the citations of the published works for their contribution to the field.

The interpretation centres on how CBDCs may contribute to reducing inequality strengthening welfare delivery mechanisms, integrating informal sectors and promoting inclusive economic growth. It also outlines the associated challenges, opportunities, and strategic considerations necessary for effective CBDC implementation. This article tries to address the research questions and reinforces the relevance of CBDCs in shaping an equitable and future-ready financial ecosystem for India.

3.5 Suggestions and Findings

This chapter presents the main results from the examination of the possible roles of Central Bank Digital Currencies (CBDCs) in enhancing social equity, decreasing financial disparities, and improving the economic performance in India. On those assessments, concrete recommendations are given to the policymakers, financial integral players, and other actors involved in the design and delivery of CBDCs in India. The recommendations are directed at alleviating the problems emerging out of the data analysis and making sure that CBDCs are instrumental in building a more inclusive and active financial system. The analysis further demonstrates that the expansion of social services in India in terms of the use of CBDCs makes them better and more effective as social equity enhancing tools. Significant findings are:

Improved Financial Inclusion: The initiative of the introduction of CBDCs would complement the achievements made by the Pradhan Mantri Jan Dhan Yojana (PMJDY) type projects by enabling even the unbanked population to transact using a digital currency. This may go a long way in eliminating the other forms of financial exclusion that exist, especially those that are experienced in the hinterlands where banks cannot reach.

Universal Access to Digital Payments: The data reveals that there is a potential that restrictions to the access of the digital payment methods may be eliminated through the introduction of CBDCs. By integrating with the present infrastructure for digital payment systems and using Aadhaar or other similar forms of identification that are already in use in the market, all members of society can enjoy financial services. CBDCs can play a positive role in reducing economic differences by minimizing the costs of economic engagement as well as enhancing the effectiveness of the social welfare systems. The findings suggest:

Cost-Effective Financial Transactions: Developments in CBDCs could decrease the expense of providing financial services and thus enhance the affordability of these services to the poor. This would broaden the scope of financial inclusion and help to bridge the income gap.

Streamlined Direct Benefit Transfers (DBTs): The viewpoint is that due to CBDCs, DBTs can be more effective in that they deliver any government transfer payments straight into the recipients' e-wallets. By doing so, this would decrease the chances of embezzlement and ensure that those who are supposed to benefit from the cash aid actually receive it in time and without obstacles.

It can be inferred that CBDCs can add value in economic development through facilitation of financial transactions and incorporation of the informal sector into the formal financial framework. Important findings include:

Increased Economic Efficiency: If CBDCs are accepted, people would become less dependent on cash, transaction costs would reduce, and the money will not be stagnant thus facilitating circulation in the economy. This would in turn enhance GDP and stability of the economy.

Integration of the Informal Economy: It has been argued that rural and informal sectors can be fully incorporated into the financial systems of CBDCs many of which would document transactions and give the Treasury detailed analyses of their finances. This would enhance transparency, enhance tax base, and allow for efficient monitoring of the economic activities thus facilitating economic development.

The successful execution of CBDCs in India is possible but the challenges have to be tackled while the possibilities pointed out in the analysis are exploited. The major highlights are:

Regulatory and Cybersecurity Challenges: The legal aspects are necessary as well as security aspects such as cybersecurity will have to be in place in order to avoid possible threats which may arise during the incorporation of CBDCs. Public confidence in the user-oriented cybersecurity solutions needs to be addressed and insisted.

Opportunities for Financial Inclusion: Nonetheless, such a mission is actually facing many difficulties, the assessment points out a great benefit for the introduction of CBDCs, which is to extend financial services in scope and especially to low-income areas such as the rural area. The scraping of the financial market in that manner is what these CBDCs may consider having a positive effect on the economy of India.

In line with the observations made in the report, the following recommendations can be made in order to improve the implementation and the effectiveness of the CBDCs in India:

Develop Clear Legal Guidelines: Clear, encompassing, and sturdy legal regulations defining the position of CBDCs in the financial system should be made available by the regulatory authorities. These regulations should provide for issuance, distribution, use of CBDCs as well as some other regulations which protect the privacy of individuals and the rights of the consumers. The most important aspects are:

Enhance Cybersecurity Measures: Intense measures must be taken also to minimize cyber-attack vulnerabilities of the CBDCs and outline the structure and provisions of the CBDCs. This should also include measures to prevent interference of agents in the internet which may lead to loss of funds during CBDC usage.

Public Education Campaigns: Public awareness programs geared toward sensitizing the particular groups of clienteles on the import of CBDCs should be organized by government and other financial institutions. This is especially needed in the areas that are low-lying and where the level of digital economic hygiene is low, more specifically, in the rural and the less served populations.

Build Public Trust in CBDCs: In fact, for the wide acceptance of CBDCs, building trust in them is of utmost priority. This can be done by enforcing the principle of accountability in the design of intervention mechanisms, allaying fears of citizens over privacy of their data, and showing how safe and usable the CBDCs are.

Integrate CBDCs with UPI and Aadhaar: In order for the CBDCs to get a wide acceptance, it would be useful to ensure that they are combined with pre-existing forms of digital payment used in the country like UPI and are also tied to Aadhaar numbers. This would make CBDCs user-friendly and equally available to a large number of people.

Target Underserved Populations: There is a need to specifically reach out to these underserved groups especially those who live in rural and remote regions. This involves see to it that the CBDCs can be used in places where access to the formal banking sector is difficult as well as help in the execution of the campaigns for improving digital competencies.

Implement CBDCs in Welfare Programs: The authorities should evaluate the possibility of deploying CBDCs in the welfare systems to facilitate the DBT systems. Such a mechanism would make the payment in kind to the electronic wallets owned by the beneficiaries hence making payments very direct, reducing transaction losses, and enhancing efficiency in welfare payments.

Monitor and Evaluate CBDC Implementation: After launching a system like a CBDC, a follow-up and appraisal process should be instituted to track the progress made and the challenges that are encountered. In addition to appeasing the CBDC users in developed areas, the responses of the "poorest" users including those in rural and underserved populations should be collected and considered.

3.6 Research Implications

The implications of this research study are based on those analyses, on the findings and suggestions offered in the previous chapter or chapters that were also under consideration. These implications illustrate the more general effect of introducing the Central Bank Digital Currencies (CBDC) in India especially in the areas of policy development, economic growth, financial inclusion, and equity in society. Such a study will help these policymakers or financial institutions and other groups that are interested in the prospects and issues of the CBDCs in the Indian context. The research identifies and explains the need for adequate legal and supervisory provisions in support of the deployment of CBDCs. In order to execute the release of a CBDC, there should be a line that expresses what the currency is intended to achieve in the ecosystem of money, how it will be plus distributed, and what the consumers' rights and privacy types of protection the law is envisaging to provide. These provisions will enable not only the seamless integration of CBDCs to the existing financial systems of India but also inspire confidence in this new currency by the populace. It is essential that regulators develop well-in-sight outlines to discuss the specific issues that CBDCs present. This often entails participation of the regulators with authority in other countries including the IMF and World Bank so that practices that are acceptable to the whole world are adopted by India. Such a medium, being digital, poses severe challenges in terms of security, the research notes. It draws attention to the importance of developing strong behavioral cybersecurity measures to protect the pathology of the CBDC architecture against possible cyber intrusions. A great deal of work will need to be done to ensure the security of online transactions and reputation of the central banks will not be at stake because of the use of CBDCs. It is essential that financial authorities and technology, including financial systems vendors join forces in order to create and put into place adequate and improved CBDC-related cybersecurity measures. Policymakers need to ensure that those measures will be continuously monitored in order to cover new types of threats.

Improved financial transaction services, as well as other possible developments, have been forecasted for CBDCs, and gradually translated into pumping up the economy of a country as the informal economy ceases to function as a bypass. Thus, it can be inferred that CBDCs will decrease the time of transactions and enhance their safety for the performers and are positively projected so to spur the economic activities, grow the gross domestic product, and maintain the economic equilibrium of the economy. Economic agents ought to adopt the issuance of CBDCs as one way of enhancing the economic development of a country. This incorporates increasing the effectiveness of government payments using CBDCs, increasing the visibility of financial transactions through CBDCs, and enhancing formalization of more individuals and businesses into the economy. The research discusses ways in which CBDCs could serve to enhance Direct Benefit Transfers (DBTs) by validating direct government payments into the digital wallets of the target beneficiaries. This would eliminate wastage, reduce opportunities for bribery, and make sure that relief funds reach deserving recipients. The government needs to consider using CBDCs in the welfare schemes of the country for better effectiveness of DBTs. Toward this end, it would be necessary to include CBDCs in relation to the present social safety programs and assess their effect on welfare in the course of time.

3.6.1 Social, Financial, and Technological Implications

The research indicates CBDCs can transform the inclusion of citizens in the economy in India. CBDCs can address this lack of financial services by offering a currency that can affect those without the normal banks hence making it a crusade in fighting the financial inclusion strife.

Implication: Social policymakers as well as institutions that offer banking services should be highly active in employing CBDC as a means to further the development of the underserviced communities. This requires embarking on specific campaigns in such places as the villages and low socioeconomic segments such that the advantages of the CBDC reach a large population.

From the research paper, it can be concluded that such systems as a central bank digital currency can also be refuges for improving economic inequality just by making it easier for people to access the economy through financial means. Therefore, the financial resources would become available to all and the disparities across various social classes would be reduced.

Implication: Financial equality should also be sought by developing CBDC systems which can help provide those who are less fortunate with low-cost financial services. The structures and implementation of CBDCs should be inclusive, affordable, and non-exploitative.

The research outlines that the successful adoption of CBDCs in India will rely on the fact that they will complement such systems as the UPI and yes, Aadhaar along the much larger digital payment systems in the country. It is easier for people to switch to a CBDC that incorporates existing systems and is therefore easier to use and more acceptable to the masses such systems.

Implication: It is the responsibility of the technology developers and financial institutions to ensure that such CBDCs will be integrated into the existing system of digital infrastructure in India very well. Partnership between governmental and non-governmental agencies, especially technology supply companies, will be required to build an integrated digital network in which CBDCs will be used widely. The research shows that there is an urgent need for campaigns directed to educating the public regarding CBDCs and improving digital literacy on the part of the people, especially in the rural and less serviced regions. The successful introduction of CBDCs would however require the public's confidence and understanding of them, hence the education is required.

Implication: Moreover, measures targeting the education of the public on the merits and applications of CBDCs as well as rectification of concerns on the aspect of safety and privacy should be taken. Such campaigns should be designed for certain categories of people so that every individual will be equipped with the understanding and capability to transact with CBDCs.

3.7 Conclusion

This study identified the purpose of assessing the viability of Central Bank Digital Currencies (CBDCs) in promoting social justice, curtailing inequitable growth and economic development in India. Its primary goal was to gather and analyze secondary information from the Reserve Bank of India (RBI), the International Monetary Fund (IMF), the World Bank, and different scholars in order to offer insights on how the said digital currencies may be used to create a more holistic and active financial environment in India. The study also sought to do a contextual analysis on the prospects and challenges of these digital currencies to the world of cyber banking and financial transactions. The emerged key research outcomes estimate that CBDCs may serve making the financial services less biased toward the poor communities thus improving social equity. They may also serve narrowing inequality of finances because of cheap transactions and more efficient operation of the welfare activities. Moreover, these currencies are also capable of creating wealth within the borders due to a speedy facilitation of monetary procedures and bringing the shadow economy to the light. However, for CBDCs to be properly depicted there is need to negate between the risks of regulation and failure of public confidence, safety, and incursion of places not to be entered. The study managed to meet its purposes through a detailed investigation of the possible effects of central bank digital currencies toward social justice, financial inequality, and particular growth of economy of India.

The research further demonstrated how it had established recommendations for the utilization of CBDCs in the provision of financial services to the underserved populations, among other purposes such as reducing inequalities in the income distribution and boosting the overall economic activities. In addition, it brought out the vital barriers which ought to be surmounted in order for CBDCs to be adopted and have an impact within a specific context. The analysis of the data from the RBI, IMF, World Bank, and relevant academic literature ensured that the research addressed both the advantages and disadvantages of CBDCs. And these findings have also provided an answer toward the research question of how these the roots of hyper-digitalization in society for financially excluded and emerged socio-economic development systems at larger present inclusive economies through strategies and options of Central Bank Digital Currencies in India.

This research has critical importance to policymakers, financial institutions, and the other interests in the stakeholders of Central Bank Digital Currencies (CBDCs) in India. The findings show that a sound legal and regulatory climate is necessary for the seamless uptake of CBDCs into the existing channels of Indian finance. The in-depth research also stresses the importance of good cybersecurity practices to secure the systems from any form of digital attacks and to help in winning the trust of the citizens while using CBDCs. In addition, the research also points out the need for engaging the public and awareness campaigns in the advantages and applications of CBDCs especially in marginalized and rural areas. The level of efficiency in the usage of CBDCs would greatly depend on their conformity with payment applications existing and their usability by the entire population. Although this research has prompted significant findings on the potential of CBDCs in India, more research is still required to investigate the effects of CBDCs on the economy and its financial system in the long term. Furthermore, there is need to conduct cross-national studies among those countries that have undertaken CBDCs for finding out best practices and challenges.

3.7.1 Final Thoughts

The Indian government has formally embraced the concept of CBDCs through a plethora of research and simulation at the RBI. Through discussing the persisting obstacles and circumventing the drawbacks of CBDCs, India can build an exciting and inclusive financial system which offers more than basic financial services to its citizens. The findings of the study offer a brief outlook not only to policymakers but also to researchers toward an emerging area of study in respect to currency remittances being substituted by other forms of monetary transference. Thus, the outcomes of this present study are vital for the planning of the design and operation of CBDCs and the provision of guidance on their impact within the financial system as they proliferate and gain prominence in India.

References

Adrian, T., & Griffoli, T. M. (2019). The rise of digital money. *Annual Review of Financial Economics*. https://doi.org/10.5089/9781498324908.063

Agur, I., Ari, A., & Dell'Ariccia, G. (2019). Designing central Bank digital currencies. *CEPR Discussion Paper Series*. https://doi.org/10.5089/9781513519883.001

Allen, S., Capkun, S., Eyal, I., Fanti, G., Ford, B., Grimmelmann, J., Juels, A., Kostiainen, K., Meiklejohn, S., Miller, A. K., Prasad, E., Wüst, K., & Zhang, F. (2020). Design choices for central Bank digital currency: Policy and technical considerations. *Banking & Insurance EJournal*. https://doi.org/10.3386/w27634

Alonso, S. L. N., Fernández, M. Á. E., Bas, D. S., & Kaczmarek, J. (2020). Reasons fostering or discouraging the implementation of central Bank-backed digital currency: A review. *Economies*. https://doi.org/10.3390/economies8020041

Auer, R. A., & Böhme, R. (2020). The Technology of Retail Central Bank Digital Currency. *Monetary Economics: Central Banks - Policies & Impacts EJournal*. https://consensus.app/papers/technology-retail-central-bank-digital-currency-auer/39e2cb48614955eca653cd598e55548a/

Auer, R. A., Cornelli, G., & Frost, J. (2020). Rise of the Central Bank Digital Currencies: Drivers, Approaches and Technologies. *CEPR Discussion Paper Series*. doi:https://doi.org/10.2139/ssrn.3724070.

Auer, R. A., Frost, J., Gambacorta, L., Monnet, C., Rice, T., & Shin, H. (2021). Central Bank Digital Currencies: Motives, Economic Implications and the Research Frontier. *Economics of Innovation EJournal*. doi:https://doi.org/10.2139/ssrn.3922836.

Barontini, C., & Holden, H. (2019). Proceeding with caution - A survey on central Bank digital currency. *European Economics: Macroeconomics & Monetary Economics EJournal*. https://consensus.app/papers/proceeding-caution-survey-central-bank-digital-currency-barontini/9b2fcffa72ea5a269f85d00547c21ad1/

Barrdear, J., & Kumhof, M. (2021). The macroeconomics of central bank digital currencies. *Journal of Economic Dynamics and Control, 104148*. https://doi.org/10.1016/J.JEDC.2021.104148

Benchmarking India's Payment System. (2022). *Department of Payment and Settlement Systems Reserve Bank of India Central Office, Mumbai. July*, 1–86.

Bianco, S. D. (2020). Central bank digital currency. *The Economics of Cryptocurrencies*. https://doi.org/10.4324/9780429200427-13

Bindseil, U. (2020). Tiered CBDC and the financial system. *ECB: Working Paper Series (Topic)*. doi:https://doi.org/10.2866/134524.

Boar, C., Holden, H., & Wadsworth, A. (2020). Impending arrival—A sequel to the survey on central Bank digital currency. *PSN: Exchange Rates & Currency (International) (Topic)*. https://consensus.app/papers/impending-arrival-sequel-survey-central-bank-digital-boar/999679e7ead35faa93318e31465d5ef0/

Boar, C., & Wehrli, A. (2021). Ready, steady, go? - results of the third BIS survey on central bank digital currency. *Research Papers in Economics.*. https://consensus.app/papers/results-survey-bank-currency-boar/e90fd34d303a585da9d4a99d1e838ad2/

Bossu, W., Itatani, M., Margulis, C., Rossi, A., Weenink, H., & Yoshinaga, A. (2020). Legal aspects of central Bank digital currency: Central Bank and monetary law considerations. *International Monetary Fund (IMF) Research Paper Series*. https://doi.org/10.5089/9781513561622.001

Brunnermeier, M. K., & James, H. (2019). The digitalization of money. *Comparative Political Economy: Monetary Policy EJournal*. doi:https://doi.org/10.3386/w26300.

Brunnermeier, M. K., & Niepelt, D. (2019). On the equivalence of private and public money. *Banking & Insurance EJournal*. https://doi.org/10.1016/J.JMONECO.2019.07.004

Chaum, D., Grothoff, C., & Moser, T. (2021). How to issue a central Bank digital currency. *ArXiv, abs/2103.00254*. https://consensus.app/papers/issue-central-bank-digital-currency-chaum/ee6b1425f0315bd79b3e8afda67f4192/

Chiu, J., Davoodalhosseini, S. M., Jiang, J. H., & Zhu, Y. (2019). Central Bank digital currency and banking. *SSRN Electronic Journal*. https://doi.org/10.2139/ssrn.3331135

Das, S. (2023). *Financial Stability Report* (Issue 27).

Fernández-Villaverde, J., Sanches, D., Schilling, L., & Uhlig, H. (2020). Central Bank digital currency: Central banking for all? *ERN: Other Monetary Economics: Central Banks - Policies & Impacts (Topic)*. https://doi.org/10.2139/ssrn.3525018

Ferrari, M., Mehl, A., & Stracca, L. (2020). Central Bank digital currency in an open economy. *Comparative Political Economy: Monetary Policy EJournal*. doi:https://doi.org/10.2866/389734.

Keister, T., & Sanches, D. (2019). Should Central Banks Issue Digital Currency? *Monetary Economics: Central Banks - Policies & Impacts EJournal*. doi:https://doi.org/10.21799/frbp.wp.2019.26.

Khiaonarong, T., & Humphrey, D. (2019). Cash use across countries and the demand for central Bank digital currency. *Macroeconomics: Monetary & Fiscal Policies EJournal*. doi:https://doi.org/10.5089/9781484399606.001.

Kiff, J., Alwazir, J., Davidovic, S., Farias, A., Khan, A., Khiaonarong, T., Malaika, M., Monroe, H., Sugimoto, N., Tourpe, H., & Zhou, P. (2020). A survey of research on retail central Bank digital currency. *Comparative Political Economy: Monetary Policy EJournal*. doi:https://doi.org/10.2139/ssrn.3639760.

Lee, D. K., Yan, L., & Wang, Y. (2020). A global perspective on central bank digital currency. *China Economic Journal, 14*, 52–66. https://doi.org/10.1080/17538963.2020.1870279

Martin, V. (2021). Central Bank digital currencies. *Bankarstvo*. https://doi.org/10.5937/bankarstvo2103109m

Meaning, J., Dyson, B., Barker, J., & Clayton, E. (2021). Broadening narrow money: Monetary policy with a central bank digital currency. *International Journal of Central Banking, 17*(2), 1–42. https://doi.org/10.2139/ssrn.3180720

Reserve Bank of India. (2022). Concept note on central Bank digital currency FinTech Department Reserve Bank of India. https://rbidocs.rbi.org.in/rdocs/PublicationReport/Pdfs/CONCEPTNOTEACB531172E0B4DFC9A6E506C2C24FFB6.PDF

Schilling, L., Fernández-Villaverde, J., & Uhlig, H. (2020). Central Bank digital currency: When Price and Bank stability collide. *Comparative Political Economy: Monetary Policy EJournal*. doi:https://doi.org/10.2139/ssrn.3606226.

Tan, B. J. (2023). *Central Bank Digital Currency and Financial Inclusion.*

Tourpe, H., Liu, Y., He, D., Mancini-Griffoli, T., Sandoval, E., & Mathai, K. (2021). The rise of digital money - a strategic plan to continue dilivering on the IMF'S mandate. July, 1–28. https://www.imf.org/en/Publications/Policy-Papers/Issues/2021/07/28/The-Rise-of-Public-and-Private-Digital-Money-462919?cid=em-COM-789-43478

Wang, Y., Lucey, B., Vigne, S., & Yarovaya, L. (2022). The effects of central Bank digital currencies news on financial markets. *SSRN Electronic Journal*. https://doi.org/10.2139/ssrn.3961648

Williamson, S. D. (2021). Central bank digital currency and flight to safety. *Journal of Economic Dynamics and Control, 104146*. https://doi.org/10.1016/J.JEDC.2021.104146

Williamson, S. D. (2022). Central Bank digital currency: Welfare and policy implications. *Journal of Political Economy, 130*, 2829–2861. https://doi.org/10.1086/720457

CHAPTER 4

Do Digital Currency and Blockchain Security Affect Financial Wellbeing: An Empirical Investigation

Suyash Mishra and Ravinder Kaur

4.1 Introduction

The junction of wireless transmission, mobile apps, and financial systems has driven the growth of digital payments which is replacing traditional cash transactions (Gupta et al., 2020). Likewise, digital currency proves to be different from established ways people handle money in society (Singh et al., 2019). The overall acceptance and widespread use of digital currency systems remains limited because these systems encounter various obstacles which hamper their potential growth. Consequently, these have minimal impact on financial services and the overall

S. Mishra (✉)
Retail and Logistics Management, Department of Vocational Studies and Skill Development, Central University of Haryana, Mahendergarh, India
e-mail: dr.suyashmishra@gmail.com

R. Kaur
Department of Commerce, Central University of Haryana, Mahendergarh, India

R. Aneja and R. Dygas (eds.), *Digital Currencies and the Green Economy*, https://doi.org/10.1007/978-981-95-2282-8_4

economy, and they may persist as a niche product serving a limited specific user base in the long term on the edge of mainstream financial services. Technological advancements have facilitated the gradual transition from cash-based to non-cash payment methods, and governments globally are actively promoting the adoption of digital payments, particularly in developing economies (Gupta et al., 2020; Mishra & Kant, 2013; Wamba et al., 2021). The digitalization of currency has the potential to separate the diverse functions fulfilled by money, precipitating heightened competition among specialized monetary instruments (Kant et al., 2013). Digital currencies affiliated with large platform ecosystems may lead to a re-bundling of monetary services, integrating payment capabilities with various other offerings. This could potentially discourage interoperability across different platforms (Alsalmi et al., 2023). Hence, in the era of digital transformation, financial organizations as well as individuals have been seeking novel technologies to improve the quality of their operational processes (Yadav et al., 2024a, 2024b). In this direction, the adoption of blockchain and distributed ledger technologies in accounting and auditing can enhance transparency, reduce fraud, and increase the clarity of financial records. Notably, blockchain technology has a substantial influence on financial sector, because it serves as the foundational infrastructure for digital currencies, commonly referred as cryptocurrencies. Following the research of Nakamoto's on Bitcoin, the blockchain concept rapidly gained prominence within technology-focused academic and industry communities. The decentralized network operating for Bitcoin transactions is what blockchain describes (Atzori, 2015; Suwanposri et al., 2021). Blockchain technology drives the transformative process of financial technologies which has created a paradigm change in the industry (Crosby et al., 2016). Blockchain technology provides multiple benefits to finance industry that lead to significant industry improvements. Today's financial systems need blockchain technology because this technological system removes the reliance on banking institutions and governments to validate deals. The decentralization model decreases overall expenses and transaction duration in bank payments because it diminishes participation from traditional financial middlemen (Alsalmi et al., 2023; Yadav et al., 2021). Moreover, the immutable and transparent characteristic of blockchain transactions assists in creating trust between financiers that aids reliable process for the financial sector to bring information lucidity. Blockchain builds trust by relying on its consensus-based decision-making system that makes decisions through most network participants without a central authority. Blockchain brings potentials across various financial operations through its technology implementation in digital currency systems and finance sectors in addition to healthcare sectors along with supply chain management and copyright protection scenarios. Blockchain technology implementation within banking will help solve multiple challenges including operational inefficiencies as well as transaction delay and fraud alongside operational risk issues when applied to payment clearing systems and trade finance and identity management systems (Guo & Liang, 2016).

The adoption of digital currency is demonstrated as the tool for enhancing the efficiency in banking system and financial wellbeing of public, although there is some academic discourse regarding the predictive association between digital currency, information transparency blockchain security, and financial wellbeing. In this direction, the scholarly literature suggests that the utilization of digital currency has precipitated augmented individual client bank account holdings and greater financial robustness (Huibers, 2021; Yamaoka, 2022). The emergence of Bitcoin and other cryptocurrencies has prompted increased scholarly examination and discussion on this subject matter. However, this framework for financial wellbeing through digital currency and blockchain is scantly analysed in India, which can suggest measures for contributing in financial stability of financial institutions through digital currency, transaction transparency, and blockchain security. On consideration of importance of these issues, the current study measures the significance of digital currency, information transparency, blockchain security, and these influences on financial wellbeing. These relationships are discussed in following section to understand the connection among these variables.

4.2 Review of Literature

4.2.1 Digital Currency and Financial Wellbeing

The research domain about the relationship between digital currencies and financial prosperity is very multifaceted and dynamic. Digital currencies have the potential advantage for facilitating financial prosperity on the one hand and present some risks and impediments on the other hand. Digital currencies may be integrated to provide access to various financial services to individuals who do not have formal banking accounts, particularly in emerging countries where conventional banking system is constrained (Yadav et al., 2021). Also, digital financial inclusion integration can contribute to the move of informal structure into the official financial system (Mhlanga, 2022; Mishra et al., 2023; Singh et al., 2022). Increased digitalization has enhanced access to financial services, thereby promoting financial inclusion and wellbeing (Kanungo & Gupta, 2021). Moreover, digital currency transactions may offer substantial cost savings compared to traditional banking methods, particularly for international payments. This has the potential to enhance the financial welfare of both individuals and businesses by diminishing the expenses associated with remittance and other economic activities (Ozili, 2018). Also, it ultimately means that digital currencies can improve people's financial freedom as a result of giving users more control over their monetary resources and operations; thereby minimizing existing reliance on third-party systems.

Further, digital currency exchange platforms together with digital asset storage solutions maintain entry points that unauthorized users exploit to steal funds leading to substantial financial harm for their customers. The absence of knowledge about digital currency operations leads people to make investment decisions which result in financial loss. The present situation underscores an urgent necessity to establish financial education programs which aim to teach both young and adult population how to comprehend the increasingly complex financial marketplace (Garg & Singh, 2018; Mireku et al., 2023). Financial literacy is crucial for making prudent financial choices, especially in the context of the volatile digital currency markets prudent financial decisions depend on financial literacy when dealing with digital currency prices that change quickly (Garg & Singh, 2018). Moreover, digital currency systems need top security levels to create their expected benefits and protect users from market dangers.

4.2.2 Blockchain Security and Financial Wellbeing

The financial wellbeing of an entity depends on various aspects linked to blockchain security. It has brought in more opportunities to humanity in the area of making financial stability and strengthening transparency, efficiency, and security of the systems but on the other side, it has also posed some new threats and challenges. It is identified that the application of blockchain in the financial system can decrease its vulnerability to systemic risk because it is not centralized. According to Walch (2015), the blockchain technology has the ability of bringing a shift to the structure of the financial markets as well as minimizes cost and wasted resources. Several of the key features of blockchain such as decentralization, transparency, and immutability can enhance the flow of information relating to the regulation and monitoring of the markets thus slashing the information deficit and thereby stability in the financial markets. Its application can also eliminate lengthy procedures in the financial transaction processes, especially on the number of days and costs of settlement. This can facilitate market efficiency and improve its fluidity as well as stability owing to reaching more individuals through electronics means. In addition to this, the implementation of cryptographic security in financial transactions decreases the chances of both cyberattacks and fraud. The cryptocurrency exchanges perform security investments due to their economic benefits (Johnson et al., 2018). Security stands as the most important element for designing blockchain systems because blockchain technology provides various benefits while imposing some risks to the stability of financial systems (Zhang et al., 2020). Further investigation of the blockchain security and financial stability association is required.

4.2.3 Blockchain Security and Information Transparency

Further, incorporating blockchain technology into banking operations can enhance efficiency and reliability for financial institutions and their clients. The increased security and pace of blockchain-based banking can assist individuals in maintaining their financial objectives and requirements (Brüggen et al., 2017). Nonetheless, rapid proliferation of blockchain technology has empowered organizations to harness its versatility across a variety of domains and sectors. Firms are proactively investing in blockchain-enabled capabilities to redefine their product and service offerings, gain innovative insights that confer a competitive advantage, and bolster their performances (Marsal-Llacuna, 2018). In addition to this, the immutable and sequential nature of blockchain ledger records has improved the safeguarding of customer data, business records, and exchange histories (Macrinici et al., 2018). Blockchain technology establishes an immutable network of shared records, which distribute data across numerous locations and employ encryption to provide enhanced security and privacy relative to centralized databases. This innovative technology is positioned to reshape the landscape of digital transactions within the emerging data-driven economy, potentially transforming the fundamental underpinnings of digital trust (Shin & Park, 2019). The decentralized distributed ledger system secured with cryptography enables blockchain to create a unique transaction management mechanism independent of central authority control (Zwitter & Hazenberg, 2020). Consequently, emerging technological innovations have substantially influenced consumers' fiscal stability and prosperity. Over the past decade, disruptive advancements have reshaped diverse facets of consumer consumption patterns, consequently impacting their financial wellbeing. In particular, the financial services experienced intense changes driven by the proliferation of financial technology.

4.3 Digital Currency, Information Transparency, and Financial Wellbeing

The accelerated adoption of digital financial instruments substantially transformed the activities of financial institutions, revolutionizing all facets of their trade frameworks (Zemlyak et al., 2022). Even, the emergence of FinTech has facilitated the digital transformation of the traditional banking model and profoundly altered the delivery of financial services (Agarwal & Zhang, 2020). The integration of digital technologies has empowered companies to achieve enhanced capabilities, enabling the virtual provision of information regarding their offerings to various markets (Zemlyak et al., 2022). Additionally, the increasing demand for easy and convenient financial services and products has contributed to the evolution of the FinTech sector, and the government is also augmenting its focus on FinTech services, concentrating efforts on reliability and information technology infrastructure to bolster the data security of individuals leveraging FinTech offerings (Akhter et al., 2022). While some businesses are afraid of using technology due to the perceived harm to society, it is also seen as an opportunity (Akhter et al., 2022). The literature on FinTech, particularly in the areas of financial services and innovations, regulation, and the global financial system, has focused on issues such as blockchain and security, which represent the current most sensitive aspects linked to the theme of digital transformation (Milian et al., 2019).

On the other hand, the advent of digital currencies, such as cryptocurrencies, has brought to the forefront the issue of information transparency in financial transactions. Previous research has highlighted the potential benefits of digital currencies in terms of increased transparency, reduced transaction costs, and enhanced financial inclusion (Agarwal & Zhang, 2020; Akhter et al., 2022; Milian et al., 2019). However, concerns have also been raised about the possible drawbacks associated with digital currencies, including their volatility, the potential for their use in illicit activities, and the need for robust regulatory frameworks to address these concerns and ensure the integrity and stability of the financial system (Agarwal & Zhang, 2020; Akhter et al., 2022; Milian et al., 2019; Zemlyak et al., 2022).

On the basis of the discussion, following hypotheses are framed:

> H1: Digital currency positively impacts financial wellbeing of individuals.
> H2: Blockchain security positively impacts financial wellbeing of individuals.
> H3: Financial transparency positively impacts financial wellbeing of individuals.

4.4 Methodology

This section summarizes the methodological part employed in the current study. The initial segment of this section mentions the population and sample size elements of the current study. It is necessary to study the research population and pick an exact number of participants to prove study's validity and usefulness while using a quantitative method. The research sample of the study included all bank account holders who resided in the Delhi-NCR metropolitan area. The reason for selecting this sample area is that the National Capital Region of Delhi sustained its dominance in India's cryptocurrency (a digital currency) adoption landscape, retaining its position as the leading market in terms of invested capital. Delhi NCR remained the epicenter of cryptocurrency adoption within the country, cementing its status as the predominant hub for digital asset investment. Notwithstanding the broader regulatory uncertainty surrounding cryptocurrencies in India, the Delhi metropolitan area has consistently outperformed other regions in attracting investor interest and driving the growth of the domestic cryptocurrency ecosystem. This investigation utilized a convenience sampling technique to gather data, consistent with previous studies (Naveed et al., 2021). The quantitative data was gathered through a questionnaire. The survey used a 5-point Likert scale, from strongly disagree to strongly agree. Before gathering the data, the researchers conducted a pilot test to make sure the questionnaire was reliable. The survey instrument is structured with questions addressing each factor and divided into two sections. The first part asks participants to provide information about themselves, thereby delineating the demographic profile of the respondents. The subsequent part encompasses statements pertaining to the constructs examined in the present study. Three hundred questionnaires were distributed to the target population, of which 215 responses were deemed appropriate for this investigation with the response rate of 71.66%. The collected data was analysed using SPSS and AMOS statistical software.

4.4.1 *Measures*

The measurement scales utilized in this study have been previously validated in the extant literature. The five items from measures established by Prawitz et al. (2006) and Gerrans et al. (2014) were used for evaluating financial wellbeing of participants. However, blockchain security was evaluated using the scale developed by Garg et al. (2021) and Shin (2019), which consisted of four items. Three digital currency items were evaluated based on a scale developed by Lober and Houben (2018); Sadiq et al. (2023). Further, the assessment of information transparency was carried out through the utilization of a four-item scale that was adapted from the work of Liu et al. (2015).

4.5 Analysis and Results

4.5.1 *Demographic Profile of Respondents*

Table 4.1 provides an overview of the basic demographic characteristics of the survey respondents. The survey participants encompassed a diverse range of age groups. The most prevalent cohort, accounting for 39.54% of respondents, was the 41 to 50 year-old demographic. The 31 to 40 and 51 to 60 age groups constituted 30.23% and 13.95% of the sample, respectively. Furthermore, 11.63% of the participants were within the 20–30 year age bracket, while 4.65% of the participants were 61 years of age or older. The data indicates that the study participants have a wide range of occupational histories. The data reveals that 40.47% of respondents are employed in the private sector, while 30.70% work for the government. Notably, 20.47% of participants are business owners, demonstrating the presence of a vibrant entrepreneurial spirit among the sample. Additionally, the inclusion of a student population (2.79%) suggests the involvement of a younger demographic in the study. The study data revealed that female participation in the study reached 34.88% and males represented 65.12% of the total participants. A notable portion of participants reported monthly incomes ranging from Rs. 60,001 to Rs. 90,000, or exceeding Rs. 90,000, indicating their strong financial position. The study results demonstrate a varied educational landscape among the respondents, with 40% holding bachelor's qualifications, 32.09% possessing master's-level credentials, 14.88% having attained senior secondary education or diplomas, and the remaining 13.02% having earned the highest academic distinction of doctoral degrees.

4.5.2 Measurement Model

In the context of structural equation modeling, confirmatory factor analysis assesses the extent to which the underlying latent variables account for the observed variables (Byrne, 2010). This approach is useful as it allows researchers to validate measurement models for latent constructs based on prior theoretical assumptions (Wasilah & Fahmyddin, 2018). To investigate the proposed relationship between variables and assess the suitability of the measurement model, a confirmatory factor analysis was conducted. Multiple fit indices can be utilized to evaluate the model's goodness of fit when performing confirmatory factor analysis (Hair et al., 2015). AMOS statistical software was used to determine the constructs' efficiency in this research. The research began with goodness-of-fit index evaluation of the model and moved to an analysis of model validity and reliability. The measurement model's goodness-of-fit statistics revealed a Chi-square/degrees of freedom ratio of 2.780, which falls below the recommended threshold of 3, indicating a robust model fit (Byrne, 2010). The model demonstrates an RMSEA value of 0.089, a GFI value of 0.873, and an AGFI value of 0.823, all of which satisfy the established threshold criteria (Hair et al., 2015). Furthermore, the incremental fit indices suggest the proposed model is well-fitted, with NFI at 0.875, TLI at 0.896, CFI at 0.915, and IFI at 0.916—all of which exceed the threshold indicative of a well-fitting model (Hair et al., 2015).

Table 4.1 Summary of respondent's profile

No	*Demographic variables*		*Frequency*	*Percentage (%)*
1	Age	20–30	25	11.63
		31–40	65	30.23
		41–50	85	39.54
		51–60	30	13.95
		61 and above	10	04.65
		Total	215	100.0
2	Occupation	Student	06	02.78
		Government job	66	30.70
		Private job	87	40.47
		Business owner	44	20.47
		Others	12	05.58
		Total	215	100.0
3	Family income	Below 30,000	15	06.98
		30,000–60,000	30	13.95
		60,001–90,000	95	44.19
		More than 90,000	75	34.88
		Total	215	100.0
4	Gender	Male	140	65.12
		Female	75	34.88
		Total	215	100.0
5	Educational Background	12th or diploma	32	14.88%
		Graduate	86	40%
		Post Graduate	69	32.09%
		Doctorate	28	13.02%
		Total	215	100.0

Source Authors' calculations

4.5.3 *Checking Scales Validity and Reliability*

Assessing the reliability and validity of the measurement tool becomes essential after performing model fit analysis. Table 4.2 demonstrates the results regarding convergent validity of measurement model. When assessing convergent validity, standardized factor loadings, composite reliability (CR), and average variance extracted (AVE) criteria must be taken into consideration. Results showed that the factor loading of all items is greater than. 05 as recommended by Hair et al. (2015). The composite reliability values for all factors were within the range of 0.811–0.899, while the average variance extracted values fell between 0.563 and 0.640. Both sets of values exceeded the recommended minimum threshold value,

Table 4.2 Reliability and validity analysis

Construct	*Item*	*Loading*	*Cronbach's alpha*	*Average variance extracted*	*Composite Reliability*	*Remarks*
Blockchain security (BCS)	BCS1	0.730	0.857	0.610	0.862	Valid and reliable
	BCS2	0.749				
	BCS3	0.758				
	BCS4	0.879				
Digital currency (DC)	DC1	0.744	0.809	0.588	0.811	Valid and reliable
	DC2	0.777				
	DC3	0.779				
Information transparency (IT)	IT1	0.720	0.828	0.563	0.837	Valid and reliable
	IT2	0.753				
	IT3	0.688				
	IT4	0.833				
Financial wellbeing (FWB)	FWB1	0.862	0.897	0.640	0.899	Valid and reliable
	FWB2	0.829				
	FWB3	0.808				
	FWB4	0.732				
	FWB5	0.762				

Note All loadings are significant at 0.001 level
Source AMOS results

indicating that the measures demonstrate adequate convergent validity (Hair et al., 2015). On the basis of these results, it can be concluded that the constructs demonstrate adequate convergent validity.

Further, discriminant validity is calculated with the help of square root of AVE and corresponding correlation coefficients. Discriminant validity reflects the extent to which each construct exhibits a unique identifying feature that differentiates it from others. Results of Table 4.3 declare that the value of square root of the average variance extracted for each construct exceeds the corresponding correlation coefficients with the other constructs in the model, which strongly confirms the discriminant validity of the measures (Fornell & Larcker, 1981).

4.5.4 *SEM Analysis and Hypotheses Testing*

Since structural equation modeling (SEM) assesses the hypothesized strength among multiple latent variables; therefore, the relationship between constructs is examined through SEM (Hair et al., 2015). In the

Table 4.3 Discriminate validity results of the measurement model

	CR	*AVE*	*MSV*	*ASV*	*DC*	*IT*	*FWB*	*BC*
DC	0.811	0.588	0.529	0.431	0.767			
IT	0.837	0.563	0.551	0.527	0.727	0.750		
FWB	0.899	0.640	0.501	0.460	0.661	0.708	0.800	
BCS	0.862	0.610	0.551	0.440	0.573	0.742	0.664	0.781

Source Authors' calculations

present study, 16 measurement items across four constructs were used to analysis. The structural model was evaluated through the application of a set of fit indices. The structural model's goodness-of-fit indicators demonstrated that the Chi-Square/df ratio is 2.80, which is within the acceptable threshold level of 3. GFI at 0.875, AGFI at 0.826, NFI at 0.875, IFI at 0.916, TLI at 0.896, CFI at 0.915, and RMSEA of 0.091 moderately meet the required level. Therefore, all of the model fit indices have attained the minimum threshold values recommended by previous scholarly investigations (Hair et al., 2015).

After evaluating the model's goodness-of-fit via confirmatory factor analysis and structural equation modeling, the hypotheses were subsequently examined through an analysis of the regression path coefficients. Table 4.4 reports regression path coefficient result. The hypothetical relationships are assessed utilizing regression beta coefficients and critical ratios. To establish the statistical significance of the causal correlations between constructs at the 1% level, the critical ratio must surpass 1.96, and the p-value must be less than 0.01 (Hair et al., 2015). Results of this study show that digital currency is found to be statistically significant in promoting financial wellbeing of individuals (H1: $\beta = 0.290$, $p < 0.01$). The next hypothesis that blockchain security significantly affects financial wellbeing of households is also found significant (H2: $\beta = 0.287$, $p < 0.01$). Further, hypothesis that information transparency significantly affects financial wellbeing of individuals is also found significant (H3: $\beta = 0.284$ $p < 0.05$). In the nutshell, the statistical results of the study confirm that all of the proposed hypotheses are statistically supported.

Table 4.4 Results of direct effects of the structural model

Hypothesis	*Path*	*Standard Coefficient*	*p value*	*Results*
H_1	DC → FWB	0.290***	0.004	Accepted
H_2	BCS → FWB	0.287***	0.003	Accepted
H_3	IT → FWB	0.284**	0.025	Accepted

Note **, *** The coefficient is significant at 0.05 and 0.01 levels, respectively
Source AMOS results

4.6 Discussion

The current research model is analysed to determine hypothetical relationships of the factors affecting financial wellbeing of individuals in the present fintech 3.0 era which is observed scantly in available literature. A structural model with digital currency, blockchain security, and information transparency constructs and their impact on financial wellbeing of people in developing country is the unique output of this empirical work. On the basis of the results of SEM, digital currency is the most crucial and significant construct to influence financial wellbeing of individuals. Earlier research of Sadiq et al. (2023) has also reported same results. CBDC and financial technology services demonstrate the potential to maintain financial stability, while cryptocurrency may pose risks to financial stability that can be addressed through appropriate regulatory measures. Further, results also declared that blockchain security significantly affect financial wellbeing of individuals and the same was discovered in the study of Sadiq et al. (2023) and Yang et al. (2024). Blockchain security can offer financial institutions a secure and transparent system for recording transactions, thereby reducing the potential for fraudulent activities. Moreover, results of this study investigated the positive and significant impact of informational transparency on financial wellbeing and supported the study of Yang et al. (2024). The integration of informational transparency and digital currencies into the financial services infrastructure holds the promise of greatly enhancing financial wellbeing for numerous individuals across the globe. However, the realization of this significant potential is contingent upon their judicious and thoughtful design and implementations, taking into account various factors and considerations to ensure their effective and beneficial integration.

4.7 Managerial Implication

This study suggests implications for policymakers in emerging markets, such as India, and contributes to the existing body of research on evolving methods of exchange in developing economies through its findings. Results highlight that digital currencies and blockchain technology are extensively utilized in the provision of financial services. The revolutionary online digital cash and payment systems have achieved unprecedented levels of speed and efficiency, transforming the financial landscape in remarkable ways and creating information transparency. Ecological issues have emerged as a significant challenge for the global community (Kaur et. al, 2022) and digital currency may create a path for sustainable development. This research establishes a compelling academic framework for the paramount significance of comprehending household acceptance of digital currencies as a payment method in developing nations. Uwamariya and Loebbecke (2020) assert that money, technology, and payment modalities have all been reconfigured premised upon the foundation of information transparency. Findings revealed that rapid progress in innovative technologies and financial infrastructures may quickly make the existing monetary system obsolete, thereby leading to the emergence of digital currencies with blockchain technology which may positively influence financial wellbeing of individuals. The findings of this study possess substantial practical applications. Financial institutions may harness blockchain security to augment households' financial transparency and economic wellbeing.

Moreover, policymakers should implement regulatory frameworks that must promote the integration of blockchain technology within the banking industry for information transparency and financial wellbeing. Executives, banking authorities, and cost-cutting strategists in banking can leverage blockchain technology to streamline their expenditures. In digital era, real-time monitoring of business transactions and optimizing operational efficiency are paramount. In critical situations like humanitarian economic crises, blockchain may serve as a facilitator, bolstering the robustness of audit trails—a boon for all stakeholders. Given the financial institutions' direct involvement in individual and corporate finances, it is vulnerable to fraud and distorted records. Our study suggests that executives can leverage blockchain to describe the industry guidelines clearly and enhance regulatory fulfilment, resulting in tangible benefits (Garg et. al, 2021).

4.8 Conclusion and Scope for Future Direction

Results of the study declared that digital currency, blockchain security, and information transparency are significant and positive predictors of financial wellbeing. The emerging technologies of blockchain and digital currencies demonstrate significant potential for future growth, considering the current rate of acceptance for novel financial systems. The investigation of the current study posits that the adoption of a blockchain-empowered banking system enhances information transparency, culminating in elevated financial wellbeing for individuals. Moreover, business leaders need to create an evaluation model to find blockchain benefits before adding it to their banking operations. The flexible design of blockchain works well in banking and helps organizations save money when they put it into practice (Garg et al., 2021). For example, the decentralized feature of blockchain can assist reduce the participation of traditional economic intermediaries, thus falling the overall transaction costs and processing time (Guo & Liang, 2016). A decentralized blockchain network helps banking systems enhance their payments supply chain by applying clear rules and acceptable practices to prevent failures (Palmié et al., 2020). Therefore, digital currency and blockchain technology demonstrate substantial power for cutting operational expenses while improving complete financial welfare. These modern technologies drive more efficient financial processing at lower costs and open doors for banking sector improvements to serve diverse groups of clients.

This research only investigates the financial wellbeing of individuals that use digital currency. Future researchers should examine the relationship between financial stability along with credit supply and monetary policy. Further exploration through academic research is needed to establish the connections between information technology, trust and information transparency, and individual financial management skills. Socio-economic characteristics of households can also be considered for future study on this topic. Expanding upon existing literature, forthcoming investigations can examine further variables that may impact the association between blockchain-enabled banking system, information transparency, digital currency, and individuals' financial prosperity.

References

Agarwal, S., & Zhang, J. (2020). FinTech, lending and payment innovation: A review. *Asia-Pacific Journal of Financial Studies, 49*(3), 353–367. https://doi.org/10.1111/ajfs.12294

Akhter, F., Waqas, M., & Sohaib, S. (2022). Factors affecting the adoption of fintech services for bank clients. *Journal of Social Sciences and Humanities, 61*(1), 45–67.https://doi.org/10.46568/jssh.v61i1.597

Alsalmi, N., Ullah, S., & Rafique, M. (2023). Accounting for digital currencies. *Research in International Business and Finance, 64*, 101897. https://doi.org/10.1016/j.ribaf.2023.101897

Atzori, M. (2015). Blockchain technology and decentralized governance: Is the state still necessary?. *Journal of Governance and Regulation, 6*(1), 45–62. https://doi.org/10.22495/jgr_v6_i1_p5

Brüggen, E., Hogreve, J., Holmlund, M., Kabadayi, S., & Löfgren. (2017). Financial well-being: A conceptualization and research agenda. *Journal of Business Research, 79*, 228–237. https://doi.org/10.1016/j.jbusres.2017.03.013

Byrne, B. M. (2010). *Multivariate applications series', Structural equation modeling with AMOS: Basic concepts, applications, and programming*. Taylor & Francis Group.

Crosby, M., Pattanayak, P., Verma, S., & Kalyanaraman, V. (2016). Blockchain technology: Beyond bitcoin. *Applied Innovation, 2*(6–10), 71.

Fornell, C., & Larcker, D. F. (1981). Evaluating structural equation models with unobservable variables and measurement error. *Journal of Marketing Research, 18*(1), 39–50. https://doi.org/10.1177/002224378101800104

Garg, N., & Singh, S. (2018). Financial literacy among youth. *International Journal of Social Economics, 45*(1), 173–186. https://doi.org/10.1108/IJSE-11-2016-0303

Garg, P., Gupta, B., Chauhan, A. K., Sivarajah, U., Gupta, S., & Modgil, S. (2021). Measuring the perceived benefits of implementing blockchain technology in the banking sector. *Technological Forecasting Social Change, 163*, Article 120407.

Gerrans, P., Speelman, C., & Campitelli, G. (2014). The relationship between personal financial wellness and financial wellbeing: A structural equation modelling approach. *Journal of Family and Economic Issues, 35*, 145–160.

Guo, Y., & Liang, C. (2016). Blockchain application and outlook in the banking industry. *Financial Innovation, 2*(24), 1–12. https://doi.org/10.1186/s40854-016-0034-9

Gupta, A., Yousaf, A., & Mishra, A. (2020). How pre-adoption expectancies shape post-adoption continuance intentions: an extended expectation-conirmation model. *International Journal of Information Management, 52*, 102094. https://doi.org/10.1016/j.ijinfomgt.2020.102094

Hair, J. F., Black, W. C., Babin, B. J., Anderson, R. E., & Tatham, R. L. (2015). *Multivariate data analysis* (7th ed). Pearson Education.

Huibers, F. (2021). Distributed ledger technology and the future of money and banking. *Accounting, Economics, and Law: Convivium, 1901*, 1–37. https://doi.org/10.1515/ael-2019-0095

Johnson, B., Laszka,A., Grossklags, J., & Moore, T. (2018). Economic analyses of security investments on cryptocurrency exchanges. In *IEEE International Conference on Internet of Things (iThings) and IEEE Green Computing and Communications (GreenCom) and IEEE Cyber, Physical and Social Computing (CPSCom) and IEEE Smart Data (SmartData)*. 1253–1262. https://doi.org/10.1109/Cybermatics_2018.2018.00220.

Kant, R., Mishra, S., & Singh, S. (2013). Microfinance: A tool of poverty alleviation with bank linkage programme in Himachal Pradesh. *SUMEDHA Journal of Management, 2*(3), 52–64.

Kanungo, R. P., & Gupta, S. (2021). Financial inclusion through digitalisation of services for well-being. *Technological Forecasting and Social Change, 167*, Article 120721. https://doi.org/10.1016/j.techfore.2021.120721

Kaur, R., Mishra, S., Yadav, S., & Shaw, T. (2022). Analyzing the impact of green marketing mix on consumer purchase intention. *International Journal of Indian Culture and Business Management, 25*(3), 403–425. https://doi.org/10.1504/IJICBM.2021.10038995

Liu, Y., Eisingerich, A. B., Auh, S., Merlo, O., & Chun, H. E. H. (2015). Service firm performance transparency: How, when, and why does it pay off? *Journal of Service Research, 18*(4), 451–467.

Lober, K., & Houben, A. (2018). *Committee on payments and market infrastructures markets committee*. CPMI. https://www.bis.org/cpmi/publ/d137.pdf.

Macrinici, D., Cartofeanu, C., & Gao, S. (2018). Smart contract applications within blockchain technology: A systematic mapping study. *Telematics and Informatics, 35*(8), 2337–2354. https://doi.org/10.1016/j.tele.2018.10.004

Marsal-Llacuna, M. (2018). Future living framework: Is blockchain the next enabling network? *Technological Forecasting and Social Change., 128*, 226–234. https://doi.org/10.1016/j.techfore.2017.12.005

Mhlanga, D. (2022). Digital financial inclusion. Springer Nature Switzerland AG. https://doi.org/10.1007/978-3-031-16687-7.

Milian, E. Z., Spínola, M. de M., & Carvalho, M. M. de. (2019). Fintechs: A literature review and research agenda. *Electronic Commerce Research and Applications, 34*, 100833.https://doi.org/10.1016/j.elerap.2019.100833

Mireku, K., Appiah, F., & Agana, J. A. (2023). Is there a link between financial literacy and financial behaviour? *Cogent Economics & Finance,11*(1). https://doi.org/10.1080/23322039.2023.2188712

Mishra, S., Singh, A. P., & Kaur, R. (2023). Does financial inclusion matter for the socioeconomic development of marginalized people? Evidence from India. *Vision—The Journal of Business Perspective*, 1–15. https://doi.org/10.1177/09722629231198609

Mishra, S., & Kant, R. (2013). Social inclusion through e-Governance: A study of the beneficiaries of Uttar Pradesh (U.P.). *SUMEDHA Journal of Management*, *2*(2), 128–136.

Naveed, M., Farah, M. F., & Hasni, M. J. S. (2021). The transformative role of firm information transparency in triggering retail investor's perceived financial well-being. *International Journal of Bank Marketing, 39*(7), 1091–1113.

Ozili, P. K. (2018). Impact of digital finance on financial inclusion and stability. *Borsa Istanbul Review, 18*(4), 329–340. https://doi.org/10.1016/j.bir.2017.12.003

Palmié, M., Wincent, J., Parida, V., & Caglar, U. (2020). The evolution of the financial technology ecosystem: An introduction and agenda for future research on disruptive innovations in ecosystems. *Technological Forecasting and Social Change., 151*, Article 119779. https://doi.org/10.1016/j.techfore.2019.119779

Prawitz, A. D., Garman, E. T., Sorhaindo, B., O'Neill, B., Kim, J., & Drentea, P. (2006). The incharge financial distress/financial well-being scale: Establishing validity and reliability. *Fin Counsel Plan, 17*, 34–50.

Sadiq, M., Aysan, A. F., & Kayani, U. N. (2023). Digital currency and blockchain security in accelerating financial stability:A mediating role of credit supply. *Borsa Istanbul Review, 23,* 1251–1262. https://doi.org/10.1016/j.bir.2023.09.00

Shin, D. D. (2019). Blockchain: The emerging technology of digital trust. *Telematics and Informatics, 45*, Article 101278. https://doi.org/10.1016/j.tele.2019.101278

Shin, D., & Park, Y. (2019). Role of fairness, accountability, and transparency in algorithmic affordance. *Computers in Human Behavior., 98*, 277–284. https://doi.org/10.1016/j.chb.2019.04.019

Singh, A., Srivastva, R., Yogendra, N., & Singh, Y. N. (2019). Prevention of payment card frauds using biometrics. *International Journal of Recent Technology and Engineering, 8*, 516–525. https://doi.org/10.35940/ijrte.c1106.1083s19

Singh, A. P., Kaur, R., & Mishra, S. (2022). Assessment of role of commercial banks for financial inclusion with special reference to Pradhan Mantri Jan Dhan Yojana. *PIMT Journal of Research, 14*(4), 47–52.

Suwanposri, C., Bhatiasevi, V., & Thanakijsombat, T. (2021). Drivers of blockchain adoption in financial and supply chain enterprises. *Global Business Review*. https://doi.org/10.1177/09721509211046170

Uwamariya, M., & Loebbecke, C. (2020). Learning from the mobile payment role model: Lessons from Kenya for neighboring Rwanda. *Information Technology for Development, 26*(1), 108–127. https://doi.org/10.1080/02681102.2018.1564725

Walch, A. (2015). The Bitcoin Blockchain as Financial Market Infrastructure: A Consideration of Operational Risk. *NYU Journal of Legislation and Public Policy*, 837, SSRN: https://ssrn.com/abstract=2579482

Wamba, S. F., Queiroz, M. M., Blome, C., & Sivarajah, U. (2021). Fostering inancial inclusion in a developing country: Predicting user acceptance of mobile wallets in Cameroon. *Journal of Global Information Management, 29*(4), 195–220.https://doi.org/10.4018/JGIM.20210701.oa9

Wasilah, S., & Fahmyddin, T. (2018). The advancement of the built environment research through employment of structural equation modeling (SEM). *IOP Conference Series: Earth and Environmental Science, 126*, Article 012001.

Yadav, J., Kaur, R., & Mishra, S. (2024a). Way for social sustainability by making rural people self-reliant: An evaluation of NABARD's initiatives in India. *World Review of Entrepreneurship, Management and Sustainable Development, 20*(6), 664–682. https://doi.org/10.1504/WREMSD.2024.10066195

Yadav, J., Kaur, R., & Mishra, S. (2024b). Contribution of self-help groups (SHGs) in addressing the several development issues: A systematic review of literature. *International Journal of Management Practice, 17*(1), 67–84. https://doi.org/10.1504/IJMP.2023.10049570

Yadav, J., Kaur, R., & Mishra, S. (2021). Self-help groups (SHGs) in India: An analysis through review of existing literature. *PIMT Journal of Research, 13*(2B), 1–4.

Yamaoka, H. (2022). Digital currencies and the future of money. In M. Heckel & F. Waldenberger (Eds.), *The future of financial systems in the digital age. perspectives in law, business and innovation.* Springer, Singapore. https://doi.org/10.1007/978-981-16-7830-1_4.

Yang, Z., Ali, S., Tao, W., & Chen, H. (2024). From transactions to transformation: Exploring the impact of blockchain on customer financial well-being. *Sage Open, 14*(2). https://doi.org/10.1177/21582440241253955

Zemlyak, S., Gusarova, O., & Khromenkova, G. (2022). Tools for correlation and regression analyses in estimating a functional relationship of digitalization factors. *Mathematics, 10*(3), 429.https://doi.org/10.3390/math10030429

Zhang, L., Xie, Y., Zheng, Y., Xue, W., Zheng, X., & Xu, X. (2020). The challenges and countermeasures of blockchain in finance and economics. *Systems Research and Behavioral Science., 37*(4), 691–698. https://doi.org/10.1002/sres.2710

Zwitter, A., & Hazenberg, J. (2020). Decentralized network governance: Blockchain technology and the future of regulation. *Frontiers in Blockchain, 3*(12). https://doi.org/10.3389/fbloc.2020.00012

CHAPTER 5

Digital Currency and Greener Environment: A Comprehensive Study of Positive and Negative Externalities of Digital Currency in India

Ananya Bhardwaj and Manas Roy

5.1 Introduction: Digital Currency

The following terminology coined by the literature is included in this research under the term "digital currency (DC)".[1] Digitalized state-issued currencies and private digital money are the two categories of DC (Gans & Halaburda, 2015). Another way to describe it is as a type of currency that incorporates modern technologies like databases, cryptography, peer-to-peer networking, and consensus-based systems. One acclaimed exemplar of DC is Bitcoin (Achord et al., 2017). In the future,

A. Bhardwaj
Department of Economics, Manipal University Jaipur, Jaipur, India

M. Roy (✉)
Department of Economics, Faculty of Management Studies, Marwadi University Rajkot, Rajkot, India
e-mail: manas.roy138@gmail.com

R. Aneja and R. Dygas (eds.), *Digital Currencies and the Green Economy*, https://doi.org/10.1007/978-981-95-2282-8_5

cryptocurrencies will undoubtedly control a sizable piece of the money market as the usage of hard currency steadily falls and the use of DC grows dramatically. What its environmental legacy will be is still up for debate (Lobo, 2022).

The term “digital economy (DE)” is now frequently used in the twenty-first century to refer to the increased usage of technology and telecommunications infrastructure to support the economic development of numerous nations worldwide. It now serves as a necessary model for both established and developing economies worldwide, acting as a catalyst for innovation in national development plans that make use of ICTs. DC’s potential impact on various economic sectors[2] increasingly portrays it as an essential element for a nation’s advancement and prosperity. It also encourages innovation and entrepreneurship. The DE has revolutionized numerous nations, and it is leading the charge in elevating nations like China to the forefront of the global economic landscape. The DE has transformed several nations and is leading the charge to make nations like China one of the world’s greatest economies. Due to the absence of the financial and infrastructure resources needed for the change, developing countries face greater challenges than industrialized ones in making the shift to a DE. Furthermore, the majority of developing nations lack the cultural norms necessary to gather and disseminate the essential dataset that assessment organizations need to gauge their progress towards a DE (Dwyer, 2014).

“Central Bank Digital Currency (CBDC)” came into the economy when the CB of a nation issued a “digital form” of “fiat money” as a matter of choice “paper or metal currency,” known to be the CB’s sincere obligation and valued in accordance with the country’s unit of account. By resolving any disagreements that may arise throughout a transaction, it offers a secure, formal, and final option for settlement. To issue and distribute a general-purpose CBDC to the public in a convenient manner, an underlying mechanism is required. This ecosystem requires that “RBI, public and private banks, and payment service providers (PSPs)” as well as other entities function. If we consider the entire economy, we can also include other financial institutions (Banerjee et al., 2023). The methods of issuing CBDCs might be quite similar to the current system, where each commercial bank and central bank work together to build a complete “end-to-end blockchain-enabled” system for distributing and issuing CBDCs. A CBDC can be established for various reasons in different countries, but some of the most common ones are to strengthen payment systems, promote financial stability, combat illicit activity, and guarantee the currency's relative power in a DE. Several technologies have surfaced that help achieve the goals of sustainable development. Fintech, private digital currencies, and digital financial services are a few of these technologies. Numerous studies have looked at how financial innovations may back the fulfilment of "sustainable development goals (SDGs)" in the literature. These studies indicate that DC modernization can contribute to achieving the SDGs, provided it meets the necessary conditions and controls environmental degradation. CBs must play a significant role in the digital transformation of "sustainable development," as "digitalization" is changing the landscape of "sustainable development."

5.2 CBDC in India

CBDC is considered a newer concept that has accrued much attention recently in India. CB issues digital equivalents of fiat currency, known as CBDCs. CBDCs can reduce cash-management expenses, enhance financial inclusion, and simplify cross-border payments. Blockchain technology is available for usage by CBDC, although it is not necessary. There exist multiple technology approaches for the implementation of CBDCs. One potential method for putting CBDCs into practice is to leverage blockchain technology, which offers a distributed, transparent ledger for tracking transactions and guaranteeing the currency's integrity. The country's residents were interested in cryptocurrency, but its ban has led to mixed feelings about it. The digitalization of the Indian rupee has been on the to-do list of the Reserve Bank of India. It is anticipated that e-₹ will contribute to a decrease in the economy's use of cash by boosting digital payments. Many people think that India's own cryptocurrency is called e ₹. However, there appears to be a subtle distinction between the e-U and other cryptocurrencies. The digital ₹ might be used in the same ways as real money, much like other CBDCs. It would be the analogy of real money in the digital realm. Like conventional fiat currencies, it would be intended to function as a "store of value" as well as a "means of exchange." The intermediary banks will distribute the e-money in similar denominations to "paper money" and "coins." Customers can buy digital ₹ online, using the official app or at reputable banks. Remember, the digital rupee is still relatively new, with limited understanding of its workings.[3] China and the Bahamas are the only two big nations that have advanced CBDCs to the next level. Similar to India, Sweden, and other nations are investigating the possibility of implementing the DC. We have also discussed the potential use of CBDCs to supply funds for specific "goods and services," specialized aid, and "subsidies." The cannabis law will shield the people from the unstable virtual currency environment in addition to enhancing payment procedures.[4] Additionally, CBDC helps enforce rules against money laundering and financial terrorism by providing a very secure way to handle international contracts, removing the need for later checks. Moreover, "distributed ledger technology (DLT)" helps expedite high-value transactions where people can benefit greatly from its use as a tool for offline payments using digital tokens (Aggarwal et al., 2021).

5.2.1 Need of CBDC in India

India, with its sixth-largest economy, may leverage its global strategic location to utilize blockchain technology to address issues related to its business climate, security, employment, and capital shortages. Because of this, the government is eager to provide the background necessary to guarantee that innovation in this field proceeds unhindered. Nevertheless, managing a blockchain is costly, requiring top-tier resources to enable full data processing. The different blockchain nodes carry out the same functions as their data copies. Numerous Indian banks[5] have approved blockchain technology. Each of these institutions anticipates significant future growth and a high growth potential. These banks have begun incorporating blockchain technology into their foreign finance dealings (Awasthy et al., 2023).

The introduction of CBDC may have the following effects on the banking industry:

a. Easier regulation and policy execution
b. Bank runs may be prevented.
c. Paper money and private bank deposits may be eliminated.
d. Increased inclusiveness

Many of the dangers and expenses associated with the old system, which was developed when clients required safe branches to deposit bags of cash, should be eliminated by these modifications.

Currency is most typically used for small-value transactions, averaging 37,000 INR,[6] according to a preliminary survey by the Reserve Bank of India on individuals' retail remittance patterns. It is important to realize that, depending on how much they are used, CBDCs may lessen the transaction demand for bank deposits. Transaction liquidity needs, like intraday liquidity, are minimized since CBDC transactions reduce settlement risk. DC payments will reduce the settlement risk of the financial system. The technology will transfer digital currencies instead of bank balances, eliminating the requirement for interbank settlement, much like it does with cash. Similarly, foreign exchange transactions would happen instantly. An exporter from India might, for instance, quickly pay an exporter from the US in digital dollars. Additionally, providing a genuinely risk-free substitute for bank savings would promote a shift away from bank deposits, which would lessen the requirement for government deposit guarantees. If a bank is having problems, depositors can easily withdraw their money because of CBDC's accessibility. Cash withdrawals cannot be completed nearly as rapidly as deposits.

5.3 Review of Literature

Otto and Nemati (2017), in their paper, have highlighted the relationship between digital money and the standard of living. This paper has covered two methods, namely Sen's Capability Approach and the Elaboration Likelihood Model. The models were used in the students' survey results, as they are the most qualified people in the country to study DC's pros and cons.

Bhowmik (2022) has edited a book on the approach of CBDCs. In the book there is a chapter written by Sandeep Poddar, which analyses the environmental impact post-COVID-19, as there has been an increase in digital payments, which has also increased the dependency on mobiles and technology even for payments.

Eichengreen (2022) contends that a great deal of the justifications for CBDCs have been made without question. Their supporters neglect to mention that there are other, less risky, and less expensive ways to achieve such objectives. This assertion holds true both generally and occasionally, particularly in the case of India with its established universal payments infrastructure and continuous endeavours to promote financial inclusion. Some arguments supporting CBDCs are illogical or unrealistic.

Few people consider the actual negative risks that come with the development of CBDCs, such as threats to institutional investors, retail CBDC end users, and the CB's reputation.

Haque and Shoaib (2023), in their paper, have highlighted the review of the e₹₹ that had been introduced by the RBI as a preliminary project to launch digital currencies and cryptocurrency in the country. Either a direct model or a hybrid model can introduce the currencies to the market. DC eliminates the need for actual cash or a physical bank at any given time or location. As a result, transactions could become more conducive and adept, specifically for the population living in distant pastoral areas. For them, purchasing digital currency in token form from commercial banks (CB) could replace the need for a bank account. Generally speaking, it would be comparable to taking money out of our bank accounts, except for handing cash. CB deposits "electronic wallets" with the money, which we could then use like any other coinage.[7]

Cyril (2023), has written a paper about the CBDC from an Indian viewpoint. CBDCs could potentially influence the behaviour of the general public and the overall state of the Indian economy. In the Indian context, the RBI issues legal currency digitally and acknowledges it as such. It further stated that the RBI will issue digital legal money as "a store of value," "unit of account," and "medium of exchange." For regular expenses, cash is still the most popular method of sending and receiving money. A Reserve Bank pilot survey conducted in six locations between December 2018 and January 2019 found that customers most commonly use cash for small-value transactions, which typically cost 37,000 Indian rupees. It is crucial to understand that the transaction demand for bank deposits may be reduced by CBDCs, depending on their usage. Because they lower settlement risk, transactions in CBDCs reduce the demand for transaction liquidity, including intraday liquidity.

5.4 Objectives of the Study

The present study aims to achieve the following:

a. To study the ongoing demand for cashless payments in India
b. To study the impact of cashless payments on the environment in India
c. To study the existing e-currency adopted by various countries

The subsequent study has highlighted the expected reach of the DC as compared to the population of the country, along with its positive and negative effects on the environment as well as costs and management. There have been subsequent case studies to supplement countries doing CBDCs to cover the third objective.

5.5 Analysis of the Study

5.5.1 *Growing Demand of Cashless Payments in India*

The primary objectives of digital currencies include enhancing transparency and enabling comprehensive tracking of transactions, which can fundamentally reshape the financial landscape. By facilitating cashless payments, digital currencies have the capacity to foster the growth of a new sector that not only streamlines financial interactions but also creates and promotes various employment opportunities within that sector (Bhat et al., 2021).

With all transactions recorded as a stable and unchangeable ledger, there is a strong potential for increased taxation in the fintech space. This is largely because the visibility of transactions significantly reduces the chances of tax evasion, resulting in a more robust tax base and improved revenue for the government. Moreover, the transition to DC means the elimination of physical cash, which directly addresses the issue of counterfeit money. By reducing the prevalence of fake currency scams, digital currencies can enhance trust in the financial system.

This shift will also provide significant cost benefits to both the administration and the RBI, as its implementation could lower the expenditure affiliated with printing and storing as well as classifying tangible currency. This reduction in costs can be redirected towards other critical areas of public investment. Ultimately, the implementation of digital currencies aligns with the vision of Atma Nirbhar Bharat, promoting self-reliance and economic resilience. By fostering a modern financial ecosystem, digital currencies can empower individuals and businesses alike, driving innovation and contributing to sustainable economic growth in India (Pachare et al., 2023).

Digital payments can help you reach the following goals:

a. Transparency
b. Employment growth

c. Boost in the taxation and fintech sectors
d. End of fake currency issue
e. Saving cost in printing of currency and supply of currency
f. Aiming towards the achievement of Atma Nirbhar Bharat

5.5.2 *Environmental Impact of Cashless Payments in India*

Initiatives to mitigate climate change, such as laws that cut greenhouse gas emissions and encourage sustainability, significantly impact economic stability. A "low-carbon economy" necessitates a large contribution in infrastructure, sustainable energy, and green technologies, all of which might spur economic expansion and create new job possibilities. But the cost of these expenses and the risk of economic disruptions during the transition phase may threaten economic stability. Additionally, different sectors may be affected differently by initiatives to mitigate climate change, which could result in changes in the monetary exercise as well as possible asymmetry. "Carbon pricing" schemes[8] have the potential to expand the price of "carbon-intensive goods and services." While companies relying on "fossil fuels" may face challenges, those utilizing energy efficiency and renewable energy sources could potentially benefit. Maintaining general economic stability depends on how well these policies accomplish their objectives while causing the fewest possible disturbances to the economy. Within the framework of global economic governance, it is essential to address the intricate and vital relationship between preserving economic stability and lessening the impacts of latitude revision. Long-term environmental sustainability depends on preventing climate change, but there are also urgent economic opportunities and issues involved. Investments in renewable energy sources and green technology are necessary to lower carbon emissions and mitigate the effects of climate change. By diversifying the economy and reducing reliance on fossil fuels, these investments have the potential to increase economic growth and create jobs in the green sector, which will increase economic stability overall. However, there are also substantial financial expenses and adjustments associated with the shift to a low-carbon economy. Companies that rely on carbon-intensive operations may encounter disruptions necessitating extensive restructuring and adjustment. Adopting climate legislation also entails upfront costs and financial risks, which could harm economic stability right away. To maintain economic stability, a balance must be struck between the short-term and long-term advantages of climate mitigation. Good management of the transition and making sure that moving to a sustainable economy positively affects overall economic stability can be done through detailed plans that link climate goals with financial strategies (Tafti et al., 2021).

5.5.3 *CBDC and Sustainable Development in India*

DC, promulgated by the Prime Bank, or CBDC, is anticipated to become the main digital infrastructure in the future and has been a hot topic in the banking and money sectors globally. Despite CBDC's significance for sustainable development, researchers, businesses, and legislators still differ over its effects on the environment. CBDC has heavily encouraged the emergence of "green bonds." Manufacturing and state-owned enterprises, in particular, have issued more green bonds as a result of CBDC. Additionally, it has been discovered that CBDC promotes sustainable development, reduces emissions of smoke, NO_x, and SO_2, and raises the percentage of green space in the overall region. Our results provide an initial overview of CBDC's effects on the environment. We propose that the CBDC help to expedite green finance, which promotes sustainable development and calls for more thorough empirical research (Yang et al., 2023).

5.5.4 *Major Usage of CBDC in India*

The RBI has maintained its opposition to "private digital currencies," arguing that "the sovereign is responsible for currency issuance." It is currently unknown if the upcoming legislation on digital currencies will outright forbid any cryptocurrency-related activities, including holding Bitcoin, which would have a significant negative influence on a large number of people. The RBI has often stated that it is accessible to CBDCs; above all, it has not yet made a firm proposal public. "As and when the technology evolves with adequate safeguards, I think it is an area that the Reserve Bank will certainly look at seriously at an appropriate time," the RBI Governor noted in a recent remark (Babu, 2021).

- *"Programmable Payments"*

"Fit-for-purpose" currency utilized for societal benefits and other purposeful pay within a nation is one potential use case for CBDC.[9] For instance, LPG subsidies might distribute pre-programmed CBDCs as direct benefit transfers (DBT). Only the authorized LPG office would be able to use this CBDC. LPG agencies could change the CBDC in terms of "fiat currency" or "general-purpose CBDC" through any commercial bank as long as the bank had the legal authority to do so. Other industries[10] may further exaggerate these subsidies, potentially using the CBDC to transfer fertilizer subsidies. Only authorized fertilizer stores could accept this CBDC, ensuring that there would be as little leakage in the subsidy program. "Programmable payments can also be utilized by other businesses for their employees' expenses, including for petrol and communication bills. Furthermore, industrial supply chain ecosystems can also take advantage of programmable payments. Pre-programmed digital CBDC in this scenario could only be used for certain things, such as gas costs and state border taxes" (Kandpal et al., 2022).

- *Cross-Border Remittances*

CBDCs could facilitate faster cross-border remittance payments. International cooperation between the world's largest economies—including India's—could contribute to the development of the arrangements and infrastructure required for the transfer and conversion of CBDC. For CBDCs to be successful, this infrastructure must guarantee that they may be transferred quickly and across countries. In this kind of setting, real-time CBDC remittances might occur, cutting down on the amount of time it takes for the intended recipient to receive the payment.

- *Retail Payments (Transaction Settlement)*

We can recycle CBDCs to facilitate trade disbursement. We could also implement deposit mechanisms to enable the use of CBDCs for payment transactions. Moreover, an offline payment feature could be one of a CBDC's universal access features. The RBI and commercial banks would distribute retail CBDC, which end users would need to store in electronic wallets or accounts. This arrangement would make the following payment methods possible:

> *The consumer-to-consumer:* Allowing customers to transfer CBDC between their wallets
> *Consumer to business:* A scenario in which customers pay for goods and services using CBDC.
> *Business-to-business:* facilitates the transfer of CBDC between companies "corporate account wallets."

Because of the fact that CBDCs provide immediate arrangements, these mitigate counterparty hazard by lowering the risk associated with retail payment clearing and settlement. The digital aspect of the currency and the underlying technology of CBDC make it better than current digital payments. Because of its unquestionable character and the ability to transfer ownership records, it can offer unquestionable evidence for partnership.

- ***"Micro, Small, and Medium-Sized Enterprises (MSME)" Grant***

MSME-sized businesses in our country may qualify for quick loans along with the support of CBDC. Since major MSMEs are going to utilize CBDC, financial institutions may develop a more precise "borrower risk profile." Financial institutions may also recycle CBDC to expedite MSME payment requirements. Additionally, the central bank (CB) might give MSMEs stimulus money right away. This approach can help businesses grow and thrive in turbulent times when capital is limited. MSMEs can establish their creditworthiness with the aid of CBDC's traceability. It also promotes transparency and has a high degree of resistance against forgeries.

- ***Offline Payments***

Another payment method that CBDC can offer is offline payment. In principle, the offline wallet would be independent and might utilize "near-field communication (NFC) technology." Use of the "digital wallet or digital application" is possible on feature phones and smartphones that support NFC technology. This appears to be very safe, as well as a convenient preference for associate payments in situations with shoddy networks or without the internet. Without requiring an internet connection, identity verification, transaction confirmation, and payment will all take place over and above the disconnected wallet in an "account-agnostic" manner.

5.6 Impact of Digital Currency: A SWOT Analysis

The table of SWOT Analysis (Table 5.1) summarizes the strengths, weaknesses, opportunities, and threats of CBDC, as analysed by many researchers individually (Sigurosson et al., 2023).

5.6.1 Strengths

The use of DC in world commerce has several benefits that include increased financial inclusion for the unbanked, decreased costs related to international transactions, improved efficiency and speed of transactions,

Table 5.1 SWOT analysis of digital currency

Strengths	*Weakness*
Quick transactions and time savings	Limited trust on it
Usage in international business	Uncertainty exists
Distance component has eased out	No back up from CB
No interference of banks, credit cards and middlemen	A kind of anonymous currency
The elimination of the "double spending problem"	
Opportunities	Threats
Ease of cross-border usage	Competing with fiat money
Easy usage in different time zones	Bank failure along with higher interest rates
No different currency complications	Risk of suppression with higher money rise
A faster way of doing transactions	Difficult for the government to control
Creation of a newer platform of trust	Bitcoin volatility

Source Sigurosson et al. (2023)

and increased transparency and traceability. As a result, in terms of overseas transactions, families and companies stand to gain from the use of CBDCs due to decreased transaction fees and reduced pricing (Table 5.1).

5.6.2 *Weakness*

Many people and companies could be reluctant to switch from conventional payment methods or might only know a limited amount about using DC. It will take the collective efforts of numerous parties, including governments, businesses, regulators, and technology developers, to address these deficiencies. The adoption of DC in global commerce heavily relies on user acceptability and familiarity. Furthermore, security and privacy issues, such as concerns about illegal activities and cyberthreats, require strong protective and supervisory measures. Furthermore, there are issues with accountability and consumer protection arising from the absence of centralized authority and governance systems in digital currencies (Table 5.1).

5.6.3 *Opportunities*

Increasing financial inclusion is a possible benefit of digital currencies, particularly for enterprises and individuals. This accessibility can provide participants in international trade more power by making it easier for them to take part in international economic activity. Additionally, by removing the need for currency conversions and lowering related costs, digital currencies enable smooth cross-border transactions that are advantageous to both households and enterprises. Due to its worldwide accessibility, firms of all sizes may now operate on an even playing field, creating new markets and increasing trade prospects. Additionally, blockchain-based digital currencies provide increased traceability and transparency for transactions involving international trade. This implies that blockchain records will probably guarantee transaction integrity, lower fraud, and foster confidence between those involved in the transaction. Therefore, enhanced transparency and strong security can be advantageous to global trade, resulting in enhanced supply chain visibility, fewer disagreements, and more effective audit procedures (Table 5.1).

5.6.4 *Threats*

The rivalry between digital and conventional currencies presents a multitude of risks and difficulties that CBs must handle. The possible erosion of CBs' power and control over traditional currencies is a major source of concern as digital currencies become more widely accepted and used. Such an outcome might lessen the power of CBs to affect important variables like interest rates, rates of inflation, and the stability of the economy as a whole. Additionally, there are concerns about consumer protection and financial stability associated with the decentralized character of some digital currencies, such as cryptocurrencies. Various factors, including market volatility, insufficient regulation, and susceptibility to fraudulent operations or cyberattacks, have the potential to compromise the integrity of financial systems. Some features of digital currencies, like their ability to keep users anonymous or semi-anonymous, make people worry about their use in illegal activities, money laundering, and funding terrorism, so authorities need to keep a close watch on them (Table 5.1).

5.6.5 *Benefits of CBDC*

One can see that the advantages of CBDC as a reliable asset during a crisis could be at risk if central banks put in place financial penalties to prevent people from changing bank currency into CBDC. Thus, several points can be considered comprehensible that bolster the CBDC claim for effective usage through trade. This includes: (i) degenerate command to usage of currency issued by bank; (ii) inadequate ingress through merchandise banking funding for important household shares, which can happen in both least-developed and highly income-dispersed nations, like the US; (iii) a retail payment infrastructure that is too concentrated or unreliable.

This is developed in the fullest detail and also assumes that the role of banknotes will be discontinued or at least significantly reduced. Naturally, if CBDC acts as a circulator as unidentified souvenir currency, alike in large quantities, this reason would not be applicable. Some writers may disagree with this particular case for CBDC because they are very concerned about reimbursement confidentiality as well as worried about network shops that the state advisory board would exploit disbursement statistics to eventually restrict people's rights. Since variable rates of interest above CBDC command offer an advanced, "non-redundant monetary policy tool" that could be able to make agreeable as well as the comprehensive effectiveness of financial policy, several researchers have suggested that CBDC expands the variety of monetary policy alternatives. In order to appease the CB of England's financial policy, which aims for price cohesion, "digital cash can be used as a tool to increase aggregate demand by making 'helicopter drops' of newly created digital cash to all citizens." Only Proponents of helicopter money will likely agree that this argument is relevant. Furthermore, since it merely makes it easier to distribute helicopter money, it is not a prerequisite, it may be claimed that it is a weak argument (Hofmann, 2023).

5.6.6 Risks of CBDC

Privacy issues have arisen because CBDCs, unlike anonymous currency, are traceable. Additionally, there may be operational hazards for data security and privacy associated with CBDCs, especially retail CBDCs (e.g., Sand Dollar, e-CNY). The protection of customers' CBDC portfolios from cyber abuse, the prevention of fraudulent CBDC pocketbooks, and many facets of ensuring the data security and privacy of CBDCs have been introduced.[11]

One of CBDC's main concerns will be how it impacts current bank deposits, or the possibility of bank disintermediation. It may lower bank lending and the profitability of the banking industry if it decreases commercial bank deposit bases. Although the impact is still mostly unknown, competition with bank deposits may arise if CBDCs are positioned as the most secure digital payment method, making them appealing as a savings vehicle. On the one hand, home savings in the form of CBDC may expand the balance sheet of the CB and displace deposits at commercial banks, endangering the commercial banks' business models because their funding source would become more costly.

A larger role for CBs in the obligations of the private banking industry may promote lending to government agendas, increasing the possibility of inefficient capital allocation. CBDCs would have the same loss of real value (due to inflation or currency weakening) as conventional paper money in cases where governments engage in financially reckless behaviour, such as printing money to finance politically motivated spending.

5.6.7 *Mitigation Measures*

As payment activities are isolated from the loan industry, a CBDC may eventually take responsibility for the continuous transformations in the business models of fintech companies. Regulators reportedly ordered some of the biggest fintech companies to develop distinct platforms for their lending operations, but it's still unclear if and how the customer data that informs the companies' lending decisions will be shared between their lending and payment divisions. A CBDC might increase ambiguity in the gathering and exchange of payment data, which might put fintech companies' current business models in jeopardy.

According to some estimates, the implementation of CBDCs should have a controllable effect on bank lending and disintermediation. A significant transition from bank security to CBDC could impact the banking sector's "lending and intermediation" practices. It also implies that at the time this new scheme is given sufficient space together with resilience to accommodate, then these things' effects perhaps become minimal for a wide range of conceivable CBDC take-up levels. The financial system has effectively managed periods of structural change over the years and is dynamic and ever-evolving. Furthermore, regardless of CBDC, advances in the private sector can create comparable deposit substitution risks, and the implementation of CBDC might open up new avenues for innovation for banks and other financial institutions (Ozili, 2023).

5.7 Area of Existing CBDC: Case Studies

A total of 134 countries and some currency unions have been exploring, researching, and are in the advanced stages of launching a digital currency for their respective economies. But as of 2024, there have only been three countries that have launched their own CBDC. Most countries are in an advanced stage of research to soon launch a CBDC, while some, like Ecuador and Senegal, have cancelled their digital currencies.

The only countries with successful operations of digital currencies are as follows:

a. The Bahamas,
b. Nigeria, and
c. Jamaica

5.7.1 *The Bahamas*

The Bahamas introduced the "Sand Dollar" in October 2020, making it the first CBDC of the contemporary era. CBs control and issue CBDCs, which are digital equivalents of cash. Compared to cryptocurrency assets, they are thought to be more secure and less volatile. It is an initiative to support more equitable access for underbanked and unbanked communities and socioeconomic categories across the nation to administer disbursements and alternative monetary services. With the advent of the commercial CBDC, the CB also hopes to curtail business consignment costs and enhance transferable capability for monetary assistance beyond the Bahamas. After an online competition, this idea was dubbed "Sand Dollar," which is also another name for CBDC.[12] The Reserve Bank of the Bahamas, which is assisted by overseas capital, has a direct obligation to issue the digital B$. The private sector is the one that creates or issues cryptocurrencies. Even when this reserve bank is endorsed by alternative resources, including reserve bank cash, that may not fall within the purview of any government or central authority. Furthermore, actual assets might not always be able to sustain cryptocurrency (Sharon et al., 2023).

5.7.2 *Jamaica*

One of just four fully launched retail CBDCs globally, Jam-Dex debuted in July 2022 and is now in competition with the Bahamian Sand Dollar, the Eastern Caribbean DCash, and the Nigerian eNaira. In certain cases, even if you construct it, they may not come. Less than 0.01% of Jamaica's $4.7 trillion in electronic market commerce in 2022, as well as 0.1% of the gross national coinage in circulation, was made through Jam-Dex, which had 190,000 customers until February 2023 and $357 million in total businesses. Compared to some of the heavyweights on that list, Jamaica's economy is far smaller, and the reasons for obtaining a CBDC vary depending on the wealth of the country. According to the BIS poll, emerging and developing economies are more likely than advanced economies to be motivated by financial inclusion concerns when it comes to CBDC work, and emerging economies are also more likely to have made progress towards CBDC than advanced ones (Sharon et al., 2023).

5.7.3 *Nigeria*

Nigeria was the first African nation and one of the first in the world to launch the CBN's[13] "e-Naira" CBDC. Designed to complement Nigeria's hard currency, not replace it, the e-Naira made its debut on 25 October 2021. About 500 million e-Naira (US$1.21 million) have minted. There are currently two mobile applications[14] available for use with the CBDC. We expect the e-Naira to accelerate economic growth and increase GDP by US$29 billion over a ten-year period. Additionally, it needs to promote international remittances, quicken the process of financial inclusion for the unbanked and underbanked, and support cross-border trade. To lower the possibility of detrimental effects on the economic and financial network, the CB of Nigeria (CBN) has released recommendations that should make its operations easier to understand, lower transaction costs, promote financial inclusion, and encourage widespread use. The CBN has not yet provided clarification on how to convert e-Naira to other cryptocurrencies or traditional naira. With transactions from the financial sector prohibited in February, e-Naira is partially an attempt to thwart the emergence of unregulated cryptocurrencies in the nation. The inherent volatility of cryptocurrencies like Bitcoin is lessened by CB regulation and the common peg to fiat currencies backed by monetary reserves in countries with CBDCs (Sharon et al., 2023).

5.7.4 *Upcoming DC Projects Worldwide*

134 nations are investigating CBDCs, according to a recent article. According to research published on September 17 by the think tank Atlantic Council, those nations are responsible for 98% of the global economy (Atlantic council, 2024). With 44 countries piloting the digital currencies, up from 36 last year, the most recent data indicates that all G20 nations are investigating CBDCs. CBDC can be implemented to encourage financial inclusion and boost the effectiveness of cross-border payments.[15]

However, adopting a CBDC necessitates considerable thought. Each of the nations in these regions, which include a wide range of economies from Pakistan and Kazakhstan to Morocco and Egypt, must consider its own particular set of conditions. CBDCs[16] may enhance the effectiveness of cross-border payment services. As already stated, this is evidenced that cross-border payments frequently encounter obstacles such as different data formats, regionally specific operating standards, and intricate compliance checks. By addressing these inefficiencies, CBDC has the capacity to drastically abate transaction costs. Transnational technology platforms have already been implemented in several nations to overcome these problems and encourage international DC payments.[17]

5.8 CBDC and Its Ways in Achieving the Various SDGs

A CBDC can eliminate poverty. The first tactic is to integrate the underprivileged into the financial system using CBDC. If effective, this approach will raise the degree of financial inclusion for the underprivileged. By explaining "financial inclusion (FI)" through CBDC, people in difficult situations can access affordable CBDC-based loans and other essential financial help, which can improve their quality of life. This may help them to surpass hardship and conclusively achieve the UN SDGs of ending distress. To ensure that no one goes hungry, a CBDC can help stock relocation to low-income families and societies more quickly and equitably. We can then use these payments to purchase food. To guarantee that no one goes hungry, CBDC may again be utilized to promote expenditure on "food banks" in both rich and poor nations.[18] To help farmers, CBDC can further be utilized if provided with sponsor credit. By enabling customers to pay expenses in identical regular proportions, innovative CBDC solutions can help users reduce their reliance on costly personal loans and afford costly fees. CBDC can help schools cut costs and give kids access to affordable education funding. CBDC can target women as a market category. The female client group can benefit from CBDC's financial solutions and improved financial services, which enhance women's job results, asset buildup, and inclination to launch a business. Micro, small, and medium-sized businesses owned by women may have greater access to microcredit thanks to CBDC. Newer avenues for residents to participate in "clean energy projects" and benefit from the generation and distribution of "clean energy" are provided by creative CBDC solutions. There is a lot of opportunity for CBDC to support investments in automation that advance the creation of inexpensive "clean energy." Additionally, CBDC also opens up new avenues for creative financing solutions in green bond markets, which lowers the cost and simplifies the financing of smaller-scale clean energy and energy efficiency projects that might hasten the energy transition.[19] Innovative CBDC solutions can help develop durable and functional infrastructure, the foundation of every successful community. Creative CBDC solutions can provide the necessary capital to enhance current infrastructure and industries. Additionally, CBDC explication could be utilized to support the progress of cutting-edge feasible proficiency that supports the growth of new infrastructure and industries, resulting in prosperity, job creation, and the establishment of a stable and prosperous society. Achieving the SDGs requires reducing inequality both within and between nations (Suratini et al., 2024).

However, these discouraging interest rates should only be used when they align with the monetary policy goals of the CBs, not in times of crisis, when they would be used to prevent an undue movement in interest towards CBDC. We recognize that the benefits of CBDC as a crisis-resilient asset could be jeopardized if CBs implemented financial disincentives to discourage the conversion of bank currency into CBDC (Yang et al., 2021).

5.9 Conclusion

There are only a handful of countries that have started with the concept of DC in their daily usage. Several countries have been trying out their ways to use the DC but also have measured a high potential risk of fraudulent services due to inadequate literacy levels. Among the principal advantages of DC in India is that the cost would be lower for the government, and all transactions would be automatically listed, reducing the number of black money transactions. Additionally, it would promote environmental sustainability by reducing paper usage, printing costs, and waste. However, the internet and payment use would increase the carbon footprint, harming the environment, and measures would need to be taken to reduce this (Otoo et al., 2017).

Potential applications of retail CBDC include the following advantages and opportunities: collaborating with international financial institutions, technology companies, and regulatory agencies can help leverage experience, share best practices, and guarantee interoperability with global payment systems. India is a developing country. India's financial system may undergo a radical transformation if the country gets a retail CBDC. There could be many benefits to implementing a CBDC in India, but there would also be obstacles in the form of technological infrastructure, user acceptability, security, and legislative (Oloyede, 2023).

All things considered, it is evident that electronic payments are replacing the need for cash in transactions, yet the incentive to keep cash on hand for storage of value does not change. As evidenced by the declining ticket sizes of these services, the share of low denomination notes has also declined, which can be largely attributed to the use of UPI and mobile wallets for small-value payments. A decline in transactional cash demand is also reflected by fewer cash disbursements at ATMs.

Cash is still in use because people still choose to save and transact with it, even in spite of the growth of digital payments. Furthermore, cash is the de facto basis for all forms of payment. It also allows transactions between the formal and informal sectors and with underserved and uninformed groups. Additionally, regions with enhanced development continue to focus on the acceptance and use of digital payments. To preserve the propulsion for DC that originated at the time of the pandemic, coordinated attempts must focus on:

a. Making payment methods and the necessary acceptance infrastructure affordable for both the supply side, for example, merchants and intermediaries, and the demand side, for example, consumers.
b. Ensuring global connections with essential facilitators[20]
c. Enhancing "financial inclusion" as well as education
d. Safeguarding "cybersecurity" and ensuring consumer safekeeping

RBI has implemented a number of measures to encourage the digital drive, including making centralized payment systems operational around the clock, launching the UPI123Pay app for feature phone users, facilitating the interoperability of prepaid payment instruments (PPIs), and initiating pilot projects for CBDC in direct sales and bulk markets. The sudden rise in interest in CBDC can be explained by the assessment of the CBs to see it in terms of accomplishing government policy behaviour, maintaining fiscal stability, and providing citizens with a convenient, secure, and steady payment mechanism.

The stance of each nation regarding the adoption of CBDC varies. While some nations are racing towards deployment, others are undertaking cycles of study and testing to establish their CBDC gradually. Determining the best time and approach to implement CBDC is the subject of continuous discussions and initiatives in India. This will open up many possibilities for ecosystem participants to provide services that facilitate consumers' ability to pay and transact online for several reasons.

It has been suggested that a DC issued by a CB may boost payment adaptability, offer appropriate access to capital, and open up funding for sustainable development. Additionally, CBDC can speed up negotiation chains along with improving capital performance for investments in projects and exercises related to sustainable development. The study's conclusion is that a CBDC could help accomplish the SDGs set forth by the UN. In pursuance of achieving the SDGs of the UN, policymakers should make sure that the CBDC in their nations is built with elements that consider sustainable development issues.

Considering the numerous advancements in India's CBDC market, more work remains before it achieves the momentum and population acceptance that it seeks. With the expansion of the pilot, the regulators may be able to address certain issues. It will be intriguing to see how various use case models—including cross-border, offline, programmable, and those that could combat financial fraud—are created in India. Regarding technology, the regulators may be able to make certain changes and modifications to the current infrastructure for CBDC, including in the areas of privacy, settlement, interface, and interoperability, to mention a few. CBDC may support numerous use cases, potentially enhancing financial inclusion in India. Although the pilot has yielded some observations thus far, the RBI's proactive actions, such as awareness campaigns and creative use cases, may aid in reducing the amount and value of CBDC adoption. It would be intriguing to see what the pilot's ultimate results show.

Abbreviation

"Central Bank"	CB
"Central Bank Digital Currency"	CBDC
"Digital currency"	DC
"Digital economy"	DE
"Micro, small, and medium-sized enterprises"	MSME
"Sustainable development goals"	(SDGs)

Notes

1. "e-money, electronic money, network money, digital money, electronic currency, digital cash, e-cash, mobile money" (Berentsen, 2005).
2. For example, "education, health, transportation, agriculture, commerce," etc.
3. There are two types of e-Rupee: "Token-based e-Rupee" and "Account-based e-Rupee."
4. The Deputy Governor of RBI recently emphasized on this issue.
5. For example, Kotak Mahindra Bank and the State Bank of India.
6. "In six cities between December 2018 and January 2019" (Pan, 2023).
7. "Real-time account settlements will be provided through e-transactions."
8. "Such as carbon taxes and cap-and-trade programs," etc.
9. "For example, the CB can pay intended beneficiaries pre-programmed CBDC, which could be accepted exclusively for a specific purpose."
10. "For example, Agriculture sector."
11. For example, "safe acquisition, repository, use of personal information against CBDC account and business, cybersecurity operators of second-tier like minor banks and non - banking associations as well as the business continuity along with security contrary to interruptions associated to climate change are just a few of them" (Bindseil, 2020).
12. "As like CBDC, the Sand Dollar is a centralized, controlled, stable, private and secure unit of account and medium of exchange."
13. "The CB of Nigeria."
14. "The e-Naira speed wallet and the e-Naira merchant wallet."
15. "Nearly two-thirds of Middle Eastern and Central Asian nations are considering a CBDC."
16. "Gulf Cooperation Council nations of Bahrain, Kuwait, Oman, Qatar, Saudi Arabia, and the United Arab Emirates, as well as oil exporters seems to be a top priority."
17. "The Arab Monetary Fund's Buna cross-border payment system," developed in 2020, serves as one illustration (Bouza et al., 2024).
18. For example, "small-scale food producers, particularly women, indigenous people, family farmers, pastoralists, and fishermen to

secure land, equipment, knowledge and other productive inputs that will double their productivity and incomes."

19. "Few such examples of innovative CBDC solutions are CBDC-based green bonds, CBDC payment systems, CBDC microloans to clean energy producers and consumers."
20. For example, "smartphones, internet connectivity," etc.

References

Achord, S., Chan, J., Collier, I., Nardani, S., & Rochemont, S. (2017). A cashless society. Benefits, Risks and Issues (Interim Paper). Institute and Faculty of Actuaries.

Aggarwal, K., Malik, S., Mishra, D. K., & Paul, D. (2021). Moving from cash to cashless economy: Toward digital India. *Journal of Asian Finance Economics and Business, 8*(4), 43–54. https://doi.org/10.13106/jafeb.2021.vol8.no4.0043

Atlantic council. (2024). *Central bank digital currency tracker*. https://www.atlanticcouncil.org/cbdctracker/

Awasthy, S., Misra, R., & Dhal, S. (2023). *Cash versus digital payment transactions in India: Decoding the currency demand paradox*, pp. 1–45

Babu, S., & Abraham, K. M. (2021). Central bank digital currencies: policy and operational perspectives for India. *CSI Transactions on ICT, 9*(2), 85–94. https://doi.org/10.1007/s40012-021-00327-6

Banerjee, S., & Sinha, M. (2023). Promoting financial inclusion through central bank digital currency: An evaluation of payment system viability in India. *Australasian Accounting Business and Finance Journal, 17*(1), 176–204. https://doi.org/10.14453/aabfj.v17i1.14

Berentsen, A. (2005). Digital money, liquidity, and monetary policy (originally published in July 1997). *First Monday*, 89–117.

Bhat, V., Nagarkar, J., & Singh, A. (2021). Prospects of digital currency in India—A way forward. *Revista Gestão Inovação E Tecnologias, 11*(4), 5247–5266. https://doi.org/10.47059/revistageintec.v11i4.2560

Bhowmik, D. (2022). Monetary policy implications of central bank digital currency with special reference to India. *Advancement in Management and Technology (AMT), 2*(3), 1–8.

Bindseil, U. (2020). *Tiered CBDC and the financial system*. SSRN 3513422.

Bouza, S., Miccoli, M., & Mircheva, B. (2024). *Central bank digital currencies can boost Middle East's financial inclusion, payment efficiency*. IMF org. 63–86. https://www.imf.org/en/Blogs/Articles/2024/06/18/central-bank-digital-currencies-can-boost-middle-easts-financial-inclusion-payment-efficiency

Dwyer, G. P. (2014). The economics of Bitcoin and similar private digital currencies. *Journal of Financial Stability, 17*, 81–91. https://doi.org/10.1016/j.jfs.2014.11.006. https://www.pymnts.com/cbdc/2024/report-digital-currency-projects-underway-in-134-countries/

Eichengreen, B. (2022). A central bank digital currency for India? *Indian Public Policy Review, 3*(4 (Jul-Sep)), 1–29. https://doi.org/10.55763/ippr.2022.03.04.001

Gans, J. S., Halaburda, H. (2015). *Economic analysis of the digital economy*. University of Chicago Press, ISBN: 0-226-20684-X; 978-0-226-20684-4, pp. i–xii. http://www.nber.org/books/gree13-1

Haque, M. A., & Shoaib, M. (2023). e₹—The digital currency in India: Challenges and prospects. *Bench Council Transactions on Benchmarks Standards and Evaluations, 3*(1), 100107. https://doi.org/10.1016/j.tbench.2023.100107

Hofmann, C. (2023). The shift from private money into 'Unlimited'CBDCs: An unviable development or a chance for reform and new opportunities? In *Central Bank Digital Currencies (CBDCs): Proceedings of a Colloquium, Christos Gortsos* (ed.), Forthcoming.

Kandpal, V., Malhotra, A., Sharma, M., & Sabiha, A. (2022). *Cashless payment systems: Emergence of a new normal in the Indian economy*, pp. 257–278

Lobo, A. (2022). *The environmental impact of cryptocurrency*. Global Research and Consulting Group Insights. https://insights.grcglobalgroup.com/the-environmental-impact-of-cryptocurrency

Nandanan, P., & Cyril. (2023). CBDC-An Indian perspective. 21.

Oloyede, A., Fark, N., Noma, N., & Tebep, E., & Nwaulune, A. (2023). Measuring the impact of the digital economy in developing countries: A systematic review and meta- analysis. *Heliyon, 9*, e17654. https://doi.org/10.1016/j.heliyon

Otoo, B. A., & Nemati, H. R. (2017). *Digital currency and its impact on quality of life*. Americas Conference on Information Systems. http://dblp.uni-trier.de/db/conf/amcis/amcis2017.html#OtooN17

Ozili, P. K. (2023). Using central bank digital currency to achieve the sustainable development goals. In *Digital transformation, strategic resilience, cyber security and risk management*, pp. 143–153. Emerald Publishing Limited.

Pachare, S., Umabrkar, S., & Jadhav, S. (2023). Challenges and risks for retail central bank digital currency (CBDC) in India. *The Online Journal of Distance Education and e-Learning, 11*(2), 2759–2770. https://www.tojsat.net/journals/tojdel/articles/v11i23/v11i23-09.pdf

Pan, S. (2023). Experts' perception on cryptocurrency trade in Bangladesh: fintech innovation or dilemma. In *Feasibility of central bank digital currency in india and abroad*, pp. 189–205. Kunal Books. https://www.researchgate.net/profile/Shapan

Sharon, B., Lynsey, W., & Allan, W. (2023). The evolution of sand dollar. *Intereconomics, 58*(4), 178–184. https://www.intereconomics.eu/contents/year/2023/number/4/article/the-evolution-of-sanddollar.html

Sigurosson, K., Eyporsson, G. P., & Kristjansdottir, H. (2023). Digital currencies, swot analysis. *Baltic Journal of Economic Studies, 9*(3), 1–9. https://doi.org/10.30525/2256-0742/2023-9-3-1-9

Suratini, Wafa, F., Ariyanti, R., Hastomo, D., & Arif, D. (2024). The impact of digital currencies, trade policies, and climate change mitigation on global economic stability. *The Journal of Academic Science, 1*(2), 152–158. https://thejoas.com/index.php/thejoas/article/view/26/31

Tafti, Z., Sarkar, K., Chowdhury, A., Bandyopadhyay, S., & Kulshreshtha, V. (2021, September). *Central bank digital currency in the Indian context* [Slide show; Online]. https://www.pwc.in/assets/pdfs/consulting/financial-services/fintech/point-of-view/pov-downloads/central-bank-digital-currency-in-the-indian-context.pdf

Yang, M., Mamun, A. A., Mohiuddin, M., Nawi, N. C., & Zainol, N. R. (2021). Cashless transactions: A study on intention and adoption of e-wallets. *Sustainability, 13*, 831. https://doi.org/10.3390/su13020831

Yang, Q., Zheng, M., & Wang, Y. (2023). The role of cbdc in green finance and sustainable development. *Emerging Markets Finance and Trade, 59*(15), 4158–4173. https://doi.org/10.1080/1540496x.2023.2185096

CHAPTER 6

The Impact of Central Bank Digital Currencies on Achieving United Nations Sustainability Goals: A Comparative Analysis

Stefan Bjarni Gunnlaugsson, Kjartan Sigurdsson, and Helga Kristjansdottir

6.1 Introduction

Central Bank Digital Currencies (CBDCs), currently under exploration by over 60 central banks and monetary authorities, represent a digital form of a nation's fiat currency. Issued and backed by the central bank, CBDCs are centralized and maintain a direct claim on the issuing authority, similar to physical cash. Unlike decentralized cryptocurrencies such as Bitcoin, which are privately issued, CBDCs are centralized, enabling

S. B. Gunnlaugsson (✉) · K. Sigurdsson · H. Kristjansdottir
Faculty of Business Administration, University of Akureyri, Akureyri, Iceland
e-mail: stefanb@unak.is

K. Sigurdsson
e-mail: kjartansig@unak.is

H. Kristjansdottir
e-mail: helga@unak.is

R. Aneja and R. Dygas (eds.), *Digital Currencies and the Green Economy*, https://doi.org/10.1007/978-981-95-2282-8_6

secure, reliable, and efficient financial transactions. This emerging method of payment has the potential to revolutionize money handling by facilitating real-time transactions that are faster, safer, and more cost-effective than traditional payment systems. These efficiencies could enhance trade, clearing, and settlement processes, reducing transaction costs (Allen et al., 2020; Kshetri, 2021). Even though many countries continue to rely on cash (Bech et al., 2018), CBDCs offer a hybrid advantage by combining the accessibility of cash with the convenience and efficiency of digital payments.

By offering a government-backed digital legal tender, CBDCs have the potential to boost efficiency, strengthen security, increase financial inclusion, and enhance the effectiveness of monetary policy (Allen et al., 2020). In particular, CBDCs could contribute to sustainable development by increasing affordable access to financial services in developing countries (Tan, 2023a, 2023b), promoting financial inclusion, and enhancing economic stability. However, the broader impact of CBDCs on sustainable growth remains to be fully understood.

The United Nations 2030 Agenda for Sustainable Development, introduced in 2015, set forth 17 Sustainable Development Goals (SDGs) to address critical environmental, social, and economic challenges. These goals encompass five key dimensions—people, prosperity, planet, partnership, and peace—and aspire to foster a healthier, more equitable future by 2030 (Cerf, 2018; Donaires et al., 2018). CBDCs have the potential to address key barriers to achieving the SDGs. They could support these goals by expanding access to affordable financial services, strengthening payment infrastructures, and enhancing financial inclusion, particularly for underbanked populations. However, the impact of CBDCs on sustainable development is likely to vary across countries, influenced by each nation's unique institutional, social, and economic context.

Financial exclusion remains a substantial challenge; according to the World Bank, approximately 1.7 billion people worldwide need access to essential banking services (World Bank, 2021). CBDCs could help close this financial inclusion gap by offering a secure, accessible, and cost-effective digital payment system, especially in underserved or underdeveloped regions. Improved financial inclusion could enable broader economic participation, enhancing quality of life and advancing goals such as poverty reduction and inclusive economic growth. Thus, CBDCs may be a powerful tool in advancing the UN SDGs (Arner et al., 2020).

While the existing literature has explored the general potential of CBDCs, it has lacked a comprehensive analysis of their relationship with the UN SDGs. This paper aims to address this research gap. In this paper, we explore the relationship between central bank digital currencies and the United Nations' Sustainable Development Goals, focusing on three key questions:

Q1 How do CBDCs contribute to the realization of the UN SDGs?
Q2 What challenges and opportunities arise when applying CBDCs to achieve the UN SDGs?
Q3 What insights have been learned from countries that have implemented CBDCs in relation to the UN SDGs?

Through a comparative analysis of select countries, this study aims to provide a comprehensive view of how CBDCs are being utilized in efforts to achieve the SDGs, examining their potential impact, outcomes, and implications across diverse national contexts.

6.2 Methodology

This study employs a qualitative research methodology and draws on a thorough review of published research papers, government and institutional records, and data from credible international organizations. It relies exclusively on secondary sources to provide a comprehensive and objective analysis of the topic, with no primary data collection involved. The study aims to comprehensively understand the link between CBDCs and the United Nations Sustainable Development Goals (SDGs) by synthesizing data from multiple reputable sources.

6.3 The United Nations Sustainable Development Goals

In 2015, the United Nations established 17 SDGs. Table 6.1 provides an overview of these goals and their intended outcomes. These goals urge nations worldwide to take action toward creating a more prosperous, equitable, and sustainable world by 2030. It is important to emphasize that these 17 goals are deeply interconnected. Reducing poverty must go hand-in-hand with strategies that improve education, enhance health outcomes, and address inequality. Achieving these goals will also require addressing the critical challenge of climate change, which poses significant threats to all dimensions of sustainable development (Cheng et al., 2021).

6.4 CBDCs and Their Contribution to UN SDGs

CBDCs could help advance the UN SDGs in several ways. Table 6.2 provides an overview of how CBDCs can contribute to the SDGs. First, financial inclusion represents a key area of impact. Particularly in underdeveloped countries, CBDCs could play an important role in expanding financial accessibility and offering affordable financial services—this is relevant to SDGs 1, 8, and 10. Through widespread access to digital payment systems, CBDCs can improve financial inclusion. The World Bank estimates that approximately 1.7 billion adults worldwide still lack bank accounts (Demirgüç-Kunt et al., 2019; Lannquist & Tan, 2023). By connecting these unbanked individuals to the formal financial system, CBDCs enable them to engage in economic activities and improve their quality of life. Reducing transaction costs and inefficiencies in the financial system can contribute to economic growth and prosperity (Tan, 2023a, 2023b).

Second, CBDCs can contribute significantly to poverty alleviation, particularly relevant to SDGs 1 and 2. CBDCs provide a vital means for the effective and secure distribution of social benefits, subsidies, and other targeted support programs directly to vulnerable communities. Through digital wallets and mobile payment systems, these digital currencies can enable the rapid distribution of government support, ensuring that funds reach their intended recipients with minimal leakage or administrative costs (Baharmand et al., 2021). In underdeveloped areas where conventional banking infrastructure is lacking, CBDC-powered digital payments can be especially effective in overcoming obstacles and directly empowering underprivileged populations. By reducing barriers and costs associated with social welfare programs, CBDCs can enhance the impact of these initiatives, helping more people escape poverty and improve overall living standards (Tan, 2023a, 2023b; Wang, 2020).

Third, CBDCs could support gender equality and women's empowerment (SDG 5). By improving women's (and other disadvantaged groups) access to personal payments and savings, CBDCs can enhance women's economic participation, reduce their vulnerability to abuse, and promote greater gender equality overall (Tan, 2023a, 2023b). By providing a

Table 6.1 The United Nations Sustainable Development Goals, their explanation and expected outcome

SDG	*Explanation*	*Expected Outcome*
1. No Poverty	Eliminate severe poverty for all people worldwide, especially by guaranteeing assistance for underprivileged groups	Significant reduction in global poverty rates, improved living standards, and reduced inequality
2. Zero Hunger	Promote sustainable agriculture, enhance nutrition, and solve food distribution inequalities to end hunger and reach food security	Elimination of hunger, enhanced food security, and increased sustainable agricultural practices
3. Good Health and Well-being	Ensure healthy lives and promote well-being for all ages by addressing maternal health, reducing mortality, and improving health systems	Reduced disease incidence, higher life expectancy, and better overall global health outcomes
4. Quality Education	Ensure inclusive and equitable quality education and promote lifelong learning opportunities for all, focusing on skill development and access to learning	Higher global literacy rates, improved education access, and a skilled, educated workforce
5. Gender Equality	Achieve gender equality and empower all women and girls by addressing gender-based violence, discrimination, and ensuring equal opportunities	Reduction in gender disparities, increased female participation in leadership, and equality across sectors
6. Clean Water and Sanitation	Ensure availability and sustainable management of water and sanitation for all, protecting natural water ecosystems and increasing safe water access	Universal access to safe drinking water, improved sanitation, and protection of water-related ecosystems
7. Affordable and Clean Energy	Ensure access to affordable, reliable, and sustainable energy for all by boosting renewable energy investments and improving energy efficiency	Increased use of renewable energy, reduced carbon footprint, and improved energy access for underprivileged communities
8. Decent Work and Economic Growth	Promote sustained, inclusive, and sustainable economic growth, employment, and decent work for all, addressing economic inequalities and labor rights	Reduced unemployment, increased economic growth, and improved working conditions globally

(continued)

Table 6.1 (continued)

SDG	*Explanation*	*Expected Outcome*
9. Industry, Innovation, and Infrastructure	Build resilient infrastructure, promote sustainable industrialization, and foster innovation for economic and technological advancement	Strengthened infrastructure, increased innovation capacity, and economic development in underserved regions
10. Reduced Inequality	Reduce inequalities within and among countries, focusing on social, economic, and political inclusion of marginalized groups	Fairer income distribution, improved social mobility, and reduced economic disparities between and within nations
11. Sustainable Cities and Communities	Make cities inclusive, safe, resilient, and sustainable, addressing urban planning, housing, and pollution control	More livable urban areas, reduced environmental impact, and improved urban infrastructure
12. Responsible Consumption and Production	Ensure sustainable consumption and production patterns by reducing waste, promoting recycling, and improving resource efficiency	Minimization of waste, sustainable resource use, and greater environmental responsibility among consumers
13. Climate Action	Take urgent action to combat climate change and its impacts by promoting climate resilience and reducing greenhouse gas emissions	Mitigation of climate change effects, greater disaster resilience, and lower carbon emissions worldwide
14. Life Below Water	Conserve and sustainably use the oceans, seas, and marine resources by addressing pollution, overfishing, and marine ecosystem protection	Healthier marine ecosystems, reduced ocean pollution, and protection of biodiversity
15. Life on Land	Protect, restore, and promote sustainable use of terrestrial ecosystems, combat desertification, and halt biodiversity loss	Preservation of forests, restored ecosystems, and reduced species extinction rates
16. Peace, Justice, and Strong Institutions	Promote peaceful, just, and inclusive societies by ensuring access to justice and building accountable institutions	Reduced conflict, stronger governance, and enhanced protection of human rights
17. Partnerships for the Goals	Strengthen global partnerships to support and achieve the SDGs, focusing on finance, technology, and capacity-building collaboration	Enhanced global cooperation, increased resource mobilization, and shared progress toward all SDGs

Sources (Caiado et al., 2018; United Nations, 2018, 2023)

Table 6.2 CBDCs and their contribution to the UN SDGs

CBDC Contributions	*Relevant SDGs*	*Description*
Financial Inclusion	SDGs 1, 8, 10	Particularly in impoverished nations, CBDCs can improve financial accessibility by allowing unbanked people to join the financial system, improving economic participation and quality of living
Poverty Alleviation	SDGs 1, 2	Through efficient distribution of social benefits, subsidies, and support programs to underprivileged populations, CBDCs reduce administrative costs and enhance project impact in poverty reduction
Gender Equality and Women's Empowerment	SDG 5	By increasing women's access to personal payments and savings, fostering economic independence, and enabling greater financial control, CBDCs empower women and advance gender equality
Environmental Sustainability	SDGs 13, 15	By facilitating green finance, reducing the carbon footprint of physical transactions, and enhancing transparency to combat environmentally harmful activities, CBDCs support environmental sustainability
Good Governance	SDGs 8, 10, 16	By enhancing cash flow transparency, reducing tax evasion, and bolstering state legitimacy, CBDCs foster citizen trust in government initiatives and promote good governance
Sustainable Economic Development	SDGs 7, 8, 9	By supporting infrastructure, driving innovation, financing renewable energy projects, and increasing financial service efficiency and accessibility, CBDCs contribute to sustainable economic growth

Sources (United Nations, 2018, 2023)

simple and secure way to make payments, CBDCs can help empower women to take greater control of household finances and build independent financial profiles (International Monetary Fund, 2019; Tan, 2023a, 2023b).

Fourth, CBDCs can support environmental sustainability—relevant to SDGs 13 and 15. CBDCs could serve as a platform for digital "green" currency initiatives encouraging environmentally friendly projects. Additionally, they can help reduce the carbon footprint associated with traditional cash and physical payment methods. CBDCs can also improve transparency in financial transactions, reducing illegal flows that might harm the environment. Furthermore, CBDCs can enhance funding efficiency for sustainability initiatives, conservation projects, and renewable energy sources (Ozili, 2022; Tan, 2023a, 2023b).

Fifth, adopting CBDCs can reinforce good governance, reduce informality and inequality, and strengthen government capacity for effective policy implementation—relevant to SDGs 8, 10, and 16. This includes enhancing the transparency of financial flows and reducing tax evasion. In these ways, CBDCs can reinforce state legitimacy and boost public trust, ultimately fostering more sustainable and equitable development outcomes (Allen et al., 2020; Kshetri, 2021; Lannquist & Tan, 2023; Tan, 2023a, 2023b).

Lastly, greater acceptance of CBDCs can promote sustainable economic development, which aligns with SDGs 8 and 9. By improving the accessibility and efficiency of financial services—especially in underserved areas—CBDCs can stimulate economic growth and job creation. CBDCs can also facilitate funding for critical targets under these SDGs, such as sustainable infrastructure, innovation, and industrialization (David-West & Nwagwu, 2018). CBDCs can contribute to SDG 7 (affordable and clean energy) by channeling resources toward renewable energy projects and programs. Furthermore, the transparent tracking of financial transactions enabled by CBDCs supports accountability and progress monitoring toward the SDGs. When carefully designed and implemented, CBDCs have the potential to advance the UN's Sustainable Development Goals across social, environmental, and economic dimensions (Arner et al., 2020; Chu, 2023; Ozili, 2022).

In conclusion, CBDCs offer significant potential to advance the UN's SDGs. By promoting financial inclusion, CBDCs can connect the unbanked to the formal economy, thereby reducing poverty. Additionally, CBDCs can empower women economically, promoting gender equality. Furthermore, CBDCs' role in green financing and financial transparency can contribute to environmental sustainability and improved governance. Overall, CBDCs can support green initiatives, broaden access to financial services, and encourage sustainable economic development, aligning with the UN's comprehensive development agenda.

6.5 Challenges and Opportunities When Using CBDCs for SDGs

CBDCs can advance global financial inclusion and economic stability, thus supporting the UN SDGs. Yet, they face several complex challenges that must be addressed to fulfill this promise. Firstly, CBDCs face significant competition from the widespread use of stable-coins, private cryptocurrencies, and fintech financial services. Many private digital currencies have gained popularity because they offer financial flexibility, low-cost transactions, and, in some cases, a hedge against local currency devaluation. Stable-coins, for instance, appeal to consumers seeking stability combined with the flexibility of digital currency because they peg their value to fiat currencies or other assets, thereby providing price stability. Meanwhile, fintech companies have emerged as strong competitors in digital payments, offering user-friendly platforms. To achieve financial inclusion and support the SDGs, CBDCs need to offer distinct advantages over these private options. This could include stronger security measures, government backing, and policy-driven incentives prioritizing public welfare over profit. CBDCs allow central banks to lower transaction costs, improve cross-border payment efficiency, and build more inclusive and stable financial systems (Allen et al., 2020; Denecker et al., 2023).

Secondly, managing the risks of financial crimes, including tax evasion and money laundering, is critical for using CBDCs to advance the SDGs. Without proper oversight, CBDCs may become tools for illegal activity. Although every digital transaction can be tracked and recorded—making CBDCs more transparent than cash transactions—this transparency could be exploited by those attempting to evade weak regulatory systems. Illicit actors could hide the origins of money or conduct complex cross-border transactions that are difficult to trace. To address this, central banks and financial authorities must develop robust anti-money laundering (AML) and counter-financing of terrorism (CFT) regulations tailored explicitly for CBDCs (Allen et al., 2020; World Bank, 2023).

Thirdly, ensuring the fair integration of CBDCs into the financial system is essential to avoid exacerbating existing social and economic inequalities. The digital divide—characterized by disparities in access to digital technology and internet connectivity—poses a major barrier to equitable CBDC adoption. Many underdeveloped nations have large populations without internet access, smartphones, or digital literacy—often prerequisites for accessing CBDCs. Without targeted policies to close these gaps, CBDCs risk unintentionally marginalizing those already facing financial exclusion, thus undermining their ability to achieve the SDGs. Alongside CBDC initiatives, central banks and governments should implement policies that promote digital inclusion. This might include subsidizing smartphone ownership, providing affordable internet access, and running digital literacy programs to enable people to understand and use digital currency systems. Some countries may also consider incorporating offline capabilities for CBDCs, enabling transactions without continuous internet connectivity (Allen et al., 2020; Maniff, 2020).

Fourthly, the successful implementation of CBDCs depends on robust technological infrastructure. Building this infrastructure can be costly and time-consuming, particularly for countries with limited financial or technological resources. CBDCs rely on advanced payment systems capable of handling potentially millions of transactions daily, requiring them to be fast, scalable, and resilient. Furthermore, the digital nature of CBDCs makes them vulnerable to cyberattacks, heightening the importance of cybersecurity measures. Establishing the necessary infrastructure ensures reliable payment systems and guarantees that central banks and financial institutions have the technical expertise to manage and monitor CBDC operations. This includes creating contingency plans for potential system failures and developing skills to oversee digital money systems. Moreover, central banks may need to collaborate with technology providers to leverage their expertise in cybersecurity and digital payments. A secure infrastructure is essential for CBDCs to become reliable tools for achieving the SDGs (Allen et al., 2020; Auer & Boehme, 2021).

Finally, cybersecurity is one of the most urgent challenges in CBDC implementation, as digital currencies are prime targets for cyberattacks. With the sensitive information involved and the financial value at stake, CBDCs are an attractive target for hackers; even a successful attack could severely damage public trust in digital currency. A major breach in a CBDC system could result in data leaks, financial losses, and severe disruptions to financial markets and daily economic activities. The risk of state-sponsored cyberattacks adds another layer of threat, as geopolitical tensions could lead to attempts to compromise a country's CBDC infrastructure as a form of economic sabotage. CBDCs must also address sophisticated threats like ransomware, distributed denial-of-service (DDoS) attacks, and phishing campaigns targeting central bank systems and individual users. Given the high level of CBDC integration into the national economy, a successful cyberattack could compromise user confidence and the overall stability of the financial system. To mitigate these risks, central banks must invest in cybersecurity measures and continuously update their defenses against evolving threats. This includes implementing advanced encryption methods, multi-factor authentication, and regular security audits and simulations to identify vulnerabilities. Furthermore, collaboration with international organizations and private cybersecurity companies is essential, as they provide critical insights and support for enhancing CBDC security (BIS, 2023; Saeed et al., 2023; Tourpe et al., 2023).

6.6 Insights Learned Regarding the UN SDGs in Countries That Have Implemented CBDCs

6.6.1 *Countries That Have Debuted CBDCs*

As of November 2024, three nations—Nigeria, the Bahamas, and Jamaica—have fully launched CBDCs. Each country's experience provides insights into how digital currencies are used, embraced, and aligned with the SDGs.

In October 2021, Nigeria launched the eNaira, becoming the first country in Africa to issue a CBDC. With a focus on transitioning to a cashless economy, the Central Bank of Nigeria (CBN) aimed to enhance financial inclusion and reduce transaction costs. Despite these goals, eNaira adoption has been challenging. By early 2024, usage remained low, with less than 0.5% of the population using the digital currency. Several factors explain this slow uptake: Public awareness of the eNaira is limited, and concerns about data privacy and trust in digital banking systems persist. Additionally, the eNaira has struggled to offer clear advantages over existing mobile money providers. The CBN has launched public education campaigns to address these issues and collaborated with financial institutions to integrate eNaira into existing payment systems. However, as of November 2024, these efforts have yet to boost adoption significantly (Ekong & Ekong, 2022; Igoni et al., 2022).

The eNaira aligns with key UN SDGs, particularly SDG 1 (no poverty), SDG 8 (decent work and economic growth), and SDG 9 (industry, innovation, and infrastructure). By providing a digital platform for financial transactions, the eNaira aims to include unbanked individuals in the financial system, potentially reducing poverty rates. It also seeks to facilitate small- and medium-sized enterprises (SMEs) transactions, supporting job creation and economic development. While establishing a digital currency infrastructure represents a significant step forward in Nigeria, limited adoption suggests that achieving these goals requires building public trust, ensuring security, and conducting educational outreach rather than solely implementing technology.

Launched in October 2020, the Sand Dollar was the first fully operational CBDC in the world. Developed to address the challenges of providing financial services across the many islands of the Bahamas, the Sand Dollar aimed to improve financial inclusion and streamline payment methods. Despite its pioneering status, adoption has been slow, with the Sand Dollar comprising less than 1% of the money in circulation by mid-2023. The Sand Dollar's objectives are closely aligned with UN SDGs, particularly SDG 1, SDG 8, and SDG 9. Barriers to broader adoption include low digital skills, cybersecurity concerns, and the need for retailers to upgrade their payment systems to accept the digital currency. In response, the Central Bank of the Bahamas has launched public outreach campaigns and is collaborating with commercial banks to integrate the Sand Dollar into their services. Regulatory policies are also being developed to require commercial institutions to support the Sand Dollar (Central Bank of the Bahamas, 2020, 2024).

Officially launched in 2022, Jamaica's central bank digital currency, JAM-DEX, was first proposed by the Bank of Jamaica (BOJ) to improve payment system efficiency, reduce transaction costs, and enhance financial inclusion. Like Nigeria and the Bahamas, JAM-DEX has faced adoption challenges. As of early 2024, JAM-DEX circulation remained low, at 230 million Jamaican dollars (approximately USD 1.47 million). Lack of public knowledge, limited business acceptance, and concerns about the advantages of using digital currency over current payment systems are among the factors affecting adoption. To address these challenges, the BOJ has launched public awareness campaigns and collaborated with banks to integrate JAM-DEX into existing financial services. Developing solutions that seamlessly integrate with existing point-of-sale systems has also encouraged businesses to adopt JAM-DEX (JIS, 2022).

JAM-DEX aligns with several UN SDGs, including SDG 8 (Decent Work and Economic Growth), SDG 9 (Industry, Innovation, and Infrastructure), and SDG 10 (Reduced Inequalities). JAM-DEX aims to stimulate economic activity and support job creation. Developing a digital currency infrastructure significantly advances Jamaica's financial sector.

JAM-DEX also seeks to reduce economic inequalities by providing access to digital financial services for diverse demographic groups. The low adoption rate highlights the importance of addressing barriers such as digital literacy and trust in digital financial systems to achieve these objectives.

The experiences of Nigeria, the Bahamas, and Jamaica in implementing CBDCs offer valuable insights for other countries considering similar projects. While the goals of CBDCs align with UN SDGs, the challenges in adoption highlight the need for comprehensive strategies that address technological, educational, and trust-related factors. Achieving the potential benefits of CBDCs requires robust infrastructure, technical support, and targeted efforts to raise public awareness of digital financial systems.

6.6.2 *Countries That Have Abandoned CBDCs*

Ecuador and Senegal have abandoned their CBDC initiatives due to technical difficulties and low adoption. Launched in 2014, Ecuador's Central Bank Digital Currency project, the Sistema de Dinero Electrónico (SDE), aimed to provide a secure, government-backed digital payment option, particularly for unbanked communities. However, public skepticism emerged as a primary obstacle, as Ecuadorians distrusted the new currency. This skepticism led to low levels of adoption. By 2016, SDE transactions accounted for only a small fraction of the currency in circulation. Minimal transaction volumes also resulted from the system's inability to attract enough merchants and customers. Faced with these challenges, Ecuador's National Assembly ultimately decided to discontinue the SDE in 2017 (Arauz et al., 2021).

In 2016, Senegal launched the eCFA digital currency via a cooperation between eCurrency Mint and the Banque Régionale de Marchés. The project aimed to modernize the payment system and improve financial inclusion. However, it faced opposition from the West African Economic and Monetary Union and its central bank, the Banque Centrale des États de l'Afrique de l'Ouest, which raised concerns about the eCFA's implementation and future trajectory. Like Ecuador's experience, the eCFA suffered from low public acceptance and transaction volumes, ultimately leading to its cancellation (BCEAO, 2023; Söderberg et al., 2024).

These cases in Senegal and Ecuador highlight important factors for successful CBDC development: strong public confidence, adequate user adoption, and favorable legal environments. The challenges underscore the need to address public mistrust, secure clear legislative backing, and engage with potential users and businesses to establish a credible digital currency ecosystem. These fundamental components are necessary for even well-intentioned CBDC projects to avoid substantial obstacles that jeopardize their viability and sustainability.

6.6.3 *Countries Exploring CBDCs*

Most countries are still exploring CBDCs and running pilot programs. Developed economies such as Sweden and the European Union are among the leading explorers of CBDCs, aiming to modernize their financial systems and address evolving economic challenges. Their regulatory solid systems and advanced technological infrastructure position them well to assess the potential benefits and implications of CBDCs.

Through its e-krona initiative, Sweden's central bank, Sveriges Riksbank, has been pioneering CBDC research. The e-krona aims to provide the public with a safe and efficient digital payment option as Sweden transitions toward a cashless society. The trial phase has focused on ensuring the security of digital payments and adapting to a cashless environment. Project findings emphasize the importance of addressing privacy concerns and ensuring financial inclusion. The initiative's success depends on ongoing evaluation and public engagement to ensure that the e-krona meets the needs of all societal groups (Sveriges Riksbank, 2023).

The European Central Bank (ECB) aims to supplement existing cash and digital payment systems in the Eurozone with the Digital Euro, a CBDC. The Digital Euro addresses the growing demand for digital payments while ensuring privacy, accessibility, and resilience. Unlike cryptocurrencies, the ECB would regulate the Digital Euro, providing price stability and legal backing. The ECB is examining the technological and legal frameworks needed to integrate the Digital Euro into Europe's financial ecosystem (ECB, 2023a, 2023b).

China has led CBDC development through its e-CNY initiative. In 2020, the People's Bank of China launched pilot programs across several cities to modernize payment infrastructure and enhance financial inclusion, particularly in rural areas. By June 2024, the e-CNY had processed 7 trillion yuan, demonstrating widespread usage. However, balancing user privacy with financial oversight remains a challenge. Investments in digital infrastructure have spurred economic growth and facilitated the integration of the e-CNY into everyday transactions (Jie, 2023; Lyu, 2024).

India's CBDC project is exemplified by the Reserve Bank of India's e-rupee pilot, launched in December 2022. The project supports SDG 4 (Quality Education) and SDG 5 (Gender Equality) by promoting financial literacy and women's economic empowerment. By June 2024, e-rupee transactions had reached 100,000 per day. The RBI emphasizes targeted education and infrastructure investments to drive broader adoption. Digital literacy initiatives and partnerships with fintech companies are important for building public trust and fostering innovation in India's financial sector (Buteau et al., 2021; DQ India, 2024).

6.7 Results

This chapter provides answers to the three main research questions on the role of Central Bank Digital Currencies in advancing the United Nations Sustainable Development Goals. First, in answering the question: "How do CBDCs contribute to the achievement of the UN SDGs?" By improving financial inclusion, fostering economic growth, and supporting good government, central bank digital currencies show great promise in helping to promote sustainable development goals. For the unbanked population, Nigeria's eNaira seeks to provide digital financial services, therefore complementing SDG 1 on poverty reduction with SDG 8 on decent jobs and economic development. Likewise, Sand Dollar from the Bahamas and JAM-DEX from Jamaica are meant to reach scattered and underprivileged communities, therefore tackling SDG 10 on lower inequality. By building public confidence in financial governance, CBDCs can also improve openness in financial transactions, therefore strengthening responsibility and helping to support SDG 16.

The second research question, "What challenges and opportunities arise when applying CBDCs to achieve the UN SDGs?" demonstrates that although CBDCs offer chances for more easily available, quick transactions and simpler government benefit distribution, their implementation is very difficult. Low digital literacy, cybersecurity issues, and competition from other digital financial services have hampered adoption in nations including the Bahamas and Nigeria, therefore restricting CBDCs' direct influence on their intended economic and social goals. Dealing with these issues calls for coordinated efforts to raise public knowledge of digital literacy, increase confidence in CBDCs by means of strong cybersecurity policies.

The third research question, "What insights have been learned regarding the UN SDGs in countries that have implemented CBDCs?" is addressed via the experiences of nations like Nigeria, the Bahamas, and Jamaica, where CBDC programs show that success relies on more than simply technology. Limited acceptance of the eNaira in Nigeria emphasizes the need of public education and financial stability in building user confidence. Likewise, the Sand Dollar project of the Bahamas demonstrated how encouraging broad use depends on technological preparedness and cooperation with commercial banks. By contrast, the discontinued CBDC programs of Ecuador and Senegal highlight how success calls on enough legislative support, public confidence, and a suitable legal environment for digital financial innovation.

These findings together show that although CBDCs have the ability to progress several SDGs, their influence mostly depends on the existence of appropriate infrastructure, public confidence, and efficient control. Implementing CBDCs with policies and methods that fit the particular technological, social, and financial situation of any nation will help them to considerably contribute to sustainable development.

6.8 Conclusion

This chapter has examined how CBDCs can support the UN's SDGs. The findings reveal that CBDCs offer benefits like enhanced financial inclusion, economic growth, and transparent governance. CBDCs can help alleviate poverty, inequality, and unfairness by integrating unbanked individuals into the financial system. Moreover, CBDCs provide a means of conducting transactions that align with the UN's 2030 goals. However, incentivizing widespread CBDC adoption faces challenges, such as low digital literacy, cybersecurity concerns, and competition from other digital finance options. To overcome these obstacles, we need to strengthen cybersecurity, raise public awareness, and invest in digital education. While CBDCs are valuable tools for sustainable development, they must be tailored to each country's unique circumstances. Overall, CBDCs have the potential to play a crucial role in achieving the SDGs and building a more inclusive, robust global economy.

References

Allen, S. E., Čapkun, S., Eyal, I., Fanti, G., Ford, B., Grimmelmann, J., Juels, A., Kostiainen, K., Meiklejohn, S., Miller, A., Prasad, E., Wüst, K., & Zhang, F. (2020). *Design choices for central bank digital currency: Policy and technical considerations*. https://doi.org/10.3386/w27634

Arauz, A., Garratt, R., & F., D. F. R. (2021). Dinero Electrónico: The rise and fall of Ecuador's central bank digital currency. *Latin American Journal of Central Banking, 2*(2), 100030. https://doi.org/10.1016/j.latcb.2021.100030

Arner, D. W., Buckley, R. P., Zetzsche, D. A., & Veidt, R. (2020). Sustainability, FinTech and financial inclusion. *European Business Organization Law Review, 21*(1), 7. https://doi.org/10.1007/s40804-020-00183-y

Auer, R., & Boehme, R. (2021). *Central bank digital currency: The quest for minimally invasive technology*. RePEc: Research Papers in Economics. https://ideas.repec.org/p/bis/biswps/948.html

Baharmand, H., Saeed, N., Comes, T., & Lauras, M. (2021). Developing a framework for designing humanitarian blockchain projects. *Computers in Industry, 131*, Article 103487. https://doi.org/10.1016/j.compind.2021.103487

BCEAO. (2023). *Membership of the BCEAO monetary policy committee*. https://www.bceao.int/sites/default/files/2020-10/BCEAO%202019%20Annual%20Report.pdf

Bech, M. L., Faruqui, U., Ougaard, F., & Picillo, C. (2018). Payments are a-changin' but cash still rules. *SSRN Electronic Journal*. https://papers.ssrn.com/sol3/papers.cfm?abstract_id=3139217

BIS. (2023). *Project polaris: Closing the CBDC cyber threat modelling gaps*. https://www.bis.org/publ/othp71.pdf

Brandon Tan. (2023). *Central bank digital currency and financial inclusion*. https://www.imf.org/en/Publications/WP/Issues/2023/03/18/Central-Bank-Digital-Currency-and-Financial-Inclusion-531104

Buteau, S., Rao, P., & Valenti, F. (2021). Emerging insights from digital solutions in financial inclusion. *CSI Transactions on ICT, 9*(2), 105. https://doi.org/10.1007/s40012-021-00330-x

Caiado, R. G. G., Filho, W. L., Quelhas, O. L. G., Nascimento, D. L. de M., & Ãvila, L. V. (2018). A literature-based review on potentials and constraints in the implementation of the sustainable development goals [Review of A literature-based review on potentials and constraints in the implementation of the sustainable development goals]. *Journal of Cleaner Production, 198*, 1276. https://doi.org/10.1016/j.jclepro.2018.07.102

Central Bank of the Bahamas. (2020). *Digital Bahamian dollar sand dollar*. https://www.sanddollar.bs/

Central Bank of the Bahamas. (2024). *The sand dollar is on schedule for gradual national release to The Bahamas*. https://www.centralbankbahamas.com/news/public-notices/the-sand-dollar-is-on-schedule-for-gradual-national-release-to-the-bahamas-in-mid-october-2020?N=C

Cerf, M. (2018). The sustainable development goals: Contextualizing Africa's economic and health landscape [Review of The Sustainable Development Goals: Contextualizing Africa's Economic and Health Landscape]. *Global Challenges, 2*(8). https://doi.org/10.1002/gch2.201800014

Cheng, Y., Liu, H., Wang, S., Cui, X., & Li, Q. (2021). Global action on SDGs: Policy review and outlook in a post-pandemic era. *Sustainability, 13*(11), 6461. https://doi.org/10.3390/su13116461

Chu, Q. (2023). Sustainable Development goals (SDGs): New Zealand outlook with central bank digital currency and SDG 8 realization on the horizon. *arXiv* (Cornell University). https://doi.org/10.48550/arxiv.2311.06716

David-West, O., & Nwagwu, I. (2018). SDGs and digital financial services (DFS) Entrepreneurship: Challenges and opportunities in Africa's largest economy. In *Contemporary issues in entrepreneurship research* (p. 103). Emerald Publishing Limited. https://doi.org/10.1108/s2040-724620180000008011

Demirgüç-Kunt, A., Klapper, L., Singer, D., Ansar, S., & Hess, J. (2019). The global findex database 2017: Measuring financial inclusion and opportunities to expand access to and use of financial services. *The World Bank Economic Review, 34*. https://doi.org/10.1093/wber/lhz013

Denecker, O., D'Estienne, A., Gompertz, P.-M., & Sasia, E. (2023). Central bank digital currencies: An active role for commercial banks. https://doi.org/10.69554/mhha2993

Donaires, O. S., Cezarino, L. O., Caldana, A. C. F., & Liboni, L. B. (2018). Sustainable development goals—An analysis of outcomes. *Kybernetes, 48*(1), 183. https://doi.org/10.1108/k-10-2017-0401

DQ India. (2024). *Powering 2024 Fintech innovation with India stack*. https://www.dqindia.com/powering-2024-fintech-innovation-with-india-stack

ECB. (2023a). *Digital euro*. https://www.ecb.europa.eu/paym/digital_euro/html/index.en.html

ECB. (2023b). https://www.ecb.europa.eu/paym/digital_euro/investigation/governance/shared/files/ecb.degov220929.en.pdf

Ekong, U. M., & Ekong, C. N. (2022). Digital currency and financial inclusion in Nigeria: Lessons for development. *Journal of Internet and Digital Economics, 2*(1), 46. https://doi.org/10.1108/jide-11-2021-0018

Igoni, S., Nwadioha, N., & Ogiri, I. (2022). Evolution of eNaira for re-engineering the nigerian emerging economy. *Journal of Economics Finance and Management Studies, 5*(10). https://doi.org/10.47191/jefms/v5-i10-06

International Monetary Fund. (2019). *How digital financial services are empowering women*. https://www.imf.org/Publications/fandd/issues/2019/03/how-digital-financial-services-are-empowering-women-hendriks

Jie, Z. (2023). How electronic CNY can leverage the development of small and micro enterprises in China. *In Frontiers in Artificial Intelligence and Applications*. https://doi.org/10.3233/faia230014

JIS. (2022). *Money moves!—Jamaica's digital currency*. https://jis.gov.jm/information/get-the-facts/money-moves-jamaicas-digital-currency/

Kshetri, N. (2021). The economics of central bank digital currency [Computing's Economics]. *Computer, 54*(6), 53. https://doi.org/10.1109/mc.2021.3070091

Lannquist, A., & Tan, B. (2023). Central bank digital currency's role in promoting financial inclusion. *Fintech Notes, 2023*(11), 1. https://doi.org/10.5089/9798400253331.063

Lyu, W. (2024). Research on the multi-stage impact of digital economy on rural revitalization in Hainan Province based on GPM model. Authorea (Authorea). https://doi.org/10.22541/au.171154002.26109604/v1

Maniff, J. L. (2020). *Inclusion by design: Crafting a central bank digital currency to reach all Americans*. 1. https://www.kansascityfed.org/documents/7583/psrb20maniff1202.pdf

Ozili, P. K. (2022). Circular economy and central bank digital currency. *Circular Economy and Sustainability, 2*(4), 1501. https://doi.org/10.1007/s43615-022-00170-0

Saeed, S., Altamimi, S. A., Alkayyal, N. A., Alshehri, E., & Alabbad, D. A. (2023). Digital transformation and cybersecurity challenges for businesses resilience: Issues and recommendations [Review of Digital Transformation and Cybersecurity Challenges for Businesses Resilience: Issues and Recommendations]. *Sensors, 23*(15), 6666. Multidisciplinary Digital Publishing Institute. https://doi.org/10.3390/s23156666

Söderberg, G., Bechara, M., Bossu, W., Che, N., Davidovic, S., Kiff, J., Lukonga, I., Griffoli, T. M., Sun, T., & Yoshinaga, A. (2024). Behind the scenes of central bank digital currency: Emerging trends, insights, and policy lessons. *SSRN Electronic Journal*. https://doi.org/10.2139/ssrn.4663923

Sveriges Riksbank. (2023). *E-krona—A digital complement to cash*. https://www.riksbank.se/en-gb/payments--cash/payments-in-sweden/payments-in-sweden-2020/3.-the-riksbank-is-adapting-to-a-changing-world/digital-money--the-riksbanks-e-krona-pilot/e-krona--a-digital-complement-to-cash/

Tan, B. (2023). *central bank digital currency adoption: A two-sided model. IMF Working Paper, 2023*(127), 1. https://doi.org/10.5089/9798400244858.001

Tourpe, H., Lannquist, A., & Soderberg, G. (2023). A guide to central bank digital currency product development. *Fintech Notes, 2023*(7), 1. https://doi.org/10.5089/9798400253690.063

United Nations. (2018). *Transforming our world: The 2030 agenda for sustainable development*. In Springer eBooks. https://doi.org/10.1891/9780826190123.ap02

United Nations. (2023). *The sustainable development goals report 2023*. https://sdgs.un.org/documents/sustainable-development-goals-report-2023-53220

Wang, W. (2020). Application of blockchain in targeted poverty alleviation. https://doi.org/10.2991/aebmr.k.200306.032

World Bank. (2021). *Global financial development report 2014 : Financial inclusion*. https://openknowledge.worldbank.org/handle/10986/16238

World Bank. (2023). *Central bank digital currencies for cross-border payments*. https://openknowledge.worldbank.org/handle/10986/36764

CHAPTER 7

Will the Digital Euro Be Green? Status Quo, Potentials, and Obstacles

Andreas Bielig

7.1 Introduction

The European Central Bank has pledged to support the environmental goals of the European Union in its area of competence and has therefore included climate protection in its list of political priorities. This is in line with a paradigm shift observed worldwide in leading national central banks. It prompted researchers from various disciplines to rethink the fundamental relationship between monetary policy and environmental protection, but also to explore the potential of digital central bank currencies in relation to the achievement of sustainability goals, such as those postulated by the 17 target categories of the UN Agenda 2030. Against the background of the current status of the ECB's project for a future digital euro, this article analyzes potential environmental impacts from an economic perspective, as well as the obstacles and conflicts that arise

A. Bielig (✉)
SGH Warsaw School of Economics, Department of German Economy Research, World Economy Research Institute, Warsaw, Poland
e-mail: abielig@sgh.waw.pl

R. Aneja and R. Dygas (eds.), *Digital Currencies and the Green Economy*, https://doi.org/10.1007/978-981-95-2282-8_7

in this context. It attempts to evaluate the findings and derives recommendations for economic policy in the context of the development of the Digital Euro project. This contribution focuses on potential environmental impacts of future Digital Euro concerning the tradeoff between security issues and energy consumption in Sect. 7.2, with respect to general ECB policy in Sect. 7.3 and the Digital Euro project design in Sect. 7.4. Furthermore it looks on the ecological footprint of the Digital Euro by highlighting the usage of renewable energy in the Euro zone in Sect. 7.5. It closes at the end with summary and conclusions.

7.2 Digital Euro and SDG—An Overview of Problems

Latest, since the European Central Bank (ECB) launched its Digital Euro project on July 14, 2021, with an initial 24-month investigation phase (ECB, 2021) beside of various monetary policy, technical, organizational, and financial market-based considerations also environmental issues increasingly came to public attention. It was not least the immense energy hunger and resulting carbon footprint of existing cryptocurrencies such as Bitcoin (BTC) or Ethereum Classic (ETC) with proof of work-consensus mechanism (PoW) that raised concerns about eco-friendly alternatives (Lu, 2021). Also transitions to other transaction validations such as proof of stake mechanisms (PoS) could not dispel the doubts about environmental friendliness fully. PoS rely on stakes of users that are willing to "stake" their crypto holdings as securities (Crypto Mines, 2023) that allow for strong reduction of energy intensity as in case of Ethereum (ETH).

The search for better environmental protection in cryptocurrencies usage at given level of technology performance has in the following led to increasing variety of so-called eco-friendly cryptocurrencies. In practice, this led to decreasing market transparency concerning disclosed technical characteristics, performance parameters, or other information relevant to potential miners, investors, and users (Brooke, 2024; Green Crypto Research, 2022; Prismecs, 2024; TRG Datacenters, 2024). Moreover, focusing exclusively on energy consumption criterion can lead to an extremely narrow view that ignores other important aspects, as green labeled cryptocurrency example Chia shows. Chia leverages a time and space consensus mechanism (PoST) by using underutilized storage space left on hard disk drives (HDD) or much faster solid state drives (SSD)

(Lilly, 2021; Sparkes, 2021). Despite of its low energy intensity and the achieved high security level of transactions provided by its strong decentralization design the applied mechanism is highly write-intensive and causes fast wear-out of hardware components. The applied PoST mechanism is therefore associated with considerable consumption of input materials and leads to large electronic waste amounts with components difficult to recycle. Furthermore, sharp demand rises for SSD components for so-called Chia farming purposes led to considerable regional bottlenecks on global markets, resulting in drastic price increases that affected conventional non-crypto-usages of SSDs negatively.

However, trade-offs caused by competing usages of technology are not limited to Chia and SSD/HDD only but are observed also for other cryptocurrencies as the Bitcoin mining example shows where excessive mining activities led to scarcities in advanced graphic cards. Revealed negative environmental effects are particularly severe because Chia use does not replace other energy-intensive cryptocurrencies, such as Bitcoin. Rather, it represents an additional source of income for crypto miners or farmers and, hence, induces additional environmental costs through extended farming activities. In this respect, it is of particular importance that increasing farming activities are taking place in world regions with low energy costs but high environmental energy production burden, such as China.

From above considerations follows that the Digital Euro project of ECB has much wider area of sustainability dimensions to take into account than that of energy-related issues but such that reach even far beyond pure environmental aspects of Central Bank Digital Currencies (CBDCs). To provide for more comprehensive global sustainability policy guidance, the 20,230 United Nations (UN) Agenda of 2015 proclaimed the United Nations Sustainable Development Goals (SDGs), consisting of 17 sustainability dimensions regarded as relevant for worldwide peace and prosperity of mankind (UN, 2024). CBDCs, together with other kinds of cryptocurrencies, are assumed to have huge potential to support the better achievement of SDGs in various ways with a strong emphasis on improved financing structures (among others Ozili, 2023; UN Secretary General, 2020; UN.ESCAP, 2017). Table 7.1 shows some main issues interlinking potential CBDCs impacts with UN SDGs achievements.

Most of the listed expected outcomes rely on positive indirect effects of CBDC usage by addressing potential solutions of financing problems for achievement of SDGs (see Table 7.1). The potential contributions to the

Table 7.1 Sustainable development goals and central bank digital currency impacts

SDG	*Topic*	*Potential CBDC impacts*
1	poverty reduction	increasing financial inclusion reducing transaction costs
2	extinction of hunger	improved distribution of aid microfinancing in agriculture
3	improved health care and well-being	increased funding transparency incentives for healthy behavior
4	higher education quality	better access to financial services in education decentralized learning platforms
5	improved gender equality	financial empowering of women female entrepreneurship
6	clean water and sanitation infrastructure	improved financing instruments
7	affordable and clean energy	increased renewable energy funding improved energy markets efficiency
8	decent work and sufficient economic growth	new economic opportunities and markets financial inclusion and reduced transaction costs
9	sustainable industry, innovation, and infrastructure	promotion of innovation decentralized funding of infrastructure
10	less inequalities	inclusive financial system structures increased cross-border remittances
11	sustainable cities and communities	transition to smart cities building resilient urban infrastructures
12	responsible consumption and production	increasing supply chain transparency promotion of circular economy
13	improved climate action	provision of carbon credits decentralized funding of climate projects
14	sustainable life below water	improved financing instruments
15	sustainable life on land	improved financing instruments
16	peace, justice, and strong institutions	increasing transparency and accountability promotion of secure voting systems
17	partnerships for SDGs	improved global collaboration joint resource mobilization

Source own depiction based on Ozili, 2023; UN.ESCAP, 2017;UN Secretary General, 2020

respective problem solutions through the use of CBDC are primarily seen in the expected effects from the improvement of financing instruments, but also in a direct or indirect addressing of existing social, ecological, economic, or technical and governance problems that are perceived as urgent. But CBDC usage may cause also various negative direct or indirect effects with respect to, first, energy and resource consumption of individual transactions and required infrastructure or, second, negative side effects due to existing conflicts of objectives within the SDGs. The latter can be triggered by interdependencies between the CBDC uses and the various political sub targets of the SDGs. Such potentially adverse effects of CBDC use can generally occur in all SDG areas and, in the author's opinion, require a more in-depth a priori analysis in the future. With regard to the first topic mentioned, energy and resources consumption, in especially areas of SDG numbers 7, 12, 13, and 15 reveal potential conflicts of CBDC usage that may cause among others the following serious problems:

ad 7) *affordable and clean energy*: high energy consumption of individual use processes and operation of the required technological infrastructure,
ad 12) *responsible consumption and production*: substantial technological effort required to realize payment processes for end users, payment service providers, and operators of backup infrastructure services,
ad 13) *improved climate action*: transactions carried out cause a considerable ecological footprint along the entire value chain in the payment process with the CO2 emissions resulting from the increased energy consumption
ad 15) *sustainable life on land*: large expenditure of energy, consumption of material resources, and the associated pollution of the environment as well as the disruption and destruction of natural ecosystems and cultural landscapes.

The above list of potential problems caused by energy and resource consumption is neither exhaustive nor does it include other challenges in the use of CBDCs caused by the above-mentioned trade-offs within the SDGs. Hence, despite of prevalent optimistic literature outlooks into future potential CBDCs impacts critical analysis of preconditions for and factual status of the Digital Euro project of ECB with respect to its specific SDG effects is required to allow for both, an evaluation of current CBDC project status and provide advisory to policymakers for necessary adjustments of CBDC development.

7.3 European Central Bank Policy and Environmental Issues

Environmental policy is not the task of central banks. The essence, formulated by US-Fed President Jerome Powell (Powell, 2023) with respect to climate policy is holding also for the ECB. However, from this perspective central banks have also "narrow, but important, responsibilities regarding climate-related financial risks, which are tightly linked to our responsibilities for bank supervision. Banks need to understand, and appropriately manage, their material risks, including the financial risks of climate change" (Powell, 2023). This interpretation of CBs risk-based approach is mirrored in ECB policy concerning environmental risks. In 2022 ECB published its Climate Agenda (ECB, 2022a) and "decided to take further steps to include climate change considerations in the Eurosystem's monetary policy framework. It decided to adjust corporate bond holdings in the Eurosystem's monetary policy portfolios and its collateral framework, to introduce climate-related disclosure requirements and to enhance its risk management practices" (ECB, 2022b). As concrete measures were among others decided, first, to decarbonize corporate bond holdings by tilting toward issuers with better climate performance and, second, to limit asset share issued by high carbon footprint entities as collateral at borrowing from Eurosystem with the aim to reduce climate-related financial risks in Eurosystem credit operations (ECB, 2022b).

However, one year later ECB reduced its environmental ambitions, applying described tilting strategy for corporate bond holdings in ECB balance sheet only shortly between October 2022 and June 2023 and abandoned in addition its envisaged haircuts introduction for climate-adjusted collaterals in December 2022 (Kedward et al., 2024) under the argument to prevent a further distraction of monetary policy from its inflation mandate. In its Climate and Nature Plan 2024–2025 of January 30, 2024, ECB defines three focus area of its work: 1. navigating transition to green economy, 2. addressing increasing physical impact of climate change, and 3. advancing work on nature loss and degradation, that together should help to assess impacts of climate change and nature degradation on price stability and associated financial risks, under regime of an adjusted risk-based approach that is now more closely linked to its core inflation mandate (ECB, 2024a) and departs obviously from an environmental derisking in European monetary policy (Kedward et al., 2024).

Nevertheless, in the roadmap for further activities in the Digital Euro project ECB mentions in its preparatory phase beside payments, banknotes, and market infrastructure topics to consider also environmental design aspects linked to the analysis of this chapter. Hence, in the following the current status of the Digital Euro project is analyzed with respect to selected aspects that have potential direct or indirect environmental implications.

7.4 Digital Euro Project Status and Environmental Aspects

Impacts of CBDC on environment and nature arise from its own technological design features, used infrastructure for payments and settlement, design of financial services of the banking industry based on the CBDC and last but not least patterns of individual user behavior. But, they are also influenced by necessary resource inputs, such as energy supply or raw materials for technological components. In UK's presidency of G7 countries in 2021 parties agreed to a set of 13 principles for retail CBDCs that address certain considerations of CBDC implications for public policy. They range from CBDC aspects of monetary and financial stability as a core area of central bank policy to international development assistance by future CBDC (UK Government, 2021). In Principle Eight concerning energy and environment issues parties agreed that energy usage of CBDC infrastructures should be designed and run efficiently to support countries transition to "net zero" economies. According them CBDC may represent a potential benchmark for design of future payment and settlement ecosystems with high energy efficiency including the usage of carbon–neutral and sustainable energy sources. For this, energy usage aspects of CBDC should be considered just in technical design features and implementation issues from outset.

For the design of Digital Euro different options for specific features of the CBDC are in general available that are considered in the current preparation phase of the project which started in November 2023

(ECB, 2024d). For the ledger infrastructure a choice between centralized systems, such as real-time gross settlement systems (RTGS) that are adopted by many central banks, and distributed ledger systems exists, such as in blockchain-based systems. Both options reveal different implications for security, computation costs, infrastructure and resource requirements, and finally energy consumption (Lee & Park, 2022). Advanced RTGS systems of many countries, such as in the Euro zone applied TARGET system (Bundesbank, 2024), combine both high resilience with large performance in terms of transactions numbers and speed at relative low transaction costs and energy usage, hence, comparable to those of large international card schemes, including debit and credit cards.

Security levels achieved by centralized systems are by design significantly lower than for distributed ledger technology (DLT) that derive its resilience against cyberattack and crime from the decentralized construction of consensus mechanism that avoids the weaknesses arising from single point of failure phenomena (SPoF) (TechTarget, 2024). Here, proof of work mechanism (PoW), such as used for Bitcoin, provides for most secure conditions at costs of transactions performance, required resource effort and energy efficiency. Therefore, other consensus mechanisms, such as proof of stake (PoS), that reduce necessary security efforts could work as potential compromise for the Digital Euro to balance security requirements with environmental costs of usage. In result of their strongly reduced decentralization of technology design—a key security feature of blockchain technology, security levels achieved by current PoS technologies deviate considerably downward with regard to levels reached by PoW mechanisms (Crypto Mines, 2023). Hence, alternative consensus mechanisms that are capable to combine both, decentralized design structures, such as for PoW, with low energy requirements, such as for PoS, may represent a feasible technological solution that could meet individual user needs, banking and finance industry requirements as well as Central Bank efforts in monetary policy provision, financial architecture stabilization, and financial supervision tasks in future Digital Euro applications.

From the above considerations it is evident that the development of an adequate CBDC technology design and successful practice implementation into existing finance and payment infrastructure is challenging. As Chia case with its PoST mechanism indicates, ambiguities in environmental impacts of DLT demand comprehensive impacts analysis of available design options for development of an "optimal" Digital Euro as

European CBDC by considering these trade-offs. Currently, ECB experiments with potential centralized and decentralized technology designs for future Digital Euro with later decision about concrete suitable solutions (Balz, 2024; ECB, 2024b). In early statements of ECB representatives that refer to achieved performance levels of TARGET as ECB's wholesale CBDC system a certain preference for centralized account-based ledger system applications is visible (Panetta, 2022). As ECB pointed out in its 2020 report on Digital Euro that retail account-based Digital Euro are implemented by opening accounts with Eurosystem directly or through supervised intermediaries, whereas bearer digital euro distribution (token-based) requires supervised intermediaries involvement (ECB, 2020. p. 25.).

In case of bearer Digital Euro usage only payer and payee verify economic transactions outside of direct control by the Eurosystem or financial intermediaries, what reduces potential influence of ECB on security issues. This suggests, together with potential synergy advantages to be expected, arising from building up of the Digital Euro design on just existing ECB backend-infrastructures, such as the RTGS system TARGET, a primarily account-based mechanism solution for the future project. That allows, first, to maintain control over security and financial stability relevant aspects of Digital Euro usage, and, second, avoids duplication of financial backend infrastructure present in parallel systems that would counter the ECB target to minimize environmental costs of the Digital Euro (ECB, 2020, p. 33). Running parallel payment systems may improve resilience in case of system default, attacks, or natural disasters but comes at high operating and maintenance costs and, last but not least, also large environmental burden. Therefore, account-based Digital Euro designs that could be build up on ECB-provided backend infrastructure may contribute to minimization of system costs, European-wide scaling up of financial instruments of Banking Sector based on the Digital Euro, reduction of environmental burden, and, finally, lowering of transaction costs for users.

However, if the target of lowering transaction costs for users is feasible depends on many technical details, e.g. Digital Euro compensation scheme for financial intermediaries. Current suggestions entail compensations at comparable electronic payments level, what can hardly regarded as active price competition driver in financial transactions and counters user cost reduction targeted by ECB (ECB, 2024c). Because account-based CBDC technologies reveal systemic disadvantages with respect to security issues in comparison with primary DLT-systems, that achieve highest security performance, ECB considers also blockchain-based design features for the Digital Euro as a bearer instrument of payment (Balz, 2024), hence, a token-based access mechanism. To allow for better ensuring ECBs task fulfillment in monetary policy and financial supervision permissioned blockchain solutions may reveal advantages in comparison with permissionless models at cost of security from decentralized structures.

On the other hand, permissionless (public) blockchain networks are considered to "provide financial market infrastructure with unprecedented efficiency" (Bindseil & Malekan, 2025, p. 15). The efficiency gains achieved from the use of permissionless public blockchain networks could therefore also be used to reduce the environmental impact of realizing financial transactions and operating the necessary technical infrastructure. In contrast, tested permissioned blockchain solutions, "while offering some of the advantages, run into the same organizational issues as existing settlement systems and do not reap all efficiency advantages of public ones" (Bindseil & Malekan, 2025, p. 16). The ECB should therefore carefully weigh up the existing advantages and disadvantages of the available optional designs for the Digital Euro.

In the decision, also the mentioned trade-off between achieved security level and environmental burden of available DLT-design options is to be taken into account by ECB (Lee & Park, 2022). Even if at early stages of project development statements about future technological Digital Euro manifestations come at high uncertainty (see ECB, 2024d and 2024e), parallel operation of blockchain technology for specific financial applications, such as offline transactions (Altcoin Buzz, 2023), in a standard account-based infrastructure environment can increase system complexity in a way that may reduce system resilience, increase maintenance, operation, and transaction costs, and, last but not least, enlarge environmental burden. During the current preparation phase ECB intends to finalize the architecture of future Digital Euro, assess the data protection impact, and develop a plan for positioning and outreach of the CBDC until end of second quarter 2025. The decisions made will therefore have a significant impact on the environmental impact of the future use of the Digital Euro. Whether the design and architecture of the Digital Euro will also take greater account of ecological aspects depends on careful consideration of its potential ecological impact in relation to the other ECB objectives discussed above. Hence, with respect to future environmental burden of

Digital Euro the statement can be confirmed that CBDCs are not simply issued but designed (Westermeier, 2024, p. 8), what underlines the essential role of the applied design concept and used infrastructure also for its ecological performance.

7.5 Digital Euro Usage and of Renewable Energies Consumption

Beyond ECBs environmental policy targets and environmental implications of concrete future CBDC design choices, large environmental impacts will derive also from eco-friendly energy inputs used for operation of related ECB infrastructure, of financial intermediaries involved, and for users individual digital transactions. Here, large shares of energy produced from renewable energy sources would contribute to reductions of ecological footprints of Digital Euro usage and support green transition of European economies (European Commission, 2022). In 2023 the average share of renewable energies on final consumption in the European Union was 24.5%, that of Euro zone members was found with 26.0% on slightly higher level (own calculation based Eurostat, 2025). From EU members and other associated states revealed in 2023 Norway (with 75.6%), Sweden (66.4%), Finland (50.8%), Albania (46.6%), and Denmark (44.9%) the highest shares of renewables (see Fig. 7.1). The lowest renewable shares had Luxembourg (11.6%), Belgium (14.7%), Malta (15.1%), Ireland (15.2%), and Poland (16.5%).

Capital keys reflect the weights of individual member states at the European Central Bank according to their size in the European Union, measured by population and Gross Domestic Product and are recalculated every five years (Bundesbank, 2014). If it is assumed that current capital keys for Euro members in the Euro area reflect also patterns of future Digital Euro dissemination and transaction usage then insights about ecological footprint of CBDC usage can derived from matching of countries renewable energy shares with capital keys as shown in Fig. 7.2. All Euro member with large renewable energy shares have small capital keys, with the leading Finland (1.8%), Latvia (0.4%), Austria (2.9%), and Estonia (0.3%). In contrast, Euro member with the largest capital keys reveal only medium renewable shares with Germany (21.5%), France (22.3%), Italy (19.6%), and Spain (24.8%).

This suggests that euro member states with high renewable shares may be due to their low capitalization in the Euro area not capable to

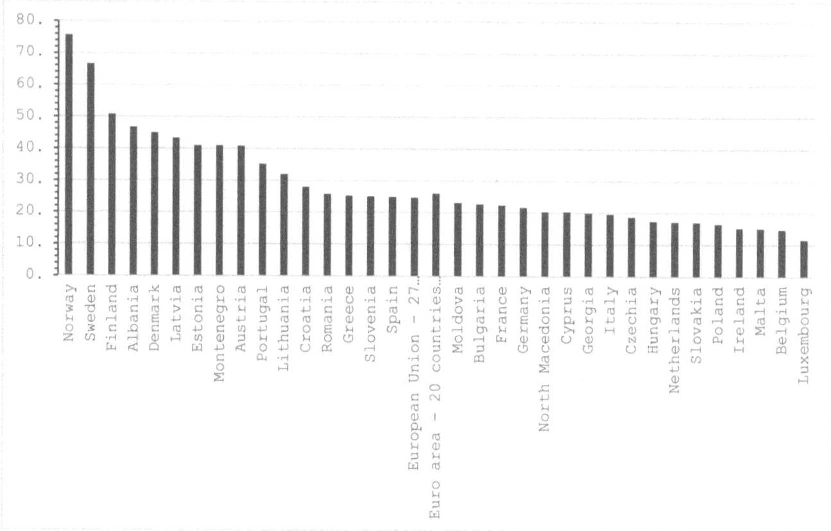

Fig. 7.1 Share of renewable energies on final consumption in EU members and associated states 2023 [%]. (*Source* own calculation and depiction on basis of Eurostat, 2025)

contribute largely to eco-friendly operation of the future Digital Euro. Contrary, larger Euro members may due to significantly lower renewable energy shares increase future environmental burden of prospected Digital Euro operation by their large representation in the Euro zone that is associated with a quantitatively greater use of the European CBDC.

To find preliminary answer on the question to what extent specific Euro member states finally could contribute with their renewable energy shares achieved in 2023 to the eco-friendly usage of the future Digital Euro in the Euro zone at given members capital keys in Fig. 7.3 countries' renewable shares are weighted with their capital keys. As visible, in result, from four countries relative large contributions in terms of high input shares of renewables for the aggregated operation of Digital Euro in the Euro area could be expected, at above given assumptions, that are: Germany (5.8%), France (4.4%), Italy (3.1%), and Spain (2.9%) (own calculation on basis of Eurostat, 2025 and ECB, 2024f). In contrast, Euro members with large renewable shares, such as Finland or Austria, are

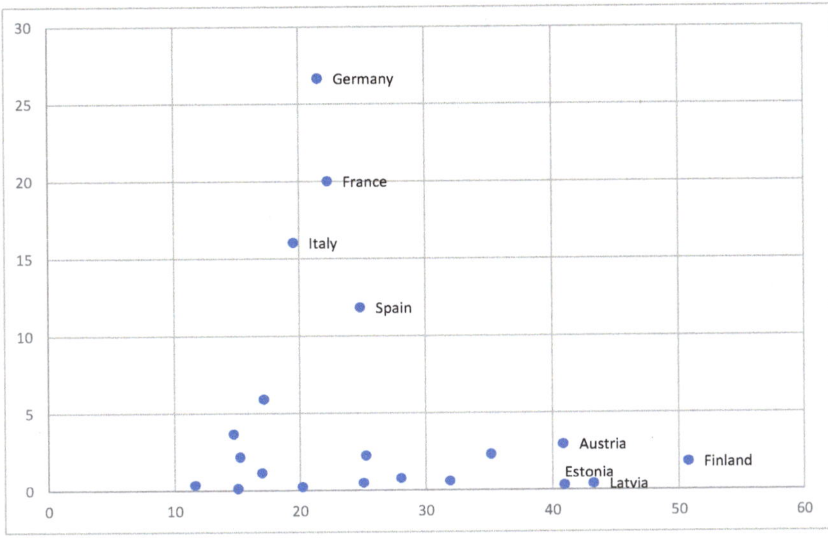

Fig. 7.2 Relation of renewable energy shares on final consumption and capital keys of Eurosystem of Euro area member states 2023, horizontal axis renewable shares [%], vertical axis capital keys [%]. (*Source* own calculation and depiction on basis of Eurostat [2025] and ECB [2024f])

under this considerations probably not in the position to render environmental impacts into positive direction significantly even in case of further expansion of green energy sources. But, huge potentials for improvement of aggregated environmental performance of the Digital Euro have large Euro member states, such as Germany, France, Italy, and Spain, due to their large capital weights in the Euro area and improvement potentials in renewable energy usage.

Hence, with respect to renewable energy input shares developments of environmental impacts of the Digital Euro will mainly depend on intensities of efforts undertaken in these large European states to promote green transition toward production and usage of renewable energies in the future. At present, based on 2023 data of Euro area members for renewable shares and capital keys, Digital Euro usage would rely on 22.8% input share of renewable energies (own calculation on basis of Eurostat, 2025 and ECB, 2024f). With respect to the existing large variance of members renewable shares of 115.8 with maximum values at 50.8% and

states weighted with capital keys of Eurosystem [%]

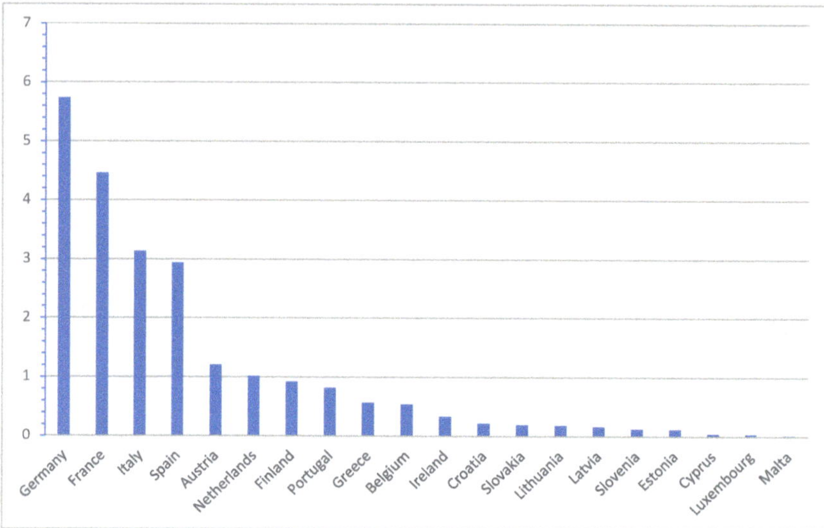

Fig. 7.3 Share of renewable energies on final consumption of Euro area member states weighted with capital keys of Eurosystem [%]. (*Source* own calculation and depiction on basis of Eurostat [2025] and ECB [2024f])

minimum at 11.6% adjustments of energy production require long and intensive efforts that are challenged by obstacles deriving from differences in national contexts and mental states. Here, in particular large Euro members have to take on responsibility for environmental performance of the Digital Euro in the future that derives from their high impacts on the project. However, also perspectives on green transition can vary and are even in case of specific European Union member states not necessarily congruent with transition toward renewable energies as current European discussion about nuclear power usage indicates.

7.6 Summary and Conclusions

The CBDC project of Digital Euro of the ECB represents an endeavor in many ways. The ECB is thus entering new, hitherto largely uncharted territory in terms of its monetary policy, ensuring international financial stability, and exercising its supervisory powers. In addition, negative experiences with substantial energy and materials consumption of many cryptocurrencies that cause large ecological footprints of digital money usage raise serious doubts about potential ecological impacts of prospective CBDCs. As consequence, the alignment of CBDC development with achievement of UN SDGs becomes an important concern also for the Digital Euro project. CBDCs may contribute to SDGs achievements by, i.e. improved financial instruments but also can hinder achievement of objectives by increased energy and materials consumption, environmental pollution, and destruction of natural ecosystems. But also at superordinated level of central bank tasks society's environmental expectations regarding a new strategic approach of European monetary policy are difficult to reconcile with the organization of its central banking mandate and available monetary policy instruments. With the return to a risk-based approach, ECB recognized these challenges and aligned the digital central bank currency project by weighing up conflicting aspects, such as preservation of monetary policy competences, adequate consideration of security aspects, and the environmental impact of provision and use of the future Digital Euro.

For the ecological impact of the prospective CBDC, among others, the chosen technological design, the payment and settlement infrastructure required for usage and last but not least the composition of energy input are particularly important. Decentralized DLT-systems may boost efficiency and innovation in European payment services provision but could come also at cost of higher energy and environmental burden as well as reduced oversight and security capability of the central bank. The use of centralized systems for the Digital Euro could avoid running of parallel systems for infrastructure that contributes to resource and cost optimizations as well as for oversight purposes but is limited in terms of innovation openness, competition, and security issues. In the current preparation phase of ECBs Digital Euro project fundamental decisions about main features, technological design constructions and infrastructural aspects are still pending but should finalized by the end of 2025 for decision of Governing Council about entering into a new phase of the project. Hence, detailed analysis of these aspects has to be postponed to the expected implementation phase.

With respect to energy composition inputs the analysis of renewable energy shares and capital keys of the Eurosystem reveals large imbalances between large Euro area members and smaller member states with the former having only small shares of renewables on final consumption and those members with large renewables shares covering small fractions of total Euro area capitalization only. Provided that future Digital Euro dissemination is associated with member states capitalization major fractions of the prospective CBDC will rely on energy originating from conventional production with large emissions and substantial ecological footprint. The ecological balance of the Digital Euro will therefore also depend in particular on further efforts to achieve an ecological transformation of energy production and utilization in large Euro states.

In sum, the analysis indicates that an orientation of the European Digital Euro Project on the fundamental level toward an ecological focus is not only desirable but also necessary to support SDG policies. Hence, ECB policy should explore carefully potential ecological impacts of available CBDC options with respect to required features, available technological designs, and infrastructural aspects and weigh these against fundamental requirements in fulfillment of its tasks in monetary policy, payment systems, and financial stability and supervision but also with innovation issues for a prospering financial industry also beyond conventional payment services. However, how green the digital euro will become depends not only on the ECB's decision, but also on the activities of many individual players in the financial industry and the fintech sector, as well as on the future users themselves.

References

Altcoin Buzz. (2023, October 4). *4 ways to make on-chain transfers without internet*, https://www.altcoinbuzz.io/bitcoin-and-crypto-guide/4-ways-to-make-on-chain-transfers-without-internet/, (accessed: 10.01.2025).

Balz, B. (2024). *Only balances of €500 allowed? What the digital euro is intended to deliver—And what not*, interview with focus online, 05.06.2024, Bundesbank, Frankfurt/Main, https://www.bundesbank.de/en/press/interviews/only-balances-of-500-allowed-what-the-digital-euro-is-intended-to-deliver-and-what-not-933704, (accessed: 10.01.2025).

Bindseil, U., & Malekan, O. (2025, February 14). *Public crypto networks as financial market infrastructures*, Available at SSRN: https://ssrn.com/abstract=5138052 or https://doi.org/10.2139/ssrn.5138052 (accessed: 10.01.2025).

Brooke, C. (2024). *Most eco-friendly cryptocurrencies to invest in 2024*, https://crypto-news.com/cryptocurrency/most-eco-friendly-crypto/, 11.10.2024, (accessed: 10.01.2025).

Bundesbank. (2014). *Understanding the capital key*, Bundesbank, Frankfurt/Main, https://www.bundesbank.de/en/tasks/topics/understanding-the-capital-key-666388, (accessed: 10.01.2025).

Bundesbank. (2024). *TARGET. The target development process*, Bundesbank, Frankfurt/Main, https://www.bundesbank.de/en/tasks/payment-systems/target/target-626752, (accessed: 10.01.2025).

Crypto Mines. (2023, July 21). *Basics of blockchain—Consensus mechanism*, https://kopalniekrypto.pl/en/blog2/bid-56-basics-of-blockchain-consensus-mechanisms, (accessed: 10.01.2025).

ECB. (2020). *Report on a digital euro*, October 2020, European Central Bank, Frankfurt/Main, https://www.ecb.europa.eu/euro/html/digitaleuro-report.en.html, (accessed: 10.01.2025).

ECB. (2021, July 14). *Press release. Eurosystem launches digital euro project*, European Central Bank, Frankfurt/Main, https://www.ecb.europa.eu/press/pr/date/2021/html/-ecb.pr210714~d99198ea23.en.html, (accessed: 10.01.2025).

ECB. (2022a, July 4). *ECB climate agenda 2022*, European Central Bank, Frankfurt/Main, https://www.ecb.europa.eu/press/pr/date/2022/html/ecb.pr220704_annex~cb39c2dcbb.en.pdf, (accessed: 10.01.2025).

ECB. (2022b, July 4). *Press release. ECB takes further steps to incorporate climate change into its monetary policy operations*, European Central Bank, Frankfurt/Main, https://www.ecb.europa.eu/press/pr/date/2022/html/ecb.pr220704~4f48a72462.en.html, (accessed: 10.01.2025).

ECB. (2024a, January 30). *Climate and nature plan 2024–2025*, https://www.ecb.europa.eu/ecb/climate/our-climate-and-nature-plan/shared/pdf/ecb.climate_nature_plan_2024-2025.en.pdf, (accessed: 10.01.2025).

ECB. (2024b, December 2). *Q14. Would the digital euro be based on a distributed ledger technology such as blockchain?*, FAQs on a digital euro,, European Central Bank, Frankfurt/Main, https://www.ecb.europa.eu/euro/digital_euro/faqs/html/ecb.faq-_digital_euro.en.html#q14, (accessed: 10.01.2025).

ECB. (2024c, July 14). *Progress on the investigation phase of a digital euro—Fourth report*, European Central Bank, Frankfurt/Main, https://www.ecb.europa.eu/press/intro-/news/html/ecb.mipnews230714.en.html, (accessed: 10.01.2025).

ECB. (2024d, June 24). *First progress report on digital euro preparation phase*, European Central Bank, Frankfurt/Main, https://www.ecb.europa.eu/euro/digital_euro/progress/html-/ecb.deprp202406.de.html, (accessed: 10.01.2025).

ECB. (2024e). *Second progress report on digital euro preparation phase*, 2.12.2024, European Central Bank, Frankfurt/Main, https://www.ecb.europa.eu/euro/digital_euro/progress-/html/ecb.deprp202412.de.html, (accessed: 10.01.2025).

ECB. (2024f). *Capital subscription*, European Central Bank, Frankfurt/ Main, https://www.ecb.europa.eu/ecb/orga/capital/html/index.en.html, (accessed: 10.01.2025).

European Commission. (2022). Towards a green and digital future, publications office of the European Union, Luxembourg, https://op.europa.eu/en/pub lication-detail//publication-/58c3af16-f692-11ec-b976-01aa75ed71a1/lan guage-en, (accessed: 10.01.2025).

Eurostat. (2025). *Share of energy from renewable sources*, Data Browser, https:// ec.europa.eu/eurostat/databrowser/view/nrg_ind_ren$defaultview/default/ table, (accessed: 10.01.2025).

Green Crypto Research. (2022). *ESG rating of polkadot: How sustainable is dot?*, Jul 27, 2022, https://www.greencryptoresearch.com/post/polkadot, (accessed: 10.01.2025).

Lee, S., & Park, J. (2022). *Environmental implications of a Central Bank Digital Currency (CBDC)*, World Bank Group Korea Office, Innovation and Technology Note Series, Juy 2022, Note Series Number 8, World Bank Group, Washington, https://openknowledge.worldbank.org/entities/public ation/b8da64b0-5ffe-54d8-9a9a-182c2113f603, (accessed: 10.01.2025).

Lilly, P. (2021, May 11). *Chia mining can wreck a 512GB SSD in as little as 6 weeks*, PC gamer, https://www.pcgamer.com/chia-mining-can-wreck-a-512gb-ssd-in-as-little-as-6-weeks/, (accessed: 10.01.2025).

Lu, D. (2021, April 6). *Bitcoin mining emissions in China will hit 130 million tonnes by 2024*, NewScientist, https://www.newscientist.com/article/227 3672-bitcoin-mining-emis-sions-in-china-will-hit-130-million-tonnes-by-2024/, (accessed: 10.01.2025).

Kedward, K., Gabor, D., & Ryan-Collins, J. (2024). *Carrots with(out) sticks: Credit policy and the limits of green central banking*, Review of International Political Economy, https://www.tandfonline.com/doi/full/10.1080/ 09692290.2024.2351838, (accessed: 10.01.2025).

Ozili, P. K. (2023). Using Central Bank digital currency to achieve the sustainable development goals. In K, Sood, B. Balusamy & S. Grima (Eds.), *Digital transformation, strategic resilience, cyber security and risk management* (*contemporary studies in economic and financial analysis, Vol. 111C*), (pp. 143–153). Emerald Publishing Limited, Leeds. https://doi.org/10.1108/S1569-37592023000111C008, (accessed: 10.01.2025).

Panetta, F. (2022, June 16). Bringing European payments to the next stage: A public-private endeavor. In *Keynote speech by Fabio Panetta, Member of the Executive Board of the ECB, at the European Payments Council's 20th anniversary conference, Frankfurt am Main*, https://www.ecb.europa.eu/press/key/date/2022/html/ecb.sp2206 16~9f8d1e277b.-en.html#footnote.11, (accessed: 10.01.2025).

Powell, J. (2023, October 24). *Statement by Chair Jerome H. Powell on principles for climate-related financial risk management for large financial institutions*, US Federal Reserve, https://www.federalreserve.gov/newsevents/pressreleases/powell-statement-20231024b.htm, (accessed: 10.01.2025).

Prismecs. (2024, February 26). *The 10 most sustainable cryptocurrencies of 2024*, https://prismecs.com/blog/the-10-most-sustainable-cryptocurrencies, (accessed: 10.01.2025).

Sparkes, M. (2021, May 10). *'Green' bitcoin alternative Chia is leading to hard disc shortages*, https://www.newscientist.com/article/2277076-green-bitcoin-alternative-chia-is-leading-to-hard-disc-shortages/, (accessed: 10.01.2025).

TechTarget. (2024). *Single point of failure (SPOF)*, https://www.techtarget.com/-searchdatacenter/definition/Single-point-of-failure-SPOF, (accessed: 10.01.2025).

TRG Datacenters. (2024). *Which cryptocurrency is the most environmentally friendly?*, https://www.trgdatacenters.com/resource/most-environment-friendly-cryptocurrencies/, (accessed: 10.01.2025).

UK Government. (2021, October 14). *G7 United Kingdom Public Policy Principles for Retail Central Bank Digital Currencies (CBDCs)*, London, https://www.gov.uk/government-/publications/g7-public-policy-principles-for-retail-central-bank-digital-currencies-and-g7-finance-ministers-and-central-bank-governors-statement-on-central-bank, (accessed: 10.01.2025).

UN. (2024). *Sustainability goals. History*, UN department of economic and social affairs, Sustainable Development, https://sdgs.un.org/goals, (accessed: 10.01.2025).

UN.ESCAP. (2017). *Digital and virtual currencies for sustainable development*. United Nations ESCAP, https://repository.unescap.org/handle/20.500.12870/575, (accessed: 10.01.2025).

UN Secretary General. (2020, August). *People's money: Harnessing digitalization to finance a sustainable future*, task force on digital financing of the Sustainable Development Goals, https://unsdg.un.org/resources/peoples-money-harnessing-digitalization-finance-sustainable-future, (accessed: 10.01.2025).

Westermeier, C. (2024). *The digital euro: A materialization of (in)security*, Review of International Political Economy, https://www.tandfonline.com/doi/full/10.1080/09692290-.2024.2345613, (accessed: 10.01.2025).

CHAPTER 8

Community Engagement and Stakeholder Collaboration for Sustainable Development

Pushp Gautam and Sanjay Bhayana

8.1 Introduction

Community engagement and stakeholder collaboration are two closely related concepts that involve actively involving and collaborating with various stakeholders within a community to address common challenges, find solutions, and make decisions. These terms are often used interchangeably and underscore the need to build relationships, establish dialogue, and work with key stakeholders. Stakeholder cooperation refers to the active involvement of any organization or individual interested in or concerned about an issue or project. Such parties could be corporations, non-profits, local government agencies, members of the public, and

P. Gautam
National Institute of Food Technology Entrepreneurship and Management, Kundli, Haryana, India
e-mail: phd-723604@niftem.ac.in

S. Bhayana (✉)
Food Business Management and Entrepreneurship Development, National Institute of Food Technology Entrepreneurship and Management, Kundli, Haryana, India

R. Aneja and R. Dygas (eds.), *Digital Currencies and the Green Economy*, https://doi.org/10.1007/978-981-95-2282-8_8

other relevant parties. Stakeholder partnerships strive to integrate these diverse perspectives and resources to create lasting and mutually beneficial outcomes. Collaboration becomes a manner of communication that invites dialogue between people. Walker (2007) asserts that cooperation is characterized by positive and open communication, typically in the form of discussion, focusing on power-sharing and a level playing field.

In contrast, community engagement is not just engaging, working with individuals in a community, with the underlying principle of developing relationships, getting input, and working to alleviate specific concerns or needs of a community. Stakeholder involvement in decision-making begins with community engagement that balances local community representation and incorporation in the decision-making process. So, the counterpart for "stakeholder collaboration and community engagement" describes the importance of participation, communicating with one another, and working together. Stakeholder participation when plastic pollution is at the lowest level and no choices are made through engaging together will improve the quality and legitimacy of the decision and thus realize better outcomes for environmental challenges and livelihood in rural society (Coenen et al., 2009).

They are founded on the proposition that when communities and other stakeholders come together, members can discover commonalities of interest and concern, reach more informed decisions, and derive more equitable and embedded results. Effective stakeholder collaboration and community engagement can produce various positive outcomes, such as a more supportive and engaged community, more equitable and sustainable solutions and interventions, enhanced stakeholder trust and knowledge, and new, effective ways to address complex problems. However, recognizing that negotiating stakeholder collaboration and community involvement also raises issues related to working through disagreements, reconciling contrasting positions, and committing adequate time and resources to the process. This brings about several challenges, such as the limited decision-making capacity of communities and the management of communal property while projects are being implemented on communal land (Zikargae et al., 2021). However, these methods are becoming increasingly acknowledged as necessary to solve the intricate social, environmental, and economic problems that communities are currently experiencing.

Community engagement ensures that local stakeholders' needs and priorities become part of digital and green economy projects. These stakeholders include residents, businesses, and community groups. Working together allows these different groups to find shared goals and reach outcomes that benefit everyone. Teaming up with many community members helps uncover creative solutions that tap into different people's special knowledge, skills, and abilities. This teamwork can get these groups moving. People can share environmental information through talks, debates, persuasion, and ongoing conversations. These dialogues help people share information and understand each other's views (Eisenhauer & Nicholson, 2005; Zikargae & Ali, 2017; Zikargae, 2018, 2021; Zikargae et al., 2021, 2022). Open and inclusive community involvement can boost the responsibility of digital and green economy projects when paired with shared decision-making. This creates a feeling of shared duty among stakeholders, leads to fair results, and helps build trust.

When combined with shared decision-making, open and inclusive community involvement impacts the accountability of digital and green economy projects. This creates a sense of shared responsibility among stakeholders, results in equitable outcomes, and helps build confidence. Community engagement is key in educating, empowering, and boosting awareness of sustainable practices and technology. When involved, stakeholders are more likely to understand and participate in the move to a more sustainable digital and green economy. The world is going through the digitalization age, and most of our day-to-day activities rely on cutting-edge digital and computer technologies. These contemporary technologies have their applications in socio-economic, environmental, sustainable, and climate research applications to enhance the productivity and efficiency of a given system (Balogun et al., 2020; Ceipek et al., 2021). To ensure digital and green economy projects fit the specific needs of a local area, getting the community involved and working with key people can help. This teamwork helps pinpoint and tackle each community's unique social, economic, and environmental issues. Digitalization brings a new set of tools that must be carefully balanced to ensure innovative applications and green character. The capability of making well-informed decisions to use resources and services more efficiently significantly impacts sustainability and equal access (Appio et al., 2021; Ardito et al., 2018).

Digital money's arrival marks the start of some significant changes in the money world. It has the power to change the way we use cash and do business big time. However, it is not just about money; these high-tech coins are also becoming valuable tools for solving the planet's significant problems, like sustainable living. With CBDCs, sending money straight to another person gets way more manageable, and it is clear as glass what is going on with the cash. That makes backing up projects that are kind to the planet a breeze so everyone can pitch in for a nicer planet. Plus, we will look at how important it is for everyone to work together when mixing digital money into the eco-friendly business scene. Global mobile phone subscriptions have increased significantly, which could make digital payments possible if adequate network coverage is obtained. In 2018, about 12.7% of people lived in places with poor mobile coverage, particularly in rural areas with low literacy and population densities, poor infrastructure, and limited access to electrical grids. As a result, there is frequently little financial motivation for mobile network operators (MNOs) to extend their services into these regions (Table 8.1).

India's transaction methods have seen a significant shift in the last two decades, moving away from a cash-focused setup and towards one bursting with digital dealings. This upgrade got a massive boost from tech advancements, government-friendly business moves, and the booming fintech scene. Sitting at the heart of all this change is the Unified Payments Interface (UPI), a system that's made buying stuff a breeze for a massive crowd of shoppers.

Table 8.1 Global comparison of CBDC adoption (2024)

Country	*CBDC stage*	*Primary use case*	*Sustainability linkage*
China	Pilot (e-CNY)	Retail payments, subsidies	Green bonds, carbon credit tracking
India	Pilot (Digital ₹)	Financial inclusion, DBTs	Farmer subsidies, renewable energy
Sweden	Testing (e-Krona)	Cash replacement	Energy-efficient blockchain design
Nigeria	Launched (eNaira)	Cross-border remittances	Agri-finance, micro-loans

Source BIS survey 2024, IMF digital currency tracker

8.2 Growth of Digital Payments in India

The global digital economy is expanding 2.5 times faster than the physical economy and currently accounts for over 15% of the world's GDP. With a 10% GDP contribution from its digital economy predicted to increase to 20% by 2026, India is a major player in this trend. India's internal economy is benefiting from this expansion and solidifying its place in the global digital economy. Expanding internet access with 199 million additional users in just three years, India's internet penetration rate has increased to 55% in 2023. The Internet connection is economical due to the nation's low data charges, which are the lowest at ₹13.32 per GB. In 2023, this resulted in an average monthly data usage of 24.1 GB per user, highlighting India's dedication to creating an equitable digital ecosystem. Rise in smartphone users, with an estimated 750 million users in 2023 and 1 billion expected by 2026, smartphones are essential to India's digital growth. For many Indians, particularly those living in rural and semi-urban regions, smartphones are their primary digital access point, contributing to the digital economy's expansion. FinTech and Digital Payments Growth With $2.6 billion in funding in 2023, India's FinTech sector is growing quickly. By managing 80% of all digital transactions in India and hitting a record-breaking 15 billion transactions in September 2024 alone, a total of over 134 billion transactions in the fiscal year 2023–2024, UPI has revolutionized digital payments. Over the last seven years, the volume of digital payment transactions has increased at a compound annual rate of 50%, positioning India as a leader (PIB Delhi, December 2024a, 2024b) (Table 8.2).

Financial inclusion through the Pradhan Mantri Jan Dhan Yojana (PMJDY), which has opened 52.5 crore Aadhaar-linked bank accounts

Table 8.2 Growth of digital payments in India (2018–2024)

Year	*UPI Transactions (in billions)*	*Value (in ₹ trillion)*	*Internet penetration (%)*	*Mobile payment users (in millions)*
2018	1.2	1.8	34%	100
2020	5.3	9.5	45%	300
2022	74.0	126.0	52%	600
2024	134.0	210.0	55%	750

Source RBI Annual Reports, PIB Delhi (2024a, 2024b), NPCI Data

which over 50% are held by women and 67% are in rural areas, has achieved significant progress towards financial inclusion. By ensuring that government assistance reaches recipients directly (PIB Delhi, August 2023), Direct Benefit Transfers (DBTs) reduce leakage and increase financial inclusion. DBTs distributed ₹6.9 lakh crore to 176 crore recipients in 2023–2024. Strengthening Digital Infrastructure Systems like India Stack, Aadhaar, UPI, and Digi locker are all part of India's strong digital infrastructure. These tools improve financial inclusion and support a range of activities. With the introduction of 5G, connection has dramatically increased, with median mobile download rates rising from 1.3 Mbps in 2014 to 107.03 Mbps in 2024. More than 2 lakh rural panchayats have been connected by Bharat Net, giving them access to e-health, e-education, and e-governance services (PIB Delhi, December 2024a, 2024b) (Fig. 8.1).

Advancements in Digital Authentication and Learning With more than 116 billion Aadhaar-based authentications and 20 billion electronic Know Your Customer (e-KYC) verifications, India has simplified service access through digital authentication. The digital lending ecosystem is also growing, with Fintech and Big-Tech companies working together to increase credit availability for individuals and enterprises.

India passed the **Digital Personal Data Protection Act (DPDP Act)** in 2023 to address privacy issues and give users more control over their

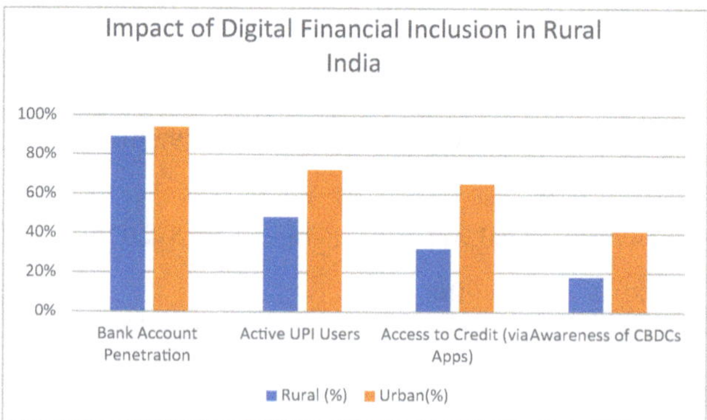

Fig. 8.1 Impact of digital financial inclusion in rural India (2023). (*Source*—PMJDY Report 2023)

data. However, cybersecurity threats are increasing as the world grows more digitally connected, underscoring the necessity of strong defences.

With initiatives to link UPI with other nations' payment systems, India's Digital Public Infrastructure model is becoming increasingly well-known worldwide. As India uses its digital infrastructure to access international markets, digital trade is predicted to contribute significantly to its GDP by 2030.

8.3 State of Digital Payments in India

Payment Systems Infrastructure With a vast array of digital payment methods and services, India boasts one of the world's most sophisticated payment systems infrastructures. The nation has established several round-the-clock payment systems, such as RTGS, NEFT, IMPS, and UPI. Because of their interconnection, these systems enable smooth money transfers between banks and other financial organizations. Expanding payment acceptance infrastructure throughout the nation, especially in rural and semi-urban areas, has been made possible mainly by the Payments Infrastructure Development Fund (PIDF), which the Reserve Bank of India (RBI) operationalized in 2021. By offering banks and payment service provider's financial incentives to deploy payment acceptance devices and infrastructure, the PIDF seeks to establish a strong digital payment ecosystem.

India's digital payment environment has changed dramatically as a result of UPI. Since its launch in 2016, which allows users to move money between bank accounts using a mobile device, it has become the nation's most widely used digital payment platform. The platform's broad popularity can be attributed to its characteristics for real-time settlement, interoperability, and ease of use.

The success of UPI is due to its open design, which promotes competition and innovation by enabling several banks and fintech businesses to provide UPI-based services. UPI's acceptance has also been expedited by the government's push for digital payments, the broad availability of cellphones, and internet connections. Additionally, UPI has been crucial in advancing financial inclusion in India. The platform has facilitated access to financial services for people, even those living in rural areas, by allowing users to link their bank accounts with a UPI ID. With the release of UPI 2.0 in 2018, the platform's functionality and attractiveness were further improved by adding new capabilities like invoice production, one-time mandates, and overdraft facilities. As UPI continues to evolve, it is expected to cement India's position as a global leader in digital payments, setting benchmarks for other nations to follow.

The Role of Government Initiatives in building the required infrastructure, increasing awareness, and providing incentives for the usage of digital payments have all been made possible by several government efforts. Promoting digital payments has also been greatly aided by the Direct Benefit Transfer (DBT) program, which deposits welfare and subsidies straight into recipients' bank accounts. Launched in 2015, the Digital India Mission sought to make India a knowledge economy and society empowered by technology. The government has undertaken several programs to advance internet access, digital literacy, and the adoption of digital payments as part of this aim.

Various entities, such as banks, payment gateways, fintech firms, and third-party service providers (TPSPs), define India's digital payment ecosystem. These companies have created a broad range of digital payment solutions to meet the various demands of both businesses and consumers. In India, banks have led the digital payment revolution by providing card-based payment, mobile, and online banking. With their user-friendly systems for online and mobile payments, payment gateways like Paytm, PhonePe, and Google Pay have also seen tremendous growth. Fintech businesses have fostered innovation and created new payment methods, including contactless, digital wallets, and Buy Now Pay Later (BNPL) services.

The development and administration of the nation's digital payment infrastructure have been greatly aided by the National Payments Corporation of India (NPCI). The foundation of India's digital payment ecosystem comprises NPCI's platforms, which enable safe and effective transactions throughout the nation. These platforms include UPI, IMPS, and AePS. The idea of Central Bank Digital Currency has surfaced as the next step in the development of digital payments, building on the success of these platforms.

8.4 Empowering Local Communities

A strong connection exists between using digital currency to empower local people and the sustainable development philosophy. These currencies can start a positive chain reaction in communities by providing a decentralized and easily accessible financial infrastructure that promotes social justice, economic growth, and environmental stewardship. Imagine a scenario where people of a distant hamlet can conveniently access financial services through their mobile phones, including micro-loans and savings accounts, due to a community-based digital currency. This accessibility empowers individuals to invest in local businesses, participate in renewable energy projects, and enhance economic resilience.

The power of digital currencies to empower communities extends beyond financial inclusion. By enabling micro-payments and incentivizing local entrepreneurship, these currencies can unlock opportunities for individuals to generate income from sustainable activities. Imagine a community of farmers utilizing a digital currency to trade locally sourced, organic produce, empowering them to access fair prices and improve their livelihoods. Beyond individual empowerment, digital currencies can foster collaboration and collective action within communities. The shared ledger technology allows for creating community-based platforms where residents can exchange information, organize events, and collectively pursue sustainable development projects. For instance, a community could use a digital currency to facilitate a local farmers' market, promoting food security and reducing reliance on external food sources. However, realizing the transformative potential of digital currencies in empowering local communities requires careful consideration of several factors. One key aspect is ensuring equitable access to digital technology. Digital literacy programs and affordable mobile devices are crucial for bridging the digital divide and ensuring all community members can participate in the digital economy.

Furthermore, fostering collaboration between community organizations, governments, and financial institutions is essential for successful implementation. This multi-stakeholder approach enables shared knowledge, resource pooling, and the development of comprehensive strategies for empowering local communities through digital currencies. The journey of empowering local communities through digital currencies is not without its challenges. Concerns about data privacy, cybersecurity, and the potential for financial instability require careful attention. However, by addressing these challenges proactively, we can unlock the immense potential of digital currencies to promote sustainable development, economic inclusion, and community empowerment. The story of community empowerment through digital currencies is still being written. As we navigate the complexities of this evolving technology, we must remain committed to its responsible and equitable application. By prioritizing community needs, fostering collaboration, and embracing innovation, we can harness the power of digital currencies to create a more sustainable and equitable future for all.

8.5 Gamification in Sustainable Development

Imagine a world where contributing to sustainable development feels less like a chore and more like an engaging game. This is where the power of gamification comes into play. Gamification, applying game design principles to non-game contexts, holds immense potential for boosting community involvement in green projects. It can transform how individuals interact with environmental initiatives, fostering a sense of purpose, motivation, and reward. Turning sustainability into a Game (Fig. 8.2).

The core principle of gamification lies in leveraging the inherent human desire for challenge, achievement, and reward. It incorporates game-like elements, such as points, badges, leaderboards, and challenges, into sustainable development projects. By framing environmental actions as a game, we can tap into intrinsic motivation and encourage active participation.

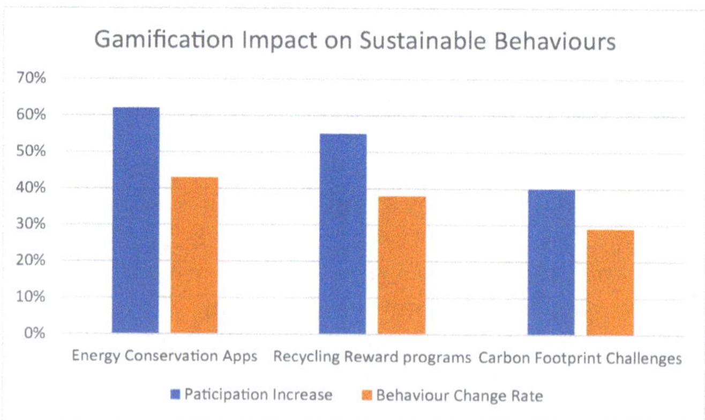

Fig. 8.2 Gamification impact on sustainable behaviours. (*Source*—Synthetic data based on MIT behavioral science lab 2023, UNEP case studies)

8.6 Examples of Gamification in Sustainable Development

1. Energy Conservation Challenges: Imagine a community where residents earn points for reducing energy consumption. This could be achieved through smart metres that track electricity usage, incentivizing individuals to compete for the lowest energy footprint. The points could be redeemed for discounts on sustainable goods, community rewards, or simply bragging rights on a public leaderboard.

2. Recycling and Waste Management Games: A city could launch a mobile app that gamifies recycling efforts. Users can scan barcodes on recyclable products, earning points based on the types of materials they recycle. The app could also provide interactive tutorials on proper waste disposal and track individual recycling performance, fostering a sense of competition and community engagement.

3. Sustainable Agriculture Initiatives: A farmer's market could introduce a "sustainable farming challenge" where participating farmers earn points based on their organic practices, water conservation techniques, and local sourcing. The points could be exchanged for access to workshops, resources, or even preferential placement at the market.

4. Biodiversity Conservation Games: A wildlife conservation organization could create a virtual ecosystem where participants adopt endangered animals, learn about their habitats, and complete tasks to contribute to their protection. The game could use virtual rewards, knowledge quizzes, and real-world volunteering opportunities to engage players meaningfully.

8.7 The Benefits of Gamification

1. Increased Participation: Gamification makes environmental actions more engaging and fun, encouraging a larger pool of individuals to participate in sustainable initiatives. Tapping into intrinsic motivation and competition can drive participation beyond traditional methods like awareness campaigns.

2. Knowledge Acquisition and Awareness: Gamification can provide a platform for educating individuals about sustainable practices through interactive elements, quizzes, and challenges. It can help demystify complex environmental concepts, making them more accessible and relatable.

3. Fostering a Sense of Community: Gamification encourages collaboration among participants, fostering a sense of community and shared responsibility for environmental stewardship. It can build bridges between individuals, organizations, and communities, promoting collective action for a common goal.

4. Data Collection and Insights: Gamification can generate valuable data on individual and community behaviours, providing insights into the effectiveness of sustainable initiatives. This data can inform future interventions, policy development, and resource allocation.

8.8 Challenges and Considerations

1. Finding the Right Balance: It is crucial to balance gamification and the seriousness of environmental issues. While gamification can be engaging, ensuring that the message of sustainability remains central is essential.

2. Inclusivity and Accessibility: Gamification strategies need to be inclusive, considering the needs and preferences of diverse populations. Accessibility should be a priority, ensuring that all community members can participate.

3. Privacy Concerns: Gamification involves collecting data on user behaviours. It is important to address privacy concerns and ensure that data is collected, used, and stored responsibly, adhering to ethical guidelines.

4. Long-Term Engagement: While gamification can initially attract a large audience, it is crucial to maintain engagement over time. This requires continuous innovation, incorporating new challenges, and adapting to changing user preferences.

8.9 Integrating Gamification into Community-Led Digital Projects

1. Sustainable Tokenized Economies: Imagine a community using a CBDC for local transactions, with rewards for sustainable actions. Individuals can earn tokens to reduce energy consumption, use public transportation, or participate in community cleanups. These tokens could be used for discounts at local businesses, access to community services, or even to participate in community-led projects.

2. Green Investment Platforms: Gamified platforms could allow individuals to invest in local green projects using CBDCs. Participants could earn points or tokens based on their investments, creating a sense of ownership and engagement. These platforms could also incorporate social impact measurement tools, making it transparent for investors to track the impact of their contributions.

3. Collaborative Environmental Mapping: Gamification can empower communities to map environmental issues and resources, using CBDCs to reward participants. Individuals could use a mobile app to report pollution, identify areas for restoration, or document biodiversity hotspots. This data could then be used to guide community-led projects and policy decisions.

8.10 Case Studies in Community-Led Initiatives

1. The Green Village Project in Kenya:

Community: A rural community in Kenya faces water scarcity and deforestation challenges.

Project: Developed a digital currency platform for community-led reforestation and water conservation initiatives.

Impact: The platform facilitated the purchase of tree saplings, water filtration systems, and sustainable agriculture techniques, empowering the community to manage their resources and build resilience against climate change.

2. **The Renewable Energy Cooperative in India:**

Community: A group of farmers in India struggling with high energy costs and unreliable power grids.

Project: Launched a digital currency-based cooperative to finance the installation of solar panels in homes and farms.

Impact: The cooperative provided a low-cost financing solution, increased access to renewable energy, and empowered farmers to take control of their energy needs.

3. **The Community-Based Tourism Platform in Costa Rica:**

Community: A rural community in Costa Rica with rich biodiversity but limited economic opportunities.

Project: Created a digital currency-based platform for sustainable tourism, allowing visitors to pay for eco-tours, lodging, and local crafts using digital currencies.

Impact: The platform generated revenue for the community, supported conservation efforts, and promoted sustainable tourism practices.

4. **The Decentralized Food System in Thailand:**

Community: A network of farmers and consumers in Thailand seeking more sustainable and equitable food systems.

Project: Developed a digital currency platform for local food production and distribution, connecting farmers directly to consumers and reducing reliance on intermediaries.

Impact: The platform empowered farmers, fostered local food markets, and promoted sustainable agricultural practices. These case studies showcase the transformative potential of community-led initiatives utilizing digital currencies. By fostering collaboration and empowering communities, these projects address local needs, enhance environmental stewardship, and contribute to a more equitable and sustainable future.

8.11 Challenges in Community-Led Digital Projects

While the promise of community-led digital currency projects is undeniably exciting, the path to realizing their full potential is challenging. Navigating these obstacles requires a keen understanding of the complexities involved and a collaborative spirit that fosters innovative solutions. One of the most significant challenges lies in the lack of widespread digital literacy and access to technology. In many communities, especially those in developing countries, the ability to use digital currencies is hampered by limited access to the internet, smartphones, and even basic computer skills. This digital divide can create a sense of exclusion, hindering participation in projects that improve lives. To bridge this gap, intensified efforts

Table 8.3 Challenges in community-led digital projects

Challenge	*Rural (%)*	*Urban (%)*	*Solution proposed*
Lack of Internet Access	42%	12%	Bharat Net expansion (2 lakh GPONs)
Low Digital Literacy	67%	28%	NGO-led training (e.g., Digital Saksharta)
Cybersecurity Risks	33%	58%	RBI's "Cyber Suraksha" awareness
Regulatory Uncertainty	25%	40%	DPDP Act 2023 compliance frameworks

Source World Bank Findex 2023, GSMA mobile money report

are needed to promote digital inclusion. This involves providing affordable access to digital devices, internet connectivity, and tailored training programs catering to diverse learning needs. Governments, technology companies, and civil society organizations must join forces to make digital literacy a shared priority, ensuring that everyone can benefit from the advancements of digital currencies. Another key challenge is establishing robust governance and regulatory frameworks that promote transparency, accountability, and trust in community-driven digital currency initiatives. Without clear rules and oversight, concerns about fraud, money laundering, and financial instability can arise, discouraging participation and undermining the integrity of the projects (Table 8.3).

8.12 Case Studies in Corporate Transformation

Case Studies in Corporate Transformation The potential of digital currencies to drive sustainable change extends beyond community initiatives. Multinational corporations, with their vast resources and global reach, have a significant role in transitioning to a greener future. Integrating digital currencies into their operations can unlock new avenues for transparency, efficiency, and positive impact. Let us explore real-world examples of corporations that have embraced digital currencies for sustainability, highlighting their strategies and achievements.

1. IBM's Blockchain for Sustainable Supply Chains IBM, a technology giant known for its commitment to innovation, is leading in leveraging Blockchain technology for sustainable supply chains. Blockchain's inherent transparency and immutability make it a powerful tool for tracking goods, materials, and emissions throughout the supply chain, empowering stakeholders to make informed decisions and reduce their environmental footprint. For instance, IBM's Food Trust platform utilizes Blockchain to trace food products from farm to table, ensuring food safety and provenance while promoting sustainable agricultural practices. This platform empowers consumers to make informed choices about the origins of their food, driving demand for sustainably produced goods and fostering responsible sourcing within the agricultural sector.

2. **Nestlé's Blockchain for Sustainable Cocoa Sourcing** Nestlé, a global food and beverage industry leader, has recognized the challenges of sustainable cocoa sourcing. Their commitment to ethical cocoa production and the elimination of child labour has led them to embrace Blockchain technology. Nestlé has partnered with other industry players and NGOs to develop the Cocoa Trace platform. This blockchain-based system tracks cocoa beans from their origin in West Africa to their final destination. This platform provides real-time data on cocoa farmers, enabling Nestlé to ensure fair compensation and responsible labour practices. By promoting transparency and traceability, Nestlé is empowering consumers to make informed choices about the origins of their chocolate while supporting sustainable cocoa production.

3. **Tesla's Integration of Bitcoin for Renewable Energy** Tesla, a pioneer in electric vehicles and clean energy solutions, has made headlines for embracing Bitcoin, a decentralized digital currency. Tesla's decision to accept Bitcoin payments for its vehicles and products was driven by recognizing the growing demand for cryptocurrencies and the potential for Bitcoin to contribute to the transition towards a more sustainable energy sector. By allowing customers to purchase its products using Bitcoin, Tesla is tapping into a new market of environmentally conscious consumers, contributing to the broader adoption of digital currencies. This move also promotes using clean energy in Bitcoin mining, further advancing Tesla's commitment to sustainability.

4. **Walmart's Blockchain for Sustainable Seafood** Walmart, the world's largest retailer, has faced challenges related to seafood sustainability. The complexity of seafood supply chains makes it difficult to ensure traceability and prevent illegal fishing practices. To address these challenges, Walmart has implemented a blockchain-based system for tracking seafood products from their source to the consumer's plate. This blockchain-powered system allows Walmart to verify the origin and

sustainability of its seafood offerings, safeguarding consumers from fraudulent practices and promoting responsible fishing practices. By leveraging Blockchain technology, Walmart demonstrates its commitment to ethical sourcing and sustainable seafood practices.

5. **Unilever's Digital Currency for Sustainable Palm Oil Sourcing** Unilever, a multinational consumer goods company, has faced criticism for sourcing palm oil, a commodity linked to deforestation and habitat loss. Unilever has addressed these concerns by integrating digital currencies into its palm oil supply chain. Unilever is working with Blockchain technology to develop systems that track palm oil from its origin in Southeast Asia to its final use in consumer products. This transparent and secure system allows Unilever to ensure responsible sourcing practices, support smallholder farmers, and minimize deforestation associated with palm oil production (Table 8.4).

Challenges and Opportunities in Corporate Sustainability While these case studies highlight the potential of digital currencies for corporate transformation, some challenges need to be addressed. Corporate leaders must carefully consider the regulatory landscape surrounding digital currencies, ensure data privacy, and develop strategies to seamlessly integrate these technologies into existing operations. Transparency and accountability are crucial, and corporations need to be prepared to demonstrate the positive impact of their digital currency initiatives. Despite these challenges, the opportunities for corporations to utilize digital currencies for sustainability are vast. Corporations can build more

Table 8.4 Corporate use of blockchain for sustainability

Company	*Initiative*	*Outcome*	*Carbon footprint reduction*
IBM	Food Trust Blockchain	28% fewer supply chain fraud cases	12% (2020–2024)
Nestlé	Cocoa Trace (Farm-to-Chocolate)	100% child-labour-free cocoa by 2025	8% (via ethical sourcing)
Walmart	Seafood Blockchain Tracking	0% traceability in Thai shrimp farms	5% (2023)

Source IBM Sustainability Report 2024, Nestlé Cocoa Trace Data resilient, transparent, and environmentally conscious operations by leveraging the power of Blockchain, smart contracts, and other emerging technologies. These initiatives can contribute to achieving sustainable development goals, empowering communities, and driving positive change across the globe.

8.13 Policy Frameworks for Digital Currencies

To address these challenges, policymakers are taking various approaches to regulating digital currencies, including:

Licensing and Registration: Many jurisdictions require digital currency exchanges and service providers to obtain licences or register with regulators, allowing for oversight and risk management.

Know Your Customer (KYC) and Anti-Money Laundering (AML) Requirements: Digital currency platforms are subject to KYC and AML regulations to prevent illicit activities and promote transparency.

Consumer Protection Measures: Regulations are being developed to protect consumers from fraudulent activities and to ensure fair and transparent digital currency transactions.

Taxation and Reporting: Governments are working to establish tax frameworks for digital currencies, including capital gains and income tax implications.

International Cooperation and Collaboration: The regulation of digital currencies is a global challenge that requires international cooperation and collaboration. Regulatory frameworks must be consistent and harmonized across borders to avoid regulatory arbitrage and ensure a level playing field for consumers and businesses.

Collaborative Platforms: Building Bridges the successful integration of digital currencies for sustainability hinges on collaboration between government, industry, and civil society. Establishing collaborative platforms that bring these stakeholders together is essential for:

Developing Shared Understanding: Collaborative platforms foster dialogue and understanding of the complexities of digital currencies, promoting a shared vision for their responsible use.

Co-creating Solutions: Through collective effort, stakeholders can co-create innovative solutions and policy frameworks that address the challenges of integrating digital currencies into the green economy.

Promoting Transparency and Accountability: Collaborative platforms enhance transparency and accountability in developing and implementing digital currency initiatives.

Case Studies: Global Insights: Several countries have made significant progress in establishing policy frameworks for digital currencies:

China: China has pioneered CBDC development, with its digital yuan (e-CNY) already undergoing pilot programs in various cities. The e-CNY aims to promote financial inclusion and efficiency.

Singapore: Singapore has established a regulatory sandbox for fintech companies, including those developing digital currency solutions, to experiment and innovate.

United States: The U.S. government is actively considering the implications of CBDCs and is engaging in policy discussions and research.

European Union: The EU has established regulations for digital currencies, including the Markets in Crypto-Assets (MiCA) regulation, aimed at harmonizing the regulatory landscape across member states.

The Role of Nongovernmental Organizations (NGOs): NGOs play a crucial role in the regulatory landscape by advocating for responsible and sustainable use of digital currencies. They work to:

Educate the Public: NGOs raise awareness about digital currencies and their potential for good, empowering communities to participate in the conversation.

Develop Best Practices: NGOs contribute to developing best practices and ethical guidelines for using digital currencies, particularly in the context of sustainability.

Monitor Regulatory Developments: NGOs monitor regulatory developments and provide feedback to policymakers, ensuring that regulations are aligned with ethical and sustainable principles.

8.14 The Future of Digital Currency Regulation

The regulatory landscape for digital currencies is in a state of constant evolution. The future holds significant opportunities and challenges: **International Harmonization:** As digital currencies become more integrated into the global financial system, the need for international harmonization of regulatory frameworks will become increasingly critical.

Emerging Technologies: The emergence of new technologies, such as artificial intelligence (AI) and Blockchain, will continue to shape the digital currency landscape, requiring adaptation and innovation in regulatory approaches.

Sustainability Focus: As the global community focuses on achieving Sustainable Development Goals (SDGs), policymakers will increasingly need to consider the role of digital currencies in advancing sustainable development.

References

Ardito, L., D'Adda, D., & Petruzzelli, A. M. (2018). Mapping innovation dynamics in the internet of things domain: Evidence from patent analysis. *Technological Forecasting and Social Change, 136*, 317–330.

Appio, F. P., Frattini, F., Petruzzelli, A. M., & Neirotti, P. (2021). Digital transformation and innovation management: A synthesis of existing research and an agenda for future studies. *Journal of Product Innovation Management, 38*(1), 4–20.

Balogun, A. L., Marks, D., Sharma, R., Shekhar, H., Balmes, C., Maheng, D., & Salehi, P. (2020). Assessing the potential of digitalization as a tool for climate change adaptation and sustainable development in urban centres. *Sustainable Cities and Society, 53*, Article 101888.

Ceipek, R., Hautz, J., Petruzzelli, A. M., De Massis, A., & Matzler, K. (2021). A motivation and ability perspective on engagement in emerging digital technologies: The case of Internet of Things solutions. *Long Range Planning, 54*(5), Article 101991.

Coenen, F. (2009). Local Agenda 21:'Meaningful and effective participation. *Public Participation and Better Environmental Decisions, 165*, 165–182.

Eisenhauer, B. W., & Nicholson, B. (2005). Using stakeholders' views: A social science methodology for the inclusive design of environmental communications. *Applied Environmental Education & Communication, 4*(1), 19–30.

Walker, G. B. (2007). Public participation as participatory communication in environmental policy decision-making: From concepts to structured conversations. *Environmental Communication, 1*(1), 99–110. https://doi.org/10.1080/17524030701334342

Zikargae, M. H., & Ali, A. C. (2017). A critical analysis of Amhara development association's development activities with a framework of participatory development communication model. *The Internet Journal Language, Culture and Society, 43*, 57–65.

Zikargae, M. H. (2018). Analysis of environmental communication and its implication for sustainable development in Ethiopia. *Science of the Total Environment, 634*, 1593–1600.

Zikargae, M. H. (2021). Assessment of applying global instruments in nongovernmental organizations for developing countries' environmental security and sustainable development. *Education Research International, 2021*(1), 9135290.

Zikargae, M. H., Woldearegay, A. G., & Skjerdal, T. (2022). Assessing the roles of stakeholders in community projects on environmental security and livelihood of impoverished rural society: A nongovernmental organization implementation strategy in focus. *Heliyon, 8*(10), Article e10987. https://doi.org/10.1016/j.heliyon.2022.e10987

PIB Delhi. (2023, August 28). The Pradhan Mantri Jan Dhan Yojana (PMJDY)—The national mission for financial inclusion. Press information bureau, government of India. https://www.pib.gov.in/PressReleasePage.aspx?PRID=1952793

PIB Delhi. (2024a, December 1). UPI: Revolutionizing digital payment in India. Press Information Bureau, Government of India. https://pib.gov.in/PressReleasePage.aspx?PRID=2079544

PIB Delhi. (2024b, December 21). BharatNet: Bridging the digital divide from remote villages to smart communities. Press Information Bureau, Government of India. https://pib.gov.in/PressReleaseIframePage.aspx?PRID=2086701

http://www.pmjdy.gov.in

http://www.pib.gov.in

http://www.rbidocs.rbi.org.in

http://www.unep.org

http://www.ibm.com

http://www.nestle.com

http://www.worldbank.org

http://www.bis.org

http://www.imf.org

http://www.npci.org.in

CHAPTER 9

Reducing and Offsetting Carbon Emissions: Pathways to a Sustainable Future

Suman Dahiya, Sushila Kumari Soriya, and Bhushan Singh

9.1 Introduction

Since the beginning of the industrial revolution, greenhouse gas emissions (GHG) have increased drastically. It has grown by 51% from the year 1990 to 2021 (Mengpin Ge, 2024). Interestingly, a few countries contribute to most emissions, including China, the United States, and the European Union (Center for Climate and Energy Solutions). In 2023, fossil CO_2 accounted for 73.7% of the total global GHG, followed by CH_4 (18.9%), N_2O (4.7%), and F gases (2.7%). Fossil CO_2 emissions have risen by 72.1% from the year 1990 (Crippa et al., 2024). Increasing

S. Dahiya (✉) · S. K. Soriya · B. Singh
Department of Commerce, Central University of Haryana, Mahendergarh, Haryana, India
e-mail: suman@cuh.ac.in

S. K. Soriya
e-mail: sushilasoriya@cuh.ac.in

B. Singh
e-mail: bhushan@cuh.ac.in

R. Aneja and R. Dygas (eds.), *Digital Currencies and the Green Economy*, https://doi.org/10.1007/978-981-95-2282-8_9

the concentration of CO_2 in the atmosphere will cause more heat absorption due to the greenhouse effect and subsequent rise in the global temperature. Therefore, taking steps towards mitigation and offsetting carbon emissions is inevitable.

Carbon reduction and offsetting are essential to achieving a carbon-free, inclusive, and sustainable future. These measures are aligned with the Sustainable Development Goals (SDGs) and address various issues relating to climate change and sustainability. Carbon reduction and offsetting strategies directly support SDG13 by contributing towards greenhouse gas reduction. Similarly, the transition from non-renewable energy to renewable energy also supports SDG7, which focuses on the promotion of affordable and clean energy.

Figure 9.1 presents the greenhouse gas emissions per capita by the leading countries. The figure shows that the United States has the highest number, followed by Russia and Japan.

As per Fig. 9.2, the cumulative emissions during the time period 1751 to 2017, the United States has the highest emissions, followed by the EU-28 and China.

Digital currencies can also play a vital role in the reduction and offsetting of carbon by making use of blockchain technology to enhance transparency, efficiency, and traceability. Using a token system, organisations and governments can democratise access to carbon markets so

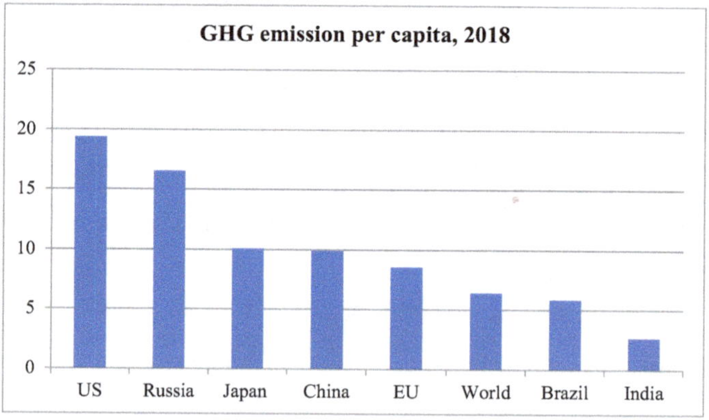

Fig. 9.1 Greenhouse gas emissions per capita, 2018. (*Source* World Development Indicators (WDI))

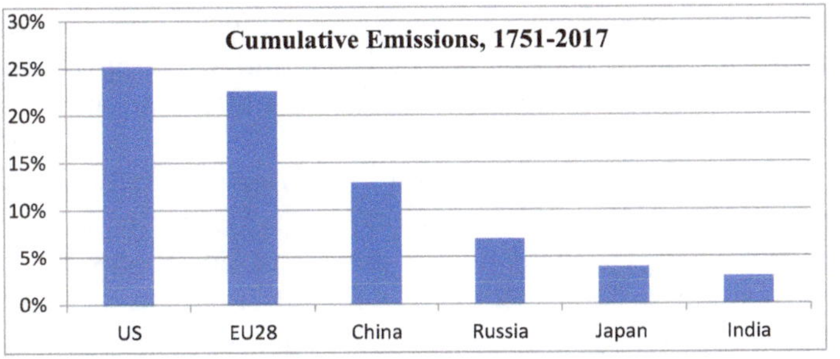

Fig. 9.2 Cumulative emissions, 1751–2017. (*Source* Our World in Data [2019])

that more people or small organisations can participate in carbon trading. However, it involves various challenges also such as the use of high energy by certain cryptocurrencies, a lack of regulatory measures, and a proper verification mechanism. Digital currencies are still in an evolutionary stage, so proper planning and a regulated framework are required to make their effective use in carbon reduction and offsetting.

9.2 Carbon Reduction Strategies

Reducing carbon emissions requires us to reshape everything at the individual, corporate, societal, and government levels. For example, we need to change what we consume, how we live, how we travel, how we grow crops, how we manufacture products in factories, and, of course, how we strengthen our economy (European Environment Agency, 2024). Nevertheless, several actions are being taken at the local and global levels to reduce carbon emissions.

Energy Efficiency: It is the most cost-saving method of carbon mitigation, as the same job is done with less energy. It is called the "first fuel" in the clean energy transition. It cuts energy bills and enhances energy security. In the year 2023, app. 200 countries at the COP28 summit agreed to work collectively to double the global average annual rate of energy efficiency by 2030 (IEA, 2024). So, energy efficiency has become a key concern for governments across nations. Besides mitigating environmental degradation, it positively impacts economic growth (Ogwu et al., 2025). It also decreases the country's dependence on energy imports and exposure to volatility in energy prices. Green finance can contribute significantly to improving energy efficiency and reducing carbon emissions through upgrading industrial structure and the adoption of green technology innovation (Wang & Xu, 2025).

Although considering the energy performance standard, energy-efficient appliances (air conditioners, coolers, refrigerators, etc.) are available in the market, the demand for inefficient appliances still coexists, which puts strain on the electricity demand. Framing of government policy targeting energy efficiency is the only solution to achieving a sustained energy intensity advantage. Rigorous policy implementation can help to accomplish climate goals across the globe while improving the lives of the people. India has also demonstrated improved energy efficiency in 2024 through its robust policies for electric vehicles and industry. Other countries are also placing policies to encourage efficient cooling, seeing drastic climatic changes causing scorching heat waves (International Energy Agency, 2024). Digital currency can also support energy efficiency by rewarding digital tokens to those who reduce energy consumption. Later, they can trade these tokens or use them to avail a discount.

Transition to Renewable Energy Sources: Shifting to sustainable energy sources is essential to reducing carbon emissions and combating climate change. Fossil fuels, including oil, coal, and natural gas, are finite energy sources responsible for the most greenhouse gas emissions. However, using sustainable energy sources like wind, solar, and hydroelectricity does not produce carbon emissions. These sources are cheaper and available in abundance. Because of increasing carbon prices, the integration of wind and solar energy into the microgrid system can reduce CO_2 and energy expenses significantly (Chung, 2024). In the year 2015, the United Nations members adopted the 2030 agenda for 17 Sustainable Development Goals (SDGs), which include SDG7, which focuses on affordable and clean energy for all (United Nations). Access to sustainable and modern energy improves the socio-economic conditions and protects from climate change.

Waste Reduction: A system of zero waste is critical to global carbon pollution as it is the easiest, most cost-effective and short-term solution to climate change. Following zero-waste strategies can reduce greenhouse gas emissions by more than 400 million metric tons of carbon per year (Eco-cycle). When organic matter is landfilled then it produces methane gas, which is a strong greenhouse gas. On the other hand, for every car, approximately 100 to 200 kg of automotive shredder residue (ASR) is disposed of in landfills, which poses a great danger to the environment (Maroufi et al., 2018). Apart from this, energy-intensive processes are involved in waste management and in the production of new products that generate enormous carbon. Therefore, bringing sustainable practices in production, consumption, and disposal can reduce carbon emissions and climate impacts. Green manufacturing can contribute towards the zero-waste circular economy. Also, Nutrient-rich soil can be created through composting, which will further help in pulling carbon from the environment. On the pattern of carbon credit, waste credits can also be created and traded. The companies that are reducing their waste can be awarded these credits.

Recycling: Waste should be segregated at the source to promote recycling at different levels. It reduces the need for further extraction of raw materials and processes that otherwise produce carbon. Recycling metals like steel, copper, and aluminium saves energy and emits less carbon, compared to basic manufacturing, which involves carbon-intensive mining and refining processes. Recycling the material will reduce the waste burden in landfills and stretch the lifespan of a material. It will reduce carbon emissions by 5.5 to 6.02 gigatons between 2020 and 2025, equal to removing one billion cars off the road for one year (Robinson & Huun, 2023). To develop and implement recycling technology, collaboration among society, government, academic, and research institutions is required to extend financial incentives, subsidies, and grants (William Li Wei Tao, 2024). Additionally, digital tokens can be given to companies that are consistent with recycling materials that can be further traded or used for a discount. For tracking the life cycle of recyclable material, blockchain technology can be used to ensure transparency.

Sustainable Transportation: Adopting environment-friendly transportation that does not produce air pollution is vital for sustainable development. In contrast to conventional vehicles, sustainable transportation like E-Vehicles, public transport, cycling, etc. decreases carbon emissions substantially. Digital currency can support sustainable transportation through the carbon credit system and the integration of a blockchain-based payment system in transportation. Sustainable transport improves accessibility and enhances economic growth. Sustainable transportation investments can advance rural-urban linkage, social equity, health, and productivity. Through various programmes such as the Vienna Programme of Action for the LLDCs, the Sendai Framework for Disaster

Risk Reduction, the Istanbul Programme of Action for the LDCs, etc., its importance is recognised at the international level (United Nations). Many countries are rigorously working for sustainable transportation, investing in green transportation infrastructure, and framing strict policies for compliance. For instance, the Ministry of Heavy Industries in India has notified various schemes in the year 2024 to promote infrastructure development and e-vehicle adoption in the country. The purpose of the PM e-Bus Sewa-Payment Security Mechanism (PSM) Scheme is to deploy more than 38,000 e-buses in the country (PIB, 2024).

Sustainable Agriculture and Fishing: Sustainable practices in agriculture and fishing reduce the carbon footprint and minimise the climate change risk. Carbon sequestration is the process of capturing and storing atmospheric CO_2 so that it does not re-emit instantly (Ayangbenro & Babalola, 2021). Soil carbon improves the health and structure of the soil and also enhances its water-holding capacity. Techniques like cover cropping, agroforestry, crop rotation, organic farming, and minimal use of chemical fertilisers can minimise the carbon footprint and manage the soil health. Similarly, overfishing may also cause emissions due to covering long distances in search of seafood items. Proper processing, storage, and distribution can minimise waste and improve the life span of seafood items. Using renewable-powered boats can also contribute towards carbon reduction.

9.3 Carbon Offsetting Strategies

Carbon offsetting is a balancing process in which the amount of carbon emissions produced is offset by investing in activities that either absorb existing emissions or prevent new ones. The Kyoto Protocol, one of the earliest international policy frameworks, addresses the issue of climate change and the environmental impact of greenhouse gas emissions and sets binding GHG emissions targets for 37 industrialised countries and economies in transition. This protocol introduced the concept of carbon offsetting by the initiation of the Clean Development Mechanism. It is the main international offset programme that exists today, which allows offsetting through investments in GHG avoidance, reduction, and sequestration projects in developing countries (Aggarwal, 2024; Gillenwater & Seres, 2011). It helps to achieve the goal of carbon neutrality and sustainability.

Reforestation and Afforestation: Reforestation and Afforestation are carbon-offsetting strategies that rely on compensating for the produced emissions either by restoring the previously destroyed forests or creating a new forest. Since 1990, afforestation has been widely used across the globe to increase the area of forest on the Earth. Digital currency can promote investment in tree planting projects by rewarding the companies with carbon credits or digital tokens for trees planted or a measurable amount of carbon absorbed.

Renewable Energy Project: One of the most effective methods of offsetting carbon is to build power plants based on renewable energy, such as wind power, hydropower, solar power, etc. Thereby, reducing the dependence on fossil-based energy, a primary source of emissions (Dan, 2024). The use of digital currency can increase the number of renewable energy projects through digital tokens and blockchain technology. It allows peer-to-peer energy trading, wherein users with excessive solar energy can sell it directly to others who are in need.

Carbon Sequestration: It means capturing and storing CO_2 from the atmosphere, which can happen naturally or by using man-made methods; biological and non-biological sequestration. Biological sequestration is cost-effective, easily applicable and uses natural processes to capture and store atmospheric CO_2. Most of the carbon released by human activities is absorbed by the terrestrial and aquatic systems (Nayak et al., 2022). For instance, photosynthesis transfers CO_2 to tree biomass, including branches, roots, and trunk. Whereas, non-biological sequestration methods are costly, less effective and require a considerable amount of mineral resources. These methods include chemical and physical reactions for capturing and storing carbon, and are based on engineering techniques such as Oceanic injection, Geological injection, Scrubbing, and Mineral carbonation (Lal, 2008).

Carbon offsetting strategies are crucial to mitigating the impact of climate change, but they are more effective when combined with carbon reduction measures. Hence, the government should make efforts in both directions, carbon reduction and offsetting, to achieve long-term environmental stability by controlling global warming. The awareness towards environmental issues and how carbon offsetting and removal mitigate their effects can promote climate protection. Jacobsen (2011) in the United States found that to improve concern about the environment and to promote voluntary carbon offsetting, some movies related to the outcomes and possibilities of the CO_2 emissions and offsetting were screened. Cheng (2020) opined that the net-zero carbon emissions target in both planetary and marine ecosystems must be raised. Carbon neutrality or net-zero carbon emissions can be realised via carbon offset and removal initiatives. But a study by (Chen et al., 2022) assessed that only a small portion, i.e. 4.5% of countries have achieved carbon neutrality so far, and the rest of the countries are still planning to do so. Many researchers (Hepburn et al., 2021; Huang & Zhai, 2021) are finding ways of neutrality in different regions, countries, and cities.

9.4 Role of Individual and Corporate in Carbon Reduction and Offsetting

Considering the drastic climate changes, it's our moral responsibility to change our lifestyle. Individuals can be important carbon footprint mitigators by changing their habits and being part of carbon offset programmes. Intergovernmental Panel on Climate Change (Harrabin, 2020) states that human influence has unequivocally contributed to increasing atmospheric CO_2 concentrations, and taking personal action is necessary in the fight against climate change. Individuals can play the most significant role by minimising energy demand at home, better insulating their houses, employing energy-saving devices, and using renewable energy (Harrabin, 2020; Seymour & Langer, 2021). If an individual is not using public transportation, walking, cycling, or driving an electric car, then it should be considered to reduce the carbon footprint (Chen et al., 2023; Tepecik, 2024). Another substantial factor is dietary choice; adopting a plant-based diet and reducing food waste can achieve major carbon footprint savings (Venter de Villiers et al., 2024). Alternatively, for emissions that cannot be avoided, people may invest in certified carbon offset initiatives, such as those for afforestation, reforestation, and renewable energy (Venter de Villiers et al., 2024). Through these measures, individuals can progress towards carbon neutrality while remaining a part of the broader strategy for global climate mitigation.

Everyone, especially corporations, has now begun to incorporate carbon offset initiatives in their efforts to reduce their carbon footprints. A global frontrunner in consulting and digital services, Infosys achieved carbon neutrality in 2020, three decades ahead of the Paris Agreement's 2050 time frame. It has achieved this after more than a decade of work in which it focused on energy efficiency, moving towards renewable energy, and implementing strong carbon offset programmes. As part of its strategy, Infosys is investing in initiatives at the community level that can achieve not only emissions reduction but also sustainable development (Infosys). Similarly, Google has contracted with Indian provider Varaha to buy carbon credits from a project that renders agricultural waste into biochar, which locks up carbon dioxide and enhances soil quality. Through this effort, Google plans to procure 100,000 tonnes of carbon credits by 2030, its first significant involvement in India's carbon dioxide removal sector (Kollmuss et al., 2008). On the global front, Microsoft is covering its carbon outlays through more than 50 projects in 30 countries, from forest conservation to renewable energy, as part of a portfolio aimed at offsetting its carbon footprint. This is part of its stated goal of being carbon-negative by 2030 (Microsoft, 2024). Moreover, TotalEnergies invested $100 million to purchase carbon credits to protect forests in ten states in the United States from deforestation (Jennifer, 2024). Etsy is the first major e-commerce company in the world to provide carbon-neutral shipping emissions by offsetting the emissions from all its shipping. The offset approach includes investments in renewable energy projects and reforestation efforts (Andrew Woods, 2019). Many industries with emission-intensive history have taken measures to significantly decrease their emissions. For instance, plants in the iron and steel sector, which account for significant industrial GHG emissions, have utilised energy savings technologies including heat recovery in coke ovens, sinter plants, and electric arc furnaces. As a result, energy consumption decreased by 18% and greenhouse gas emissions by 12%. Likewise, biofuels are already being used in Finland and Sweden's forestry for energy generation, and these countries are urged to decarbonise by introducing electrification for transportation (Chen et al., 2023).

New technology developments are also speeding up efforts to offset CO_2. The rising CO_2 emissions from industrial processes are among the major challenges facing today, and therefore Carbon Capture, Utilisation and Storage (CCUS) is poised to emerge as an indispensable solution to capture and store such emissions. Certain industries like glass manufacturing contribute millions of tonnes of CO_2 emissions every year and have also started implementing decarbonisation techniques, including carbon capture, batch preheating, and electric furnaces. Governments, financiers, and businesses are taking clean energy investments more seriously, integrating wind and solar energy into their energy mix. Adaptation of transportation to being fully electric and industrial efficiency improvements stand out as necessary steps towards a low-carbon economy (Chen et al., 2023).

9.5 Conclusion

Reaching a sustainable future relies deeply on effective carbon reduction and responsible carbon offsetting. Reducing carbon through energy efficiency, adoption of renewable energy, waste reduction, recycling, and sustainable transportation and agriculture is imperative to mitigate climate change. While offsetting is also essential and plays a complementary role through reforestation, afforestation, and carbon sequestration. Evolving technologies, such as digital currency and blockchain, enable individuals and corporations to access the credit market and trade carbon credits, and improve the transparency in the entire process.

Furthermore, CO_2 reduction and offsetting are no silver bullet—it calls for individuals to embrace sustainable lifestyles, businesses to cut carbon emissions as a part of their long-term strategy, and technological progress to open the door to enhanced mitigation. With the help of regulatory frameworks, voluntary market mechanisms, and cutting-edge innovations, societies can dramatically cut their carbon footprint and contribute to the achievement of global climate goals. This is something that requires the combined will of people, companies, governments, and technology to create a carbon-neutral world.

References

Aggarwal, R. (2024). Carbon offsets compatible with the Paris agreement to limit global warming: Call for a direct action. *Environmental Challenges, 17*(July), Article 101034. https://doi.org/10.1016/j.envc.2024.101034

Andrew Woods. (2019). *Etsy to offset 100% of its carbon emissions from shipping*. Energy Digital. https://energydigital.com/sustainability/etsy-offset-100-its-carbon-emissions-shipping

Ayangbenro, A. S., & Babalola, O. O. (2021). Reclamation of arid and semi-arid soils: The role of plant growth-promoting archaea and bacteria. *Current Plant Biology, 25*, Article 100173. https://doi.org/10.1016/j.cpb.2020.100173

Center for Climate and Energy Solutions. (n.d.). *Global Emissions*. https://www.c2es.org/content/international-emissions/

Chen, L., Chen, Z., Zhang, Y., Liu, Y., Osman, A. I., Farghali, M., Hua, J., Al-Fatesh, A., Ihara, I., Rooney, D. W., & Yap, P. S. (2023). Artificial intelligence-based solutions for climate change: A review. *Environmental Chemistry Letters, 21*, 2525–2557. https://doi.org/10.1007/s10311-023-01617-y

Chen, L., Msigwa, G., Yang, M., Osman, A. I., Fawzy, S., Rooney, D. W., & Yap, P. S. (2022). Strategies to achieve a carbon neutral society: A review. *Environmental Chemistry Letters, 20*(4), 2277–2310. Springer International Publishing. https://doi.org/10.1007/s10311-022-01435-8

Cheng, H. (2020). Future earth and sustainable developments. *Innovation, 1*(3), Article 100055. https://doi.org/10.1016/j.xinn.2020.100055

Chung, I. H. (2024). Using break-even analysis to explore the cost and carbon reduction benefits of solar and wind energy integration in microgrids for convenience stores. *Heliyon, 10*(21), Article e39644. https://doi.org/10.1016/j.heliyon.2024.e39644

Crippa, M., Guizzardi, D., Pagani, F., Banja, M., Muntean, M., Schaaf, E., Monforti-Ferrario, F., Becker, W.E., Quadrelli, R., Risquez Martin, A., Taghavi-Moharamli, P., Köykkä, J., Grassi, G., Rossi, S., Melo, J., Oom, D., Branco, A., San-Miguel, J., & Man, F. (2024). GHG emissions of all world countries. *Publications Office of the European Union*. https://doi.org/10.2760/0115360

Dan, B. (2024). Carbon offsetting. *Ethics, Policy and Environment, 27*(3), 281–298. https://doi.org/10.1080/21550085.2023.2223805

Eco-cycle. (n.d.). *Zero waste is a climate change solution*. Retrieved January 28, 2025, from https://ecocycle.org/learn-about-zero-waste/zw-is-a-climate-change-solution/#:~:text=Reducing methane emissions from landfills represents a huge opportunity to,focus in the next decade.

European Environment Agency. (2024). *Climate change mitigation: Reducing emissions*.

Gillenwater, M., & Seres, S. (2011). The clean development mechanism: A review of the first international offset programme. *Greenhouse Gas Measurement and Management, 1*(3–4), 179–203. https://doi.org/10.1080/20430779.2011.647014

Harrabin, R. (2020). Climate change: Top 10 tips to reduce carbon footprint revealed. *BBC*. https://www.bbc.com/news/science-environment-52719662

Hepburn, C., Qi, Y., Stern, N., Ward, B., Xie, C., & Zenghelis, D. (2021). Towards carbon neutrality and China's 14th five-year plan: Clean energy transition, sustainable urban development, and investment priorities. *Environmental Science and Ecotechnology, 8*. https://doi.org/10.1016/j.ese.2021.100130

Huang, M. T., & Zhai, P. M. (2021). Achieving Paris agreement temperature goals requires carbon neutrality by middle century with far-reaching transitions in the whole society. *Advances in Climate Change Research, 12*(2), 281–286. https://doi.org/10.1016/j.accre.2021.03.004

IEA. (2024). Energy efficiency. https://www.iea.org/energy-system/energy-efficiency-and-demand/energy-efficiency

Infosys. (n.d.). *ESG Report 2020–21, Climate change : In the forefront of ecological transformation.*

International Energy Agency. (2024). *Energy Efficiency*. 1–134.

Jacobsen, G. D. (2011). The Al gore effect: An inconvenient truth and voluntary carbon offsets. *Journal of Environmental Economics and Management, 61*, 67–78. https://doi.org/10.1016/j.jeem.2010.08.002

Jennifer L. (2024). *TotalEnergies invests $100 million in U.S. Forestry as part of net zero push.* Carbon Credits.Com. https://carboncredits.com/totalenergies-invests-100-million-in-sustainable-u-s-forestry-to-boost-carbon-sinks-and-net-zero/

Kollmuss, Zink, & Polycarp. (2008). Making sense of the voluntary carbon market. In *WWF Germany Title*. http://www.wwf.de/fileadmin/fm-wwf/pdf_neu/A_Comparison_of_Carbon_Offset_Standards_lang.pdf

Lal, R. (2008). Carbon sequestration. *Philosophical Transactions of the Royal Society B: Biological Sciences, 363*(1492), 815–830. https://doi.org/10.1098/rstb.2007.2185

Maroufi, S., Echeverria, C. A., Pahlevani, F., & Sahajwalla, V. (2018). Green manufacturing: From waste to value added materials. *Unmaking Waste in Production and Consumption: Towards The Circular Economy*, 261–279. https://doi.org/10.1108/978-1-78714-619-820181021

Mengpin Ge, J. F., & L. V. (2024). *Where do emissions come from? 4 charts explain greenhouse gas emissions by sector*. https://www.wri.org/insights/4-charts-explain-greenhouse-gas-emissions-countries-and-sectors#:~:text=Carbon dioxide (CO2) comprises 74,Source: Climate Watch.

Microsoft. (2024). *Environmental sustainability repor, how can we advance sustainability ?*

Nayak, N., Mehrotra, R., & Mehrotra, S. (2022). Carbon biosequestration strategies: A review. *Carbon Capture Science and Technology, 4*(July), Article 100065. https://doi.org/10.1016/j.ccst.2022.100065

Ogwu, S. O., Okolo, C. V., & Agan, B. (2025). The role of debt burden, green financing, and energy efficiency in reducing carbon footprints in MINT & BRICS economies: New evidence from panel QARDL method. *Sustainable Futures, 9*(October 2024). https://doi.org/10.1016/j.sftr.2024.100417

PIB. (2024). *New electric vehicle policy*. https://pib.gov.in/PressReleaseIframePage.aspx?PRID=2082743

Robinson, C., & Huun, K. (2023). *The impact of recycling on climate change*. www.colorado.edu/ecenter/2023/12/15/impact-recycling-climate-change#:~:text=The benefits of recycling&text=Project Drawdown estimates that recycling,the streets for one year.

Seymour, F., & Langer, P. (2021). Consideration of nature-based solutions as offsets in corporate climate change mitigation strategies. *World Resources Institute, February*, 1–27. https://doi.org/10.46830/wriwp.20.00043

Tepecik, A. (2024). The role of transportation in environmental sustainability and climate change mitigation. In *Interdisciplinary Approaches to Transportation and Urban Planning* (pp. 1–22). https://doi.org/10.4018/979-8-3693-6695-0.ch001

United Nations. (n.d.-a). *Energy*. Retrieved January 27, 2025, from https://sdgs.un.org/topics/energy

United Nations. (n.d.-b). *Sustainble transport*. Retrieved January 29, 2025, from https://sdgs.un.org/topics/sustainable-transport

Venter de Villiers, M., Cheng, J., & Truter, L. (2024). The shift towards plant-based lifestyles: Factors driving young consumers' decisions to choose plant-based food products. *Sustainability (Switzerland), 16*(20), 1–15. https://doi.org/10.3390/su16209022

Wang, P., & Xu, X. (2025). Green finance and energy efficiency improvement: The role of green innovation and industrial upgrading. *Innovation and Green Development, 4*(1), Article 100200. https://doi.org/10.1016/j.igd.2024.100200

William Li Wei Tao. (2024). Carbon capture and recycling technology of carbon resources under the target of carbon neutrality. *International Journal of Low-Carbon Technologies, 19*, 2693–2701. https://doi.org/10.1093/ijlct/ctae229

CHAPTER 10

Environmental Impact of Digital Currency Mining

Sunil Kumar and Rajender S. Godara

10.1 Introduction

In recent times, a significant number of digital currencies, commonly termed as cryptocurrencies, have gained substantial power as a medium of exchange, functioning similarly to traditional money. However, unlike conventional currencies, working of cryptocurrencies is independent of national territory, central banks, governments, or fiat currency (Maese et al., 2016).

The process of creating digital currency is known as mining. At its core, mining involves calculating the value of digital currency assets using cryptographic methods. These methods typically generate the desired digital currency in units called blocks, which are essentially basic ledger files containing records of recent transactions. Mining is a crucial part of

S. Kumar (✉) · R. S. Godara
Department of Economics, Mittal School of Business, Lovely Professional University, Phagwara, India
e-mail: kaindalsunil54@gmail.com

R. S. Godara
e-mail: godaras@gmail.com

R. Aneja and R. Dygas (eds.), *Digital Currencies and the Green Economy*, https://doi.org/10.1007/978-981-95-2282-8_10

any digital currency system and is often seen as costly and time-intensive (Malone & O'Dwyer, 2014).

In the Bitcoin network, transactions are organized into blocks, which are then connected to previously recorded blocks, forming a continuous chain known as the blockchain. The information within these blocks, along with the complete history of all transactions, is stored on users' devices, referred to as nodes. These nodes play a crucial role in maintaining the network by verifying new transactions against existing data to ensure their accuracy and legitimacy. Once a transaction is successfully validated, the nodes are rewarded for their efforts. This entire process is what is commonly known as mining (Yli-Huumo et al., 2016).

Mining is the process of verifying transactions on the blockchain. When a Bitcoin payment is made, it triggers an energy-intensive process to prevent fraud and double-spending. This involves a Proof-of-Work (PoW) mechanism where computers race to solve complex mathematical problems to verify transactions (Vervoort et al., 2021). The Proof-of-Work (PoW) system intentionally rewards miners with Bitcoins for each block they successfully verify. As more miners participate, the mathematical problems increase in complexity (Nakamoto, 2008), and the sense of competition intensifies as shareholders actively compete to secure the minimum reward available for the day, driving a race to maximize their gains (Goodkind et al., 2020a, 2020b).

Today, mining operations heavily rely on application-specific integrated circuits (ASICs) to achieve optimal efficiency and speed. These specialized microchips are designed solely for mining at incredible rates, maximizing profitability. However, operating this hardware consumes substantial energy, particularly given the vast industrial scale it has reached. The energy production required for these operations, depending on whether it is derived from sustainable sources, that can have both direct and indirect effects on the environment and human health, including contributing to air pollution and exacerbating related health issues (Stoll et al., 2019a, 2019b).

First cryptocurrency, Bitcoin, was created by Satoshi Nakamoto during the 2008 Sub-Prime Crisis, a period marked by widespread distrust in banks and the financial system. Bitcoin represented a groundbreaking digital currency that operates independently of any central authority, such as banks or governments, and allows for secure, unchangeable transactions. Today, with more than 20,000 different cryptocurrencies in circulation, there is a growing body of research focused on examining the environmental effects of cryptocurrency mining, including the significant amount of energy ingesting connected with the hardware used for this process, (Goodkind et al., 2020a, 2020b).

From the past ten years, the market capitalization of cryptocurrencies has experienced a remarkable transformation, growing at an unprecedented pace. This rapid evolution has raised concerns for the federal government, prompting efforts to develop a central bank digital currency (CBDC). The primary goal of this initiative is to mitigate the potential risks and disruptions caused by the emergence of a parallel financial system, ensuring greater stability and control within the economic framework (Fig. 10.1).

Mining is widely recognized as a highly energy-intensive process. With digital currencies and cryptocurrencies gaining significant attention in the global economy, the challenge lies in integrating this parallel financial system with traditional financial structures. Beyond the economic implications, a critical concern is the environmental impact of digital currency mining, which is heavily reliant on substantial energy consumption.

Several factors influence the sustainability of cryptocurrency mining include energy costs, the sources of energy production, local climate

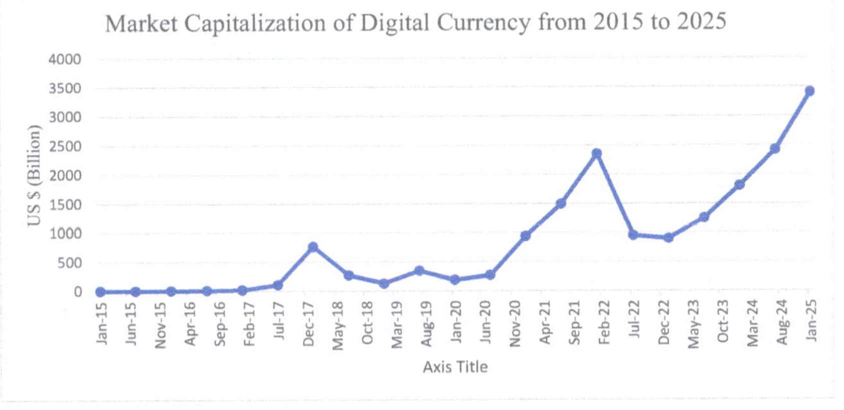

Fig. 10.1 Trends of market capitalization of digital currency. *Source* Crypto market cap 2010–2025 | Statista

conditions, regulatory frameworks, capital investment, and the involvement of research and development stakeholders. These elements collectively determine whether cryptocurrency mining can be pursued in an environmentally sustainable manner. According to (Alonso et al., 2021) adopting sustainable mining practices can significantly reduce the negative environmental impacts.

The environmental effects of mining particularly impact three key sustainable goals ensuring clean and affordable energy, promoting responsible consumption and production, and advancing climate action. Addressing these challenges is essential to mitigate the ecological consequences of mining while aligning with global sustainability efforts.

The environmental impacts of mining activities related to digital currencies, focusing on the broader implications for the global community. It will delve into the possible environmental significances of mining, such as excessive energy ingesting, greenhouse gas emissions, and electronic waste. A particular emphasis will be placed on how these activities disproportionately affect least-developed and developing nations, where access to affordable energy and robust regulatory frameworks is often limited, exacerbating environmental degradation and energy inequality.

Examine pathways to promote sustainable mining practices, emphasizing the increased reliance on renewable energy sources such as solar, wind, and hydroelectric power is essential for reducing the environmental impact of mining. By aligning with the United Nations Sustainable Development Goals—particularly those focused on clean energy, responsible consumption, and climate action—this discussion will emphasize effective strategies to mitigate the negative consequences of mining while promoting sustainability and environmental responsibility. This will also include adopting energy-efficient technologies, improving recycling systems for mining hardware, and implementing policies that incentivize greener operations. The goal is to provide a roadmap for neutralizing the adverse effects of digital currency mining while fostering sustainable economic growth and technological innovation.

10.2 Digital Currency Mining

Mining is the process that makes digital currency transactions possible by ensuring their execution, validity, and agreement within the system. It is a complex process because it combines elements from various fields. To fully grasp how mining works, one needs to understand concepts from computer science, economics and cryptography (Berentsen & Schar, 2018).

There are two types of mechanisms worldwide which is used in block for creating the digital currency.

(i) Proof of Work (PoW)

The Proof-of-Work (PoW) system is the most widely used and recognized method for mining. In a Proof-of-Work (PoW) system, network participants compete to solve complex cryptographic puzzles to secure the right to add new blocks to the blockchain. This process, known as mining, ensures the integrity and security of transactions within the network. As the network grows, the input data for these puzzles increases, making the calculations progressively more difficult (Houben & Snyers, 2018).

The PoW mechanism relies on significant computing power, which in turn consumes large amounts of electricity. When a network participant (also known as a node) successfully solves the cryptographic puzzle, it demonstrates that they have completed the required work. As a reward, they receive digital value, such as newly created coins in the case of cryptocurrencies. This reward system incentivizes participants to maintain the network and ensure its security and reliability.

(ii) Proof of Stake (PoS)

Proof-of-Stake (PoS) system, a transaction validator, also known as a network node, must demonstrate ownership of a certain asset—in the case of cryptocurrencies, a specific number of coins—to participate in validating transactions. Unlike in Proof-of-Work systems, this process is referred to as "forging" rather than "mining." (Houben & Snyers, 2018).

According to Ernst and Young Global limited, in a cryptocurrency network, a validator must prove their "stake," or share of the total coins in circulation, to gain the right to validate transactions. A validator who owns more coins has the higher chances of being selected in validate of the next block. This is because a larger stake indicates greater seniority and trustworthiness within the network. As compensation for their validation services, the transaction validator receives a transaction fee paid by the parties involved in the transaction (Table 10.1).

Table 10.1 Difference between Proof of Work (PoW) and Proof of Stakes (PoS)

Aspects	*Proof of Work (PoW)*	*Proof of Stakes (PoS)*
Block validation	Determined by how much computational work is done by a single miner	Determined by the size of a validator's stake in the network
Reward system	Miners receive a reward for solving cryptographic puzzles	No mining reward; validators earn transaction fees instead
Security against attacks	Hackers need 51% of the network's computational power to alter the blockchain	Hackers would need to own 51% of the total cryptocurrency supply, which is nearly impossible
Energy efficiency & cost	Less energy efficient but widely tested and proven	More energy efficient but costlier and relatively newer
Notable cryptocurrencies	Bitcoin is the most well-known cryptocurrency using PoW	Cryptocurrencies using PoS include EOS, Tezos (XTZ), and Cardano (ADA)

Source https://www.geeksforgeeks.org

Some other mechanism in the blockchain is Delegated Proof of Stakes (DPoS), Proof of Burn (PoB), Proof of Capacity (PoC) and Proof of Elapsed time.

10.3 Global Distribution of Mining

Cryptocurrency mining stands out from other forms of mining due to its exceptionally high energy demands. This is primarily because the process involves the operation of tens of thousands of interconnected computers, working together like data center. Miners perform complex calculations to verify transactions within the network, ensuring they are completed and allowing new cryptocurrency to be generated Bloomberg (2022) (Fig. 10.2).

Currently, the United States leads the world in cryptocurrency mining, accounting for a significant 37.84% share of global mining activities. China, which previously held the top spot and once mined over half of the world's Bitcoin, now ranks second. Kazakhstan follows in third place, contributing 13.22% to the global mining share, with Canada and other countries rounding out the top contributors. In comparison, India ranks far lower at 38th position, with a modest share of just 0.03%.

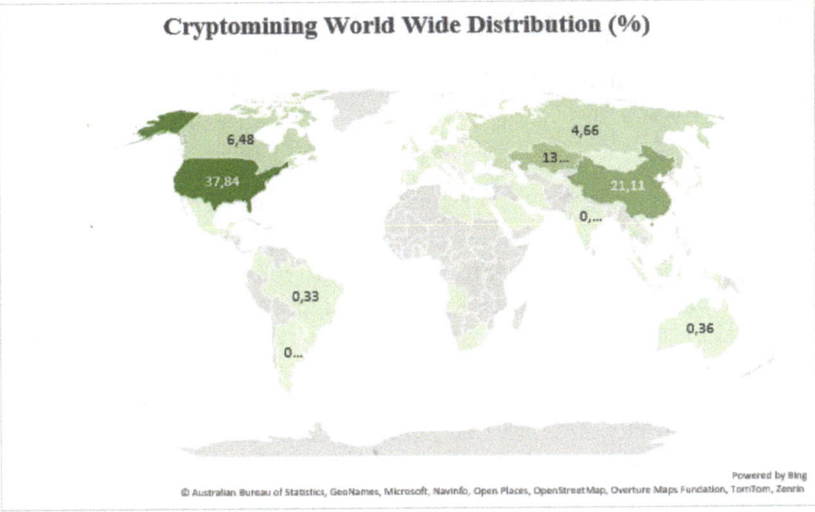

Fig. 10.2 Country wise digital currency mining trends. *Source* World Population Review

10.4 Environmental Concerns

If Bitcoin adoption continues at the modest pace observed in some widely accepted technologies, the cumulative emissions from its mining activities could contribute to a 2 °C rise in global temperatures within the next 22 years. However, if Bitcoin adoption grows as rapidly as the fastest-emerging technologies, this temperature increase could occur in just 11 years. These projections, however, are based on the assumption that the energy sources used for mining will remain constant and unchanged over this period (Mora et al., 2018).

Bitcoin mining, as well as mining for other digital currencies, is an extremely energy-intensive process, requiring a substantial amount of energy to mine a single block on the blockchain. With the rise in mining activity across the globe, energy consumption has surged significantly. Much of the electricity used in mining comes from fossil fuels, such as coal in Kazakhstan, which generates higher carbon emissions compared to other energy sources (Wiwoho et al., 2024).

Additionally, mining is entirely technology-driven, necessitating advanced hardware and equipment. This reliance on technology also results in a growing amount of electronic waste, raising significant environmental concerns. Addressing the energy demands, carbon emissions, and e-waste associated with mining will need to be a primary focus moving forward.

10.5 High Use of Energy

Cryptocurrency transactions are considered to be more energy intensive than any other cashless or internet banking transaction adding mining activities for any digital currency need huge amount of energy (Kohli et al., 2022). A clear example of the immense electricity consumption in cryptocurrency mining can be observed in the United States. In 2021, mining activities consumed between 8 and 11 billion kilowatt-hours (kWh) of electricity, a figure that surged to 33–55 billion kilowatt-hours (kWh) in 2022. This significant energy usage has led to an annual increase in carbon emissions of 21–35 million metric tons of CO_2. To put this into perspective, every 42 billion kilowatt-hours (kWh) of electricity consumed produces approximately 17 million metric tons of CO_2 annually in upstate New York and as much as 38 million metric tons annually in the central Great Plains (The White House Washington, 2022).

According to an analysis conducted by Cambridge University, the total electricity consumed by Bitcoin mining exceeds the entire electricity consumption of Argentina. If Bitcoin were considered a country, its electricity consumption would place it among the top 30 energy-consuming nations in the world. Studies suggest that mining just one US dollar's worth of Bitcoin consumes four times more energy than extracting the same value of copper and twice as much energy as mining an equivalent value of platinum or gold. The same value of copper and twice as much as extracting an equivalent amount of platinum or gold. This highlights the immense energy demands of Bitcoin mining compared to traditional resource extraction (Stoll et al., 2019a, 2019b).

Bitcoin mining is a major contributor to carbon emissions, producing approximately 13 thousand kg of CO_2 for every bitcoin mined and around 40 thousand kilograms (kg) of CO_2 every hour. On a world level scale, the electricity required for Bitcoin mining reaches an estimated 32.56 terawatt-hours (TWh) annually, surpassing the total electricity consumption of entire countries like Ireland or Denmark (Sergio et al., 2019). From 2016 to 2018 mining of four cryptocurrencies contributes about 3–15 million tons of carbon emission (Krause &Tolaymat, 2018).

Increase in the energy consumption due to the mining and trading of cryptocurrency has huge consequence to the environment. Empirical data shows that there is direct relationship between trading and energy consumption (Schinckus et al., 2020).

10.6 Increase in Carbon Emission

The method of energy generation—whether from fossil fuels, coal, hydro-electric power, or other non-renewable sources—often results in some form of pollution, such as air pollution or other environmental impacts (Goodkind et al., 2020a, 2020b). The process of validation in Bitcoin or any other cryptocurrency needed special type of hardware and a higher amount of electricity which transact into a higher carbon footprint (Stoll et al., 2019a, 2019b). With a direct relationship of mining with higher electricity consumption there are also other factors which negatively affects the sustainability. Which is termed as negative effect on the social, economic and environmental interests of people of specific region (Joshi et al., 2019).

According to *The Conversation*, digital currency mining using the Proof-of-Work (PoW) method has a significant harmful impact on the environment. In the UK alone, mining operations consume approximately 300 terawatt-hours (TWh) of electricity annually, primarily sourced from fossil fuels. This results in an estimated 114 million tons of carbon emissions, equivalent to the environmental impact of 380,000 space rocket launches. Additionally, the International Monetary Fund (IMF) has highlighted that Bitcoin, one of the most widely used cryptocurrencies, consumes a million times more energy than a single credit card transaction (O'Dwyer & Malone, 2014). Crypto mining activities were responsible for emitting approximately 139 million tons of CO_2-equivalent in 2021, accounting for about 0.4% of global carbon emissions that year (Landon, 2023). Mining activity involved with different types of minerals, silver, and other materials who help in building computing equipment increase green-house gas emissions. There is a fluctuation activity triggered by the change in price of crypto or marketing activity. Which cause to fluctuate electricity use and green house gas emissions hence increase the carbon footprint globally (Vries et al., 2022).

Carbon emissions are a major global concern, particularly for least-developed countries, where energy needs are largely met through fossil fuels, coal, and other non-renewable sources. While large-scale mining operations in countries like China and the United States contribute significantly to carbon emissions, the most severe impact is felt by nations with limited resources to adopt advanced technologies for reducing emissions. Studies suggest that the current level of mining activity could lead to a temperature rise of up to 2 degrees Celsius, accelerating climate change and worsening its consequences for vulnerable regions.

10.7 Increase in E-Waste

For digital currency mining there is a need of advanced computing instrument which consist of chips, cables, computer circuit, semiconductors, and other chemical which can pollute the soil, air, and water after the disposal. Globally 54.6 MMT electronic waste was produced in 2019 and just one-sixth part was recycled and it will be doubled by 2050 (Vries & Stoll, 2021). Electronic devices used in cryptocurrency mining typically have a limited lifespan (maximum of two years). So, there will be more electronic waste than the tradition transaction electronic devices (Digiconomist, 2022). Toxic substances such as lead and mercury not only affect the environment but also pose serious health risks to workers through indirect exposure (Althaf et al., 2020). According to the Global E-Waste Monitor 2024 total E-Waste generated is 92 billion Kg globally and just 23% globally collected and recycled and after 2010 it is increasing at the rate of five times per year which is alarming. Adding crypto mining also has a significant contribution in this regard.

The combined impact of electricity consumption, carbon emissions, and electronic waste from cryptocurrency mining poses a serious threat to the environment and exacerbates climate change-related issues. The high energy demands, reliance on fossil fuels, and rapid turnover of mining hardware contribute to resource depletion, pollution, and global warming. There are also some indirect environmental impacts like increase in resource extraction of earth metals, high water usage, and land usage ecological impact. To address these challenges effectively, a coordinated international effort is essential.

10.8 Mitigation Strategies

10.8.1 Use of Renewable Energy

We know mining of digital currencies needs more than significant amount of energy but use of such amount of energy also depends on how it was produced. Implementing a site regulation policy that enforces changes in the energy consumption structure of mining activities has been found to be a more effective approach to reducing carbon emissions from cryptocurrency and blockchain mining. By regulating where and how mining operations source their energy, such policies can encourage the use of renewable energy, improve energy efficiency, and ultimately lower the environmental impact of mining activities (Jiang et al., 2021).

Canada's focus on using green energy for Bitcoin mining is not just a smart choice, this is the step toward a sustainable future. With climate change becoming a major concern, adopting eco-friendly practices in industries like cryptocurrency is no longer optional but essential.

10.8.2 Efficient Mining Hardware

As we discussed mining hardware has a short life span means they are of no use after some time. So, focus of scientific communities should be in more effective mining hardware, computer circuit, advance in ASIC's (Application Specific integrated Circuit) in place of FGPA (Field-Programmable Gate Array). Because FGPA is not suited for bulk production where ASIC is designed for application's specific need and is also ideal for bulk production.

These advanced circuit consumes less amount of energy than the traditional one, means decrease in carbon emissions. ASIC has more life than FGPA, so this also can solve the problems of increase in E-waste.

10.8.3 Energy Efficient Consensus Mechanism

Bitcoin is one of the crypto currency which mining activities is highest globally and it work on Proof of Work which is not energy efficient consensus mechanism. Shifting of consensus mechanism from Proof of Work (PoW) to Proof of Stake (PoS) can drastically change the scene of overusing electricity. Where Proof of Stake is risk free from hacking operation because there is a need of 51% access of whole network system not just a 51% access of personal desktop.

10.8.4 Regulatory Measure

Counties should focus on cryptocurrency mining supervision policy. Policymakers should focus on the aspect of crypto and possible impact on the current financial system after the implementation (Imran et al., 2024). Maximum countries are planning to launch their central bank digital currencies (CBDCs) and some are in research phase what will be possible impact of CBDC on their financial system as well as international trade of their economy (Kumar & Godara, 2024). Countries need to implement policies that incorporate key environmental indicators to promote sustainable cryptocurrency transactions. By designing regulations that prioritize eco-friendly practices, governments can work towards reducing the environmental impact of digital currencies (Sergio, 2023).

Policy recommendation given by White House for mining must be eco-friendly are as:

(i) Green-house gas emission control.
(ii) Enhance the use of Renewable Energy.
(iii) Transparency promotion for better environmental performance.
(iv) Energy Efficient Measure Enforcement.
(v) Monitor and mitigation.

10.8.5 Introduction of Carbon Tax

Mining of any cryptocurrency needs high amount of electricity and specialized hardware which resulted increase in carbon footprint. Energy used for mining is equivalent to the electricity usage of a country (O'Dwyer & Malone, 2014). Purposing of a carbon tax in a nation can justify the commitment of a country toward nationally determined contribution (NDC) as stated by Paris Agreement (Putranti, 2022).

This principle highlights the importance of addressing environmental damage as a priority, ensuring that those responsible for pollution bear the costs of their actions. It enforces the "polluter pays" concept, where mining operations must take responsibility for the environmental harm they cause. By implementing taxes and penalties on excessive energy consumption and carbon emissions, governments can increase state revenue while incentivizing a transition toward renewable energy sources. This approach not only holds miners accountable but also reduces the financial burden on society, encouraging a more sustainable and responsible approach to cryptocurrency mining.

10.9 Conclusion

Cryptocurrency mining requires massive amounts of electricity, much of which is generated from fossil fuels, coal, and other non-renewable sources. This poses a significant challenge for countries that lack energy efficiency, leading to increased carbon emissions and environmental degradation. Additionally, the rapid use and disposal of mining hardware contribute to the growing problem of electronic waste. Together, these factors accelerate climate change on both a national and global scale.

To mitigate these environmental impacts, the shift toward renewable energy sources and energy-efficient mining hardware is crucial. Renewable energy can help reduce carbon emissions, while advanced, sustainable mining technology can minimize resource wastage. Furthermore, government intervention is essential to regulate cryptocurrency mining effectively. Policies such as carbon taxes, transaction fees on mining, and other mitigation strategies should be implemented to curb environmental damage and support climate action efforts. By addressing these issues through regulation and innovation, the cryptocurrency industry can become more sustainable and environmentally responsible.

References

Alonso, S. L. N., Jorge-Vázquez, J., Echarte Fernández, M. Á., & Reier Forradellas, R. F. (2021). Cryptocurrency mining from an economic and environmental perspective analysis of the most and least sustainable countries. *Energies*, *14*(14), 1. https://doi.org/10.3390/en14144254

Althaf, S., Babbitt, C. W., & Chen, R. (2020). The evolution of consumer electronic waste in the United States. *Journal of Industrial Ecology, 25*(3), 693–715. https://doi.org/10.1111/jiec.13074

Berentsen, A., & Schar, F. (2018). A short introduction to the world of cryptocurrencies. *Review, 100*(1), 1–19. https://doi.org/10.20955/r.2018.1-16

Bloomberg. (2022). Why bitcoin's energy problem is so hard to fix. *Sustainable finance*. Retrieved from https://www.bloomberg.com/ (open in a new window).

Cambridge Bitcoin Electricity Consumption Index. (2024). Retrieved from https://ccaf.io/cbnsi/cbeci/ghg

De Vries, A., Gallersdörfer, U., Klaaßen, L., & Stoll, C. (2022). Revisiting bitcoin's carbon footprint. *Joule, 6*(3), 498–502. https://doi.org/10.1016/j.joule.2022.02.005

Digiconomist. (2022). *Bitcoin energy consumption index*. Retrieved from https://digiconomist.net/bitcoin-energy-consumption

Goodkind, A. L., et al. (2020a). Cryptodamages: Monetary value estimates of the air pollution and human health impacts of cryptocurrency mining. *Energy Research & Social Science, 59*, Article 101281.

Goodkind, A. L., Jones, B. A., & Berrens, R. P. (2020b). Cryptodamages: Monetary value estimates of the air pollution and human health impacts of cryptocurrency mining. *Energy Research & Social Science, 59*, Article 101281.

Houben, R., & Snyers, A. (2018). *Cryptocurrency and blockchain: Legal context and implications for financial crime, money laundering and tax evasion*. European Parliament.

Imran, Y., et al. (2024). Environmental attention and uncertainties of cryptocurrency market: Examining linkages with crypto-mining stocks. *Finance Research Letters, 59*, 1–11. https://doi.org/10.1016/j.frl.2023.104672

Jiang, S., Li, Y., Lu, Q., Hong, Y., Guan, D., Xiong, Y., & Wang, S. (2021). Policy assessments for the carbon emission flows and sustainability of Bitcoin blockchain operation in China. *Nature Communications, 12*, 1–10.

Joshi, A., Kalauni, D., & Tiwari, U. (2019). Determinants of awareness of good agricultural practices (GAP) among banana growers in Chitwan, Nepal. *Journal of Agriculture and Food Research, 1*, 100010. https://doi.org/10.1016/j.jafr.2019.100010

Kohli, V., Chakravarty, S., Chamola, V., Sangwan, K. S., & Zeadally, S. (2022). An analysis of energy consumption and carbon footprints of cryptocurrencies and possible solutions. *Digital Communications and Networks*. https://doi.org/10.1016/j.dcan.2022.06.017

Krause, M. J., & Tolaymat, T. (2018). Quantification of energy and carbon costs for mining cryptocurrencies. *Nature Sustainability, 1*, 711–718.

Kumar, S., & Godara, R. S. (2024). RBI's digital currency and its significance in global trade. In R. Aneja & R. Dygas (Eds.), *Digital currencies in the new global world order*. Palgrave Macmillan. https://doi.org/10.1007/978-981-97-4810-5_11

Landon et al., (2023). The water and carbon footprint of cryptocurrencies and conventional currencies. *Journal of Cleaner Production, 411*, 137268. https://doi.org/10.1016/j.jclepro.2023.137268

Maese, V. A., Avery, A. W., Naftalis, B. A., Wink, S. P., & Valdez, Y. D. (2016). Cryptocurrency: A primer. *The Banking Law Journal, 133*, 468–471.

Malone, D., O'Dwyer, K. J. (2014). Bitcoin mining and its energy footprint. In *25th IET Irish signals & systems conference 2014 and 2014 China-Ireland international conference on information and communities technologies (ISSC 2014/CIICT 2014)* (pp. 280–285). https://doi.org/10.1049/cp.2014.0699

Mora, C., Rollins, R. L., Taladay, K., Kantar, M. B., Chock, M. K., Shimada, M., & Franklin, E. C. (2018). Bitcoin emissions alone could push global warming above 2c. *Nature Climate Change, 8*(11), 931.

Nakamoto, S. (2008). *Bitcoin: A peer-to-peer electronic cash system.* https://ssrn.com/abstract=3440802 or https://doi.org/10.2139/ssrn.3440802

O'Dwyer, K. J., & Malone, D. (2014). Bitcoin mining and its energy footprint, Limerick, June 26–27. In *Irish signals & systems conference 2014 and 2014 China-Ireland international conference on information and communications technologies (ISSC 2014/CIICT 2014).*

One node "forges" each block. See: EY, "IFRS—Accounting for crypto-assets", March 2018. IFRS: Accounting for crypto-assets (pp. 1647–1661).

Putranti, I. R. (2022). Crypto mining: Indonesia carbon tax challenges and safeguarding international commitment on human security. *International Journal of Business, Economics and Social Development, 3*(1), 10–18.

Schinckus, C., Nguyen, C. P., & Ling, F. C. H. (2020). Crypto-currencies trading and energy consumption. *International Journal of Energy Economics and Policy, 10*, 355–364.

Sergio, L. N. A. (2023). Can central bank digital currencies be green and sustainable? *Green Finance, 5*(4), 603–623.

Sergio et al. (2019). Activities and operations with cryptocurrencies and their taxation implications: The Spanish case. *Laws, 8*(3), 16. https://doi.org/10.3390/laws8030016

Stoll et al. (2019a). The carbon footprint of bitcoin. *Joule, 3*(7), 1647–1661. https://doi.org/10.1016/j.joule.2019.05.012

Stoll, C., KlaaBen, L., & Gallersdörfer, U. (2019b). The carbon footprint of bitcoin. Available at SSRN 3335781.

The White House Washington. (2022). *Climate and energy implications of crypto-assets in the United States.* The White House.

Vervoort, D., et al. (2021). Blockchain, health disparities and global health. *BMJ Innovation, 7*, 506–514. https://doi.org/10.1136/bmjinnov-2021-000667

Vries, A. D., & Stoll, C. (2021). Bitcoin's growing e-waste problem. *Resources, Conservation & Recycling, 175*, Article 105901. https://doi.org/10.1016/j.resconrec.2021.105901

Wiwoho, J., Trinugroho, I., Kharisma, D. B., & Suwadi, P. (2024). Cryptocurrency mining policy to protect the environment. *Cogent Social Sciences, 10*(1), 2323755. https://doi.org/10.1080/23311886.2024.2323755

World Population Review. (2024). https://worldpopulationreview.com/country-rankings/bitcoin-mining-by-country

Yli-Huumo, J., Ko, D., Choi, S., Park, S., & Smolander, K. (2016). Where is current research on blockchain technology? A systematic review. *PLoS ONE, 11*(10), Article e0163477. https://doi.org/10.1371/journal.pone.0163477

CHAPTER 11

Blockchain and Sustainable Development Goals—Synthetic Approach

Grzegorz Sobiecki and Marta Kotlarska

11.1 Introduction

Blockchain technology is often discussed in the context of achieving sustainable development goals (SDGs), primarily in relation to its high energy consumption and carbon footprint. Much of the discourse focuses on the need to reduce blockchain's environmental impact through energy-efficient consensus mechanisms, reliance on renewable energy sources, or, in extreme cases, eliminating its use altogether. However, beyond these environmental concerns, blockchain also possesses unique properties that enable new types of assets and services while enhancing transparency, security, immutability, and integrity. These characteristics

G. Sobiecki (✉)
Department of Financial System, SGH Warsaw School of Economics, Warsaw, Poland
e-mail: gsobie@sgh.waw.pl

M. Kotlarska
Revolut Ltd, Kraków, Poland

R. Aneja and R. Dygas (eds.), *Digital Currencies and the Green Economy*, https://doi.org/10.1007/978-981-95-2282-8_11

contribute to increasing certainty and equality in business and social relations. As a result, blockchain applications have the potential to support the realisation of multiple SDGs.

This chapter aims to provide a comprehensive analysis of blockchain's potential in achieving the 17 SDGs. We begin by presenting the fundamentals of blockchain technology, including its core principles, mechanisms, and key functionalities, as well as the conditions necessary for its effective operation. Following this, we examine the essence of each SDG to assess where blockchain can contribute most significantly and the mechanisms through which it facilitates progress towards these goals. Additionally, we explore instances where blockchain applications may hinder or counteract SDG achievements, either by creating barriers or generating unintended negative consequences. We provide examples of real-world implementations and conceptual applications of blockchain that actively contribute to SDG fulfillment.

The growing academic and professional interest in this intersection is reflected in a significant rise in publications on the topic. Between 2017 and 2023, the number of studies on blockchain and SDGs increased by an average of 90.64% per year, underscoring the expanding recognition of blockchain's potential role in sustainable development. This chapter synthesises existing knowledge while offering a structured perspective on how blockchain can either facilitate or challenge SDG realisation, ultimately aiming to provide a balanced and well-researched foundation for further discussions on the topic.

11.2 Sustainable Development Goals (SDGs)

The Sustainable Development Goals (SDGs) were identified in response to global challenges that threaten social, economic, and environmental stability. Population growth, social inequalities, environmental degradation, climate change, and insufficient access to education and healthcare have become worldwide concerns. Recognising these threats, the international community acknowledged the need for coordinated action to address them effectively. The SDGs emerged from a prolonged negotiation process involving UN member states, non-governmental organisations, and experts who recognised the necessity of establishing common priorities for humanity. Their objective is to create a fairer, more inclusive, and more sustainable world. As stated in the UN's, 2015 declaration:

"This Agenda is a plan of action for people, planet and prosperity. It also seeks to strengthen universal peace in larger freedom" (UN, 2015).

At their core, the SDGs aim not only to improve the quality of life for present generations but also to ensure that future generations have access to natural resources and well-functioning institutions. Each goal is interconnected—eradicating poverty requires access to education, better healthcare, and economic stability, while environmental protection cannot be effective without responsible consumption and production. Through the SDGs, countries can shape their policies in a way that simultaneously addresses the needs of various economic and social sectors, fostering the conditions necessary for sustainable development (UN, 2015).

11.3 Blockchain and its characteristics

Blockchain is a technology with transformative and revolutionary potential. It introduces entirely new properties and functionalities, among which the following are particularly significant:

- It serves as an immutable and tamper-proof database that records transactions in a permanent ledger.
- It relies on extensive data redundancy, preventing accidental loss or intentional deletion.
- It is based on hash functions—the core of the entire system—which ensure data integrity and historical consistency without the need to store their full content.
- It guarantees a high level of security through advanced cryptography, often resistant even to quantum computing threats.
- It remains continuously available, without interruptions.
- Data is recorded and accessible for reading with no delays.
- It enables the tracking of historical records, including transfers of value, products, documents, data, rights, and financial instruments.
- Transactions recorded in the ledger are irreversible.
- It is decentralised and not subject to control by a single entity.
- It allows direct peer-to-peer (P2P) relationships between parties without operational intermediaries.
- It facilitates decentralised value transfers.
- Automation is enabled through a predefined and widely accepted network protocol, as well as smart contract code.
- It allows for the management of transparency and anonimity.

- Smart contracts enable decentralised automation of relationships between entities and the creation of autonomous market platforms.
- It provides mechanisms for managing the level of decision-making centralisation.
- By design, all participants in the system are treated equally by the algorithm.
- It ensures equal access to the ledger from multiple locations worldwide.
- Each user is responsible for their own actions, assets, and data (self-custody).
- It enables the creation of autonomous structures for coordinating group activities (DAOs).
- It represents a broader trend in the digitalisation of economic life.
- Blockchain systems incorporate built-in mechanisms for digital identity management, including identification, authentication, and authorisation.
- Public blockchain networks function as financial systems, facilitating the transfer of value and rights without relying on external financial infrastructures.
- It enables the development of new business models, such as decentralised finance (DeFi).

Furthermore, blockchain introduces a new class of assets—crypto-assets—which, despite having a similar format (stored in a crypto wallet), can represent various values, rights, and digital goods. However, crypto-assets are a distinct type of asset. Their essence does not lie in data, as is the case with files, music streams, but rather in the record of the number of units in a decentralised ledger, supplemented with a structured description of additional characteristics and assigned rights.

All these distinctive features and properties form the foundation for blockchain's potential in advancing the Sustainable Development Goals (SDGs).

11.4 Literature Review

The potential of blockchain technology in achieving the Sustainable Development Goals (SDGs) has been widely explored by various scholars. Below, we present selected studies on this topic.

Adams et al. (2018) examined the potential applications of blockchain technology in achieving the SDGs. The authors highlight that previous research and implementations of blockchain have predominantly focused on cryptocurrencies, particularly Bitcoin. However, the technology has far broader applications that could contribute to positive social and environmental change. They introduced the concept of "*Blockchain for Good*" (B4G), which refers to the use of blockchain for social and environmental purposes. The study emphasises that blockchain has the potential to transform business models and enhance the transparency of organisations working towards SDGs.

Jiang et al. (2022) conducted a meta-analysis of literature reviews (a so-called tertiary review) that examined the impact of blockchain technology on SDG implementation. The primary aim of their study was to systematically synthesise existing academic literature on blockchain and its potential effects—both positive and negative—on various aspects of sustainable development. The authors analysed 42 prior literature reviews, identifying 76 positive and 10 negative interactions between blockchain and the SDGs. They also explored key barriers and facilitating factors for blockchain adoption in the SDG context, as well as research gaps and future directions for studying blockchain's role in sustainable development.

Joshi et al. (2023) conducted a literature review aimed at identifying, mapping, and synthesising the available literature to understand how blockchain can support SDG implementation. The authors analysed 1,277 publications from the Scopus and Web of Science databases. After applying selection criteria, they included 157 studies in their detailed analysis. Their findings indicate that blockchain technology has the potential to positively impact nearly all 17 SDGs, though certain aspects may also have negative consequences.

Salim et al. (2023) also examined the relationship between blockchain technology and the SDGs, using a bibliometric analysis of the literature. They reviewed 271 articles published between 2017 and 2023, ultimately selecting 183 for detailed bibliometric examination. Their study underscores that blockchain can be a key tool in improving transparency, accountability, and efficiency in sustainable development processes, though further research and technological adaptation are needed.

Campos and Proença (2024) conducted a systematic analysis of academic literature on blockchain applications across various economic sectors and their impact on SDG implementation. Using the PRISMA methodology, they reviewed 441 articles from the Scopus and Web of Science databases, identifying major research trends and the most frequently studied SDGs.

This chapter synthesises the findings of the aforementioned studies while incorporating additional mechanisms that take into account the specific characteristics of blockchain technology.

11.5 SDGs Supported by Blockchain

All 17 SDGs have some degree of connection to blockchain technology, though its impact is not always positive. Below is a synthesised assessment of blockchain's potential applications in achieving the SDGs.

11.5.1 SDG 1—No Poverty

According to the World Bank, approximately 1.7 billion people worldwide lack access to banking services, and more than 780 million people live below the international poverty line. In many developing countries, individuals without official documents are unable to open bank accounts. In poorer regions, the high cost of maintaining bank branches prevents financial institutions from operating there. Traditional banks and payment systems impose high fees, making financial services unaffordable for low-income individuals (World Bank, 2024).

Integrating blockchain into financial service providers' business models—through existing crypto-assets and, potentially, decentralised finance (DeFi)—can contribute to financial inclusion by eliminating intermediaries and enabling access to banking services and microloans for financially excluded individuals. Unbanked individuals can use cryptocurrency wallets instead of traditional bank accounts. Decentralised finance (DeFi) facilitates borrowing without intermediaries, where lenders are other network users rather than traditional banks. With blockchain, users can take out loans by securing them with crypto-assets (*collateralised lending*) without undergoing conventional credit procedures. They can also take out loans relying on decentralised credit-scoring mechanisms, though this sector is still in its early stages of development (Sobiecki, 2022). Examples of DeFi lending models include protocols such as Aave (2025) and Compound (2025), which operate on liquid collateral, and CreDA—Credit Data Alliance (2024), a decentralised credit-scoring service based on blockchain data.

Another major obstacle to poverty reduction is international remittances, which, when processed through traditional mechanisms such as SWIFT, can take several days and incur high fees. Peer-to-peer (P2P) payments bypass intermediaries, allowing for faster and cheaper transactions compared to conventional banking systems. Blockchain-based financial models could significantly improve remittance processes and reduce costs—an essential factor for developing economies. Depending on the blockchain technology used, transactions could compete effectively with existing payment systems in four key areas: cross-border payments, instant payments, large-scale payments, and micro transactions (Sobiecki, 2022). Any established cryptocurrency with low transaction fees—particularly those using layer-two solutions to minimise costs—can facilitate affordable cross-border payments. Some existing crypto-assets already offer transfer fees as low as a fraction of a dollar (Stellar, Tron, Cardano, Ripple), while certain platforms are designed to enable fee-free crypto transfers (e.g., EOS, Nano, Iota, Algorand).

Unbanked individuals often have limited investment opportunities despite possessing liquid assets. Blockchain enables asset tokenisation (e.g., real estate, commodities, bonds), allowing individuals with limited capital to invest with small amounts. Tokenisation fractionalises assets, broadening access to investment markets. For example, RealT (2025) is a platform that allows global investors to participate in the US real estate market.

The distribution of humanitarian aid faces numerous unresolved challenges. Funds often pass through multiple intermediaries, increasing the risk of embezzlement and inefficient allocation, while donors lack certainty that their contributions are being used as intended. Bureaucratic hurdles can delay the delivery of aid to the area most in need. Additionally, in some regions, fraudulent registrations or ghost beneficiaries distort the fair allocation of assistance. At the same time, many individuals lack access to banking systems, making it difficult for them to receive aid funds.

Blockchain can address these issues by establishing a transparent, secure, decentralised, and partially automated tracking system through smart contracts. Such a system would monitor the flow of humanitarian funds and resources, eliminating unnecessary intermediaries and minimising corruption.

Several notable blockchain-based humanitarian initiatives have emerged. Building Blocks (BB) (World Food Programme, 2025) is the largest blockchain-based humanitarian initiative globally, implemented by the World Food Programme (WFP). It enables food aid distribution tracking for refugees in Jordan, ensuring that funds are spent exclusively on food purchases. Giveth (2025) is a blockchain platform that automates donations to aid organisations while providing full transparency over expenditures. UnBlocked Cash—Oxfam International (Oxfam International, 2024) is a blockchain-driven initiative by Oxfam, tested in Vanuatu, designed to streamline humanitarian aid through fast, transparent, and cost-effective fund transfers.

According to the 2030 Agenda, poverty reduction requires effective social protection mechanisms. In this regard, blockchain can enhance the targeting and distribution of financial aid, ensuring that assistance reaches those who need it most. A dedicated tracking system for aid distribution could significantly improve transparency and efficiency. One specific blockchain application in this area is Central Bank Digital Currencies (CBDCs). If properly implemented and programmed, CBDCs could function as programmable aid funds, restricting spending to predefined categories of essential goods and services.

11.5.1.1 SDG 2—Zero Hunger

Despite the fact that one-third of the world's food is wasted, 735 million people suffer from hunger (FAO, 2016). The causes of hunger are diverse, but blockchain can help address several key factors—enhancing transparency in food supply chains, reducing corruption, and preventing unfair distribution. Additionally, blockchain can contribute to reducing food waste by improving monitoring systems, ensuring that food is not damaged during transport or storage, and minimising delivery delays through reliable supply chain tracking.

By preserving historical records, blockchain also prevents manipulation of expiry dates, incentivising retailers to optimise their sales processes. Similar to humanitarian aid distribution efforts aimed at poverty reduction, food aid and nutrition programmes could also benefit from blockchain in ensuring greater transparency. Food that is nearing its expiry date but remains safe for consumption can be directed to those in need through aid organisations. Blockchain can help track and monitor food distribution, ensuring it reaches the intended recipients.

Ensuring data integrity in supply chains and tracking the history of food products can also contribute to sustainable agriculture. By enabling better resource management, raw material monitoring, and product quality control, blockchain allows farmers to adjust production based on demand and distribution trends, leading to more efficient food systems.

The 2030 Agenda, under SDG 2, highlights the importance of equitable access to and fair distribution of benefits derived from genetic resources and traditional knowledge. In this area, blockchain could provide tokenisation solutions for knowledge (e.g., genetic code) and platform-based intellectual property management, enabling tracking and verification of its use. Another key aspect of SDG 2 is the development of mechanisms to ensure well-functioning food commodity markets. Blockchain can automate transactions in these markets, facilitating fair participation for both small-scale and large-scale producers and buyers.

Some blockchain-based platforms supporting SDG 2:

- IBM Food Trust—A platform designed to enhance transparency and safety in the global food supply chain. Used by Walmart, Carrefour, and Nestlé, among others, to track the origin of food products (IBM, 2024b).
- Agriledger—A blockchain-based system for farmers that supports supply tracking, reduces food losses, and improves transparency and fairness in global agricultural supply chains (Agriledger, 2024).
- TE-FOOD—A blockchain platform enabling traceability and verification of food origins at every stage of the supply chain. It has been deployed in Vietnam and Africa (TE-FOOD, 2025).

11.5.1.2 SDG 3—Good Health and Well-Being

In the pursuit of SDG 3, blockchain can enhance the security of medical data and enable interoperability within healthcare systems.

Modern healthcare systems are highly complex, with medical data fragmented across various platforms, including electronic health records (EHRs), laboratory results, physicians' notes, and diagnostic images. Thousands of healthcare organisations use their own IT platforms, standards, and privacy protection mechanisms, leading to a situation where no single medical institution has a comprehensive view of a patient's health (Carrara & MD, 2024; Hayden, 2025; Prior et al., 2023). Blockchain could facilitate the integration of disparate systems without requiring a complete overhaul of software infrastructure in different institutions, nor the centralisation of medical records. Similar in the Interplanetary File System (IPFS) (2025), data could remain stored in its original locations (where it was generated), while allowing authorised access to all relevant records with built-in data management controls.

According to HIPAA Journal, one of the most common violations of HIPAA regulations is unauthorised access to patient records by healthcare staff, posing a significant threat to patient privacy (Alder, 2025). A study by the Clearwater Cyberintelligence Institute found that 54% of all reported data breaches in the healthcare sector involved server vulnerabilities, pointing out the high susceptibility of these systems to cyberattacks (Alder, 2019). Furthermore, in 2023 alone, 725 data breaches were reported in the healthcare sector, exposing or improperly sharing over 133 million records (Alder, 2019).

Patients often do not know who has accessed their medical records, nor can they trace past access. Blockchain can address this issue by enabling the encryption of patient data, ensuring that records can only be accessed by authorised individuals (e.g., doctors, insurers, or the patient). It also allows for selective data sharing, granting specific entities access to specific records for a limited time, while maintaining a transparent and auditable record of all interactions.

According to an article published in the *Journal of the American Medical Informatics Association*, medical data lacks consistency across different healthcare systems. Hospitals, clinics, laboratories, and insurers all use separate IT systems that are not interoperable, preventing seamless communication between them (Wei et al., 2012). The lack of access to a patient's complete medical records often forces doctors to order duplicate diagnostic tests, as previous results are not readily available (Medivault, 2024). This not only extends treatment times but also reduces overall system efficiency. An integrated and standardised solution could significantly improve healthcare system interoperability. Blockchain could serve as a foundational layer that ensures transparency, data redundancy (preventing accidental loss or intentional deletion), and authorised access—even if such a system were managed by a central institution.

Blockchain could also streamline and automate medical processes. Patient registration, record-keeping, prescription issuance, and insurance settlements consume significant time and resources. Smart contracts could help accelerate these processes by, for example, automating patient eligibility verification for treatment reimbursement, approving hospital payments through predefined conditions, and issuing tamper-proof prescriptions that are verifiable and traceable. Examples of platforms facilitating health data management include: MedRec (Azaria et al., 2016; Ekblaw, 2017), BurstIQ (Johnson, 2025), and Gem Health Network (Prisco, 2016).

Blockchain can also track and regulate the distribution of medicines and vaccines, preventing counterfeit drugs from entering the supply chain. Counterfeit pharmaceuticals pose a significant global issue. According to the World Health Organization (WHO), approximately 10% of medical products in low- and middle-income countries are substandard or falsified (WHO, 2024). The lack of a universal drug-tracking system makes it difficult for patients to verify the authenticity of their medications. Blockchain can record a drug's entire history, from licensed manufacturers to pharmacies, allowing for instant authenticity verification—for example, using QR codes (Abdallah & Nizamuddin, 2023). One of the blockchain-based solutions for tracking pharmaceuticals is Infosys Pharma Supply Chain Distributed, which aims to create a seamless network for suppliers, manufacturers, regulators, quality control laboratories, and logistics operators. This system is based on a shared ledger, allowing for the traceability of specialised medicines at the packaging level while reducing revenue losses from counterfeit pharmaceuticals (Infosys, 2025).

Blockchain can also be used to monitor health indicators and track pandemics. Many countries lack civil registration systems and comprehensive health statistics, making it difficult to collect consistent epidemiological data (Sankoh, 2017). Some studies suggest that certain governments deliberately underreported COVID-19 cases (Price & Gargiulo, 2021; Wigley, 2022). The lack of an integrated global system for data collection, exchange, and reporting can cause delays in pandemic response, postponing effective containment measures (Alvarez et al., 2023). Blockchain can provide a transparent and decentralised system for data exchange, independent of any single institution or authority. In such a system, all infections, deaths, and recoveries could be immutably recorded on the blockchain, ensuring public accessibility (or restricted access for designated health institutions, depending on regulations). This would mean that reporting pandemic-related events would not require prior government approval, facilitating faster and more reliable data sharing with the WHO and other health organisations, including governments, laboratories, hospitals, and pharmaceutical manufacturers. An example of a blockchain-powered platform for integrating epidemiological data is

MiPasa, developed by HACERA in collaboration with IBM, Oracle, and the WHO. During the COVID-19 pandemic, MiPasa was used to track and verify real-time infection data (Singh, 2020).

Beyond case tracking, blockchain can also aid in predicting potential future infections through location-based data (GPS) voluntarily shared by infected individuals, recording their movement history and contacts with others. Blockchain allows these records to be stored anonymously, alleviating privacy concerns. A conceptual system for digital health passport management and infectious disease contact tracing is Block-HPCT, developed and tested by researchers from Pukyong National University and Dong-A University in South Korea (Rashid et al., 2022).

Another issue in pandemic control is the forgery of vaccination certificates and test results, as well as the lack of a global system for verifying health passports. In the United States, numerous cases of fraudulent COVID-19 vaccination cards were reported. In August 2021, customs agents seized over 30,000 counterfeit vaccination cards imported from China (Sapp, 2022). Once again, blockchain's notarisation capabilities prove crucial in achieving SDG objectives. These systems—by design, transparent, and immutable—can store records of test results, vaccination records, and issued health certificates, making them easily verifiable in real time. In addition to centralised solutions, several blockchain-based health passport platforms have been developed, including the Digital Health Passport (Jadhav, 2021), the IBM Digital Health Pass and CommonPass (Hackett, 2020).

A less obvious application of blockchain in healthcare is its role in supporting addiction prevention and treatment. Blockchain could facilitate digital reward and certification systems, granting regularly issued certificates to individuals overcoming addiction. These certificates could serve as a verified record of their progress, providing both motivation and proof of commitment to recovery.

Blockchain could also reduce road accident casualties and injuries by enabling a mandatory registration system for spare vehicle parts, ensuring that only high-quality components are used in vehicles. Additionally, blockchain can be used to record and track a vehicle's history, ensuring that only roadworthy cars remain in circulation. Examples of such concepts include BCVehis (Chen et al., 2020) and a vehicle-tracking framework proposed by researchers from China and Taiwan (Chen et al., 2022).

Blockchain can also aid in the fight against drug trafficking and illicit substance use by providing greater transparency in supply chains, enabling the tracking of precursor substances used in drug production, eliminating prescription fraud, and improving the regulation of medical narcotics. Additionally, law enforcement agencies can benefit from on-chain data on financial transactions, particularly in tracking payments for illicit substances and subsequent money laundering via crypto-assets. An increasing number of blockchain-based applications are already assisting law enforcement agencies in monitoring financial transactions linked to drug trade and money laundering. A notable example is Elliptic, a platform that facilitates cryptocurrency transaction analysis to support financial crime investigations (Elliptic, 2025).

11.5.1.3 SDG 4—Quality Education

Blockchain technology, through crypto-assets and its ability to generate, store, and transfer them, enables the creation of tamper-proof and easily verifiable digital education and training certificates. These certificates are simple to issue, transfer, and authenticate while also supporting advanced identification and authentication methods, such as qualified electronic signatures and electronic seals. However, they can also function independently of these systems, making it easier to achieve international recognition of qualifications. Currently, both private solutions and publicly developed initiatives operate in this field. Notable examples include:

- Doxychain (2024),
- Diploma Safe (Mortensen, 2023),
- Blockcerts (2025),
- DC4EU (Digital Credentials for Europe)—a public project aimed at testing the interoperability of digital identity systems and educational certificates to facilitate the recognition of vocational and academic qualifications across the European Union (DC4EU Consortium, 2025).

Blockchain can enhance access to online education by supporting transparent data management systems, ensuring access to secure and authenticated (certified) educational content. One such platform, Odem (2021), was designed to connect educators, employers, students, and educational institutions, but it is no longer operational.

Blockchain-secured certificates can reflect comprehensive skill sets, including diplomas, degrees, and training certificates, as well as micro-credentials for specific skills. This allows for verification of the issuing institution or the individual validating the competencies. In 2023, Cracow University of Technology implemented blockchain-based micro-credentialing for skill certification (Szarata, 2023).

One of the objectives of SDG 4 is to increase the number of scholarships for citizens of developing countries. While blockchain cannot directly increase the availability of scholarships, it can improve transparency in their distribution by ensuring a fair and accountable allocation system. Through public expenditure tracking and monitoring the use of international funds, blockchain can help ensure that financial aid is equitably distributed and used as intended.

Blockchain technology has the potential to support bottom-up governance and finance for research in niche fields—particularly in regions or contexts where political priorities or budget constraints lead to insufficient support. One illustrative example is AthenaDAO (2025), a decentralised autonomous organisation (DAO) that employs blockchain-based tools to fund and amplify research in women's health. The project addresses substantial gaps in both financial support and research focus across numerous domains related to women's health (Philbin et al., 2024). By sourcing partnerships and recruiting researchers, AthenaDAO provides comprehensive support, funding, and incubation services, thus offering a novel alternative to traditional research-funding pathways. As a DAO, AthenaDAO entrusts governance decisions to a community of token holders who use the native ATH token to vote on strategic directions. This structure fosters a community-centric model aligned with the early anti-establishment ethos of many cryptocurrency initiatives. Additionally, the organisation issues IP-NFTs (non-fungible tokens certifying intellectual property and on-chain ownership), creating an innovative framework for managing and potentially monetising research outputs. Such models of research funding are particularly crucial in fields at risk of being underfunded or banned—including women's health studies in certain developed countries, such as the United States—demonstrating how decentralised approaches can circumvent political or institutional barriers to critical research.

11.5.1.4 SDG 5—Gender Equality

Blockchain supports gender equality by helping women gain legal, secure, and immutable digital identities, which is particularly vital in developing countries, where the lack of formal identification documents remains a significant barrier. Through decentralised solutions, women can access financial services, own digital wallets, and store funds securely without requiring a traditional bank account. Blockchain enables them to make payments, conduct international transfers without intermediaries, and protect assets from confiscation. Since a digital wallet is a fundamental component of any decentralised system (including cryptocurrencies), women who join the blockchain ecosystem automatically gain financial autonomy. Beyond these financial solutions, women can also benefit from decentralised identity (DID) systems, which do not rely on centralised authorities.

Notable private (commercial) projects in this field include Microsoft Entra Verified ID *(formerly Microsoft Azure Active Directory Verifiable Credentials)* (Microsoft, 2025) and Veramo *(formerly uPort Identity)* (Hamza, 2019). Discussions on global and public decentralised identity solutions are ongoing within initiatives such as Decentralized Identity Foundation (2025) and ID4Africa (2025).

In 2022, the European Self-Sovereign Identity Framework (ESSIF) project was completed as part of the European Blockchain Services Infrastructure (EBSI) under the European Blockchain Partnership (EBP). The project aimed to develop a framework for Self-Sovereign Identity (SSI) in Europe. The results and insights gained from ESSIF and eSSIF-Lab are now being used to further develop and integrate SSI solutions across Europe. Following the project's completion, its alumni launched the "eSSIF-Lab-to-Market" initiative to continue work on SSI adoption (European Commission, 2022). A similar initiative offering a public utility SSI service is the Sovrin Network, a decentralised digital identity system that enables self-managed identity data. However, the network is scheduled to shut down in March 2025 (Perala, 2024). In 2022, the European Cooperative IDunion Consortium was established by the German Ministry of Economic Affairs, bringing together multiple stakeholders to develop and implement SSI solutions (IDunion, 2025).

In many countries, women face legal and cultural barriers that prevent them from owning land or property. For example, in Tonga, a law from 1875 prohibits women from owning land, restricting their financial independence and economic opportunities (Sefeti, 2024). Blockchain can help secure women's property rights by recording ownership in an immutable ledger, ensuring direct access and transparency, and protecting against illegal seizures. Propy—a platform using blockchain to enhance transparency and security in real estate transactions (Singh, 2023)—is one example of blockchain-based real estate solutions. Another project is Bitland (Ghana), launched in 2016 to digitally register land ownership and provide legal security. The pilot programme initially covered 28 communities in Kumasi, with plans to expand across other regions of Africa. However, publicly available information on the current status of Bitland remains limited (Aitken, n.d.; Miller, 2020).

Women often earn lower wages than men for the same positions. The lack of pay transparency means that many employees remain unaware of salary disparities. A public or private blockchain-based payroll registry could enhance salary transparency, allowing employees to compare wages and promotions within similar roles, enabling them to advocate for equal pay and fair career advancement. Additionally, storing performance evaluations on the blockchain ensures objective and fair assessments of employees' work history. Smart contracts in human resources (HR) can automate salary increases and bonuses based on predefined criteria, eliminating managerial bias in pay adjustments.

Discriminatory hiring practices—such as excluding women from recruitment due to potential pregnancy—remain a significant barrier to gender equality. Blockchain can record and track recruitment processes, ensuring that hiring decisions are made based on qualifications rather than gender. Moreover, blockchain-based data management systems allow for the selective disclosure of applicant credentials, revealing only relevant professional qualifications while concealing demographic details such as gender and age. At the same time, blockchain enables quick and verifiable confirmation of formal qualifications, reducing the risk of credential fraud.

Women who experience sexual harassment often refrain from reporting incidents due to fear of retaliation, while employers may conceal cases of harassment or manipulate records. An immutable harassment report registry would allow for secure and anonymous reporting of abuses, increasing the credibility of cases in legal proceedings.

Although most of SDG 5 focuses on combating discrimination against women, it is important to acknowledge that gender discrimination can also affect men. Men may face challenges in entering professions traditionally viewed as "female-dominated", such as nursing, early childhood education, and social care.

In family court proceedings, men often encounter bias in child custody and alimony cases. A lack of transparency in judicial processes can lead to unfair rulings. Blockchain could help improve transparency in court documentation, ensuring that evidence and rulings are securely recorded and protected from manipulation. As a result, men would have better access to fair legal proceedings, and their rights in child custody cases would be better safeguarded.

According to a 2023 Axios report, the United States is one of the few countries that does not guarantee paid paternity leave, limiting fathers' ability to care for their newborns (Peck, 2023). Blockchain could introduce greater transparency in the allocation of parental leave, eliminating gender-based discrimination and helping reduce bias against women as potential maternity leavers. If both men and women have equal access to parental leave, there would be no incentive to discriminate against one gender over the other. Additionally, smart contracts could automate the management of parental leave policies, ensuring that leave entitlements are granted fairly to both women and men.

Examples of blockchain-based projects that aim to combat gender discrimination include:

- Chrono.tech (formerly ChronoBank)—an Australian blockchain-based HR system designed to prevent hiring discrimination. It integrates LaborX—a global recruitment platform, PaymentX—a cryptocurrency payroll tool, TimeX—a hybrid cryptocurrency exchange, and AUDT stablecoin, pegged to the Australian dollar.
- Smashboard—a non-profit platform founded in 2019 by Indian journalist and activist Noopur Tiwari. Its goal is to support survivors of sexual violence by providing a secure space for reporting incidents and access to a support network (Nagaraj, 2020).

Some blockchain initiatives that previously aimed to improve workplace transparency and verification but are no longer active include WorkChain.io—a platform that enabled real-time salary payments for employees (Petrovic, 2018)—and APPII—a blockchain solution for verifying CVs and employment history (Free-Work, 2017).

Additionally, a persistent gender gap remains evident within the blockchain sector itself, affecting both cryptocurrency users and technology practitioners such as project founders. Although this technology aspires to promote financial empowerment, it has not yet systematically addressed unequal internal participation. For instance, a global survey indicates that while approximately 22% of men own or use cryptocurrencies, only 10% of women do so (Al Tamime et al., 2024). This disparity is rooted in broader socio-cultural factors, including limited decision-making power over household finances, reluctance to engage in high-risk investments, and insufficient female-focused education in finance and technology. Moreover, studies identify further barriers for women aspiring to careers in crypto, such as gender bias, insufficient technological literacy, lack of confidence, and a "crypto bro" culture dominated by affluence and outspoken behaviour.

Bridging the blockchain gender gap, therefore, necessitates simultaneously bridging the gap within the blockchain space itself. In response, a growing movement has emerged to create dedicated spaces for women in blockchain, with the objectives of fostering inclusion, networking, specialised training, and entrepreneurial support. Illustrative examples include SheFi, which offers robust educational resources and a community to help women build careers in the sector, and DLT Talents, an introductory online programme launching its 9th cohort in April 2025. Each cohort includes several hundred participants, many of whom cite this experience as an entry point into the broader crypto ecosystem.

11.5.1.5 SDG 6—Clean Water and Sanitation

In many cities, a significant portion of water is wasted due to leaks, poor management, or misuse. According to the Infrastructure Report Card (2019), the United States loses approximately 2.1 trillion gallons of water annually due to leaks, resulting in financial losses of $7.6 billion. Some cities lose up to 70% of their water due to leaks and illegal connections, which severely impacts both utility companies and consumers (Duffy, 2016).

Water losses can be attributed to unauthorised consumption, measurement errors, or data mismanagement, leading to inaccurate billing and financial discrepancies rozliczeń (Burke & Burks, 2023). Many cities lack early fault detection systems, resulting in significant losses and expensive repairs. In some countries, water is illegally extracted without payment, while in others, a substantial portion of water supplies remains undocumented, contributing to water crises—as seen in Johannesburg, South Africa (Rose & Mark, 2024). Blockchain, integrated with IoT sensors and smart meters, can enable immutable and transparent recording of water usage. It allows for precise tracking of consumption at household, district, and city levels, eliminating billing errors and fraudulent manipulations, and promoting a fairer water management system. Blockchain-based systems can automatically track water flow in real time, log all water infrastructure events, aiding in identifying high-loss areas, and prevent data manipulation regarding leaks and water losses.

Another urban water challenge is the inefficiency of sewage systems, leading to river and groundwater pollution. Furthermore, inadequate monitoring and oversight mechanisms fail to hold polluters accountable (Ducci et al., 2023). Blockchain-based systems can permanently record and share data on water quality and treatment processes, enable real-time automatic wastewater and pollution monitoring through IoT integration, and prevent corruption and manipulation of wastewater treatment data (Xia et al., 2022). Similarly, blockchain can help address inequitable access to clean water in drought-affected regions, unfair distribution of water resources by governments or corporations, and water wastage in agriculture and industry at the expense of local communities.

Water management systems can be particularly beneficial in countries, regions, or cities lacking its centralised oversight, such as Libya (Singh et al., 2023). One example of a blockchain-based water tracking system that eliminates inefficiencies in distribution, improves billing accuracy, and ensures a transparent and immutable record of water transactions is Water Ledger (2025). This platform also serves as a water trading marketplace and supports investment in water infrastructure.

Various types of infrastructure, including water systems, can leverage blockchain technology to facilitate financing and funding mechanisms. While most blockchain-based funding initiatives rely on ICO (Initial Coin Offering), STO (Security Token Offering), or other DeFi-based schemes, blockchain could also support integrated infrastructure financing systems, particularly for local community projects. Such solutions could provide transparency in crowdfunding and investment processes, accountability in infrastructure development and operational costs, and fair cost-sharing models based on actual water consumption (Srokosz et al., 2025). Currently, no fully integrated blockchain-based infrastructure financing models exist. However, some initiatives raise funds through cryptocurrency donations to support clean water access. An example is The Clean Water Coin Initiative, a project under The Water Project, which collects crypto-based donations for water accessibility programmes (The Water Project, 2025).

11.5.1.6 SDG 7—Affordable and Clean Energy

In modern energy markets, large utility companies control energy production, transmission, and distribution. Energy must pass through wholesalers, grid operators, and suppliers before reaching consumers. While these markets are generally regulated to ensure a degree of competition, prosumers—such as owners of photovoltaic installations—often have limited options and can only sell surplus energy to the grid at low rates. Blockchain has the potential to revolutionise the renewable energy sector by enabling decentralised peer-to-peer (P2P) energy trading. With this technology, prosumers—individuals who both produce and consume electricity (e.g., solar panel owners)—can sell excess energy directly to other consumers without intermediaries. This not only reduces costs and increases market efficiency but also accelerates the transition to clean, renewable energy sources. Eliminating intermediaries can lead to somewhat better prices for consumers; in large-scale networks, removing intermediaries reduces customer service costs and maintenance fees associated with centralised power generation, and in local energy-sharing systems, blockchain-based solutions could eliminate network fees entirely, making transactions more cost-effective.

Blockchain, combined with smart contract-based automated settlement systems, can also support energy communities—groups that collectively invest in renewable energy installations and microgrid management systems. These can be either connected to national energy grids or operate off-grid. Blockchain ensures transparent and fair participation among community members, automated energy settlements, as well as decentralised governance of energy production and consumption.

Beyond facilitating direct transactions between energy producers and consumers, blockchain can also enable dynamic energy storage management. This allows for optimised battery charging and discharging within integrated energy management systems. A distributed energy network—consisting of homes equipped with solar panels and battery storage systems—can collaborate as a single power plant and virtual energy storage system (VPP). Through blockchain-enabled coordination, participants can share stored energy as a resource during peak demand and generate revenue by contributing to the distributed energy network. Blockchain presents an optimal solution for managing decentralised energy ecosystems (Lozanova, 2024).

Examples of blockchain initiatives that promote decentralised clean energy trading systems include:

- Energy Web—A non-profit organisation developing an open-source digital infrastructure based on blockchain technology to accelerate decarbonisation and decentralisation of global energy markets. The platform provides tools for integrating distributed energy resources, such as solar installations, battery storage systems, and electric vehicles, as well as a public blockchain optimised for the energy sector. This blockchain enables the identification, registration, and management of energy assets in a decentralised manner (Energy Web, 2020);
- Power Ledger—A blockchain-based platform facilitating peer-to-peer (P2P) energy trading, supporting Virtual Power Plant (VPP) operations by enabling users to trade surplus energy (Lozanova, 2024);
- Brooklyn Microgrid (USA)—One of the first blockchain-based P2P platforms for energy exchange among residents within a single neighbourhood (Brooklyn Microgrid, 2025; Molly, 2017). However, no recent information is available regarding the current status of the project.

Traditional CO_2 emission tracking systems are prone to fraud in emission reporting. Manipulation of CO_2 emission reports by companies is a major issue, undermining trust in corporate environmental declarations and hindering effective climate action.

Discrepancies between changes in revenue and reported emission reductions suggest that such risks are not merely hypothetical. Calculating the full carbon footprint requires data collection from multiple sources, a process that is both time-consuming and costly. As a result, some companies may opt for simplified reporting, omitting key emission sources. Central authorities may also manipulate data, for example, by underreporting national emissions. By providing an immutable and decentralised

CO_2 emission ledger, blockchain—when integrated with IoT sensors that automatically measure and record real emissions—can ensure transparency and consistency in emissions reporting, resilience against data manipulation and corruption, public access to verified emission data, allowing any market participant to check the actual CO_2 emissions of specific companies.

Beyond emission reporting issues, traditional systems also lack transparency in CO_2 reduction claims, which can be exploited to obtain larger carbon credit allocations. Additionally, the buyers and sellers of carbon credits are not always identifiable, and transactions require brokers and institutions, leading to higher costs. Blockchain can address these issues by enabling an automated, transparent, and decentralised carbon credit trading system, a crypto-asset and smart contract-based framework, and an intermediary-free marketplace, reducing transaction costs. Several blockchain initiatives aim to create a transparent and secure ecosystem for tracking and verifying carbon credits (Antier, 2023), including IBM Blockchain for Climate, Veridium, CarbonX, and Climatecoin.

Similar issues to those seen in the CO_2 credit market can arise in the green certificate market. Green certificates can be forged or used multiple times, while manual reporting of renewable energy consumption complicates the verification of actual emission reductions. Additionally, consumers are not always certain whether they are genuinely purchasing renewable energy. Tokenisation of green energy certificates and the organisation of markets through decentralised platforms could help resolve these issues. Furthermore, smart contracts could automatically verify and enforce renewable energy support schemes, such as tax incentives.

An example of a platform enabling the trading of a wide range of renewable energy and carbon emission certificates is ATP GreenX—the first digital green energy marketplace in Turkey, leveraging blockchain technology to secure transactions (ATP GreenX, 2025).

Blockchain could also introduce a "second life" for green certificates through systems that generate tokenised proof of certificate retirement. These could be purchased by companies looking to demonstrate their commitment to supporting renewable energy production.

11.5.1.7 SDG 8—Economic Growth and Decent Work

SDG 8 (Sustainable Economic Growth and Decent Work) aims to increase productivity, create fair employment opportunities, eliminate exploitation, and improve working conditions globally. Blockchain can support this goal by enhancing transparency, reducing labour market abuses, and improving access to financing.

Public blockchain networks naturally integrate with markets, as their core function is the transfer of value. Low-cost global value transfers have the potential to significantly reduce transaction costs in international trade, thereby boosting efficiency and economic productivity. Similarly, blockchain's ability to automate market exchanges, particularly in financial markets, can reduce the role of intermediaries, minimise delays, enhance market liquidity and efficiency, and lower operational costs.

One of the key challenges to economic growth, particularly for small businesses, is access to early-stage financing. Global stock markets are not well-suited for small enterprises, and local markets often lack liquidity. Furthermore, a lack of reliable credit history makes it difficult for micro-enterprises to secure bank loans. Even when banks provide financing, it is often expensive and restrictive. Decentralised Finance (DeFi) has introduced new opportunities for business financing. One of the most commonly used is ICO (Initial Coin Offering)—the issuance of utility tokens in exchange for crypto-assets with recognised market value. Other forms include STO (Security Token Offering)—issuance of tokens classified as financial instruments—and IEO (Initial Exchange Offering)—token issuance through cryptocurrency exchanges, allowing for immediate listing on the exchange. Additionally, there are numerous lending and deposit protocols within DeFi. However, most of these are designed for on-chain trading, relying on over-collateralisation and primarily serving crypto-asset investors rather than real-world businesses. Nonetheless, emerging solutions go beyond these limitations, offering unsecured loans based on alternative credit assessment models (Sobiecki, 2022). These innovations provide small businesses with access to credit and financing without requiring a traditional bank account.

Due to its technical characteristics and natural integration with markets, blockchain has been driving the creation of new business models based on decentralised financial systems (DeFi) for years. While most current blockchain-based services operate within closed-loop value ecosystems inside DeFi, the potential of blockchain extends far beyond these applications, particularly in off-chain economic activities. The solutions and examples presented in this chapter illustrate how blockchain can provide real-world utility beyond existing financial services. Beyond its role in achieving Sustainable Development Goals (SDGs), blockchain also supports the automation of business network relationships and enhances coordination in management processes.

The second major area related to SDG 8 concerns working conditions, labour rights, recruitment, and fair wages.

Many companies—particularly those selling consumer-facing (B2C) products—lack full visibility into working conditions across their supply chains. Issues such as forced labour, worker exploitation, and child labour remain hidden in some regions. Even when businesses require formal declarations from suppliers regarding labour conditions, there is a risk of false claims about ethical practices—a phenomenon known as greenwashing (misleading environmental claims) or fairwashing (misrepresenting fair labour practices). By integrating supply chains, blockchain enables registration and verification of key labour conditions in factories and plantations, ensuring data consistency to prevent exploitation from being concealed. At the same time, it increases transparency for ethical producers, allowing them to prove compliance with fair labour standards. Workers and consumers may also feel empowered to verify whether a company respects labour rights.

Examples of blockchain projects used to verify and track labour conditions include:

- diginexLUMEN—a platform developed by Diginex that enables labour condition monitoring in supply chains, ensuring transparency and compliance with ESG standards. It has been used by companies such as Coca-Cola (Ledger Insights, 2022);
- Provenance—a blockchain-based platform that tracks product origins, providing supply chain transparency so consumers can verify ethical production practices and working conditions at various stages of production (Crudu, 2024).
- eMin—a platform created by The Mekong Club, a non-governmental organisation fighting modern slavery. It allows employment contracts to be securely stored on the blockchain, ensuring that workers have access to verified versions of their agreements. This tool helps businesses audit their supply chains and prevent worker exploitation. The platform has been tested in Thailand, Malaysia, and Bahrain (Angotti & Aydin, 2020).
- EthicHub—a Spain-based social enterprise that functions as a peer-to-peer crowdlending platform. It connects smallholder coffee

farmers, who are excluded from traditional financial opportunities and often face poverty, with funders willing to finance their agricultural activities (EthicHub, 2025).

Just as blockchain can help prevent gender discrimination in hiring, it can also combat other fraudulent practices in recruitment, such as fake job listings, illegal fees imposed on workers, and difficulties in verifying candidate skills and experience. Blockchain can authenticate job postings and facilitate the secure transmission of verified credentials for professional qualifications. An example of a platform that helps manage professional identities is Truvera (formerly Dock.io). It allows users to control their digital credentials, decentralised identities (DID), and professional achievements, enabling them to share their data publicly or privately (Truvera, 2025).

In some countries, workers do not receive their wages on time. Similarly, gig economy workers—such as freelancers, drivers, and couriers—often struggle with payment delays, and international transaction fees can be high, extending the waiting time for their earnings. Blockchain can automate salary payments in cryptocurrencies and stablecoins, while smart contracts can automatically process payments upon task completion, reducing delays and exploitation and increasing efficiency and purchasing power. Examples of platforms that enable global teams and freelancers to receive payments automatically in cryptocurrencies, stablecoins, or local currencies, simplifying international transactions, include Bitwage (2025) and Request Network (2025).

Another issue in the labour market is that employers can unilaterally change employment terms, such as lowering salaries or extending working hours without consent, often through contracts containing unfair clauses. Additionally, in many countries, employment agreements are informal, or workers lack access to their contracts, leading to exploitation. A notable example is the Kafala system in the Middle East, where migrant workers can be deceived about their working conditions (Robinson, 2022). Some employers confiscate workers' identity documents (e.g., passports), preventing them from leaving their jobs. While blockchain cannot eliminate employer misconduct, employment contracts stored as smart contracts can prevent unilateral changes to employment conditions without mutual consent, ensure both parties have permanent access to the contract, and automatically enforce penalties for contract breaches (e.g., late wage payments) when mandated by labour market regulators or adopted voluntarily by ethical employers.

Examples of decentralised employment and contract management platforms include Chrono.tech (previously mentioned) and LaborX (LaborX, 2025).

11.5.1.8 SDG 9—Industry, Innovation, and Infrastructure

Blockchain itself is an innovative technology that broadly supports digitalisation, meaning that its adoption and development inherently contribute to the achievement of this goal. One of the most frequently cited applications of blockchain is its ability to enhance the integrity of supply chains, logistics, and transport systems.

Due to the independent nature of entities involved in supply chains, it is rarely possible to monitor the entire process end-to-end. Neither end customers nor companies often have full visibility into the status of orders, the transportation of raw materials and semi-finished products, or the condition of goods being sold. This lack of oversight leads to losses, inefficiencies, delays, lost shipments, and counterfeit trade. Additionally, fraudulent modifications to transport documentation, such as falsifying the origin of goods, are difficult to detect and eliminate, particularly when records are kept in paper form. The lack of trust among partners necessitates costly audits and verification processes. Blockchain, with its ability to maintain data integrity within a system, combined with automated data entry through IoT integration (e.g., GPS, temperature, and humidity sensors), can ensure that every stage of transportation and storage conditions is recorded immutably. At the same time, blockchain can preserve the integrity of documentation, making it resistant to tampering. If a common platform is built using smart contracts, it can automate payments and formal procedures, triggering transactions only when predefined conditions are met—such as successful delivery of a shipment. In cases where payments rely on traditional financial systems, blockchain could be used to enable decentralised forms of letters of credit. As a result, customers would gain greater confidence in the origin and authenticity of goods.

Another challenge caused by a lack of supply chain integration is high freight costs, which result from poor synchronisation between carriers, freight forwarders, and ports. This lack of coordination generates delays, increased storage expenses, and customs issues that could otherwise be avoided (Salazar, 2024). A fully integrated supply chain, using tokenised transport documents, can reduce the number of intermediaries, increase automation in document approval, and eliminate administrative inefficiencies.

A similar issue arising from the large number of entities involved in supply chains, particularly in international logistics, is the lack of global route optimisation. Goods are sometimes transported via unnecessarily long or indirect routes simply because freight forwarders are unaware that an alternative path, which appears longer, could actually shorten the journey (Arviem, 2020). By integrating supply chains through blockchain, it is possible to merge data from GPS systems and artificial intelligence, enabling the selection of the most efficient routes for transportation (Moudoud et al., 2019).

Several blockchain-based tracking systems have already been implemented to enhance supply chain transparency and efficiency. IBM Food Trust provides end-to-end traceability for food shipments (IBM, 2024a), while Everledger tracks the origin of diamonds, minerals, and luxury goods (Wong, 2024). Similarly, DHL and Accenture have developed a blockchain solution for tracking pharmaceutical shipments (DHL, 2024). UPS has incorporated blockchain to secure shipment data (UPS, 2023). However, not all initiatives in this area have succeeded—the Maersk and IBM TradeLens project for container tracking was discontinued in 2023, as it failed to secure full cooperation from the global shipping industry (PierNext, 2023).

One of the objectives of SDG 9 is to increase the number of researchers and professionals working in research and development (R&D). This can be achieved by expanding access to funding for scientific and technological projects. Blockchain has the potential to optimise grant allocation and research funding processes, reducing bureaucratic inefficiencies and ensuring greater transparency, speed, and global access to funds. It could also facilitate the formation of research teams. Currently, researchers often wait several months for funding decisions, with additional delays due to lengthy proposal preparation processes. Many research projects remain underfunded, and access to resources is often restricted to specific countries or institutions. Even when funding decisions claim to follow methodological selection criteria, transparency issues persist, sometimes leading to biases and favouritism towards particular research institutions. A potential solution is direct community-driven funding through grant crowdfunding, eliminating intermediaries. A decentralised assessment platform based on Decentralised Autonomous Organisations (DAOs) could coordinate fund allocation automatically. A distributed network of experts could collectively evaluate projects, making decisions in a transparent and easily auditable process. Research grants could be disbursed progressively, in line with achievements and project milestones, verified by peer evaluations—with reviewers also receiving incentives for their participation in the system.

Such a blockchain-based research funding system would ensure that funds reach the selected researchers directly, while enhancing transparency and accountability in the use of public funds. This could increase the number of professionals working in R&D. Furthermore, researchers could receive a blockchain-based certificate (NFT token) upon completion of a grant, validating their contributions to the project. In cases where the research leads to publications, patents, or other intellectual property, this system would also make it easier to assess individual contributions to scientific knowledge. An existing example of such implementation is the previously mentioned AthenaDAO.

In line with the previously discussed initiatives, the Decentralized Science (DeSci) movement has emerged as an innovative approach to conducting scientific research. This model uses blockchain technology and Web3 tools to create a more open, transparent, and community-driven scientific ecosystem, facilitating easier funding for research and decentralised publication of results. By integrating tokens, non-fungible tokens (NFTs), and decentralised autonomous organisations (DAOs), DeSci seeks to democratise scientific research, allowing for greater community participation and fairer compensation for contributions to scientific advancements (Strauss, 2023). An example of a DeSci initiative is Bloxberg, a blockchain-based infrastructure developed by the Max Planck Institute to support scientific collaboration and research data verification (Kleinfercher, 2025).

11.5.1.9 SDG 10—Reduced Inequalities

Just as blockchain contributes to gender equality by ensuring fair wages and eliminating workplace discrimination, it can also strengthen social, economic, and political inclusion, regardless of age, disability, race, ethnicity, nationality, religion, or economic status. Additionally, it can help reduce existing inequalities by eliminating discriminatory laws, policies, and practices.

SDG 10 highlights the need for equal access to essential services, the elimination of social and economic barriers, and greater support for marginalised groups. According to the World Bank, approximately one billion people worldwide lack official identification documents. Without a recognised identity, these individuals cannot open bank accounts, establish businesses, secure loans, or legally work, leaving them vulnerable to exploitation. They also face limited access to education, healthcare, and civil rights, including voting rights. Blockchain, through decentralised digital identity systems (SSI-/-DID), provides individuals with an independent and tamper-proof digital identity, even without government-issued documents. These identities are immutable and resistant to manipulation. Furthermore, users retain full control over their personal data, eliminating the need for government databases while allowing them to selectively disclose specific information. With the appropriate interfaces, the authenticity of these digital identities can be verified not only by authorised entities but also by businesses required to verify customer or contractor information in compliance with legal requirements. A similar mechanism can apply to corporate passports, enabling institutions to maintain a verifiable digital identity.

On the other hand, undocumented or unverified immigrants may attempt to manipulate data regarding their origin, age, medical history, or past criminal activities, creating risks and uncertainty for society. The ability of authorised agencies to verify personal data, even from unofficial digital identity records (SSI), could reduce social risks and ensure that all individuals are treated equally under the law.

Additionally, low-cost value transfers enabled by blockchain facilitate cheaper international remittances, not only for businesses and institutions but also for migrant workers, ensuring greater financial inclusion.

A fair taxation system also plays a crucial role in reducing inequality and combating tax evasion. Blockchain allows for the development of transparent tax systems, limiting corruption and money laundering, and thus helping to equalise economic opportunities and reduce income disparities. This can be achieved through dedicated international platforms and programmable digital currencies (Sobiecki & Szwed-Ziemichód, 2019).

11.5.2 SDG 11—Sustainable Cities and Communities

Blockchain can play a key role in supporting the development of smart cities through digitalisation of public services. By leveraging digital identity systems, cities can authenticate residents and grant access to local digital resources, including participatory budgeting and digital voting systems. These solutions can increase the efficiency of urban services by automating processes, reducing operational costs, and improving transparency and data security.

Decentralised technologies can also be used to manage public transportation, public (urban) infrastructure, and municipal data through decentralised ledgers. By decentralising urban registries with blockchain, cities can enhance protection against cyberattacks, ensure transparency in the use of public data, and increase automation in urban administrative processes. Additionally, they can guarantee data permanence and integrity and enable full traceability of historical records.

A blockchain-based registry for building permits enables citizens to verify which companies have received permits and under what conditions, thereby eliminating opportunities for corruption. Additionally, smart contracts can autonomously update registry entries once the required payment has been made by the property owner. If an individual changes their residence, blockchain can automatically notify tax authorities about the need to update official records. An example of such an application can be found in Georgia, where a blockchain-based land registry system ensures the immutability and accessibility of property ownership records (Shang & Price, 2019). In Sweden, a pilot project for blockchain-based real estate transactions was conducted in 2016 (Lantmäteriet, 2016).

Blockchain solutions could also allow drivers to reserve parking spaces without intermediaries or locate available parking spots in real time, reducing traffic congestion and the time spent searching for parking. Smart contracts could automatically calculate fees based on the actual duration of parking. This application would be particularly beneficial in cities with multiple independent parking operators, including small private car parks. While there are no significant implementations in this area yet, several conceptual studies have been proposed (Amiri et al., 2021; Gaurav & Baranwal, 2024; Kalbhor et al., 2024).

The integration of IoT and blockchain allows for real-time data collection on traffic conditions, vehicle maintenance status, and delays, enabling dynamic route adjustments based on actual urban mobility needs. A blockchain-based solution would be particularly useful in metropolitan areas with multiple independent public transport providers, ensuring they coordinate effectively to maintain a seamless urban transportation system.

Similar to blockchain applications in water supply and wastewater management, the technology can also be used to track pollution emissions and improve air and soil quality, as well as enhance waste management efficiency. Decentralised networks of environmental sensors can continuously monitor air quality in real time, ensuring secure data transmission and immutability of recorded measurements. An example of such an implementation is a system described by Vaneeta et al., which employs machine learning algorithms to predict air quality categories and then stores the data on a blockchain platform, eliminating any possibility of data manipulation (Vaneeta et al., 2023). Blockchain can also be used to create transparent pollution reporting systems for businesses. Organisations could track, store, and share emission data in an immutable and verifiable manner, promoting better environmental management practices. Locus Technologies, for example, has proposed a blockchain-based system for aggregating emissions reports, allowing for faster and more reliable sharing of environmental data with regulatory agencies (Duplan, 2018).

In waste management, blockchain can ensure full transparency and traceability at every stage—from waste generation to transportation and disposal. By registering each step in a decentralised ledger, the system minimises fraud and illegal dumping practices. In the context of a circular economy, blockchain facilitates tokenisation systems that assign digital value to recycled materials, incentivising reuse and promoting sustainable practices. An example of this is Plastic Bank, which rewards individuals collecting plastic waste in developing countries by issuing digital tokens exchangeable for goods or services (Taylor et al., 2020).

11.5.3 SDG 12—Responsible Consumption and Production

Blockchain's ability to track products and documentation throughout supply chains has already been discussed in previous sections. However, this capability is also directly relevant to SDG 12, supporting responsible production and consumption. By preserving the history of documentation, products, and raw materials within supply chains—including diamonds, food, and textiles—blockchain helps eliminate unethical practices such as conflict diamonds ("blood diamonds") or illegal fishing. It also contributes to reducing raw material waste, minimising environmental damage, and increasing transparency in sustainability reporting. With permanent records of production and emissions, consumers can make informed purchasing decisions, while companies are incentivised to maintain high ethical and environmental standards. Blockchain enables businesses to monitor and report their sustainability practices transparently, increasing stakeholder and consumer trust (Toher, 2024).

Beyond tracking product histories, blockchain also supports secondary product circulation by enabling the tokenisation of recycled materials, incentivising recycling through reward programmes, and monitoring waste processing. These functionalities help eliminate illegal dumping sites and reduce environmental pollution.

An example of a blockchain-powered circular economy solution is KleanLoop. This platform utilises blockchain and data analytics to optimise material recovery and recycling processes. Originally designed for end-of-life tyres, KleanLoop provides a transparent and secure marketplace for trading recycled materials and recycling services (Klean Industries, 2025). The platform enables direct information and resource exchange among producers, logistics providers, and recyclers, eliminating the need for intermediaries. KleanLoop also introduces digital tokens representing real-world secondary raw materials, simplifying tracking, valuation, and global trading. Furthermore, it incorporates artificial intelligence (AI) for market data analysis, providing users with up-to-date insights into the recycling sector and supporting informed business decisions (Klean Industries, 2019). Another relevant initiative is RecycleGO, which, like KleanLoop, focuses on creating a transparent and secure marketplace for secondary raw materials. However, RecycleGO specialises in logistics management within the recycling industry, offering route optimisation tools and automated invoicing solutions (RecycleGO, 2025). A third example is Circularise, a blockchain solution designed to support the circular economy by providing digital product passports. These passports contain key data on materials, components, and final products, allowing companies to share information about raw material origins, production processes, and certifications while protecting confidential data and intellectual property (Circularise, 2025).

The first key task under SDG 12 is the implementation of ten-year programmes promoting sustainable consumption and production. Long-term initiatives involving multiple sovereign entities with a shared goal create ideal conditions for blockchain adoption. The technology can provide a decentralised and tamper-proof registry, storing critical data on progress towards the ten-year plan. Due to data redundancy, such a system would be resilient against manipulation and changes in stakeholder groups. Each participant holds a copy of the records, and blockchain synchronisation mechanisms ensure consistency. Additionally, smart contracts can streamline policy implementation procedures, ensuring automatic enforcement. In cases of non-compliance, these contracts could trigger penalties or environmental fees, reinforcing sustainable development commitments.

11.5.3.1 SDG 13—Climate Action

Many climate-related initiatives align with those promoting clean energy and sustainability, making blockchain-based solutions supporting SDG 13 similar to those discussed previously. The technology can facilitate carbon credit tokenisation to improve emissions offset mechanisms, enhance transparency in corporate environmental reporting, enable precise tracking of pollution levels and energy consumption in enterprises, and monitor and verify corporate sustainability initiatives, ensuring compliance with regulations.

11.5.4 SDG 14—Life Below Water

As a general-purpose technology, blockchain can play a key role in marine ecosystem protection by tracking the legality of fishing activities and combating illegal practices, supporting ocean pollution reduction initiatives, and facilitating real-time monitoring of marine ecosystems.

Blockchain enables the registration and verification of every stage of the seafood supply chain—from fishing to sale—making it difficult for illegally caught fish to enter the market (Ismail et al., 2023). A notable example is Indonesia's pilot project using blockchain to track tuna provenance, implemented through the Provenance platform. This initiative helped identify and eliminate illegal fishing activities, ensuring greater sustainability in the industry (Provenance, 2016).

The integration of blockchain with IoT devices enables the real-time collection and analysis of environmental data, such as water temperature and pollution levels, supporting the sustainable management of marine resources. Furthermore, blockchain can track the journey of plastic waste from collection through recycling to reuse, ensuring transparency and efficiency in waste management processes.

Tracking products in secondary circulation and waste streams is a key feature of previously mentioned solutions, such as Circularise. However, several other blockchain initiatives specifically focus on marine conservation. One such example is Plastic Bank, a blockchain-powered platform incentivising ocean clean-up efforts. It allows residents in impoverished regions to collect plastic waste and exchange it for essential goods and services, including school fees, healthcare, internet access, and cooking fuel. To date, Plastic Bank has helped collect nearly eight billion plastic bottles. The collected plastic is reprocessed and reintroduced into supply chains as "Social Plastic®", which companies can use to manufacture sustainable packaging and products. In collaboration with IBM, Plastic Bank has developed a blockchain-based platform to ensure traceability and transparency at every stage of the plastic collection and recycling process. Each transaction is recorded on a blockchain ledger, enabling auditability and fostering trust among stakeholders and local communities. Additionally, Plastic Credits function within the system. Companies seeking to reduce their environmental footprint can purchase Plastic Credits, with each credit representing a specific amount of collected and processed plastic. This model supports the financial sustainability of plastic collection initiatives, ensuring that collectors are fairly compensated for their efforts (Plastic Bank, 2024).

Other blockchain-powered initiatives aimed at reducing plastic pollution include:

- Plastiks—a platform that enables companies to monitor and document plastic recovery and recycling efforts (Plastiks, 2025).
- ReSea Project, mobilising local communities to collect marine waste, while ensuring verification and documentation of these activities (ReSea Project, 2025).
- Empower, building a global plastic recycling ecosystem based on blockchain technology, allowing plastic waste to be exchanged for digital tokens (Empower, 2025).

11.5.5 SDG 15—Life on Land

Just as blockchain facilitates tracking of raw materials, luxury goods, food, plastics, chemicals, water, energy, and CO_2, it can also support land conservation efforts, particularly forest protection initiatives. The technology can monitor deforestation activities in real-time, prevent illegal logging, and enhance accountability in cases of environmental violations. By recording data on forest health and land use, blockchain ensures that any unauthorised deforestation can be detected and investigated efficiently.

Blockchain technology enables the tracking of every stage in the harvesting and transportation of timber, from logging to the final product, making it more difficult to introduce illegally sourced wood into the market. A notable example comes from Brazil's pulp and paper industry, which is investing in blockchain solutions to comply with the European Union's deforestation-free product requirements (Mendes, 2024). Additionally, blockchain can be used to monitor the trade of endangered species and regulate timber markets, helping to identify the origin of wood and curb illegal logging. While there are currently few fully operational blockchain-based timber marketplaces, there are already supply chain tracking solutions in development. One key initiative is the Forest Stewardship Council (FSC) blockchain platform, designed to facilitate traceability compliance for FSC certificate holders. This platform enables the verification of supplier certification status, the generation of product statements, and the recording of essential raw material data, such as the origin plot and tree species. This ensures alignment with new regulations, including the EU Deforestation Regulation (EUDR) (FSC, 2023). Another innovative approach has been proposed by Shibano, Nakajima, and Mogi (2022), who developed a blockchain system incorporating zero-knowledge proofs (ZKP) for timber traceability verification. By combining ZKP with NFC technology, their system guarantees data integrity while preventing unauthorised entities from falsifying records.

Beyond supply chain tracking, the integration of blockchain with satellite technology and the Internet of Things (IoT) enables real-time forest cover monitoring. This allows for the rapid detection of unauthorised logging and deforestation activities. For example, Forest 4.0, a project led by researchers from Lithuania and Sweden, employs big data, artificial intelligence, IoT, and blockchain to create a transparent forest management model (Gaurav & Baranwal, 2024). Moreover, blockchain's capacity for immutable data storage supports long-term monitoring of endangered species populations, preventing data manipulation and strengthening biodiversity conservation efforts.

11.5.6 SDG 16—Peace, Justice, and Strong Institutions

In the implementation of the previously described SDG goals, the potential of blockchain for coordinating activities or decentralising processes was not explicitly accentuated (although it can be indirectly utilised in each of them). However, when it comes to supporting efforts towards peace, justice, and strong institutions—where decision-making plays a crucial role—this potential can be particularly useful.

Blockchain can enhance the transparency of government systems and electoral processes, significantly reducing the risk of election fraud at various administrative levels. It enables the creation of digital identities, voter registries, and decentralised voting mechanisms, ensuring tamper-proof and verifiable elections. By using cryptographic security mechanisms, blockchain protects the integrity of votes, preventing modifications after they have been recorded in the system. This transparency and automation can increase public trust in electoral processes and reduce concerns about manipulation or fraud (Singh et al., 2024). One of the most notable real-world applications of blockchain-based e-voting was West Virginia's pilot test in the United States in 2018, which used the Voatz platform to allow overseas citizens to vote remotely (Nguyen, 2018). Several other countries have also experimented with blockchain-based voting, including Switzerland (2018) (swissinfo.ch, 2018), Japan (2018) (Ledger Insights, 2020), and Russia (2020) (Ledger Insights, 2021).

Blockchain-based e-voting can be applied to national elections, local elections, citizen-driven initiatives, and even corporate governance voting. In 2018, the city of Tsukuba in Japan introduced a blockchain-based online voting system, allowing residents to participate in decision-making for social initiatives (AWS, 2025). Additionally, in November 2018, Thailand's Democratic Party conducted an internal leadership election using blockchain, with over 120,000 votes cast securely (Panyaarvudh & Chanwanpen, 2018).

On the other hand, blockchain is a registry-based technology. The database created by blockchain mechanisms primarily stores records, and most solutions are not designed to handle large amounts of data. This makes the creation of immutable public ownership registries (e.g., land records) in developing countries a particularly optimal use of this technology. Beyond increasing automation and facilitating citizen services, it can also help reduce corruption risks and strengthen institutions by improving their efficiency. In this context, blockchain serves as a layer that preserves records, provides tokenised entries and transactions that reflect registry changes, and secures a highly transparent public access to data. An example of a land registry using blockchain is the previously mentioned initiatives in Georgia and Sweden. Another notable case is the state of Andhra Pradesh in India, which, in collaboration with the company Zebi, implemented a pilot project utilising blockchain for land registration. This project resulted in a 50% reduction in land ownership disputes and a 30% increase in transaction efficiency (Common Share, 2024).

Ensuring a fair and transparent aid process in humanitarian organisations, as discussed in the context of blockchain's support for SDG 1, is a key application of this technology. Beyond the example of *Building Blocks*, which focuses on fighting hunger and poverty, other projects contribute to strengthening humanitarian institutions in alternative ways, such as by facilitating the collection and tracking of funds.

For instance, the organisation *Finn Church Aid*, in collaboration with the company *Solita*, has explored the potential of blockchain technology in enhancing the speed and transparency of financial donations, as well as improving operational efficiency and tracking the allocation of aid funds (Solita, 2025).

11.5.6.1 SDG 17—Partnerships for the Goals

The final SDG, which blockchain helps to achieve, leverages many of the mechanisms previously described. Blockchain enables transparent tracking of aid funds and international grants directed towards organisations supporting the implementation of SDG-related initiatives, such as sustainable development projects and ESG programs. It can facilitate the monitoring of grant execution and automate payments through smart contracts, ensuring that disbursements occur according to a predefined schedule or only when specific conditions are met. Additionally, blockchain can support global collaboration platforms by eliminating intermediaries in cross-border fund transfers.

A particularly relevant application of blockchain in achieving SDG 17 is its ability to create platforms that connect sovereign entities—including governments, public institutions, investors, and communities—allowing them to collectively store and permanently record evidence of progress towards SDG 17 and other sustainability goals. This capability enhances the tracking of Agenda 2030 implementation and ensures accountability in global partnerships.

11.6 SDGs That Blockchain May Hinder

While blockchain can support the achievement of the Sustainable Development Goals (SDGs), it can also pose challenges to their realisation. Research suggests that blockchain may impede at least six SDGs due to factors such as high energy consumption, CO_2 emissions, and environmental impact (SDG 7, SDG 12, SDG 13), digital exclusion and unequal access to technology (SDG 10), the speculative nature of cryptocurrencies, as well as regulatory challenges, anonymity issues, and risks associated with financial crimes (SDG 16, SDG 17). Below is an analysis of how blockchain implementation may hinder the progress of certain SDGs.

11.6.1 SDG 7—Clean and Affordable Energy

The primary issue is the high energy consumption of consensus mechanisms, particularly Proof of Work (PoW), which requires immense computational power to validate transactions. According to the Cambridge Bitcoin Electricity Consumption Index (CBECI), at the beginning of 2025, Bitcoin's network had an annualised electricity consumption of 175 terawatt-hours (TWh), exceeding the yearly energy use of countries such as Sweden, Belgium, or Finland (CBECI, 2025). This intensive energy demand significantly increases CO_2 emissions, contradicting global efforts to decarbonise the economy. Cryptocurrency mining, especially for Bitcoin and Ethereum before its transition to Proof of Stake (PoS), has driven up electricity consumption. In countries with low energy costs, such as China and Kazakhstan, mining operations often rely on non-renewable sources, exacerbating environmental harm. Such practices hinder the energy transition and the shift towards cleaner energy sources.

Although alternative consensus mechanisms like Proof of Stake are far less energy-intensive and can reduce the carbon footprint by up to 99.9%, their adoption remains limited. The dominance of energy-hungry blockchains may weaken global climate initiatives and slow the development of sustainable solutions in the energy sector. As a result, a technology with the potential to enhance transparency and efficiency across various industries simultaneously poses an obstacle to achieving clean energy goals. However, it is worth noting that an increasing number of cryptocurrency mining operations now rely on renewable energy. According to a 2022 report by the Bitcoin Mining Council, the ban on cryptocurrency mining in China led to a significant rise in the use of renewable energy for Bitcoin extraction (Buckler, 2022). One such initiative is Genesis Digital Assets Limited (GDA), which in 2023 opened an environmentally friendly Bitcoin mining facility in Sweden powered by hydroelectric energy.

11.6.1.1 SDG 10—Reduced Inequalities

Its implementation requires internet access, advanced digital infrastructure, and appropriate technical skills. In developing countries, where access to these resources is limited, this can exacerbate digital exclusion and social inequality. According to a report by UNCTAD, the lack of adequate infrastructure and technological skills in these regions constitutes a significant barrier to the adoption of blockchain technology (UNCTAD, 2024). Moreover, the still persistent issue of mobile gender gap which results in women and girls being less likely than men and boys to own or use a smartphone, further hinders their adoption of blockchain. Since a mobile phone is often the primary means of accessing cryptocurrencies, this disparity limits their participation in blockchain-based financial ecosystems (GSMA, 2024).

Moreover, the speculative nature of cryptocurrencies may contribute to widening wealth disparities. Individuals with financial knowledge and capital can profit from cryptocurrency investments, while less experienced investors, often from lower-income groups, are more vulnerable to financial losses due to the high volatility of these assets. Research highlights the potential for cryptocurrency price manipulation and the use of schemes that would be either prohibited or impossible in traditional markets, leading to unfair gains for privileged market participants at the expense of less informed investors (Makarov & Schoar, 2020).

Additionally, a significant portion of cryptocurrency holdings is concentrated in the hands of a small group of individuals. An analysis conducted by *The Wall Street Journal* reveals that 0.01% of Bitcoin holders control 27% of all available coins, which can further entrench wealth concentration and deepen economic inequality (Vigna, 2021).

Consequently, despite the potential of blockchain technology to promote financial inclusion, its current applications may, in some cases, contribute to growing inequality, particularly in communities with limited access to modern technology and financial education.

11.6.1.2 SDG 12—Responsible Consumption and Production

As previously mentioned, cryptocurrency mining requires significant energy inputs and specialised computer hardware. This equipment often becomes obsolete quickly, leading to the generation of substantial amounts of electronic waste (e-waste). According to research published by Greenpeace, in 2021, the Bitcoin network produced approximately 30.7 kilometric tonnes of e-waste annually due to outdated ASIC (Application-Specific Integrated Circuit) devices (G. Singh, 2024).

Furthermore, the absence of uniform regulations and sustainability standards in blockchain projects can result in greenwashing practices. Some companies may present their solutions as environmentally friendly without genuinely meeting the relevant environmental criteria. Greenwashing undermines consumer trust and hinders the development of truly sustainable products and markets (Nygaard & Silkoset, 2023).

To address these challenges, the introduction of global standards and regulations promoting transparency and sustainability in blockchain technologies is essential. Only through such measures can technological advancements align with the goals of responsible consumption and production.

11.6.1.3 SDG 13—Climate Action

Blockchain technology, particularly in the context of cryptocurrencies such as Bitcoin, poses challenges to achieving SDG 13. The primary concern, as previously mentioned, is the high energy consumption of blockchain networks.

Additionally, the lack of effective carbon offset mechanisms within the blockchain ecosystem makes it difficult to mitigate its climate impact. While some initiatives leverage blockchain to enhance transparency and efficiency in carbon markets, their effectiveness remains limited, and the technology is still in its early stages of implementation in this domain (Mills, 2022).

Moreover, certain blockchain projects may engage in greenwashing practices. The absence of standardised regulations and verification mechanisms makes it difficult to assess their actual environmental impact, potentially delaying efforts to protect the climate.

11.6.1.4 SDG 16—Peace, Justice, and Strong Institutions

One of the main challenges is the anonymity of blockchain transactions, which makes it difficult to identify users and may facilitate criminal activities such as money laundering, terrorism financing, and tax evasion. As noted in a Europol report, cryptocurrencies are frequently used for money laundering and the trade of illegal goods and services online (Europol, 2021).

The decentralised nature of blockchain and the lack of uniform regulations hinder governments and international organisations from effectively overseeing its applications. This situation can lead to financial fraud, market manipulation, and other unethical practices, ultimately undermining trust in financial institutions and legal systems.

Smart contracts and the widely adopted DAO structures for coordinating DeFi services raise questions about the legal accountability of stakeholders within these frameworks. In cases of coding errors, fraud, or unforeseen circumstances, determining liability for resulting damages is challenging. The absence of standardised regulatory frameworks for smart contracts across jurisdictions further complicates their enforcement and dispute resolution (Perrin & Agnihotri, 2022; Townsend & Hanna, 2023). Finally, the irreversible nature of blockchain transactions means that erroneous or fraudulent transactions cannot be easily reversed, potentially leading to permanent financial losses for affected parties. This lack of appeal mechanisms may discourage users and erode trust in blockchain-based systems.

11.6.1.5 SDG 17—Partnerships for the Goals

One of the main challenges in achieving SDG 17 is the lack of uniform international regulations on blockchain technology and cryptocurrencies. Governments and international organisations have not established consistent guidelines in this area, leading to legal discrepancies between countries and hindering global cooperation.

Additionally, some nations, such as China, have imposed a complete ban on cryptocurrency transactions, limiting the potential use of blockchain technology in international projects. In 2021, the People's Bank of China prohibited all cryptocurrency-related transactions, citing the need to curb financial crime and safeguard the country's economic stability (Shin, 2022).

The absence of unified standards and regulations at the international level, combined with differing national approaches to blockchain technology, presents significant barriers to global collaboration. These discrepancies make it difficult to implement standardised solutions and slow the development of partnerships essential for achieving the Sustainable Development Goals.

11.7 The Role of Public Institutions and Regulations in Achieving SDGs Through Blockchain

Many solutions that support the achievement of the SDGs do not necessarily require blockchain technology. However, as demonstrated in this chapter, blockchain offers specific utilities that centralised technologies cannot provide. When adopting blockchain technology, businesses can choose from a wide range of features, utilities, and functionalities. They have the option to select only those that align with the SDGs. Proper adaptation of the technology—such as using more environmentally friendly consensus algorithms, implementing regulations, and increasing public education about blockchain—can help minimise negative impacts while enhancing its positive contribution to the SDGs.

However, businesses operate within market constraints and are driven by profit. If the market demands blockchain utilities that conflict with the SDGs, companies are likely to prioritise them. On the other hand, blockchain's potential to support a particular goal does not automatically guarantee its technical feasibility or financial viability. A solution that benefits customers does not always provide sufficient returns for the service provider to justify the costs of its development and maintenance, making investment in such solutions less likely.

Additionally, blockchain's features are not always sought after by customers. Transparency, anonymity, and personal control may be less important than a provider's reputation, convenience, or the ability to verify users' identities. In the financial sector, individual clients often prefer traditional banks and payment institutions over decentralised DeFi platforms, as they value stability, deposit insurance, and the ability to regain account access if they lose their credentials. Similarly, in the healthcare sector, patients may not be interested in full control over their medical records if it entails greater responsibility and the need to manage access themselves.

Blockchain applications are not always strictly consumer-oriented (B2C) or fit within the traditional B2B model—some solutions do not readily align with commercial applications. Blockchain's greatest utility lies in its role as a "trust technology"—a system that enables automation and the immutable recording of interactions between sovereign entities, such as companies within supply chains. Its primary value emerges in platform-based solutions that create markets or integrate different environments.

For this reason, public institutions can play a crucial role. Their involvement is particularly important because projects funded and developed by businesses primarily reflect commercial goals rather than social ones. The SDGs, by contrast, are universal, public, and social in nature, and their realisation often conflicts with business objectives. For instance, an HR system that allows employees to monitor salary structures may not necessarily be welcomed by companies using it. Public institutions, therefore, have a role in encouraging and promoting "Blockchain for Bood" (Adams et al., 2018; Seyedsayamdost & Vanderwal, 2020).

On the one hand, these institutions can develop blockchain-based solutions themselves. Blockchain has inherent features that make it well-suited for products that involve multiple independent parties (Sobiecki et al., 2024). In some cases, supporting SDG implementation through blockchain is not feasible without regulatory intervention from central authorities or supervisory bodies—for example, the introduction of employment contracts in the form of smart contracts, a decentralised land registry system, or blockchain-based electoral processes. The challenges associated with developing large-scale Self-Sovereign Identity (SSI) systems illustrate that the creation of such solutions requires national and, at times, international cooperation, involving investors, developers, and public institutions. Ultimately, these institutions are responsible for meeting the public needs of citizens (Sobiecki et al., 2024).

On the other hand, regulators of crypto-asset markets and other blockchain applications can introduce regulations that promote or even mandate solutions supporting the SDGs. Such regulations are already being implemented, although they do not always explicitly reference the achievement of SDG targets.

The EU Regulation 2023/1114, commonly referred to as "Markets in Crypto-Assets" (MiCA) (EU, 2023), has introduced disclosure requirements regarding environmental impact for token issuers and Crypto Asset Service Providers (CASPs). Financial institutions will be required to report their energy consumption and carbon footprint related to crypto activities, particularly in the case of Proof of Work (PoW) algorithms. At the same time, the EU is actively promoting more energy-efficient technologies, such as Proof of Stake (PoS), to reduce blockchain's negative environmental impact. These measures contribute to the achievement of SDG 13 (Climate Action).

MiCA has also introduced more transparent regulations to protect investors and reduce the risk of market manipulation. By ensuring access to secure financial services, it fosters the growth of cryptocurrency-based and fintech-driven economies, supporting SDG 8 (Decent Work and Economic Growth).

Similarly, regulating a market that has so far operated without clear legal frameworks supports the achievement of SDG 16 (Peace, Justice, and Strong Institutions). Establishing regulations for crypto-assets enhances financial stability, reduces the risk of money laundering and terrorism financing (AML/CFT), and aims to prevent fraud and unfair practices, thereby strengthening the rule of law and market transparency.

The EU considers sustainable development a key element of its economic policy, and MiCA is part of a broader regulatory framework that incorporates Environmental, Social, and Governance (ESG) principles. It is likely that additional future regulations will address the environmental impact of crypto-assets, potentially including CO_2 emissions limitations or the promotion of low-energy blockchain technologies.

11.8 Conclusion

The analysis above demonstrates not only the theoretical and logically justified potential of blockchain technology but also its real-world applicability, as confirmed by the examples provided. However, this remains an evolving field. Blockchain has the capacity to impact all 17 Sustainable Development Goals (SDGs). Its effectiveness, however, depends on appropriate regulations and standards, the ability to mitigate blockchain's negative impacts, particularly on the environment, the education of all stakeholders, and the engagement of public institutions. As a relatively young general-purpose technology, blockchain also requires further research and innovation to maximise its positive effects and minimise its drawbacks.

Public institutions play a crucial role in harnessing this potential by creating conditions that support businesses aligned with SDG objectives while preventing the growth of those that hinder their achievement. Blockchain is fundamentally dependent on the existence of a physical network, without which it cannot function. Access to energy and network infrastructure is essential and must be systemically (market-driven) ensured. Without these, the benefits of blockchain remain purely hypothetical or highly limited. At the same time, blockchain-based solutions must offer a highly refined, intuitive user experience (UX) due to the complexity of blockchain systems. Finally, continuous education based on reliable sources can serve as a catalyst for advancing SDG implementation through blockchain applications.

Several recommendations can be drawn from the analysis for further research and regulators. Research and development efforts should focus on optimising blockchain technology through energy-efficient consensus mechanisms to mitigate environmental impacts. Scholars should systematically assess the socioeconomic implications of blockchain applications, identifying conditions under which blockchain contributes positively or negatively to achieving the SDGs. Furthermore, academic research should strive to develop robust frameworks and methodologies for evaluating blockchain's transparency, accountability, and inclusivity outcomes. This involves interdisciplinary collaboration to address technical, ethical, economic, and social dimensions comprehensively.

A future research agenda addressing these recommendations should encompass several critical avenues. First, there is a need for empirical studies evaluating blockchain's long-term impact on social equity, particularly concerning marginalised and economically disadvantaged populations. Second, researchers should prioritise developing scalable decentralized digital identity systems (DIDs) that promote financial and social inclusion, especially in developing economies. Third, future research must explore blockchain's integration with other emerging technologies (such as artificial intelligence and the Internet of Things) to enhance sustainability and efficiency across sectors including agriculture, healthcare, energy, and governance. Lastly, comparative studies examining different blockchain governance models—including decentralised autonomous organisations (DAOs)—could provide valuable insights into optimising democratic participation and accountability within blockchain-enabled ecosystems.

Policymakers, on the other hand, are urged to establish clear, enabling regulatory environments that support responsible blockchain adoption, and not blocking the development of the technology. Such regulations should emphasise transparency, data security, digital inclusion, and equitable access, ensuring that blockchain solutions are accessible even in resource-constrained regions. Policy efforts should also include support for public–private partnerships to scale successful blockchain initiatives effectively. Additionally, policymakers must remain vigilant against unintended consequences, such as digital exclusion or increased socioeconomic disparities resulting from the uneven distribution of blockchain's benefits.

Addressing these areas through coordinated academic research and informed policymaking will significantly contribute to maximising blockchain's benefits while proactively managing its risks, thus ensuring its sustainable integration into global development efforts.

References

Aave. (2025). *Aave*. Aave.Com. https://aave.com/

Abdallah, S., & Nizamuddin, N. (2023). Blockchain-based solution for Pharma Supply Chain Industry. *Computers & Industrial Engineering, 177*, Article 108997. https://doi.org/10.1016/j.cie.2023.108997

Adams, R., Kewell, B., & Parry, G. (2018). Blockchain for good? Digital ledger technology and sustainable development goals. In W. Leal Filho, R. W. Marans, & J. Callewaert (Eds.), *Handbook of Sustainability and Social Science Research* (pp. 127–140). Springer. https://doi.org/10.1007/978-3-319-67122-2_7

Agriledger. (2024). *Agriledger*. https://agriledger.com/

Aitken, R. (n.d.). *Bitland's African blockchain initiative putting land on the ledger*. Forbes. Retrieved 15 February, 2025, from https://www.forbes.com/sites/rogeraitken/2016/04/05/bitlands-african-blockchain-initiative-putting-land-on-the-ledger/

Al Tamime, R., Strohmaier, M., & Weber, I. (2024). Exploring Global gender gaps in the blockchain domain: Insights from LinkedIn advertising data. In *2024 IEEE International Conference on Big Data (BigData)* (pp. 3075–3081). https://doi.org/10.1109/BigData62323.2024.10825073

Alder, S. (2019, June 24). Vulnerabilities in servers behind majority of healthcare data breaches. *The HIPAA Journal*. https://www.hipaajournal.com/vulnerabilities-in-servers-behind-majority-of-healthcare-data-breaches/

Alder, S. (2025, January 2). The most common HIPAA Violations you must avoid—2025 update. *The HIPAA Journal*. https://www.hipaajournal.com/common-hipaa-violations/

Alvarez, E., Bielska, I. A., Hopkins, S., Belal, A. A., Goldstein, D. M., Slick, J., Pavalagantharajah, S., Wynfield, A., Dakey, S., Gedeon, M.-C., Alam, E., & Bouzanis, K. (2023). Limitations of COVID-19 testing and case data for evidence-informed health policy and practice. *Health Research Policy and Systems, 21*(1), 11. https://doi.org/10.1186/s12961-023-00963-1

Amiri, W. A., Baza, M., Banawan, K., Mahmoud, M., Alasmary, W., & Akkaya, K. (2021). *Privacy-preserving smart parking system using blockchain and private information retrieval*. arXiv:1904.09703. arXiv. https://doi.org/10.48550/arXiv.1904.09703

Angotti, A., & Aydin, B. (2020, September 16). *Using technology to battle forced labor in supply chain*. https://guidehouse.com/insights/financial-crimes/b20/technology-to-battle-forced-labor-in-supply-chain?utm_source=chatgpt.com

Antier. (2023, July 17). Blockchain carbon credit software: The future of sustainable business. https://www.antiersolutions.com/blogs. https://www.antiersolutions.com/blogs/blockchain-carbon-credit-software-the-future-of-sustainable-business/

Arviem. (2020, July 22). *Common inefficiencies of logistics networks and how visibility helps to address them! | Arviem Cargo Monitoring*. https://arviem.com/common-inefficiencies-of-logistics-networks-and-how-visibility-helps-to-address-them/

AthenaDAO. (2025). *AthenaDAO | Advancing Women's Health Research*. https://www.athenadao.co/

ATP GreenX. (2025). ATP GreenX. *ATP*. https://www.atptech.com/atp-greenx/?lang=en

AWS. (2025). *AWS implementation case study: Tsukuba City | AWS*. Amazon Web Services, Inc. https://aws.amazon.com/solutions/case-studies/tukuba/

Azaria, A., Ekblaw, A., Vieira, T., & Lippman, A. (2016). MedRec: Using blockchain for medical data access and permission management. In *2016 2nd International Conference on Open and Big Data (OBD)* (pp. 25–30). https://doi.org/10.1109/OBD.2016.11

Bitwage. (2025). *Simplify global payroll & workforce payments | bitwage*. https://bitwage.com/en-us/

Blockcerts. (2025). *Blockchain credentials*. Blockcerts. http://blockcerts.org/

Brooklyn Microgrid. (2025). *Brooklyn Microgrid | Community Powered Energy*. Brooklyn Microgrid. https://www.brooklyn.energy

Buckler, N. (2022, August 9). *Mining Bitcoina wykorzystuje teraz 10,9% więcej źródeł energii odnawialnej*. BeInCrypto Polska. https://pl.beincrypto.com/mining-bitcoina-wykorzystuje-teraz-109-wiecej-zrodel-energii-odnawialnej/

Burke, E. B., & Burks, B. (2023). *Lost water: Challenges and opportunities* (Sustainability Insights). S&P Global. https://www.spglobal.com/_assets/documents/ratings/research/101585883.pdf?utm_source=chatgpt.com

Campos, A., & Proença, J. (2024). Sustainable development goals and blockchain: A systematic literature review from a business studies perspective. *European Conference on Innovation and Entrepreneurship, 19*(1), 881–891. https://doi.org/10.34190/ecie.19.1.2719

Carrara, G. J. & MD. (2024). *Impact of data fragmentation in healthcare*. https://www.boyden.com/media/impact-of-data-fragmentation-in-healthcare-24386669/

CBECI. (2025, February). *Cambridge blockchain network sustainability index*. https://ccaf.io/cbnsi/cbeci

Chen, C.-L., Zhu, Z.-P., Zhou, M., Tsaur, W.-J., Wu, C.-M., & Sun, H. (2022). A secure and traceable vehicles and parts system based on blockchain and smart contract. *Sensors*, *22*(18), Article 18. https://doi.org/10.3390/s22186754

Chen, J., Ruan, Y., Guo, L., & Lu, H. (2020). BCVehis: A blockchain-based service prototype of vehicle history tracking for used-car trades in China. *IEEE Access, 8*, 214842–214851. https://doi.org/10.1109/ACCESS.2020.3040229

Circularise. (2025). *Circularise | Product traceability platform for supply chain compliance*. https://www.circularise.com/

Common Share. (2024, September 9). *India's blockchain revolution: Transforming land registry for greater transparency*. https://news.commonshare.com/blog/india-s-blockchain-revolution-transforming-land-registry-for-greater-transparency?utm_source=chatgpt.com

Compound Labs. (2025). *Compound*. https://compound.finance

CreDA. (2024, April 18). CreDA, the Credit Data Alliance. *Medium*. https://creda-app.medium.com/creda-is-back-as-an-ai-powered-data-service-fc4724ddb3ae

Crudu, V. (2024, April 15). *Exploring the use of blockchain for ethical labor practices in the supply chain | MoldStud*. https://moldstud.com/articles/p-exploring-the-use-of-blockchain-for-ethical-labor-practices-in-the-supply-chain?utm_source=chatgpt.com

DC4EU Consortium. (2025, February 13). *Digital credentials for Europe*. DC4EU. https://www.dc4eu.eu/

DHL. (2024, February 20). *Blockchain in supply chain management: Streamline logistics with DHL*. https://www.dhl.com/discover/en-id/logistics-advice/logistics-insights/how-dhl-express-streamline-the-supply-chain

DIF. (2025). *DIF—Decentralized Identity Foundation*. https://identity.foundation/

Doxychain. (2024, April 8). *Unlock the benefits of blockchain for digital certificates*. https://www.doxychain.com/blog/benefits-of-blockchain-for-digital-certificates

Ducci, L., Rizzo, P., Pinardi, R., Solfrini, A., Maggiali, A., Pizzati, M., Balsamo, F., & Celico, F. (2023). What is the impact of leaky sewers on groundwater contamination in urban semi-confined aquifers? A test study related to fecal matter and Personal Care Products (PCPs). *Hydrology*, *10*(1), Article 1. https://doi.org/10.3390/hydrology10010003

Duffy, D. P. (2016, May 26). *Non-revenue water loss: its causes and cures*. WaterWorld. https://www.waterworld.com/home/article/14070145/non-revenue-water-loss-its-causes-and-cures

Duplan, N. (2018, August 21). Blockchain: Aggregate emissions reporting. *Locus Technologies*. https://ltweb-stage.locustec.com/blog/blockchain-aggregate-emissions-reporting/

Ekblaw, A. (2017). *MedRec: Blockchain for medical data access, permission management and trend analysis* [MIT]. https://www.media.mit.edu/publications/medrec-blockchain-for-medical-data-access-permission-management-and-trend-analysis/

Elliptic. (2025). *CipherTrace Alternative*. https://info.elliptic.co/schedule-demo-elliptic-ciphertrace-alternative

Empower. (2025). *The future of plastic is circular*. https://www.empower.eco/

Energy Web. (2020, June). *EW-DSO: The energy web decentralized operating system*. https://cdn.prod.website-files.com/65e5b22cf7f0480a007420fc/66636832be155a40f00ea44e_EnergyWeb-EWDOS-PART2-TechnologyDetail-202006-vFinal.pdf

EthicHub. (2025). *EthicHub—Create social impact investing online or buying to our farmers*. https://www.ethichub.com/en

EU. (2023). *Regulation (EU) 2023/1114 of the European Parliament and of the Council of 31 May 2023 on markets in crypto-assets, and amending Regulations (EU) No 1093/2010 and (EU) No 1095/2010 and Directives 2013/36/EU and (EU) 2019/1937*. https://eur-lex.europa.eu/eli/reg/2023/1114/oj/eng

European Commission. (2022). *Final Common SSI Framework*. CORDIS | European Commission. https://cordis.europa.eu/project/id/871932/reporting

Europol. (2021). *Cryptocurrencies—Tracing the evolution of criminal finances*. Publications Office of the European Union; https://doi.org/10.2813/75468. https://www.europol.europa.eu/cms/sites/default/files/documents/Europol%20Spotlight%20-%20Cryptocurrencies%20-%20Tracing%20the%20evolution%20of%20criminal%20finances.pdf?utm_source=chatgpt.com

FAO. (2016, June 30). *FAO Food policy series: Food loss and waste*. FoodLossWaste. https://www.fao.org/platform-food-loss-waste/resources/multimedia/video/fao-food-policy-series-food-loss-and-waste/en

Free-Work. (2017, December 14). *Create a blockchain verified CV*. Free-Work. https://www.free-work.com/en-gb/tech-it/blog/it-skills/create-a-blockchain-verified-cv

FSC. (2023, March 16). *Home | Forest Stewardship Council*. https://fsc.org/en

Gaurav, K. K., & Baranwal, G. (2024). A blockchain-enabled private parking space allocation with improved parking space utilization. *Computers & Industrial Engineering, 197*, Article 110613. https://doi.org/10.1016/j.cie.2024.110613

Giveth. (2025). *Giveth: Future of giving with zero-fee crypto donation*. https://giveth.io/

GSMA. (2024). *The mobile gender gap report 2024*. https://www.gsma.com/r/wp-content/uploads/2024/05/The-Mobile-Gender-Gap-Report-2024.pdf?utm_source=website&utm_medium=button&utm_campaign=gender-gap-2024

Hackett, M. (2020, October 7). Digital health passport CommonPass begins testing to help travel and trade resume. *MobiHealthNews*. https://www.mobihealthnews.com/news/digital-health-passport-commonpass-begins-testing-help-travel-and-trade-resume

Hamza, M. (2019, February 6). All you need to know about uPort Identity management. *Medium*. https://medium.com/@hamzamaslah/all-you-need-to-know-about-uport-identity-management-3fc49db25332

Hayden, C. (2025, February 10). Data fragmentation: The key healthcare challenge of our time? *Digital Health*. https://www.fiercehealthcare.com/digital-health/data-fragmentation-key-healthcare-challenge-our-time

IBM. (2024a, February 2). *IBM Food Trust*. https://www.ibm.com/docs/en/food-trust?topic=overview

IBM. (2024b, November 8). *Food logistics on blockchain*. https://www.ibm.com/blockchain/resources/food-trust/food-logistics/www.ibm.com/blockchain/resources/food-trust/food-logistics

ID4Africa. (2025). *ID4Africa—identity for all in Africa*. https://id4africa.com/

IDunion. (2025). *Historie—IDunion*. https://idunion.org/en/historie/

Infosys. (2025). *Blockchain in the Pharmaceutical Industry | Infosys*. https://www.infosys.com/services/blockchain/offerings/pharma-supply-chain.html

IPFS. (2025). *An open system to manage data without a central server*. IPFS. https://ipfs.tech

Ismail, S., Reza, H., Salameh, K., Kashani Zadeh, H., & Vasefi, F. (2023). Toward an intelligent blockchain IoT-enabled fish supply Chain: A review and conceptual framework. *Sensors, 23*(11), 5136. https://doi.org/10.3390/s23115136

Jadhav, S. (2021, October 4). Digital Health Passport on Amazon Managed Blockchain. *IBM Blog*. https://www.ibm.com/blog/digital-health-passport-on-amazon-managed-blockchain/

Jiang, S., Jakobsen, K., Bueie, J., Li, J., & Haro, P. H. (2022). A Tertiary review on blockchain and sustainability with focus on sustainable development goals. *IEEE Access, 10*, 114975–115006. https://doi.org/10.1109/ACCESS.2022.3217683

Johnson, L. (2025). *BurstIQ*. BurstIQ. https://www.burstiq.com/Build-Solutions-With-LifeGraph®/

Joshi, P., Tewari, V., Kumar, S., & Singh, A. (2023). Blockchain technology for sustainable development: A systematic literature review. *Journal of Global Operations and Strategic Sourcing, 16*(3), 683–717. https://doi.org/10.1108/JGOSS-06-2022-0054

Kalbhor, A., Nair, R. S., Phansalkar, S., Sonkamble, R., Sharma, A., Mohan, H., Wong, C. H., & Lim, W. H. (2024). PARKTag: An AI–blockchain integrated solution for an efficient, trusted, and scalable parking management system. *Technologies, 12*(9), Article 9. https://doi.org/10.3390/technologies12090155

Klean Industries. (2019, September 19). *KleanLoop a decentralized blockchain DApp for creating transparency in tyre and plastic recycling*. RecyclingInside. https://recyclinginside.com/recycling-technology/instrumentation-and-control/kleanloop-a-decentralized-blockchain-dapp-for-creating-transparency-in-tyre-and-plastic-recycling/

Klean Industries. (2025, February 11). *Klean Industries' SaaS Klean Loop™ blockchain garners interest for new sustainability solutions beyond end-of-life tires | Klean Industries*. https://kleanindustries.com/investors/press-releases/saas-klean-loop-blockchain-new-sustainability-solutions-beyond-end-of-life-tires/

Kleinfercher, F. (2025). *The Max Planck decentralized science initiative: DeSci Connect—MPDL*. https://www.mpdl.mpg.de/45-service/1019-desci-service.html?utm_source=chatgpt.com

LaborX. (2025, January 31). *Crypto Jobs: Web3 & Blockchain & Cryptocurrency Jobs list*. LaborX. https://laborx.com/

Lantmäteriet. (2016). *The Land Registry in the blockchain*. Lantmäteriet. https://ica-it.org/pdf/Blockchain_Landregistry_Report.pdf?utm_source=chatgpt.com

Ledger Insights. (2020, November 9). *Japan's Tsukuba City to use blockchain-based electronic voting*. Ledger Insights—Blockchain for Enterprise. https://www.ledgerinsights.com/japans-tsukuba-city-to-use-blockchain-based-electronic-voting/

Ledger Insights. (2021, September 24). *Russia trials blockchain voting in controversial parliamentary elections*. Ledger Insights—Blockchain for Enterprise. https://www.ledgerinsights.com/russia-trials-blockchain-voting-in-controversial-parliamentary-elections/

Ledger Insights. (2022, March 17). *Coca-Cola partners Diginex for ESG supply chain traceability using blockchain*. Ledger Insights—Blockchain for Enterprise. https://www.ledgerinsights.com/coca-cola-partners-diginex-for-esg-supply-chain-traceability-using-blockchain/

Lozanova, S. (2024, October 10). *Virtual Power Plants (VPPs) Explained*. GreenLancer. https://www.greenlancer.com/post/virtual-power-plants-vpps

Makarov, I., & Schoar, A. (2020). Trading and arbitrage in cryptocurrency markets. *Journal of Financial Economics, 135*(2), 293–319. https://doi.org/10.1016/j.jfineco.2019.07.001

Medivault. (2024). *The Hidden Barrier to Effective Healthcare | Medivault*. https://medivault.org/post/fragmented-medical-records-the-hidden-barrier-to-effective-healthcare

Mendes, K. (2024, December 16). *Brazil paper and pulp industry invests in blockchain to comply with EUDR*. Mongabay Environmental News. https://news.mongabay.com/2024/12/brazil-paper-and-pulp-industry-invests-in-blockchain-to-comply-with-eudr/

Microsoft. (2025, January 27). *Introduction to Microsoft Entra Verified ID - Microsoft Entra Verified ID*. https://learn.microsoft.com/en-us/entra/verified-id/decentralized-identifier-overview

Miller, M. (2020, September 24). Bitland: Property rights for the world's poor. *The Borgen Project*. https://borgenproject.org/property-rights-for-the-worlds-poor/

Mills, R. (2022, November 11). *Beyond the Buzz: What can blockchain do for carbon markets?* RMI. https://rmi.org/what-can-blockchain-do-for-carbon-markets/

Molly. (2017, April 11). The Brooklyn microgrid: Blockchain-enabled community power. *Power Technology*. https://www.power-technology.com/features/featurethe-brooklyn-microgrid-blockchain-enabled-community-power-5783564/

Mortensen, K. S. (2023, November 22). *Blockchain for digital certificates*. Diplomasafe. https://diplomasafe.com/blockchain-certification-process/

Moudoud, H., Cherkaoui, S., & Khoukhi, L. (2019). An IoT blockchain architecture using oracles and smart contracts: The Use-Case of a Food Supply Chain. In *2019 IEEE 30th Annual International Symposium on Personal, Indoor and Mobile Radio Communications (PIMRC)* (pp. 1–6). https://doi.org/10.1109/PIMRC.2019.8904404

Nagaraj, A. (2020, January 8). Encrypted app aims to boost sex crime reporting in India. *Reuters*. https://www.reuters.com/article/world/encrypted-app-aims-to-boost-sex-crime-reporting-in-india-idUSKBN1Z720R/

Nguyen, T. (2018, August 10). West Virginia to offer mobile blockchain voting app for overseas voters in November election. *Washington Post*. https://www.washingtonpost.com/technology/2018/08/10/west-virginia-pilots-mobile-blockchain-voting-app-overseas-voters-november-election/

Nygaard, A., & Silkoset, R. (2023). Sustainable development and greenwashing: How blockchain technology information can empower green consumers. *Business Strategy and the Environment, 32*(6), 3801–3813. https://doi.org/10.1002/bse.3338

Odem. (2021). Online Education & Course Marketplace | What is ODEM? *Odem.Cloud*. https://wp.odem.cloud/c/odem-trust-network/

Oxfam International. (2024, February 13). *UnBlocked Cash Project: Using blockchain technology to revolutionize humanitarian aid*. Oxfam International. https://www.oxfam.org/en/unblocked-cash-project-using-blockchain-technology-revolutionize-humanitarian-aid

Panyaarvudh, J., & Chanwanpen, K. (2018, November 30). *Reliable voting TECHNOLOGY*. Nationthailand. https://www.nationthailand.com/in-focus/30359633

Peck, E. (2023, February 28). *Majority of countries guarantee paid paternity leave—But not the U.S.* https://www.axios.com/2023/02/28/majority-of-countries-guarantee-paid-paternity-leave-but-not-the-us?utm_source=chatgpt.com

Perala, A. (2024, October 21). *'The Community Moved On': Sovrin Announces MainNet's 'Likely Shutdown'*. https://idtechwire.com/the-community-moved-on-sovrin-announces-mainnets-likely-shutdown/

Perrin, C. R., & Agnihotri, R. (2022, May 20). Liability for digitally autonomous organizations. *Blockchain and Banking Blog*. https://frostbrowntodd.com/liability-for-digitally-autonomous-organizations/

Petrovic, I. (2018, October 18). Introducing WorkChain.io: The blockchain solution for the future of payroll—Make Everyday Payday. *WorkChain.Io*. https://medium.com/workchain-io/introducing-workchain-io-the-blockchain-solution-for-the-future-of-work-89df3ba9e2ea

Philbin, M. M., Everett, B. G., & Auerbach, J. D. (2024). Gender(ed) science: How the institutionalization of gender continues to shape the conduct and content of women's health research. *Social Science & Medicine (1982), 351*(Suppl 1), 116456. https://doi.org/10.1016/j.socscimed.2023.116456

PierNext. (2023, January 26). Why Maersk and IBM's blockchain platform TradeLens is closing down. *PierNext*. https://piernext.portdebarcelona.cat/en/technology/the-closure-of-tradelens/

Plastic Bank. (2024, September 4). *Plastic Bank | 7 Billion Plastic Bottles Gathered by Hand*. https://plasticbank.com/

Plastiks. (2025). *Plastiks—Plastic Recycling Traceability*. https://www.plastiks.io/

Price, M., & Gargiulo, M. (2021, June 24). Lies, Damned Lies, and "Official" Statistics—Health and Human Rights Journal. *Health and Human Rights*. https://www.hhrjournal.org/2021/06/24/lies-damned-lies-and-official-statistics/

Prior, A., Vestergaard, C. H., Vedsted, P., Smith, S. M., Virgilsen, L. F., Rasmussen, L. A., & Fenger-Grøn, M. (2023). Healthcare fragmentation, multimorbidity, potentially inappropriate medication, and mortality: A Danish nationwide cohort study. *BMC Medicine, 21*, 305. https://doi.org/10.1186/s12916-023-03021-3

Prisco, G. (2016, April 26). *The Blockchain for Healthcare: Gem Launches Gem Health Network with Philips Blockchain Lab—Bitcoin Magazine—Bitcoin News, Articles and Expert Insights*. https://bitcoinmagazine.com/business/the-blockchain-for-heathcare-gem-launches-gem-health-network-with-philips-blockchain-lab-1461674938

Provenance. (2016, July 15). *From shore to plate: Tracking tuna on the blockchain*. Provenance. https://legacy.provenance.org/tracking-tuna-on-the-blockchain

Rashid, M. M., Choi, P., Lee, S.-H., & Kwon, K.-R. (2022). Block-HPCT: Blockchain enabled digital health passports and contact tracing of infectious diseases like COVID-19. *Sensors, 22*(11), 4256. https://doi.org/10.3390/s22114256

RealT, Inc. (2025). *RealT*. RealT, Inc. https://realt.co/

RecycleGO. (2025). *Blockchain tracks entire life cycle of recycled materials*. https://www.recyclego.com/post/blockchain-tracks-entire-life-cycle-of-recycled-materials

Request Network. (2025). *Request Network Foundation*. https://request.network/

ReSea Project. (2025). *Our project | How we do it | ReSea Project*. ReSea Project Main. https://www.reseaproject.com/our-project

Robinson, K. (2022, November 18). *What Is the Kafala System? | Council on Foreign Relations*. https://www.cfr.org/backgrounder/what-kafala-system

Rose, R., & Mark, M. (2024, December 30). Johannesburg bears brunt of South Africa's water crisis. *Financial Times*.

Salazar, D. (2024, October 30). *How port congestion & capacity constraints impact freight rates | ExFreight | USA*. https://www.exfreight.com/how-port-congestion-capacity-constraints-impact-freight-rates/?utm_source=chatgpt.com

Salim, M., Khan, P. A., Jalil, N. A., Johl, S. K., Jafar, S. H., Irfan, F., & Khan, M. (2023). Fusion of blockchain and sustainable development goals: A bibliometric analysis for future trends. *KnE Social Sciences*, 633–654. https://doi.org/10.18502/kss.v8i20.14629

Sankoh, O. (2017). Why population-based data are crucial to achieving the Sustainable Development Goals. *International Journal of Epidemiology, 46*(1), 4–7. https://doi.org/10.1093/ije/dyx010

Sapp, S. (2022, January 14). Philadelphia CBP Intercepts Fake COVID Vax Card—One of 30K Seized Nationally. *U.S. Customs and Border Protection*. https://www.cbp.gov/newsroom/local-media-release/philadelphia-cbp-intercepts-fake-covid-vax-card-one-30k-seized

Sefeti, S. (2024, September 13). 'We can't even buy our own land': The Tongan women pushing for change. *The Guardian*. https://www.theguardian.com/world/2024/sep/14/we-cant-even-buy-our-own-land-the-tongan-women-pushing-for-change

Seyedsayamdost, E., & Vanderwal, P. (2020). From good governance to governance for good: Blockchain for social impact. *Journal of International Development, 32*(6), 943–960. https://doi.org/10.1002/jid.3485

Shang, Q., & Price, A. (2019). A blockchain-based land titling project in the Republic of Georgia: Rebuilding public trust and lessons for future pilot projects. *Innovations: Technology, Governance, Globalization*, *12*(3). https://doi.org/10.1162/inov_a_00276

Shibano, K., Nakajima, T., & Mogi, G. (2022). *Wood traceability system using blockchain and zero-knowledge proof*. arXiv:2211.11136. arXiv. https://doi.org/10.48550/arXiv.2211.11136

Shin, F. (2022, January 31). What's behind China's cryptocurrency ban? *World Economic Forum*. https://www.weforum.org/stories/2022/01/what-s-behind-china-s-cryptocurrency-ban/

Singh, A.-T., Eskenazi, A., Ruttenberg, F., Kort, M., & Sitanggang, R. V. (2023). *Blockchain and IoT for drinking water: A game-changing opportunity or a risky proposition*.

Singh, G. (2020, March 27). MiPasa project and IBM Blockchain team on open data platform to support Covid-19 response. *IBM Blog*. https://www.ibm.com/blog/mipasa-project-and-ibm-blockchain-team-on-open-data-platform-to-support-covid-19-response/

Singh, G. (2024, April 22). *Bitcoin's E-Waste Problem is Hiding in Plain Sight—Greenpeace*. Greenpeace. https://www.greenpeace.org/usa/bitcoins-e-waste-problem-is-hiding-in-plain-sight/

Singh, I., Kaur, A., Agarwal, P., & Idrees, S. M. (2024). Enhancing security and transparency in online voting through blockchain decentralization. *SN Computer Science, 5*(7), 921. https://doi.org/10.1007/s42979-024-03286-2

Singh, S. (2023, March 8). How blockchain empowers women in developing economies. *Cointelegraph*. https://cointelegraph.com/explained/how-blockchain-empowers-women-in-developing-economies

Sobiecki, G. (2022). Zdecentralizowane finanse osobiste (eng. Decentralized personal finance). In K. Waliszewski (Ed.), *Finanse osobiste (eng. Personal Finance): Vol. 2 (14)* (2022nd ed., p. 450). Polska Akademia Nauk. https://publikacje.pan.pl/chapter/124238/waliszewski-red-krzysztof-finanse-osobiste-2022?language=pl

Sobiecki, G., & Szwed-Ziemichód, M. (2019). Wykorzystanie technologii blockchain do eliminacji wybranych problemów systemu podatkowego—Przegląd i analiza rozwiązań (eng. Using Blockchainl Technology to Eliminate Selected Problems of the Tax System). *Analizy i Studia CASP (eng. Analyses and Studies CASP)*, *7*(1), 3–32. https://doi.org/10.33119/ASCASP.2019.1.1

Sobiecki, G., Wisła, J., & Marucha-Jaworska, M. (2024). Państwo w sieci blockchain (eng. The state in the blockchain network). In *Raport SGH i Forum Ekonomicznego 2024 (ang. Report for the XXXIII Economic Forum in Karpacz in 2024)* (1st ed., pp. 233–290). Oficyna Wydawnicza SGH; https://doi.org/10.33119/978-83-8030-678-3.2024. https://www.forum-ekonomiczne.pl/projekty/raport-sgh-i-forum-ekonomicznego

Solita. (2025). *How blockchain can increase trust and transparency in humanitarian aid*. Solita. https://www.solita.fi/work/how-blockchain-can-increase-trust-and-transparency-in-humanitarian-aid/

Srokosz, W., Lenio, P., & Sobiecki, G. (2025). *Blockchain technology in project finance. A legal and practical model for financing mega-investments.* (1st ed.). Routledge. https://doi.org/10.4324/9781003568797

Strauss, C. (2023, July 27). *Unlocking scientific innovation through decentralized science—Part I*. Stanford Law School. https://law.stanford.edu/2023/07/27/unlocking-scientific-innovation-through-decentralized-science-part-i/

swissinfo.ch. (2018, July 2). Switzerland's first municipal blockchain vote hailed a success. *SWI Swissinfo.Ch*. https://www.swissinfo.ch/eng/business/crypto-valley-_-switzerland-s-first-municipal-blockchain-vote-hailed-a-success/44230928

Szarata, A. (2023, October 30). *Doświadczenia Politechniki Krakowskiej związane z opracowywaniem i wydawaniem mikropoświadczeń (eng. Experience of the Krakow University of Technology in developing and issuing micro-credentials)*. https://www.gov.pl/attachment/0389bef6-6260-4d10-8c3b-15bf70909197

Taylor, P., Steenmans, K., & Steenmans, I. (2020). Blockchain technology for sustainable waste management. *Frontiers in Political Science*. https://doi.org/10.3389/fpos.2020.590923

TE-FOOD. (2025). *TE-FOOD*. https://te-food.com/

The Water Project. (2025). *Clean Water Coin—myWaterProject*. The Water Project. https://thewaterproject.org/community/profile/clean-water-coin

Toher, J. P. (2024, October 9). *Can blockchain improve transparency in sustainability reporting?* Human Kind. https://thehumankind.co/2024/10/09/can-blockchain-improve-transparency-in-sustainability-reporting/

Townsend, M., & Hanna, R. (2023, June 15). Managing DAO-related risks. *Perspectives | Reed Smith LLP*. https://www.reedsmith.com/en/perspectives/2023/06/managing-dao-related-risks

Truvera. (2025, January 22). *Truvera overview | Truvera Documentation portal*. https://docs.truvera.io

UN. (2015). *A/RES/70/1 Transforming our world: The 2030 Agenda for Sustainable Development*.

UNCTAD. (2024). *Harnessing blockchain technologies for sustainable development*.

UPS. (2023, December 22). How UPS forwarding hub utilizes blockchain technology. *FreightAmigo*. https://www.freightamigo.com/blog/how-ups-forwarding-hub-utilizes-blockchain-technology/

Vaneeta, M., Deepa, S. R., Sangeetha, V., Kamalakshi, N., S, V. K., J, A., M, N., & R, S. H. (2023). Tamper proof air quality management system using blockchain. *International Journal of Advanced Computer Science and Applications*, *14*(2). https://doi.org/10.14569/IJACSA.2023.0140232

Vigna, P. (2021, December 20). Bitcoin's 'One Percent' Controls Lion's Share of the Cryptocurrency's Wealth. *Wall Street Journal*. https://www.wsj.com/articles/bitcoins-one-percent-controls-lions-share-of-the-cryptocurrencys-wealth-11639996204

Water Ledger. (2025). *Water Ledger | Blockchain Platform for Water Management*. https://www.waterledger.com/

Wei, W.-Q., Leibson, C. L., Ransom, J. E., Kho, A. N., Caraballo, P. J., Chai, H. S., Yawn, B. P., Pacheco, J. A., & Chute, C. G. (2012). Impact of data fragmentation across healthcare centers on the accuracy of a high-throughput clinical phenotyping algorithm for specifying subjects with type 2 diabetes mellitus. *Journal of the American Medical Informatics Association : JAMIA*, *19*(2), 219–224. https://doi.org/10.1136/amiajnl-2011-000597

WHO. (2024, December 3). *Substandard and falsified medical products*. https://www.who.int/news-room/fact-sheets/detail/substandard-and-falsified-medical-products

Wigley, S. (2022). *Regime type and data manipulation: Evidence from the COVID-19 pandemic* (p. 2022.12.11.22283310). medRxiv. https://doi.org/10.1101/2022.12.11.22283310

Wong, G. (2024, July 13). *Radical transparency? Blockchain is making diamond sourcing more accountable*. South China Morning Post. https://www.scmp.com/magazines/style/luxury/jewellery/article/3267986/blockchain-tech-making-diamond-sourcing-more-accountable-and-major-players-gia-luxury-brands-are

World Bank. (2024, October 15). *Measuring Poverty* [Text/HTML]. World Bank. https://www.worldbank.org/en/topic/measuringpoverty

World Food Programme. (2025). *Building Blocks*. https://www.wfp.org/building-blocks

Xia, W., Chen, X., & Song, C. (2022). A framework of blockchain technology in intelligent water management. *Frontiers in Environmental Science, 10*, 909606. https://doi.org/10.3389/fenvs.2022.909606

CHAPTER 12

Digital Currencies Challenges for Green Economy in Poland

Robert Dygas

12.1 Introduction

The concept of the "green economy" has become central to Poland's economic and environmental policy in recent years. Defined by the United Nations Environment Programme (UNEP) as an economy that results in "improved human well-being and social equity, while significantly reducing environmental risks and ecological scarcities" (UNEP, 2011), a green economy seeks to harmonize economic growth with sustainable practices. Poland, with its long-standing reliance on coal as a primary energy source, faces particular challenges in transitioning to a low-carbon economy. Yet, as digital currencies gain traction worldwide, they introduce both challenges and opportunities for Poland's green economic ambitions. Historically, Poland's economy has depended on coal, which accounted for nearly 70% of its energy production as of 2020 (International Energy Agency [IEA], 2020). While this dependency on coal has contributed significantly to the national GDP, it has also

R. Dygas (✉)
SGH Warsaw School of Economics, Warsaw, Poland
e-mail: Rdygas1@sgh.waw.pl

R. Aneja and R. Dygas (eds.), *Digital Currencies and the Green Economy*, https://doi.org/10.1007/978-981-95-2282-8_12

resulted in some of the highest levels of greenhouse gas emissions in the European Union. Consequently, transitioning towards renewable energy sources is crucial for Poland to meet EU-wide commitments under the European Green Deal, which aims for net-zero greenhouse gas emissions by 2050 (European Commission, 2019). However, the shift from coal to renewable energy is complex and costly, necessitating investments in infrastructure, policy reform, and public–private partnerships (European Commission, 2019).

At the same time, Poland's digital economy, particularly the use and mining of digital currencies such as Bitcoin, adds a layer of complexity to its environmental goals. Cryptocurrency mining, a process requiring significant computational power and, therefore, energy, predominantly relies on electricity from fossil fuels in Poland, further complicating the path to a green economy (Cambridge Centre for Alternative Finance [CCAF], 2022). As demand for digital currencies grows, it is essential to consider their environmental impact and explore ways to integrate renewable energy sources into their production.

Digital currencies, especially those using Proof of Work (PoW) mechanisms, require intensive energy consumption, which in Poland primarily translates to a higher carbon footprint due to coal-based electricity. Research by Stoll et al. (2019) highlights that Bitcoin mining alone consumes more electricity annually than some entire nations, exacerbating environmental issues in coal-reliant countries like Poland (Stoll et al., 2019). Since digital currencies are borderless, the environmental implications of mining activities are globally distributed. However, Poland's heavy coal dependence means that its contribution to the global environmental footprint of digital currencies is disproportionately high.

According to a study from the Cambridge Bitcoin Electricity Consumption Index, Poland ranks among the top 20 countries in Bitcoin mining, with its energy primarily sourced from non-renewable sources (Cambridge Centre for Alternative Finance, 2022). This positioning makes it imperative for the country to explore alternative energy sources, such as solar, wind, or hydroelectric power, to align cryptocurrency operations with green economic goals. As such, fostering a green economy in Poland requires a dual strategy: shifting general energy production to renewables and incentivizing the digital currency sector to adopt cleaner, less energy-intensive technologies.

Digital currencies, while energy-intensive, also present opportunities for innovation in green financing. Blockchain technology, which underpins most cryptocurrencies, offers transparent and traceable systems that can aid in sustainable development initiatives. For instance, blockchain can facilitate carbon credit trading, renewable energy certifications, and green financing, aligning digital assets with Poland's environmental objectives (Schletz et al., 2020). By embracing these applications, Poland could leverage blockchain to support its green economy transition.

However, realizing these synergies requires regulatory frameworks that balance environmental sustainability with technological innovation. The Polish government has initiated steps to regulate digital currencies, including a tax on cryptocurrency transactions. Nevertheless, there is an urgent need for comprehensive policies that incentivize sustainable practices in the sector. As highlighted by Hassler and Volkova (2021), policy measures that promote Proof of Stake (PoS) over Proof of Work (PoW) in cryptocurrency mining could drastically reduce the environmental impact of digital currencies, making them more compatible with green economy goals (Hassler & Volkova, 2021).

Despite these potential benefits, digital currency integration into Poland's green economy faces multiple challenges. The lack of renewable infrastructure and the prevalence of energy-intensive PoW mechanisms pose significant barriers. Moreover, as Poland increases its adoption of digital currencies, it risks exacerbating its carbon footprint unless it shifts towards more sustainable mining practices (Schulz, 2021). Thus, achieving a green economy will require Poland not only to modernize its energy infrastructure but also to introduce targeted regulations in the digital currency sector.

For Poland, the journey towards a green economy necessitates a multipronged approach, balancing traditional industry reform with the innovative potential of digital technologies. Digital currencies can either hinder or accelerate Poland's green economy transition, depending on the energy sources used and the regulatory frameworks adopted. While the government is advancing renewable energy goals, there is a clear need for policies specific to digital currencies that encourage sustainable practices, potentially transforming Poland into a pioneer of green finance in Eastern Europe.

By addressing these interrelated issues, Poland could achieve a model of economic growth that is both sustainable and technologically advanced. This would position the country not only as a responsible participant in the European Green Deal but also as a leader in sustainable digital finance. Digital currencies, notably cryptocurrencies like Bitcoin, Ethereum, and others, represent an evolving segment of the financial landscape that provides a decentralized framework for transactions. These currencies utilize blockchain technology, which underpins their transparency, security, and resistance to fraud. However, digital currency mining, particularly under the Proof of Work (PoW) protocol, is computationally intensive and demands substantial energy resources, raising concerns about its environmental impact.

Poland's energy profile, characterized by a high dependency on coal, poses specific challenges in integrating digital currencies into an economy striving to meet EU-mandated carbon reduction targets. As a European Union member, Poland is committed to the Green Deal, which emphasizes a transition to a low-carbon economy, aiming for net-zero emissions by 2050. The inherent contradiction between energy-intensive digital currencies and sustainable economic development creates a pressing need for regulatory and technological solutions that address environmental externalities.

This chapter aims to evaluate the environmental challenges posed by digital currencies to Poland's green economy goals. It explores the implications of cryptocurrency mining's carbon footprint on Poland's environmental objectives and examines regulatory measures that could mitigate these impacts. Additionally, the chapter considers alternative blockchain mechanisms and policy frameworks to support sustainable digital finance practices in Poland.

12.2 Methodology

The study adopts a mixed-methods approach, combining a literature review, data analysis, and case studies. This multifaceted approach enables a comprehensive examination of both the theoretical and practical implications of digital currencies for Poland's green economy. Data is gathered from primary and secondary sources. Primary sources include reports and statistics from Poland's Ministry of Climate and Environment, Narodowy Bank Polski (NBP), and EU environmental agencies. Secondary sources comprise academic journals, technical papers, and reports from environmental organizations such as Greenpeace and Cambridge Centre for Alternative Finance. The analytical framework focuses on key variables, including energy consumption metrics (kWh per transaction), carbon emissions (metric tonnes of CO_2 equivalent), and economic externalities. Environmental impact assessments (EIAs) and carbon footprint models are used to quantify the potential effect of cryptocurrency activities in Poland. A comparative analysis is also conducted to contrast the environmental costs of PoW with less energy-intensive models, such as Proof of Stake (PoS).

12.3 Literature Review

Digital currencies, encompassing cryptocurrencies and central bank digital currencies (CBDCs), are increasingly intersecting with the green economy, particularly in Poland. This literature review examines the challenges digital currencies pose to Poland's green economy, drawing from scholarly works published between 2020 and 2024. The review highlights key themes such as regulatory frameworks, technological integration, public perception, and financial instruments, providing insights into the complexities of aligning digital currencies with sustainable development goals. The National Bank of Poland (NBP) has adopted a cautious stance on issuing a digital zloty, citing a lack of clear benefits and potential risks to the financial system (NBP, 2024). This prudence reflects concerns about financial stability and the readiness of existing infrastructures to support CBDCs. Polish regulators, such as the Financial Supervision Authority (KNF), continue to view crypto-assets as high-risk, emphasizing consumer protection and financial security (Chambers & Partners, 2024). This regulatory hesitancy may impede the integration of digital currencies into green financial initiatives. The successful deployment of digital currencies in support of the green economy necessitates robust technological infrastructure. Poland has made strides in digitalization, with significant investments in gigabit connectivity and the digitalization of SMEs (European Commission, 2024). However, the adoption of advanced technologies like artificial intelligence and blockchain remains limited, potentially hindering the scalability and efficiency of digital currency platforms. Furthermore, the energy consumption associated with blockchain technologies raises environmental concerns. Studies have highlighted the need for sustainable blockchain solutions to mitigate the carbon footprint of digital currencies (Kozar & Wodnicka, 2024). Balancing technological advancement with environmental sustainability is crucial for aligning digital currencies with green economy objectives.

Public perception plays a vital role in the adoption of digital currencies. Research indicates a growing awareness of cryptocurrencies among Poles, with 94.2% having heard of them and 11.7% owning some form of cryptocurrency (Łukasik & Witczak, 2023; Zborowski & Chmielarz, 2024). However, concerns about volatility, lack of regulation, and potential for misuse persist, affecting public trust and willingness to engage with digital currencies. The COVID-19 pandemic further influenced perceptions, with a notable increase in interest in cryptocurrencies as alternative investment options (Maciejasz et al., 2024). Understanding and addressing public concerns is essential for fostering a supportive environment for digital currencies within the green economy. Digital currencies have the potential to revolutionize green financing by facilitating transparent and efficient transactions. Poland's green bond market has seen growth, yet faces challenges such as higher issuance costs and lack of uniform standards (Chamera, 2023). Integrating digital currencies could streamline processes and attract more investors to green projects. FinTech companies are also emerging as catalysts for ESG principles in the financial sector. Their innovative approaches, including digital payments and crowdfunding, can support sustainable initiatives and enhance financial inclusion (Hazla, 2023). Leveraging FinTech solutions may bridge gaps in green financing and promote the adoption of digital currencies aligned with environmental goals. Complementary currencies like the *Polish Zielony* (PLZ) demonstrate how localized digital currencies can support sustainable development. Operating since 2015, the Zielony has positively influenced local economies by promoting job creation and economic resilience, particularly during the COVID-19 pandemic (Stępnicka et al., 2023). Such models highlight the potential of digital currencies to drive green economy objectives at the community level. The integration of digital currencies into Poland's green economy presents both opportunities and challenges. While technological advancements and innovative financial instruments offer pathways to sustainability, regulatory uncertainties and public scepticism pose significant hurdles. A collaborative approach involving policymakers, financial institutions, and the public is essential to harness the potential of digital currencies in achieving green economy goals. The broader perspective on energy source and emissions for cryptocurrency mining facilities in Poland, and Poland's renewable energy growth needs to be analysed.

12.4 Energy Source and Emissions for Cryptocurrency Mining Facilities in Poland

The starting point can be the link between Poland's green economy and the digital currencies. This link is not obvious and requires more description. The graphic visualization of such link was presented by Fig. 12.1.

The core of the link is the policy and technology bridge which enables to implement the goals of the green economy, e.g. reduction of the CO2 emission and allows the new technology as the blockchain to be used for the evaluating and measure the environmental impact. As the concept itself seemed rather straightforward the most tough is the implementation of such concept and transferring that into the government policy which allows to be used in the green economy mechanism. In Poland there are some pilots approaches with the created mining facilities and efforts to have such concept implemented.

This Table 12.1 provides an analysis of various cryptocurrency mining facilities in Poland, highlighting their energy sources, annual energy consumption, and resulting carbon emissions. The data emphasizes the significant environmental impact of coal-based operations compared to those that utilize renewable energy.

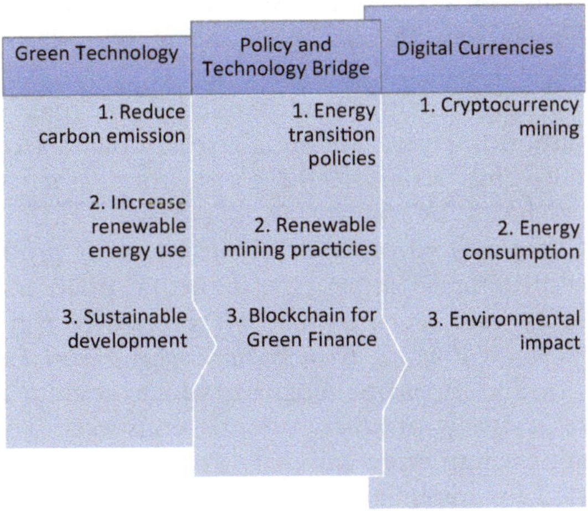

Fig. 12.1 The link between Poland's green economy and the digital currencies. *Source* Author's concept

Table 12.1 Comparative analysis of mining facilities in Poland (2019–2023)

Facility name	*Location*	*Energy source*	*Annual energy consumption (MWh)*	*CO_2 emissions (metric tonnes)*	*Emission reduction potential with renewables (%)*
BitHub Warsaw	Warsaw	Coal	5,000	4,600	80%
Krakow Mining Co	Krakow	Hydro	2,500	150	N/A
GreenCoin Gdansk	Gdansk	Mixed (Coal 60%, Wind 40%)	3,200	1,800	55%
EcoMine Poznan	Poznan	Wind	1,800	10	N/A
VarsityCrypto Katowice	Katowice	Coal	6,500	5,980	85%

Source Author's findings based on the reports and data 2019–2023

This Table 12.1 shows the distinct difference in CO_2 emissions based on the energy source used by each facility. In particular coal-based facilities, renewable energy-based facilities, and the mixed energy sources. *The Coal-Based Facilities* like BitHub Warsaw and VarsityCrypto Katowice heavily rely on coal, resulting in high carbon emissions. For instance, VarsityCrypto Katowice emits close to 6,000 metric tonnes of CO_2 annually due to its dependence on coal, which is among the most carbon-intensive energy sources. Poland's coal-fired power plants typically emit around 0.92 metric tonnes of CO_2 per MWh of electricity produced. By contrast, wind and hydro facilities have negligible emissions. Coal-powered mining facilities not only produce high emissions but also contribute to other environmental pollutants, including sulfur dioxide (SO_2) and nitrogen oxides (NOx), which further exacerbate air quality issues in Poland. *Renewable Energy-Based Facilities* like Krakow Mining Co. and EcoMine Poznan, which operate on hydro and wind power respectively, produce minimal emissions. These renewables-based operations align more closely with Poland's environmental objectives and are vital for minimizing the ecological footprint of digital currency mining. For example, EcoMine Poznan's wind-powered operation has negligible emissions (around 10 metric tonnes per year), a stark contrast to the emissions from coal-reliant facilities. If more facilities transitioned to wind or hydro, Poland could see significant reductions in its overall carbon footprint from the mining sector. *The Mixed Energy Sources* include Green Coin Gdansk exemplifies a hybrid model, using both coal and wind energy. Although its emissions are lower than coal-only facilities, they remain substantial. Transitioning this operation entirely to renewables could reduce its carbon footprint by up to 55%. Hybrid energy models like this underscore the gradual shift in some sectors towards renewable sources, although coal reliance remains high.

Coal-based cryptocurrency mining in Poland is a major contributor to greenhouse gas emissions. Transitioning such facilities to renewable energy could reduce emissions by approximately 80–85%, providing a significant environmental benefit. Coal-based mining facilities, such as BitHub Warsaw and VarsityCrypto Katowice, exhibit CO_2 emissions far above renewable-powered facilities, underscoring the unsustainable nature of coal dependency. Coal's high emissions per MWh make it one of the most environmentally damaging sources of energy, releasing around 0.92 metric tonnes of CO_2 per MWh. The comparison highlights the stark environmental cost, with coal facilities producing up to 98% of emissions from the mining sector. By adopting renewable sources, these coal-based facilities could reduce emissions by up to 85%. Facilities like Green Coin Gdansk demonstrate that mixed energy sources can significantly lower carbon footprints, but they still fall short of the minimal emissions achievable by facilities that rely fully on renewables. In Poland, coal is economically entrenched and heavily subsidized, which presents challenges to large-scale transitions to renewables for mining. Yet, the findings suggest that even partial shifts to renewables in mining facilities could substantially mitigate environmental impact without requiring a complete overhaul. The fact is that cryptocurrencies energy consumption can have the environmental impact. Table 12.2 presented Cryptocurrency Energy Consumption by Consensus Mechanism.

This table provides a comparative view of the energy consumption per transaction and the environmental impact of different cryptocurrencies based on their consensus mechanisms. Proof of Work (PoW) currencies consume far more energy compared to those using Proof of Stake (PoS), making them less sustainable in a coal-heavy energy mix like Poland's. Bitcoin and Ethereum (prior to the transition to Ethereum 2.0) are two of the most energy-intensive cryptocurrencies, primarily due to the PoW

Table 12.2 Cryptocurrency energy consumption by consensus mechanism

Cryptocurrency	*Consensus mechanism*	*Energy consumption per transaction (kWh)*	*Annual carbon emissions (metric tonnes)*	*Environmental impact*
Bitcoin	PoW	707	62,000	Very High
Ethereum (pre-2.0)	PoW	62	5,400	High
Ethereum 2.0	PoS	0.1	< 1	Very Low
Cardano	PoS	0.1	< 1	Very Low
Polkadot	Nominated Proof of Stake (NPoS)	0.5	5	Low

Source Based on Mora et al. (2018), Stoll et al. (2019), CBCEI https://ccaf.io/cbnsi/cbeci, Hassler and Volkova (2021), Sims and Sani, (2022) Carbon Tracker Initiative (CTI)

protocol. Bitcoin, for example, consumes 707 kWh per transaction, a consumption level that exceeds that of entire nations for some facilities. High energy consumption in PoW-based cryptocurrencies significantly escalates carbon emissions, especially in coal-reliant countries like Poland. For instance, Bitcoin mining in Poland, if powered predominantly by coal, would release about 0.65 metric tonnes of CO_2 per MWh. The environmental cost of PoW cryptocurrencies is disproportionately high. In countries with a renewable energy infrastructure, this burden could be lessened, but for Poland, which relies heavily on coal, PoW mining imposes a high environmental toll. Cryptocurrencies like Ethereum (post-2.0 transition) and Cardano, which utilize PoS mechanisms, consume a fraction of the energy per transaction compared to PoW cryptocurrencies. For example, Ethereum 2.0 now operates with an estimated 0.1 kWh per transaction, drastically reducing its energy footprint. Since PoS validators are selected based on coin ownership rather than computational power, this model does not require extensive energy resources, making it significantly more sustainable, especially in regions dependent on fossil fuels. PoS models are better suited for Poland's green economy goals, as they align with the EU's carbon reduction objectives by minimizing additional energy demand on the grid. Switching to PoS-based cryptocurrencies in Poland would greatly reduce the environmental impact of digital currency mining. If miners in Poland adopted PoS-based cryptocurrencies, the carbon footprint could be reduced by over 90%, a critical step towards sustainable digital finance. For Poland to align with EU-wide carbon reduction targets, adopting PoS cryptocurrencies over PoW is imperative. Policies encouraging PoS adoption, such as lower taxation for PoS miners, could accelerate this transition and make the digital currency ecosystem more sustainable. Important aspect is the renewable energy production and future growth for Poland which was presented in Table 12.3. It highlights the potential of using renewable energy for cryptocurrency mining operations, which could significantly cut down emissions.

Poland has made strides in renewable energy development, with wind and solar power capacities showing consistent growth since 2015. In 2020, Poland's renewable energy installed capacity surpassed 12 GW, largely due to substantial investments in solar and wind. Offshore wind, in particular, plays a significant role in Poland's strategy, especially for achieving energy transition goals by 2030. Offshore wind capacity is expected to boost Poland's total renewable generation significantly, aligning with EU mandates for reducing reliance on coal (Ministry of Climate & Environment, 2021). The rapid increase in solar installations aligns with Poland's commitment to diversify its energy mix, driven by decreasing costs and government incentives. By 2030, solar is expected to provide a substantial share of renewable capacity. The Energy Policy of Poland until 2040 (EPP, 2040) outlines that renewable capacity could reach approximately 27 GW by 2030, driven by policies favouring wind and solar growth (Energy Policy of Poland,

Table 12.3 Poland's renewable energy growth and its potential for cryptocurrency mining

Year	*Total renewable energy capacity (GW)*	*Wind power capacity (GW)*	*Solar power capacity (GW)*	*Hydro power capacity (GW)*	*Projected carbon emissions reduction potential (%) to 2015 base year*
2015	7.2	4.8	0.1	2.3	–
2020	12.6	6.3	3.9	2.4	15%
2025F	20.0	7.6	10.0	2.4	25%
2030F	27.0	11.5	13.0	2.5	30%

Source Based on EEA (2024) and IRENA (2024) reports; (Ministry of Climate and Environment EPP 2040, 2021)

2021). With this level of capacity, renewable energy could support a substantial portion of the country's energy-intensive industries, including cryptocurrency mining. Assuming a shift from coal to renewable energy for mining facilities, Poland could reduce its mining-related carbon emissions by up to 75% by 2030. Such a reduction aligns well with EU emissions targets and Poland's own green economy objectives. Leveraging Poland's growing renewable energy capacity could make cryptocurrency mining more sustainable. With wind and solar power expansions, the country has a viable pathway for reducing the environmental impact of its digital currency mining sector. Poland's renewable growth would not only support environmental goals but could create economic opportunities in the digital finance sector. Increased renewable infrastructure could make Poland an attractive hub for environmentally responsible mining, drawing investment and positioning the country as a leader in sustainable cryptocurrency operations.

12.5 Conclusions

The shift towards a green economy in Poland faces significant challenges, partly due to its strong historical reliance on coal and the economic and political implications tied to energy resources. Poland's green transition is impacted by high costs associated with reducing coal dependency and meeting European Union (EU) emissions targets. The country has historically been one of the EU's most coal-dependent nations, with coal-fired plants producing a significant portion of its electricity. This dependence has influenced both its economy and policies, as seen in recent plans to phase out coal mining by 2049, a slower timeline than in many neighbouring EU nations (Hernandez-Moralez, 2020).

In conclusion, coal-powered mining operations in Poland have a far higher environmental cost than renewable-powered facilities, making them unsustainable in the long run. The tables and analyses underscore the urgency of transitioning Poland's cryptocurrency mining sector towards renewable energy. A regulatory push, coupled with financial incentives for renewable-based operations, could significantly support Poland's green economy goals while reducing the ecological footprint of digital currency activities. The data underscores the need for targeted interventions in Poland's cryptocurrency mining sector to reduce carbon emissions and align with the EU's climate targets. Key actions include:

- **Policy Shifts**: Introducing policies that favour PoS cryptocurrencies over PoW, and providing incentives for renewable-powered mining, could help transition Poland's digital currency sector to a more sustainable model.
- **Infrastructure Development**: Continued investment in renewable energy infrastructure will be crucial for reducing emissions from energy-intensive industries, including cryptocurrency mining.
- **Public–Private Partnerships**: Encouraging collaborations between the government, renewable energy providers, and cryptocurrency firms can expedite the shift to a green economy.

The integration of comprehensive references supports a nuanced understanding of Poland's unique energy landscape and the actionable insights to address the environmental challenges posed by digital currencies. The entire effort of CO2 reduction was not spectacular in case of Poland. In the period of two last decades according to the International Energy Agency data, Poland reduced the CO2 emissions from fuel combustion by 1.7% (290 Mt CO2 in 2000 and 285 Mt CO2 in 2022) (IEA, 2024). The integration of digital currencies, particularly cryptocurrencies, into Poland's economy presents both significant opportunities and challenges, especially in the context of a green economy. On one hand, digital currencies offer potential for innovation, financial inclusion, and decentralized financial systems, which are aligned with a sustainable future. However, the environmental impact of these technologies, particularly energy consumption, is a major concern. Cryptocurrencies like Bitcoin rely heavily on Proof-of-Work (PoW) algorithms, leading to substantial electricity consumption, which, in Poland's case, is still predominantly sourced from fossil fuels. This exacerbates the country's carbon footprint, counteracting its efforts to transition to a greener energy mix.

One of the primary challenges Poland faces is the high carbon intensity of its energy sector, heavily reliant on coal. While Poland has committed to increasing its renewable energy share, including wind and solar, the pace of this transition is slow. The digital currency mining process, especially PoW-based currencies, often relies on non-renewable energy sources, raising concerns about their compatibility with Poland's green economy goals. Additionally, Poland's limited infrastructure for clean energy, combined with high energy prices, presents a further barrier to the widespread adoption of sustainable blockchain technologies.

In the short term, Poland must address the energy demands of digital currencies by investing in more sustainable and efficient technologies, such as Proof-of-Stake (PoS) models or hybrid consensus mechanisms, which are less energy-intensive than PoW. Furthermore, the government could introduce regulations to encourage cryptocurrency mining operations to use renewable energy sources. In parallel, Poland should increase investments in its renewable energy infrastructure, reducing the carbon intensity of its overall power generation, which would mitigate the impact of energy-hungry technologies like digital currencies. Looking ahead, Poland could integrate blockchain technologies in ways that support environmental sustainability, such as utilizing them in carbon trading systems, transparent supply chains, and energy trading platforms. These applications align with the broader goals of a green economy, enhancing energy efficiency and reducing emissions. However, without clear policy frameworks, technological advancements, and significant investments in clean energy, Poland risks undermining its green economy objectives through the unchecked growth of energy-intensive digital currency markets.

In conclusion, while digital currencies present significant potential for Poland's financial and technological landscape, their environmental impact must be carefully managed. The country's success in reconciling these emerging technologies with its green economy goals depends on strategic investments in renewable energy and the adoption of energy-efficient cryptocurrency protocols. Only through a collaborative effort between government, industry, and environmental stakeholders can Poland navigate the challenges posed by digital currencies and steer its economy towards a more sustainable future. Although Poland has committed to EU climate goals, its energy policies remain deeply influenced by economic and social factors linked to coal. Transitioning too quickly to a green economy could jeopardize jobs in coal-dependent regions, increase energy costs, and lead to economic instability. Germany's energy policies, particularly the *Energiewende* (energy transition) strategy, have a substantial impact on Poland. Germany's shift to renewable energy has at times led to electricity imports from neighbouring countries, including Poland, which still relies on coal. This cross-border dynamic can pressure Poland to adjust its energy policies more rapidly than it might otherwise choose, even as Germany benefits from a more robust economy capable of investing heavily in green technology. Additionally, Poland often imports German technology for renewable energy infrastructure, making it financially and technically dependent on Germany for green economy initiatives. In essence, while the green economy ideals are theoretically beneficial, Poland's reliance on coal, combined with external influences such as Germany's energy policies, creates challenges for the country's ability to fully embrace a green economy without risking economic setbacks and energy security concerns.

References

Cambridge Centre for Alternative Finance. (2022). Bitcoin electricity consumption index (CBECI). Retrieved May 3, 2025, from https://cbeci.org

Chambers and Partners. (2024). *Fintech 2024—Poland. Global practice guides*. Retrieved May 3, 2025, from https://practiceguides.chambers.com/practice-guides/fintech-2024/poland/trends-and-developments/O16358

Chamera, K. (2023). The development of the Polish green bond market in comparison to selected European countries. *Central European Review of Economics & Finance, 45*(4A), 21–34. https://doi.org/10.24136/ceref.2023.032

European Commission. (2019). The European Green Deal. (p. 5). Retrieved May 3, 2025, from https://ec.europa.eu/info/strategy/priorities-2019-2024/european-green-deal_en

European Commission. (2024). *Poland 2024 Digital Decade Country Report*. Retrieved from May 3, 2025, from https://digital-strategy.ec.europa.eu/en/factpages/poland-2024-digital-decade-country-report

Hassler, M., & Volkova, E. (2021). Analysis of PoS and PoW environmental impact. *Journal of Cleaner Production, 268*, 118–130. Retrieved from https://www.sciencedirect.com/journal/journal-of-cleaner-production

Hazla, M. W. (2023). *Can FinTechs become a catalyst for ESG rules in the Polish financial sector? Blue Europe*. Retrieved May 3, 2025, from https://www.blue-europe.eu/analysis-en/short-analysis/can-fintechs-become-a-catalyst-for-esg-rules-in-the-polish-financial-sector/

Hernandez-Moralez, A. (2020). *Coal-dependent Poland pivots toward green energy*. Retrieved November 9, 2024, from https://www.politico.eu/article/coal-dependent-poland-green-energy-pivot/, published September 25, 2020 6:58 pm CET.

IEA, International Energy Agency. (2020). *Poland energy profile*. Retrieved from https://www.iea.org/countries/poland

Kozar, Ł., & Wodnicka, M. (2024). Blockchain in energy: literature review in the context of sustainability. *Economics and Environment, 90*(3), 1–18. https://www.ekonomiaisrodowisko.pl/journal/article/view/866

Łukasik, K., & Witczak, J. (2023). *Popularność kryptowalut w Polsce*. Polski Instytut Ekonomiczny (pp. 1–49). https://pie.net.pl/wp-content/uploads/2023/09/PIE-Raport_kryptowaluty_2023.pdf

Maciejasz, M., Poskart, R., & Wotzka, D. (2024). Perceptions of Cryptocurrencies and Modern Money before and after the COVID-19 Pandemic in Poland and Germany. *International Journal of Financial Studies, 12*(3), 64. https://doi.org/10.3390/ijfs12030064

Ministry of Climate and Environment. (2021). Energy Policy of Poland until 2040 (EPP2040). Retrieved November 8, 2024, from https://www.gov.pl/web/climate/energy-policy-of-poland-until-2040-epp2040

Mora, C., Rollins, R. L., & Taladay, K. (2018). Bitcoin emissions alone could push global warming above 2°C. *Nature Climate Change, 8*, 931–933. https://doi.org/10.1038/s41558-018-0321-8

Narodowy Bank Polski. (2024). Central Bank Digital Currency. Retrieved from May 3, 2025, from https://nbp.pl/en/payment-system/statistical-data/analyzes-and-studies/central-bank-digital-currency/

Schletz, M., Brodsky, L., & Camhi, J. (2020). Blockchain and the transition to a green economy: Opportunities and challenges. *Environmental Innovation and Societal Transitions, 36*, 80–92. Retrieved from https://www.sciencedirect.com/journal/environmental-innovation-and-societal-transitions

Schulz, K. (2021). Energy consumption and environmental impact of Bitcoin mining in Poland. *Energy Policy Journal, 42*(2), 250–270. Retrieved from https://www.journals.elsevier.com/energy-policy

Sims, J., & Sani, L. (2022). *Poland's Energy Dilemma: New gas power traps taxpayers in a costly future, Carbon Tracker 2022*. Retrieved from November 7, 2024, from https://carbontracker.org/reports/polands-energy-dilemma/

Stępnicka, N., Sadowska, B., Walasek, R., Zimon, G., & Brzozowiec, D. (2023). Sustainable local development in relation to complementary currencies on the example of the Polish currency Zielony. *Technological and Economic Development of Economy, 29*(2), 618–652. https://doi.org/10.3846/tede.2023.18341

Stoll, C., Klaaßen, L., & Gallersdörfer, U. (2019). The carbon footprint of Bitcoin. *Joule, 3*(7), 1647–1661. Retrieved from https://www.cell.com/joule/fulltext/S2542-4351(19)30285-3

UNEP. (2011). *Towards a green economy: Pathways to sustainable development and poverty eradication* (p.16). Retrieved from https://www.unep.org/resources/report/towards-green-economy-pathways-sustainable-development-and-poverty-eradication

Zborowski, M., & Chmielarz, W. (2024). Identification of awareness of the conditions for using cryptocurrencies in Poland. *Szkoła Główna Handlowa w Warszawie, e-Mentor, 104*(2), 4–13.

Data References

CTI. (2024). https://carbontracker.org, accessed 07.11.2024

EEA. (2024). https://www.eea.europa.eu/themes/energy/renewable-energy, accessed 07.11.2024

IEA. (2024). https://www.iea.org/countries/poland, accessed 08.11.2024

IRENA. (2024). Renewable capacity statistics 2024, International Renewable Energy Agency, Abu Dhabi, https://www.irena.org//media/Files/IRENA/Agency/Publication/2024/Mar/IRENA_RE_Capacity_Statistics_2024.pdf, accessed 08.11.2024

CHAPTER 13

Digital Ecosystems for Social Justice: Analysing the Intersection of Technology, Law, and Sustainability

Arun Kumar Singh and Wagisha

13.1 Introduction

The vast digitisation of financial systems has opened the doors for new transformative shifts in the global economy. They challenge traditional monetary mechanisms while building new financial inclusion and economic sustainability models. Digital currencies, which function exclusively in electronic form and use crypto technologies, stand at the forefront of this transformation (Grant, 2024). In contrast to the fiat currencies issued by the central banks, these currencies facilitate instantaneous, borderless transactions (Dionysopoulos et al., 2023). Thus, they are redefining the process of exchange of economic value. This development has marked a radical shift from conventional financial systems (Dionysopoulos et al., 2023). Hence, it has compelled governments,

A. K. Singh · Wagisha (✉)
Department of Law, North-Eastern Hill University, Shillong, India
e-mail: wagisha.w70@gmail.com

R. Aneja and R. Dygas (eds.), *Digital Currencies and the Green Economy*, https://doi.org/10.1007/978-981-95-2282-8_13

financial bodies, and regulatory institutions to ponder monetary policies and economic structures. In India, the digital currency has gained a significant salience with approximately 115 million crypto investors, majorly falling within the age group of 18–60 years (Bhardwaj, 2022). This rise highlights the infusion of digital economic instruments into the mainstream economy. This showcases their potential in expanding financial inclusion. Hence, they not only serve as a method of transactional convenience but also as a key player in realising broader socio-economic aims. One of the most crucial prospects of digital financial development lies in its capability to facilitate economic accessibility for the marginalised groups. Numerous civil society organisations (hereinafter CSOs) and non-government organisations (NGOs) in India grapple with financial restrictions (Banks et al., 2015). This also restricts their capability to support the marginalised communities. Parallel sustainable monetary systems, which are driven by community-backed digital currencies, offer a feasible solution to this issue. They seek to integrate financial mechanisms with ecological economics. This, in turn, will not just solve the problems of CSOs and NGOs but also challenge the conventional growth-centric economic models.

Though there is a plethora of scholarly articles on digital currencies and sustainable economic models. However, there remains a dearth of understanding of their intersectionality in the Indian context. Hence, the current chapter seeks to add to the existing scholarship by conducting a holistic and comparative analysis of global best practices dealing with digital currency and their effect on sustainability models like the green economy, doughnut economy, and circular economy. With the help of case studies from Asia and Europe, the present research strives to evaluate the efficiency of economic paradigms. It also seeks to examine the alignment processes of India's evolving digital financial frameworks with these models. Also, this study seeks to inquire into the role of digital currencies in promoting socio-economic equity and social justice.

The current research adopts doctrinal and analytical methods. This would aid in examining the process of structuring modern economic frameworks through digital financial developments. Models like Circular Economy (hereinafter CE) and Doughnut Economy (hereinafter DE) give important insights into the evolution of linear economic systems into more inclusive and sustainable forms. CE stresses the induction of environmental sustainability within the economic structures, yet it lags in terms of its non-consideration of the social components' role in the said process (Everett, 2021). Conversely, DE aligns environmental and social dimensions with the economic model (Everett, 2021). They stress the importance of respecting the planetary boundaries and human welfare (Everett, 2021). Yet, DE faces challenges in the form of practical implications, especially in the context of the business sector (Everett, 2021). This is mainly due to the nuances associated with the integration of sustainability with corporate structures (Everett, 2021). This research rests on a dual framework that integrates both conceptual and theoretical perspectives. A theoretical undergirding is drawn from institutional economics and legal pluralism in explanatory accounts of how various legal systems affect the legitimation and evolution of digital currencies. Conceptually, this research captures the intersection of sustainability (through SDGs), technology (via blockchain and fintech innovation), and law (particularly regulatory governance), demonstrating the interaction in the creation of sustainable monetary ecosystems.

Finally, through this work, the current chapter argues for the requirement of a holistically integrated model that considers socio-economic and environmental dimensions. A parallel sustainable monetary system has the potential to facilitate such model and foster a long-tern economic stability and equity. With the help of analysis, the chapter seeks to unravel as to how digital currencies can act as a catalyst for inducing sustainable financial transformation based on economic inclusivity, regulatory adaptability, and social justice.

13.2 Theoretical Framework

13.2.1 Ecological Economics and Its critique of Traditional Growth-Oriented Models

Ecology-based economics proposes a major transition from traditional neoclassical environmental economics. Though it has progressed beyond the conventional economic models, it continues to be deeply seated in historical and developmental matters. Initially, the economic growth was perceived in consonance with the expansion of goods and services, however, contemporary developmental scholarships now infuse the sustainability and quality of life with the economic growth (Clower, 1967). Despite the existence of constant growth-fetishism in policy circles, sustainable development has gained momentum, marking a significant shift in economic scholarship over the last century (Goodhart,

1998). The foundation of political economy could be traced back to the propositions of Adam Smith and David Ricardo, who stressed economic development even though their perspectives contrasted with the contemporary modern development theory (Dionysopoulos et al., 2023). Early scholarship on economics primarily focused on developed nations, with a restricted approach and attention towards the Global South (Goodhart, 1998). With Colin Clark's quantitative study in 1940, this approach started shifting from the mid-twentieth century (Dionysopoulos et al., 2023). From this timeline onwards, economists started recognising the stark disparities in economic dimensions between the capitalist countries and the rest of the globe.

The notion of development economics further shifted post-World War II and the decolonisation (Eichengreen & Flandreau, 2005). The economists explored ways to resolve poverty and economic disparities after witnessing issues in numerous newly independent countries. The emergence of prominent global institutions, viz. the United Nations, International Monetary Fund, International Labor Organisation, and World Bank, enabled thorough studies on development. Concurrently, the dominant views preferred industrialisation and capital formation as the base of development (Savini, 2024). This resulted in the categorisation of countries into developed and underdeveloped groups. The "stage theory of growth", as advocated by Rostow and Gerschenkron, stressed that economies shift by linear stages of development (Mukhopadhyay et al., 2017). Nonetheless, this perspective was fraught with criticisms owing to its reductionist assumption, whereby it ignored the socio-political nuances influencing the economic trajectories (Mukhopadhyay et al., 2017). Other fragments consisting of economists like Nurkse, Lewis, and early Keynesians favoured "role of capital formation, savings and government intervention for inducing growth processes" (Dionysopoulos et al., 2023). Both Marxist and Keynesian perspectives stressed the salience of state involvement in planning and transformation of economic growth (Dionysopoulos et al., 2023).

Following the war period, the development economics was majorly shaped by the Central European economists, viz. Kalecki, Mandelbaum and Rosentein-Rodan (Alacevich, 2018). Their propositions were heavily influenced by their experience with late industrialisation (Alacevich, 2018). This led to the development of state-centric economic models, especially in newly independent countries like India, which opted for a Soviet-style economic planning. Both state intervention in agriculture, infrastructure, and industry, and sovereignty over natural resources were common practices in this type of model (Alacevich, 2018). Yet, on a practical note, many countries were fraught with challenges in the form of external pressure and policy infringements (Alacevich, 2018). Near the end of the twentieth century, the neoclassical development theorists stressed for "international trade and market liberalisation" (Thomas & Vogel, 2018). They argued that the reduction of trade barriers and removal of price distortions would boost growth (Thomas & Vogel, 2018). This ultimately structured export-driven approaches across South East Asia and China (Thomas & Vogel, 2018). However, there were occasional disruptions to it owing to factors like capital mobility and currency devaluations (Thomas & Vogel, 2018). This highlights the challenges of full capital account mobility.

All these timelines of the evolution of development economics approaches reflect a transition from growth-centric classical political economy to equity, global integration, and sustainability-driven contemporary approach. Though industrialisation and trade continue to have significance. However, modern economists are increasingly recognising the need for a more holistic and sustainable form of development. For this approach, it becomes important to explore the recent development of the theoretical frameworks seeking to accommodate the contemporary approaches. To this end, the next segment stands crucial.

13.2.2 *Alternative Economic Models: Green Economy, Doughnut Economy, Circular Economy*

As per Robins, "economics is the science which studies human behavior as a relationship between ends and scarce means which have alternative uses" (Robbins, 1935). Other definitions also have a similar kind of implication whereby society and human dimension are closely related to economics (Marshall, 1890). Also, they highlight the aspects of scarcity and the requisites for attaining well-being (Marshall, 1890). They seek to link scarcity as an immediate cause of the current linear economy (Bade et al., 2002). They seek to suggest the need for an economic model to consider the society and human behaviour while responding to the 'scarcity of resources'. However, the current models only focus on economic scarcity and ways to tackle it while ignoring the social dimension and issues of resource scarcity. Hence, the current economic models place the dimensions of economic development as the core of business and decision-making processes while undermining the salience of the environment and society. This linear form of economy entails three short but destructive stages, i.e., 'take, make, and dispose'. It is based on the 'fossil fuel inputs', yielding a huge depletion in both natural resources and natural capital (Ellen McArthur Foundation, 2012). Per the ARUP report titled "50 scenarios: four plausible futures", we are on our track towards 2050 being "shaped by three decades of gradual social advancement, coupled with half-hearted environmental stewardship" (ARUP, 2019). Its future attributes have a huge possibility of making both the people and the planet suffer.

The development of major countries across the globe is measured by their Gross Domestic Product (GDP). However, it has its shortfalls owing to the ignorance of other factors associated with the success and well-being of a country, by simply emphasising the economics of a country. In today's era, evaluation of the development of a country should not only be based on its financial stability but also on its capability to cope with resource scarcity, natural resources, and social well-being. Doing this would infuse the pillars of sustainability, i.e., social, economic, and environmental, into the economic model. To this end, the circular economy offers a better approach.

The Circular Economy (CE) is an alternative model that stresses the integration of the environment into economics with the aid of cascades and feedback loops (Ellen McArthur Foundation, 2012). Hence, it offers a model representing both sustainability and business opportunities. Its popularity and momentum are exponentially increasing, and various countries, governments, institutions, and businesses are adopting it. This could be demonstrated by the 'EU Circular Economy Action Plan, the Circularity Gap Report, and the Ellen MacArthur Foundation' (Ellen McArthur Foundation, 2012). The concept of cascades and feedback loops permits the return of the biological materials to the biosphere while maximising the technical materials' value and decreasing the demand for the raw material with the help of 'maintenance, reuse and refurbishment' (Ellen McArthur Foundation, 2012). It promotes innovation and boosts business prospects and value creation while minimising environmental damage. The aspects of natural capital and the salience of nature within economics are the basis of this model. The integration of nature into the economy is done by alleviating the 'productivity and life cycle of raw materials and natural resources and transitioning towards renewable forms of energies' (Benyus, 1997). Contrasting with the linear economy, this model proposes an economy whereby economic and environmental parameters are set for assessing the success (Benyus, 1997). Despite its entailing the infusion of the economic and environmental pillars of sustainable development, this model still lacks the elements of the social pillar. To this end, Murray has argued for accommodating social justice and a social element as a crucial part of sustainability (Murray et al., 2017). Yet, it remains unclear as to how this model could yield social equality (Murray et al., 2017). Per Schroeder, this model has strong coherence with certain Sustainable Development Goals (hereinafter 'SDGs') like SDG no. 6, 7, 8, 12, 15 as they have a close connection with aspects of economy and environment (Schroeder et al., 2019). However, SDGs 3, 5, 10, 11, and 16 are not related to CE and come under the social pillar of sustainability (Schroeder et al., 2019). Also, Padilla-Rivera has stressed that social elements necessary for impactful results and strategies are not encouraged within this model (Padilla-Rivera et al., 2020). Also, the lack of integration of the social dimension there lies an uncertainty as to how CE is more sustainable over the linear model for future generations (Padilla-Rivera et al., 2020). This strongly highlights the lack of consensus over a suitable model integrating the economic, environmental, and social dimensions. Accordingly, future studies are required to focus on the definition and way to measure social parameters and CE practices' endeavour to enhance 'human wellbeing in the society' (Padilla-Rivera et al., 2020). Accordingly, CE could be considered a huge development over the linear model, yet, with the need to consider social parameters for transforming into a full, holistic model.

The Doughnut Economy (DE), proposed by Raworth, is another model that offers both inclusivity and sustainability (Raworth, 2017). It seeks to integrate social and environmental dimensions into the economic model (Raworth, 2017). This, in turn, would aid in developing both planet-centric and people-centric worlds with the induction of boundaries into them. For integrating the social aspect with the economic model, it highlights the existence of SDGs-based social boundaries that a society should be confined within for meeting the requirements of every person. For the introduction of environmental dimensions into the economic model, this model highlights the planetary boundaries, which should not be broken to ensure that economic advancement is not happening at the cost of the planet. Per Raworth,

> "Last century's adopted policy goal of never-ending Gross Domestic Product (GDP) growth has been leading us far off course, resulting in economies that are degenerative, running down the living world on which human wellbeing fundamentally depends, and that are also divisive, enriching the 1 per cent at the expense of the rest." (Raworth, 2017)

DE has a sharp contrast to that of the linear model, which solely focuses upon GDP and financial economics, as it places people and the planet at the core. It seeks to balance the development of place and people with the well-being and health of people and the whole planet (Raworth, 2017). Despite its holistic approach, which is based on the society, management of scarcity, and living within the planetary limits, it has limitations in terms of its application in the business world. The 'Doughnut Economics Action Lab' currently permits the use of DE by businesses only in the form of an internal tool within the business organisation (Everett, 2021). This seeks to prevent greenwashing and promote the regenerative and distributive designs for businesses. Yet, it also indicates that there is an inadequacy in terms of understanding the impact of DE on businesses and their revenue, or the aspects of sustainability. This model clarifies the goals while remaining within the doughnut, yet it is unclear over the means to achieve it. The 'how' aspect depends on the motivation and innovation within the businesses (Everett, 2021). For this, Raworth has emphasised that for building a regenerative business and economy, it is necessary to create a circular design with the help of loops for transforming from the linear model (Raworth, 2017). This indicates the parallelism with the CE while also going a step ahead by promoting the integration of social pillars into the economics for building a regenerative and distributive design.

These models demonstrate the evolution of the traditional linear economy to meet its limitations effectively. Both CE and DE offer these kinds of alternative models. Though CE focuses on infusing the dimensions of environmental sustainability with economic processes, it remains deficient in terms of its strong emphasis on the social aspects. On the other hand, DE integrates both environmental and social boundaries, seeking a balanced way of economic development that reflects set boundaries and human well-being. However, DE, despite being conceptually strong, is fraught with challenges in the form of practical implementation in the context of the business sector. For building an efficient, sustainable, and inclusive economic framework, it is required that future research and policies emphasise the holistic integration of socio-economic and environmental pillars. For this, a parallel sustainable monetary system is essential as it would align these principles with financial structures. This would ensure economic stability, which fosters a long-term form of equitable and regenerative growth.

13.3 Understanding Digital Currencies and Ecosystems:

13.3.1 Definition and Evolution of Digital Currencies

The paradigm shift of the economic model integrates with the necessity for an "alternative economic model" which aligns socio-economic and environmental sustainability (Salminen, 2023). The challenges posited by both CE and DE showcase the need for a 'parallel sustainable monetary system' which fosters equitable distribution of resources and long-term resilience. Digital currencies have the potential to support such transitions owing to their decentralised nature and capability of enabling transparent, secure, and efficient transactions (Salminen, 2023). They can encourage financial inclusion and ensure economic opportunities to marginalised communities through the reduction of the dependency on conventional financial intermediaries (Dionysopoulos et al., 2023). This aspect is often an ignored facet in traditional economic models. Moreover, blockchain-based systems have the potential to boost accountability and traceability in economic transactions (Dionysopoulos et al., 2023). This would reinforce the regenerative and distributive form of the economic model, which DE advocates for. Hence, the infusion of digital currencies into the alternative economic models provides a potent force for bridging the prevailing shortfalls. This builds a holistic structure balancing social well-being, economic growth, and environmental sustainability.

Digital currencies signify an innovative overhaul of the methods of conducting financial transactions. They are a type of money solely existing in electronic form, harnessing cryptographic technologies and decentralised networks for facilitating secure and efficient transactions (Molnar, 2022). In contrast to the central banks' issued and tangible form defining the traditional fiat currency, digital currencies are characterised entirely by their digital form (Molnar, 2022). This facilitates international transactions instantaneously and seamlessly. Their evolution could be traced back to the initial conception of electronic money in the late twentieth century (Molnar, 2022). In this context, the earliest attempt could be reflected in the 1980s in the form of David Chaum's e-cash (Molnar, 2022). This launched cryptographic techniques for anonymous transactions (Molnar, 2022). However, the revolutionisation of such currency was done only with the launch of Bitcoin in 2009 by an anonymous entity with the pseudonym 'Santoshi Nakamoto' (Molnar, 2022). Bitcoin introduced new characteristics of digital currencies marked by 'blockchain technology, a decentralised ledger mechanism enabling peer-to-peer transactions without intermediaries' (Molnar, 2022). Post the success of Bitcoin, numerous cryptocurrencies were developed, including Ethereum (Molnar, 2022). This also marked the expansion of blockchain's functionality, accommodating smart contracts, i.e., self-executing agreements running on blockchain networks. These developments led to the rise of systems like decentralised finance (DeFi), non-fungible tokens (NFTs), etc., in the domain of digital economy (Molnar, 2022).

Moreover, contrary to the initial development, even sovereign authorities with the help of central banks across the globe have entered as new players in launching their own Central Bank Digital Currencies (CBDCs). CBDCs are a digital form of a country's fiat currency, which are issued and controlled by the central banks (Corbett et al., 2024). Contrary to the other cryptocurrencies operating on decentralised networks, they are centralised to build a safe, stable, and secure digital alternative to cash. Apart from this category, there exists another one in the form of 'community-based digital currencies' (Corbett et al., 2024). They are developed to serve particular local groups or economies (Corbett et al., 2024). Instead of being regulated by the central authority, they are backed by the trust within a community. They seek to foster financial inclusion and economic resilience at the local level. Regional digital currencies in Japan and African mobile money systems like M-Pesa exemplify this system (Corbett et al., 2024).

Overall, the evolutionary process of digital currencies can be marked right from the niche technological experiments to its rise as a global financial tool having significant economic outcomes. Their evolution has reached a stage whereby it is directly challenging the traditional financial mechanism as it is stimulating deliberation among the governments and institutions for revisiting their monetary policies, economic systems, and regulations. Moreover, it has also introduced a new ecosystem in the economic structure, namely the digital ecosystem. Exploring their mechanism becomes crucial for tracing the linkage of digital currencies with that of sustainability, which shall be part of the next section.

13.3.2 Overview of Digital Ecosystems and Their Economic Impact

A digital ecosystem involves a series of interconnected digital infrastructure, stakeholders, and platforms enabling economic transactions within a digital economy. They include various factors like 'digital currencies, payment networks, blockchain platforms, e-commerce systems, and Financial Technology (FinTech) services' (Petrova et al, 2022). One of the major advantages of such an ecosystem lies in its capability to boost the financial accessibility and efficiency (Petrova et al, 2022). It could be illustrated from the fact that blockchain and mobile technology-enabled digital payment systems have cut down the transaction costs and boosted the speed of cross-border transactions (Petrova et al, 2022). This has led to significant business implications, especially in terms of e-commerce and global trade. In these domains, digital transactions have facilitated a seamless form of international transactions. Also, their economic impact can be seen in terms of their extension to numerous industries. For instance, in the financial sector, blockchain-enabled decentralised finance (DeFi) has equipped the users with accessibility to financial services without intermediaries (Petrova et al, 2022). Such platforms provide services like lending, borrowing, and investment backed by a smart contract. This, in turn, democratises access to financial resources (Petrova et al, 2022). Such democratisation reflects its use in achieving the sustainable development goals like SDG no. 1 (associated with eradication of poverty), SDG no. 5 (seeks to achieve gender equality), SDG no. 8 (seeks to achieve decent work and economic growth), SDG no. 9 (seeks to promote industry, innovation and infrastructure), SDG no. 10 (seeks to reduce inequalities), SDG no. 16 (seeks to establish peace, justice and strong institution), and SDG no. 17 (for achieving global and regional financial cooperation). Digital ecosystem also fosters economic growth by supporting innovation and entrepreneurship. The surge of digital assets like cryptocurrencies and NFTs has developed new business models and revenue streams (Dulsrud & Bygstad, 2022). Also, tokenisation of assets, which involves digital tokens representing real-world assets like real estate, art, and intellectual property, has boosted investment and liquidity opportunities (Abbas et al., 2025). However, they are also fraught with certain limitations in the form of regulatory uncertainties, cybersecurity risks, and issues surrounding the digital divide (Abbas et al., 2025). To this end, government and financial institutions are striving to build legal mechanisms that balance both consumer protection and the promotion of innovation. Yet, they continue to be in a vulnerable state, mainly due to issues over cybersecurity in the form of hacking, fraud, and breach of data and privacy (Abbas et al., 2025). Despite these issues, this form of ecosystem is significantly reshaping the global economic frameworks. The constant integration of artificial intelligence, blockchain technology, and machine learning with financial services has a strong potential to secure transparency, security, and efficiency. With the gradual evolution of digital ecosystems, their prominence in economic growth will also be rising by affecting policies, financial strategies, and international partnerships.

13.3.3 Relationship Between Digital Currencies and Social Inclusion

The emergence of digital currencies can be marked as the rise of a strong instrument for achieving social inclusion, especially in regions with limited traditional banking infrastructure (Shaw, 2016). They can provide unbanked and underbanked population access to financial resources leading to increased economic participation and empowerment (Shaw, 2016). This promising future of digital currencies lies in the fact that they have the potential to leverage blockchain technology and mobile financial services (Shaw, 2016).

The digital currencies can majorly contribute to the process of social inclusion by facilitating financial services for marginalised communities (Shaw, 2016). In various developing countries, a major part of the population has limited access to the formal banking system (Shaw, 2016). The factors contributing to such limitations are high cost, geographical limitations, and poor documentation. Digital currencies like mobile money systems and cryptocurrencies enable individuals to store, send, and receive money without involving the formal banking institutions (Shaw, 2016). Another area where they can contribute significantly to social inclusion is remittance. Migrant workers often transfer funds to their families (Shaw, 2016). However, traditional remittance routes involve high fees and lengthy processing times. Cryptocurrencies have the potential to negate these challenges as they offer a more cost-effective alternative with near-instant transactions (Shaw, 2016). This would directly affect the economic stability of numerous families across the globe. Digital financial inclusion also entails promises for uplifting the condition of women and marginalised groups. They foster opportunities for women entrepreneurs with restricted financial resources on account of social norms (Shaw, 2016). Services like blockchain-enabled lending platforms and decentralised finance (hereinafter DeFi) effectuate this by facilitating microloans and crowdfunding (Shaw, 2016). This aids small-scale businesses in developing independently from the traditional banks' influences.

However, certain challenges still seek to limit their potential in realising social inclusion. Factors like the digital divide (on account of disparities in internet accessibility), digital literacy, and technological inefficiency are major contributors to such challenges (Mattsson et al., 2022). Also, compliance risks and security threats in the form of fraud and cybercrime add to this limitation. Hence, a robust policy intervention and training campaigns are needed for the protection of users.

Overall, digital currencies have a great deal of salience in achieving social inclusion. They provide accessible and affordable financial services. However, certain challenges continue to realise their full potential in this direction. For this, it is required to address regulatory challenges, improve digital literacy, and expansion of internet connectivity. By employing this solution, digital currencies would be effective enough to bridge economic gaps and enhance global financial equity.

13.4 Intersectionality of Law, Technology, and Economic Rights in the Digital Era

The digital era is marked by fundamental changes in the functioning of societies. This has not just opened doors for new opportunities but also posed some its challenges. Since digital technologies are developing rapidly, they have now reached an intersecting point with legal frameworks and economic structures. They have the potential to influence the process of recognition, protection, and exercise of rights. This intersectionality becomes more important while ensuring equitable access, regulatory compliance, and securing fundamental economic rights in a rapid digital world.

13.4.1 *Legal Frameworks in the Digital Economy*

The legal framework in this digital age is undergoing constant transformations to meet the pace of technological developments. Since conventional legal landscapes were designed only to cater pre-digital economy, hence struggle to deal effectively with new issues associated with cybersecurity, data privacy, and intellectual property rights (Adelakun et al., 2024). The emergence of blockchain, artificial intelligence, and DeFi also poses certain nuanced legal issues associated with liability, governance, and jurisdiction (Adelakun et al., 2024). However, data protection stands out as the most critical issue about the digital economy (Adelakun et al., 2024). Since digital platforms entail a vast amount of personal data collection, legal frameworks like the European General Data Protection Regulation (GDPR) and India's Digital Personal Data Protection Act (DPDA) aim at securing individual control over such personal data (Adelakun et al., 2024). Yet, their enforcement continues to be a challenge, especially in the context of those countries having weak regulatory oversight. Additionally, the growing salience of digital contracts and smart contracts limits the conventional legal interpretations of contract law. These developments require certain legal adaptation that ensures the enforcement of rights and duties in digital transactions.

13.4.2 *Technology as an Enabler and Barrier to Economic Rights*

Technology acts both as a barrier and an enabler to economic rights. The digital platforms foster financial inclusion by extending the accessibility of banking, credit, and investment opportunities to those fragments who were previously excluded from the conventional financial institutions (Evdokimova et al., 2023). For instance, India's digital payment platform, i.e., Unified Payment Interface (UPI), and Africa's mobile money services like M-Pesa have reinvented the financial accessibility for the marginalised communities (Evdokimova et al., 2023). However, they can also intensify economic inequalities (Evdokimova et al., 2023). The emergence of automation and AI imperils the displacement of the workforce of various industries (Evdokimova et al., 2023). This can intensify the inequality between those with digital skills and those without them (Evdokimova et al., 2023). The platform economy, marked by gig work, often works in legally ambiguous situations (Evdokimova et al., 2023). The workers, in this kind of economy, are devoid of conventional labour protections like social security and minimum wage (Evdokimova et al., 2023). This posits crucial issues concerning fair compensation, job security, and algorithmic biases influencing economic participation.

13.4.3 Digital Rights and Economic Justice

The digital economy is not just limited to economic transactions but also concerns digital rights and economic justice. Digital monopolies in the form of big technology firms significantly control the global economic pursuits (Taylor, 2017). They often design market trends, consumer behavior, and policy decisions (Taylor, 2017). This has prompted the revisitation of antitrust laws and competition regulations globally for the prevention of exploitative practices and securing fair market competition (Taylor, 2017). Moreover, the right to access to internet has emerged as one of the fundamental components of basic economic rights (Taylor, 2017). The digital divide, which is marked by limiting certain fragments of the population from accessing the internet or digital devices, has majorly affected the economic opportunities, education, and social mobility (Taylor, 2017). Hence, the focus of the government and international institutions or organisations has shifted towards securing digital literacy, infrastructure development, and affordable internet access to meet these new challenges.

The convergence of law, technology, and economic rights in the digital age has both negative and positive implications. On one hand, technology can be seen as a prime force driving financial inclusion and economic empowerment. On the other hand, insufficient legal frameworks and uncontrolled technological development can result into exclusion and exploitations. Hence, it is required for the policymakers, legal experts, and technologist to work at a combined front for ensuring an inclusive, equitable technological development that fosters fundamental human rights and economic justice principles.

13.5 Global Practices in Digital Currency for Sustainability and Social Justice

13.5.1 Case Studies: Asia and Europe

The integration of digital currencies with sustainability and social justice varies in degrees across the globe (Shilina, 2024). Asia and Europe exhibit distinct models in it. On one hand, Asian countries emphasise the financial inclusion and economic resilience. On the other hand, Europe focuses more on environmental sustainability and regulatory frameworks.

13.5.2 Asia: China's Digital Yuan and India's UPI-Linked CBDC

China's establishment of its own CBDC in the form of Digital Yuan (e-CNY) exemplifies one of the major case studies for the digital economic model of Asia. Their initiative aims at cutting down the dependence on cash, augmenting financial transparency, and suppressing corruption (Gupta et al., 2023). The digital Yuan also fosters financial inclusion for both rural and unbanked communities by making banking services accessible through digital wallets (Gupta et al., 2023). Yet, issues about state surveillance and data privacy continue to threaten this positive progression in China (Gupta et al., 2023).

India also has its integrated system of CBDC in the form of UPI, which seeks to foster economic accessibility (Gupta et al., 2023). The UPI system had expanded significantly to bring millions into the formal economy. Additionally, the Reserve Bank of India (RBI) introduced a Digital Rupee pilot to integrate with its UPI system (Gupta et al., 2023). Indian model successfully showcases the salience of digital payments in promoting economic participation while retaining the traditional banking structures.

13.5.3 Europe: Sweden's E-Krona and the EU's Digital Euro

In Europe, Sweden's digital currency, namely e-Krona, exemplifies European countries' endeavours to expand their currency system in the digital domain. This currency aims at scaling down the reliance on cash (Ozturkcan et al., 2019). They have significantly showcased the success in achieving their aim at a very rapid pace (Ozturkcan et al., 2019). This currency is designed in a manner that it seeks to ensure all-inclusive accessibility, including the elderly and remotely located populations, by providing both online and offline payment options (Ozturkcan et al., 2019). It also fosters sustainable economic practices by minimising the environmental effects of cash production.

Another case study from Europe stands in the form of the European Union's Digital Euro. This initiative is still at the developmental stage, yet it seeks to secure privacy, security, and financial sovereignty (Ozturkcan et al., 2019). Diverging from the commercial digital wallet, this initiative will demonstrate a state-regulated and decentralised system counterbalancing both the prominence of private digital currencies and fair financial access (Ozturkcan et al., 2019).

13.5.4 Comparative Analysis of Different Monetary Systems Integrating Digital Currencies

Various economies have adopted digital currencies in different ways based on their financial systems, technological expertise, and policy preferences.

1. CBDCs v. Private cryptocurrencies: On one hand, both China and the EU strive to maintain a state-regulated CBDC. On the other hand, countries like Japan and Switzerland demonstrate their openness towards private cryptocurrencies like Bitcoin and Ethereum (Sharma, 2025). Japan has controlled crypto exchanges that seek to ensure both consumer protection and promote innovation.
2. Cashless vs. Hybrid Models: Countries like Sweden and China seek to achieve an almost cashless economy, while India and Germany strive for a hybrid model accommodating both digital currency adoption and constant use of physical cash (Sharma, 2025).
3. Regulatory Stringency: Europe executes strict regulations over digital currencies. They seek to secure data privacy and financial stability. On the other hand, Asian countries like Thailand and Singapore have endorsed regulatory sandboxes which allows the growth of fintech innovations within a controlled environment (Sharma, 2025).
4. Sustainability Practices: Some European states are aligning digital currencies with green finance schemes. For illustration, the EU's digital finance strategy stresses carbon neutral transactions and sustainable investments. While Asian countries prefer economic empowerment with the help of digital inclusion (Sharma, 2025).

13.5.5 Impact on Financial Inclusion and Marginalised Communities

Digital currencies yield significant implications for financial inclusion, especially for marginalised communities like women, migrant workers, the rural population, and low-income groups. The following are listed major advantages of it:

- Access to Banking Services: Digital wallets and mobile-enabled financial tools have empowered even unbanked individuals to participate in the formal economy (Pantin, 2023). Africa's M-Pesa and India's UPI demonstrate this transformation of increased financial accessibility.
- Lower Transaction Costs: Formal banking systems require high costs for remittances and cross-border transactions. Blockchain-based digital currencies cut these costs significantly and boost financial autonomy (Pantin, 2023).
- Empowerment of Women: In countries where women confront socio-economic barriers, digital currencies open opportunities for them. It enables them to have an independent decision-making stance without relying on male guardians or intermediaries (Pantin, 2023).

Despite having a promising stature to secure financial inclusion, it has its own set of limitations, which are listed as follows:

- Digital Divide: The digital divide can be severely noted by the fact that numerous marginalised groups continue to lack digital literacy, smartphones, or internet access. This limits their capability to use digital currencies (Pantin, 2023).
- Cybersecurity and Fraud: Digital ecosystem also faces significant amount of cybersecurity-based risks owing to the factors like hacking, phishing, and data breaches. This asymmetrically affects those unaccustomed to cybersecurity (Pantin, 2023).
- Regulatory Exclusion: Lack of effective and efficient regulation reinforces the exclusion of informal workers and low-income groups from the mainstream digital financial system. This is mainly because of the complex Know Your Customer (KYC) requirements (Pantin, 2023).

The worldwide practices over the adoption of digital currencies to achieve sustainability and social justice showcase both the potential and shortfalls of digital economic transformations. Though the Asian and European models highlight distinctive preferences, i.e., financial inclusion and economic empowerment versus regulatory oversight and sustainability, they also demonstrate the need for achieving an inclusive, balanced, and transparent digital currency system. The major limitation lies in terms of securing the full participation of marginalised communities in the digital economies while protecting their financial rights, privacy, and security.

13.6 The Indian Context: Digital Currencies, Legal Framework, and Social Justice:

13.6.1 *India's Approach to Digital Currencies (Crypto, CBDCs, Digital Rupee)*

The Indian system of digital currencies is based on a complex interplay of regulatory vigilance, financial innovation, and economic security considerations. The nation has observed a significant boost in cryptocurrency adoption, whereby Bitcoins, Ethereum, and Stablecoins have become popular among retail investors. Yet, the scepticism of the Reserve Bank of India and the Indian government cannot be ruled out concerning cryptocurrencies. This is mainly due to factors like their volatility, financial crimes, and their ability to destabilise the monetary structure (Bilgin, 2022). Also, the ambiguity in the legal landscape while dealing with such currencies adds a layer of risk (Bilgin, 2022). Though they are not explicitly forbidden, yet are imposed with heavy taxation and policy restrictions. The union budget of 2022 imposed a thirty per cent capital gains tax on cryptocurrencies and a one per cent Tax Deducted at Source (TDS) on every trade (Das, 2024). This significantly demotivates the active involvement in the crypto market (Das, 2024). Also, India introduced CBDC, the Digital Rupee, in 2022 to meet the risks posed by unchecked digital currencies (Das, 2024). Being a state-supported and regulated digital asset, the Digital Rupee seeks to improve transaction efficiency, financial inclusion, and minimise cash dependency. Moreover, the CBDC is further categorised into retail CBDC (CBDC-R) (meant for public use) and wholesale CBDC(CBDC-W) (meant for interbank transactions) (Das, 2024). On one hand, the Digital Rupee seeks to achieve India's aim of establishing a cashless economy, while on the other hand, it also poses heightened risks in the form of increased government surveillance over transactions. Though the Digital Rupee provides some promises for achieving digital financial integration, yet, it is fraught with challenges in the form of being a mere tool for financial surveillance and centralised control. This challenges its endeavour to achieve economic accessibility and social justice.

13.6.2 Role of NGOs and Civil Society in Financial Inclusion Through Digital Means

Financial exclusion continues to be a major concern for India despite fast digital developments. It becomes a graver reality, especially in the context of marginalised communities like women, informal workers, and rural populations. A major digital divide exists in India, whereby millions are still devoid of smartphones, digital literacy, and access to secure online financial services. In this direction, Non-governmental Organisations and Civil Society Organisations (CSOs) stand as key players in bridging this divide as they can provide financial education, facilitate microfinance access, and advocate for the adoption of digital payment. Their prominent role can be demonstrated through the works of organisations like the Self-Employed Women's Association (SEWA) and Pratham. These organisations have extensively trained people in digital banking, mobile payment platforms, and government subsidy transfers. Likewise, microfinance institutions and cooperative banks also demonstrate their prominent role in meeting these challenges. They have leveraged digital platforms for advancing loans to the self-help groups (SHGs) and low-income entrepreneurs. Further strengthening of financial accessibility could be marked by the integration of Aadhaar-linked digital wallets, Direct Benefit Transfers (DBTs), and community-based fintech solutions. However, certain systemic barriers persist. For NGOs, these can be chalked out in the form of internet connectivity issues, cybersecurity risks, and restrictive regulations on foreign funding of NGOs. This restricts their capability to scale the digital financial inclusion initiatives. Moreover, the marginalised groups continue to remain vulnerable to digital financial fraud on account of their limited awareness about cybersecurity practices. Also, the role of NGOs needs expansion beyond financial literacy to fostering decentralised and community-centric financial structures.

This will empower local economies, minimise dependency on centralised financial institutions, and boost economic resilience.

13.7 Legal and Regulatory Challenges in India:

Indian legal stance towards digital currencies persists as fragmented and restrictive, whereby their focus remains on monetary control rather than supporting financial innovation. Though the Digital Rupee is significantly backed by government policy, private cryptocurrencies continue to remain in a legally grey zone. The lack of effective and focused cryptocurrency regulation law has built an environment of uncertainty among investors and fintech businesses. This has limited India's potential to establish itself as a global hub for blockchain innovation. One of the major challenges lies in the form of conflict between the RBI's monetary policies and the increasing prominence of decentralised digital assets. The RBI has constantly shown its restraint towards cryptocurrencies by arguing that they diminish financial stability and support illegal transactions. This has resulted in a hostile investment environment, whereby the Indian crypto startups have had to relocate their operations to crypto-friendly nations like Dubai and Singapore. The heavy taxation and TDS policy further added to this challenge and demotivated retail participation. This has significantly decreased the domestic trading volumes of the Indian crypto transactions. In addition to the crypto regulation, consumer protection and financial fraud prevention also pose severe issues. The emergence of crypto scams, Ponzi schemes, and phishing attacks highlights a critical demand for strong digital asset regulation. Moreover, Indian laws on data protection continue to be inadequate. This raises issues regarding privacy, financial surveillance, and government overreach in digital transactions. Regulatory institutions are required to balance financial security with technological advancement. This would only ensure a transparent, progressive, and investor-friendly regulatory mechanism in India.

13.7.1 Scope of Parallel Sustainable Monetary Systems in the Indian Framework

The system of 'Parallel sustainable monetary system' denotes an "alternative form of financial ecosystem whereby multiple forms of digital, community-driven and decentralised currencies coexist with traditional banking systems". There is a vast potential for such a system in India, as it would aid in dealing with financial exclusion, local economic empowerment, and sustainable economic practices. One such prominent approach lies in the form of community-driven digital currencies. Such currencies work within the local economies, cooperative and self-help groups. They have the potential to support local trade, financial resilience, and reduce dependence on volatile national and global markets. For example, if digital community currencies are integrated with the Indian SHG movement, they would aid the rural entrepreneurs and small-scale producers in exchanging their goods and services independently of conventional banking networks.

Moreover, blockchain-based DeFi solutions can be a significant player in boosting peer-to-peer lending, microfinance, and community savings groups. This would offer an alternative to an exploitative traditional credit mechanism. Also, it eliminates intermediaries, which significantly brings down the transaction costs and expands access to credit for marginalised communities. Additionally, a well-structured and regulated hybrid financial framework (based on the co-existence of decentralised financial models) could create a more inclusive, transparent, and resilient monetary system.

For this kind of development, the government must support an open and collaborative form of financial ecosystem which fosters alternative monetary models instead of getting stifled by restrictive regulations. A more democratic and accessible financial future can be achieved with the help of policies that fosters interoperability between CBDCs, cryptocurrencies, and community-based financial mechanisms.

India's stance on digital currencies is currently at a very critical juncture. Though the Digital Rupee demonstrates a structured and regulated step towards achieving a secure digital economy, yet, the restrictive crypto taxation policies and regulatory vagueness limit financial innovations. NGOs and CSOs are key players in meeting certain challenges like the digital divide and expansion of financial access for marginalised communities. However, their programs need backing from systemic reforms in India's financial ecosystem. One major avenue of sustainable financial inclusion remains in terms of a parallel monetary system based on the coexistence of CBDCs, digital community currencies, and DeFi models. Such a system provides opportunities for local economic empowerment, minimises financial exclusion, and increases financial resilience. Yet, the success of such models in India requires the adoption of a regulatory framework promoting financial inclusion, innovation, and sustainability. A robust and inclusive financial ecosystem balancing economic growth with social justice can be established in India with the help of the integration of progressive regulatory policies, community-based financial solutions, and digital infrastructure development.

13.8 Digital Currencies and Sustainable Development Goals (SDGs): A Case for Parallel Sustainable Monetary Systems:

13.8.1 The Role of Digital Financial Ecosystems in Advancing SDGs

Digital financial ecosystems are pivotal in promoting the SDGs. They have the potential to advance financial inclusion, reduce economic inequalities, foster sustainable economic growth, and ensure transparent governance (Bhargava, 2019). The assimilation of digital currencies, blockchain technology, and DeFi can bring progress across SDGs more expeditiously (Mattila et al., 2021). This could be most effectively witnessed in securing SDG 1 (No Poverty), SDG 8 (Decent Work and Economic Growth), and SDG 10 (Reduced Inequalities). Though these digital innovation boosts financial accessibility, they pose new challenges in the form of financial exclusion, cybersecurity risks, and centralised financial regulation. For mitigating these challenges, the Parallel Sustainable monetary system (hereinafter PSMS) can work as a complementary system (Mattila et al., 2021). This would ensure the alignment of digital finance with SDGs without intensifying the socio-economic disparities. One of the most crucial ways to foster the contribution of digital financial ecosystems in achieving SDGs is by bringing the unbanked and the underbanked population within the domain of the formal financial sector. Traditional banking models tend to exclude marginalised groups on account of barriers in the form of geographical, economic, and bureaucratic barriers. Yet, systems like mobile-based payments, blockchain-based remittance, and community-driven digital currencies can empower individuals from rural and low-income backgrounds to access financial services (Mattila et al., 2021). The contribution of parallel sustainable monetary systems in the form of community currencies or cooperative blockchain finance is significant in this regard. Contrary to the centralised digital currencies, these systems guarantee financial autonomy and adaptability. This enables the communities to evolve the financial structures that cater to the local economic needs while alleviating the reliance on large financial institutions. Also, digital currencies boost financial transparency and minimise corruption. This facet is critical for achieving SDG 16, i.e., peace, justice, and strong institutions. Blockchain-driven transactions reduce illegal financial activities like money laundering, fraud, and financial management. In this manner, it maintains traceability and security. In terms of government welfare schemes, community-based digital finance systems hinder fund leakages and ensure targeted delivery of financial aid. On the other hand, blockchain-driven cooperative lending networks can improve the efficiency of social schemes. For this, it can ensure a direct and transparent delivery mechanism of the financial aid to the marginalised population.

13.8.2 Policy and Regulatory Measures for Effective Integration

A robust regulatory framework is required to ensure an effective contribution of digital currencies to the SDGs. However, over-dependence on the highly centralised and state-regulated digital finance model may induce risks associated with privacy, financial surveillance, and monopolisation (Vinnyk et al., 2021). A parallel sustainable monetary system can solve these by fostering a decentralised, community-driven financial structure (Binswanger-Mkhize et al., 2010). Such structures can operate simultaneously with the mainstream financial systems and at the same time are designed per the local and ethical economic needs (Binswanger-Mkhize et al., 2010). One major regulatory issue persists in the form of consumer protection and cybersecurity (Binswanger-Mkhize et al., 2010). The governments are required to implement anti-money laundering (AML) and KYC regulations to tackle the increasing digital financial fraud, hacking, and crypto-assets' misuse (Binswanger-Mkhize et al., 2010). However, such policies should not prevent the growth of community-driven financial ecosystems. It can operate securely with local governance models and blockchain-driven identity verification systems. DeFi platforms associated with such parallel systems can improve security while lessening the financial surveillance threats.

Another crucial factor for assuring a seamless assimilation of digital finance services lies in the form of interoperability. Regulatory mechanisms should induce the coexistence between CBDCs, private cryptocurrencies, and community-centric monetary systems. Unlike the CBDCs being solely confined within the state-controlled mechanisms, a parallel sustainable monetary system offers dynamic financial alternatives (Binswanger-Mkhize et al., 2010). They allow communities for local circulation of wealth while staying connected with global financial networks. Moreover, there is a need to structure taxation policies and financial incentives in a manner that boosts responsible digital currency adoption instead of stifling innovation (Binswanger-Mkhize et al., 2010). Since a heavy taxation on crypto transactions has discouraged crypto adoption. Hence, a more balanced stance is needed, which should be inclusive of regulatory sandboxes, blockchain-based sustainable finance models, and ethical financial guidelines. This would promote digital infrastructure, ensuring digital financial inclusion while mitigating risks.

13.9 Comparing India's Progress with Global Initiatives

India had made crucial strides in ensuring digital financial inclusion. This could be especially demonstrated through schemes like UPI, Aadhar-linked banking, and CBDC. Also, the Pradhan Mantri Jan Dhan Yojana (PMJDY) has inducted millions into the formal banking system. On the other hand, the DBT system has boosted the efficiency of social schemes. Such schemes align with SDG 1 (no poverty) and SDG 8 (Decent work and economic growth). This has facilitated direct financial aid and economic participation for marginalised groups. However, India continues to be cautious and highly regulated compared to global digital currency systems (Gupta, 2023). Nations like Sweden, China, and El Salvador have demonstrated an aggressive form of integration of digital currencies with their economic systems (Gupta, 2023). For example, China's digital yuan is embraced for public purposes and has been integrated into major e-commerce and payment platforms. Sweden's e-Krona program pilots with blockchain-driven financial solutions for financial transactions while striving to build a secure and efficient financial governance (Gupta, 2023).

India continues to acknowledge its commitment to digital finance. However, India's restrictive stance over cryptocurrencies and the decentralisation of financial models has blocked significant development of blockchain-based sustainable financial solutions. The dearth of parallel sustainable monetary systems in India denotes a digital financial system marred with severe state control and reduced financial diversity. Contrastingly, Germany and Switzerland have established systems involving blockchain-based green bonds and tokenised carbon credits (Gupta, 2023). This demonstrates ways to link the digital economy directly with the environmental sustainability endeavours (SDG 13- climate action). India can completely optimise the potential of digital currencies for achieving SDGs by considering and developing a parallel sustainable monetary approach. This approach must accommodate community-based financial networks, DeFi solutions, and blockchain-based sustainable investment systems together (Gupta, 2023). Moreover, more inclusivity and sustainability in the economic model could be promoted by enabling local digital currencies to complement national economic mechanisms. This would ultimately benefit the marginalised sections while securing financial stability for them.

Overall, digital currencies exhibit promising potential in the context of transforming sustainable development. Yet, their success relies upon factors like progressive regulations, decentralised financial alternatives, and ethical governance mechanism. The overly centralised approach to digital currency adoption restricts financial diversity and adaptability in India despite its strides to achieve digital financial inclusion. A parallel monetary system, coexisting with mainstream financial mechanisms, has the potential for ensuring more inclusive, ethical, and resilient economic models. In India, financial exclusion can only be challenged with the help of the integration of community-based digital currencies, blockchain-based financial cooperatives, and decentralised finance models. Moreover, such integration would also enhance economic equity and ensure a digital economic ecosystem backed SDGs. The adoption of global best practices by causing an indigenous development in it would providing global solutions for local socio-economic needs effectively. This would project India as a champion of sustainable digital finance. It will also ensure a financial transformation that is socially equitable, technologically advanced, and environmentally cautious.

13.10 Challenges and Ethical Considerations in Digital Financial Systems: A Case for Parallel Sustainable Monetary Systems

13.10.1 *Risks of Financial Exclusion and the Digital Divide*

The digital financial mechanism is often applauded for its capability to expand accessibility and economic inclusion. Yet, they pose certain potential challenges associated with financial exclusion. This is further deepened based on lower digital literacy, unstable internet access, and a lack of formal financial credentials. The transition to achieve cashless economies, blockchain-based transactions, and digital wallets has yielded certain negative outcomes (Sahid & Maleh, 2024). These can be chalked out in the form of the digital divide, which has disproportionately impacted rural populations, the informal sector workforce, and economically disadvantaged communities (Sahid & Maleh, 2024). This is especially grave in countries like India due to the major reliance of the population on cash-based transactions and uneven development of digital infrastructure across the rural and urban areas. A parallel sustainable monetary system has the potential to meet these challenges effectively. Since they operate alongside the conventional financial systems, they ensure the economic inclusion of communities with restricted access to traditional banking services. For instance, local digital currencies and blockchain-driven cooperative banking models can potentially build an inclusive financial structure (Sahid & Maleh, 2024). Such a structure would be independent of the commercial banks and regulatory obstacles, which could offer cost-efficient financial solutions for the marginalised communities.

13.10.2 *Concerns Regarding Regulation, Fraud, and Cybersecurity*

The emergence of cryptocurrencies, fintech platforms, and AI-backed banking systems has also unveiled some new forms of issues associated with cybersecurity, financial fraud, and regulatory inconsistencies (Sahid & Maleh, 2024). Digital economic models, especially those decentralised and blockchain-based, often work beyond the traditional legal frameworks (Sahid & Maleh, 2024). This exposes them to illegal financial activities like money laundering, ransomware attacks, and fraudulent transactions (Sahid & Maleh, 2024). Also, the DeFi system, devoid of consumer protection mechanisms, has intensified the cases of investor losses on account of cyber intrusions, Ponzi schemes, and volatile digital assets (Sahid & Maleh, 2024). To this end, parallel sustainable monetary systems offer a solution. It has the potential to introduce alternative financial structures based on factors like transparency, security, and local economic resilience. A decentralised system of finances focuses on securing community governance, ethical banking models, and sustainable financial transactions. This can reduce risks posed by the centralised system while strengthening responsible digital finance. For instance, integration of blockchain-driven identity verification with the community-backed financial system can minimise fraud risks while expanding accessibility to underprivileged communities.

13.10.3 Ethical Concerns in Implementing Digital Financial Systems

Apart from security and regulatory issues, there are certain ethical concerns also associated with digital finance. They are primarily associated with privacy, surveillance, and financial autonomy. Numerous governments and financial institutions are adopting CBDCs for enhancing transaction efficiency (Sahid & Maleh, 2024). However, it also enables state surveillance and regulation over financial behaviours (Sahid & Maleh, 2024). A certain authoritarian regime may leverage programmable money within CBDCs to strengthen restrictions over individual financial freedom by tracking spending patterns or enforcing politico-economic controls. In this context, a parallel sustainable monetary system provides an alternative. Local digital currencies, viz. The UK's Bristol Pound and Italy's Sardex have exemplified that local economies can thrive with independent and community-driven financial systems (Miller, 2020). This reduces reliance on government-regulated financial systems. In the Indian context, a state-backed and community-governed digital financial mechanism could balance digital inclusion with state overreach effectively.

13.10.4 Environmental and Social Sustainability in Digital Finance

One of the most critical ethical implications of the digital economy concerns its environmental impact. This is especially grave in the context of the high energy consumption of cryptocurrency mining (Ozili, 2021).

It could be exemplified by the fact that Bitcoin mining accounts for energy consumption exceeding that of some small countries (Ozili, 2021). This also contributes to carbon emissions and ecological degradation. These models, being environmentally unsustainable, have spearheaded the exploration of alternative blockchain consensus models like Proof-of-Stake (PoS) and eco-conscious digital currencies (Ozili, 2021). Also, parallel sustainable monetary systems could contribute significantly to evolving green financial solutions. Community-backed digital currencies, by fostering sustainable local businesses, carbon credit-linked blockchain initiatives, and digital cooperatives by investing in renewable energy projects, provide a sound ethical financial alternative (Miller, 2020). Such systems integrate financial inclusion with environmental responsibility. This ensures a positive contribution of digital finance towards socio-economic development and ecological sustainability.

The surge of digital financial models provides a paradox of both inclusion and exclusion. On one hand, they guarantee efficiency, financial accessibility, and security. On the other hand, they also pose challenges by deepening economic inequalities, digital divides, and regulatory futilities. The surging centralisation of digital financial regulations with the help of CBDCs and AI-powered banking algorithms poses issues regarding privacy, financial autonomy, and state surveillance. Simultaneously, cybersecurity risks and ethical concerns also pose some grave issues that government and regulatory authorities are grappling to address fully. The parallel sustainable monetary systems provide some viable solutions to many such challenges. It seeks to integrate decentralisation, community backing, and environmental sustainability with the financial models. This also demonstrates how society can counteract the challenges of exclusion and state control while strengthening a resilient and equitable economic ecosystem. If properly executed, these models could act as a financial safety net for vulnerable groups. They can also ensure better transparency and security, and sustainability in the long run.

13.11 Research Gap: Towards a Sustainability-Oriented Legal and Institutional Framework for Digital Currencies

Even as scholarship continues to grow regarding the digital currencies and their technological infrastructure or financial innovations. A significant lacuna could be noted regarding the integration of law and sustainability research. This lacuna especially appears in context of the Global South including India. Most literatures on digital currencies focus on efficiency, security, and financial inclusion (Dionysopoulos et al., 2023; Molnar, 2022). However, they pay very little attention as to how such instruments engage with the environment and legal frameworks.

Moreover, even though the Circular Economy and Doughnut Economy are extensively debated models of discussion (Everett, 2021; Raworth, 2017), these models are seldom applied to digital monetary systems in comparative or policy-driven ways. For instance, the Doughnut Economy's attempt at fostering an integrated vision of social and planetary limits (Raworth, 2017). There is very little empirical or doctrinal scholarship examining how community-based digital currencies or Central Bank Digital Currencies (CBDCs) might engage with these models or operate within institutional frameworks configured by law and governance. At the same time, critical scholarship of Circular Economy models tends to demonstrate the failure to address social justice (Padilla-Rivera et al., 2020). This gap which the community-based digital currencies could help fill, but only if properly governed.

The Indian example highlights this divide starkly. On one hand, India is characterised by the rapid adoption of the Digital Rupee alongside wide-scale acceptance of UPI (Gupta et al., 2023). On the other hand, the country's responses to regulation remain fragmented and are largely focused on monetary control, paying little attention to innovation or sustainability in financial frameworks (Bilgi, 2022; Das, 2024). While the RBI's initiative with the CBDC pilot intends to enhance financial inclusion. However, fostering of environmental sustainability or considering systemic exclusion within this context is largely absent. This is aggravated by the inability to formulate coherent policies. Such policies should be aimed at supporting community-based digital currencies alongside decentralised financial (DeFi) systems that serve environmental conscious localised economies (Corbett et al., 2024).

Additionally, Corbett et al. (2024) observe that the imbalance is characterised by a lack of emerging frameworks. Such frameworks require a combination of various branches of existing disciplines such as digital ecosystem governance and financing methods. They need to align with the Sustainable Development Goals. Although some global practices exist such as Sweden's e-Krona and the EU's Digital Euro which focus on eco-conscious social access. However, the gaps in providing systematic evaluative benchmarks for replicability within the Indian context and other developing nations remain unbridged (Ozturkcan et al., 2019).

This research, as a result, has attempted to address these gaps in research by assessing how technology, law, and sustainability intertwine in the context of digital currencies. This research aims to sought to propose a cohesive model that integrates legal scholarship with theories of sustainability and economic entitlements. In this regard, the study augments the discussion on creating just, decentralised, and ecologically responsible currency systems adaptable to various socio-economic settings.

13.12 Conclusion

The creation of digital currencies signifies more than a sophisticated technological development. It is an opportunity that challenges the globe to reconsider how economies work while ensuring equity, inclusion, and sustainability. Parallel sustainable monetary systems (PSMS) are no longer a speculative or futuristic dream. They now offer a viable replacement to more outdated forms of finance within today's world. Rooted in ecological economics, decentralisation, and social justice, these systems provide an avenue to construct stronger, more inclusive, and greener economies. PSMS need not replace existing frameworks. They can work in harmony with Central Bank Digital Currencies (CBDCs) and other traditional structures. The strength of PSMS lies in community-based digital currencies and blockchain cooperatives, which bolster local economies, circumvent predatory credit systems, and provide required financial services in the absence of banks. These systems not only help in achieving the SDGs. They also address chronic challenges of financial exclusion, income inequality, and environmental decline. To harness these opportunities, affirmative policy action and institutional commitment are required. The following interventions could be noted as a starting point in this regard:

a. Regulatory Coherence and Interoperability: Draft laws that foster the interoperability between CBDCs, cryptocurrencies, and community currencies. They should also create a balance between the financial surveillance potential as well as overpowering control mechanisms.

b. Decentralised Innovation Hubs: Establish regulatory sandboxes and innovation zones to pilot PSMS within urban and rural settings, especially focusing on informal economies.

c. Green Finance Integration: Encourage blockchain-backed carbon credits, ESG-linked token economies, and local currencies that promote circular and doughnut economic models.

d. Community Ownership and Digital Literacy: Promote public–private partnerships that support community-managed fintech platforms, while investing in digital education and secure access infrastructure to close the digital divide.

e. Incentivised Participation: Provide tax reliefs or subsidies for institutions adopting sustainability-linked digital currency models, especially those serving marginalised communities.

India is a digitally innovative and regulation-ripe country. It allows the country to pioneer a blended monetary framework with centralised control and decentralised resilience. Observing international practices and adapting them to local socio-economic settings can help India develop a digital financial system for its people and the planet. It needs to be emphasised that the design and architecture of digital currency must focus on empowerment and sustainability, and not just efficacy. Sustainable parallel monetary systems are not a far-off dream. They are an urgent and viable tool for transformative systemic change. The call for action requires harmonised effort, responsible leadership, and creative collaboration. Only then will digital currencies become catalysts for economic equity, environmental responsibility, and inclusive prosperity in the digital era.

References

Abbas, A., et al. (2025). Assets Tokenization: Prospects and Challenges. In S. Boubaker, D.K. Nguyen (Eds.), *Transformation in Banking Finance and Regulations* (pp. 387–406). World Scientific Connect. https://doi.org/10.1142/9781800616257_0014

Adelakun, B. O., et al. (2024). Legal frameworks and tax compliance in the digital economy: A finance perspective. *Engineering Science & Technology Journal, 5*(3), 844–853.

Alacevich, M. (2018). The birth of development and economics: Theories and institutions. *History of Political Economy, 50*, 114–132. https://doi.org/10.1215/00182702-7033884

ARUP. (2019). *Four Plausible Futures 2050 scenarios*. https://www.arup.com/perspectives/publications/research/section/2050-scenarios-four-plausible-futures. Accessed January 21, 2025.

Bade, R., et al. (2002). *Foundations of Microeconomics*. Addison Wesley.

Banks, N., et al. (2015). NGOs, states and donors revisited: Still too close for comfort? *World Development, 66*, 707–718. https://doi.org/10.1016/j.worlddev.2014.09.028

Benyus, J. M. (1997). *Biomimicry: Innovation Inspired by Nature*. William Morrow and Co.

Bhardwaj, S. (2022, August 23). 33 percent of the estimated 115 mn crypto users in India are worried about regulations. Forbes India, 23 August, https://www.forbesindia.com/article/crypto-made-easy/33-percent-of-the-estimated-115-mn-crypto-users-in-india-are-worried-about-regulations/79243/1. Accessed January 3, 2025.

Bhargava, V., et al. (2019). Expanding civil society contributions to the governance agendas of the Sustainable Development Goals and international financial institutions. *Partnership for Transparency*. Washington, https://ptfund.org/wp-content/uploads/2018/07/Expanding-Civil-Society-Contributions-to-Good-Governance.pdf. Accessed January 30, 2025.

Bilgi, R. (2022). *An analysis of the launch of digital currency as legal tender in India* (Doctoral dissertation, Dublin, National College of Ireland).

Binswanger-Mkhize, H. P., et al. (Eds.) (2010). Local and community-driven development: Moving to scale in theory and practice. World Bank Publications.

Clower, R. (1967). A reconsideration of the microfoundations of monetary theory. *Economic Enquiry, 6*(1), 1–8. https://doi.org/10.1111/j.1465-7295.1967.tb01171.x

Corbett, S., et al. (2024). Understanding the rapid development of CBDC in emerging economies. *Finance Research Letters, 70*, 16266. https://doi.org/10.1016/j.frl.2024.106226

Das, S. (2024). Significance of digital currencies in sustainable finance and investment Indian perspective. In E.D.R.S. Gonzalez, et al. (Eds.), *Fintech for ESG and the Circular Economy* (pp. 225–245). Wiley Publications. https://doi.org/10.1002/9781394234035.ch12.

Dionysopoulos, L., et al. (2023). Central Bank Digital currencies, A critical review. *International Review of Financial Analysis, 91*, Article 103031. https://doi.org/10.1016/j.irfa.2023.103031

Dulsrud, A., & Bygstad, B. (2022). Digital ecosystems as social institutions: Exploring the role of consumption through four research streams of digital ecosystems. *Consumption and Society, 1*(1), 99–119. https://doi.org/10.1332/QUPH6141

Eichengreen, B., & Flandreau, M. (Eds.). (2005). *Gold Standard in Theory and History*. Routledge Publications.

Ellen MacArthur Foundation. (2012). An economic and business rationale for an accelerated transition. *Towards Circular Economy, 1*, 14–20.

Evdokimova, E. N., et al. (2023). Enablers and Barriers of Digital Transformations Industry: A Study of Regional Development. In *Unlocking Digital Transformation of Agricultural Enterprises: Technology Advances, Digital Ecosystems, and Innovative Firm Governance* (pp. 95–104). Springer.

Everett, E. (2021). Combining the Circular Economy, Doughnut Economy, and Permaculture to create a Holistic Economic Model for Future Generations. *Paper presented at the 9th International Conference on Sustainable Development; 20–21 September, Virtual.* https://doi.org/10.3390/environsciproc2022015019.

Goodhart, C. A. E. (1998). The two concepts of money: Implications for the analysis of optimal currency areas. *European Journal of Political Economy, 14*(3), 407–432. https://doi.org/10.1016/S0176-2680(98)00015-9

Grant, M. (2024). *Digital Money: What It Is How It Works, Types, and Examples*. Investopedia, 15 March, https://www.investopedia.com/terms/d/digital-money.asp. Accessed January 3, 2025.

Gupta, M., et al. (2023). Does Previous Experience with the Unified Payments Interface (UPI) affect the usage of Central Bank Digital Currency (CBDC)? *Journal of Financial Management, 16*(6), 286. https://doi.org/10.3390/jrfm16060286

Marshall, A. (1890). *Principles of Political Economy*. Macmillan.

Mattila, V., et al. (2021). *The Role of Blockchain in Sustainable Development Goals (SDGs). 9*(2), 231–241. https://www.researchgate.net/publication/356790274_The_Role_of_Blockchain_in_Sustainable_Development_Goals_SDGs.

Mattsson, C. E., et al. (2022). Sarafu community inclusion currency 2020–2021. *Scientific Data, 9*(1), 426–450.

Miller, N. (2020). *Are community currencies a better way to shop? BBC, 27 April.* https://www.bbc.com/worklife/article/20200427-how-community-currencies-help-keep-businesses-afloat. Accessed January 31, 2025.

Molnar, N. A. (2022). The Evolution of Digital Currency. *UCBE, 3*(1), 1–11. https://hrcak.srce.hr/file/410496.

Mukhopadhyay, P., et al. (2017). *Global Change, Ecosystems, Sustainability: Theory, Methods, Practice*. https://doi.org/10.4135/9789353280284.

Murray, A., et al. (2017). The circular economy: An interdisciplinary exploration of the concept and application in a global context. *Journal of Business Ethics, 140*, 369–380. https://doi.org/10.1007/s10551-015-2693-2

Ozili, P. K. (2021). Digital finance, green finance and social finance: Is there a link? *Financial Internet Quarterly, 17*(1), 1–7. https://doi.org/10.2478/fiqf-2021-0001

Ozturkcan, S., et al. (2019). Digital National Currency: Example of Sweden and e-Krona. *Paper presented at the 2nd International Conference on Digital Innovation, Entrepreneurship and Financing; 2 December, Valencia, Spain*. http://lnu.diva-portal.org/smash/get/diva2:1370128/FULLTEXT02.pdf.

Padilla-Rivera, A., et al. (2020). Addressing the Social Aspects of A Circular Economy: A Systematic Literature Review. *Sustainability, 12*(19), 7912. https://doi.org/10.3390/su12197912

Pantin, L.P. (2023). Financial Inclusion, Cryptocurrency, and Afrofuturism. *North Western University Law Review, 118*(3), 621–690. https://scholarlycommons.law.northwestern.edu/cgi/viewcontent.cgi?article=1548&context=nulr.

Petrova, M., et al. (2022). Digital Ecosystem: Nature, Types and Opportunities for Value Creation. In: Rodionov, D., et al. (Eds.) *Innovations in Digital Economy. SPBPU IDE 2021. Communications in Computer and Information Science 1619*. Springer. https://doi.org/10.1007/978-3-031-14985-6_5.

Raworth, K. (2017). *Doughnut Economics: Seven Ways to Think Like a 21st-century Economist*. Chelsea Green Publishing.

Robbins, L. C. (1935). *An Essay on the Nature and Significance of Economic Science*. Macmillan and Co.

Sahid, A. & Maleh, Y. (2024). Emerging Fintech and Digital Money: Current Trends and Future Perspectives. In A. Sahid, & Y. Maleh, (Eds.), *Advances in Emerging Financial Technology and Digital Money* (pp. 1–24). CRC Press.

Salminen, H. et al. (2023). Connecting the Circular Economy and Sustainability: Finnish Stakeholder Perceptions. In J. Kujala, et al. (Eds.) *Stakeholder Engagement in a Sustainable Circular Economy*. Palgrave Macmillan. https://doi.org/10.1007/978-3-031-31937-2_13

Savini, F. (2024). Post-Growth, Degrowth, the Doughnut and Circular Economy: A short Guide for Policymakers. *Journal of City Climate Policy and Economy, 2*(2), 113–123. https://doi.org/10.3138/jccpe-2023-0004

Schroeder, P., et al. (2019). The Relevance of Circular Economy Practices to the Sustainable Development Goals. *Journal of Industrial Ecology, 23*(1), 77–95. https://doi.org/10.1111/jiec.12732

Sharma, T. K. (2025). *Top 10 countries Leading Blockchain Technology in the World*. Blockchain Council, 29 January, https://www.blockchain-council.org/blockchain/top-10-countries-leading-blockchain-technology-in-the-world/. Accessed January 30, 2025.

Shaw, L. (2016). *The meanings of new money: Social constructions of value in the rise of digital currencies (Doctoral dissertation).*

Shilina, S. (2024). Economic, Social, and Environmental Impacts of CBDCs: Implications and Considerations. In *Exploring Central Bank Digital Currencies: Concepts, Frameworks, Models, and Challenges* (pp. 253–281). IGI Global.

Taylor, L. (2017). What is data justice? The case for connecting digital rights and freedoms globally. *Big Data & Society, 4*(2), 2053951717736335.

Thomas, J., & Vogel, B. (2018). Intervention Gentrification and Everyday Socio-economic Transactions in Intervention Societies. *Civil Wars, 20*, 217–237. https://doi.org/10.1080/13698249.2018.1466089

Vinnyk, O. M., et al. (2021). Economic and legal policy of the state in the field of digital economy. *International Journal of Criminology and Sociology, 10*, 383–392. https://www.lifescienceglobalca.com/index.php/ijcs/article/download/7087/3706.

CHAPTER 14

Unveiling Green Financial Development in South Asia: An Empirical Analysis

Jaishree and Satyanarayana Murthy Dogga

14.1 Introduction

The pursuit of the diminution of CO2 emissions, a significant contributor on a global scale, is imperative to accomplish the Sustainable Development Goals (SDGS), specifically 'SDG-13', which addresses the mitigation of climate change risk. As society advances, the pursuit of financial gain has assumed a diminished role in driving economic expansion. Financial methods prioritising sustainable development and environmental conservation are called green finance, environmental finance, and sustainable finance. The investigation of GF transmission mechanisms in advanced economies often adopts a market-oriented approach and concentrates on the market dynamics. The influence of shareholder voting rights and investor financing on firm decision-making is evident in

Jaishree (✉) · S. M. Dogga
Department of Economics, Central University of Rajasthan, Ajmer, India
e-mail: 2021phdec004@curaj.ac.in

S. M. Dogga
e-mail: satyanarayana_eco@curaj.ac.in

R. Aneja and R. Dygas (eds.), *Digital Currencies and the Green Economy*, https://doi.org/10.1007/978-981-95-2282-8_14

the development of GF. To advance policy in emerging nations such as South Asia, green funding is typically directed through financial institutions and government agencies (Zhang & Liang, 2023; Zhang, 2023a, 2023b).

Green finance is essential in fostering sustainable economic development and mitigating environmental problems. It involves various financial mechanisms, investments, and operations to fund eco-friendly endeavours and projects. It is crucial to measure and analyse trends and outcomes of GF to evaluate the current state, find gaps, and form relevant policies. Present-day green finance research is primarily concerned with advancing green finance practice and engaging in theoretical discussions regarding GF's development history, connotation, policy, and transmission mechanism. The scholarly contributions of these works have assisted in elucidating GF concepts and summarising prior experience and methodologies. GFDi necessitates a comprehensive theoretical investigation and evaluation of its progress.

Efficient measurement of the GFDi can analyse the dynamic relationship between the advancement of GF and macroeconomic operations, thereby facilitating the evaluation of GFD. The assessment of GFD broadens and intensifies concepts.

Even though numerous efforts have been made to bridge the aforementioned gap, there is still no consensus regarding a universally accepted definition or standardised approach to quantifying GF. Additional research is essential to establish robust and comprehensive frameworks for assessing the progress or impact of GF initiatives, particularly in the emerging nations of South Asia. The primary objective of this research endeavour is to enhance the current corpus of knowledge by establishing an alternative framework for assessing the progress of GF in the South Asian region, which is by quantifying GFD using PCA. Many factors are considered, such as carbon finance, green investment, green trade, and green credit, out of which green trade has not been used in the literature so far, for the measurement of GFD. Green trade refers to the international exchange of environmentally friendly goods and services. It reflects a country's dedication to protecting the environment and promoting sustainable development (Olasehinde-Williams & Folorunsho, 2023). When we include green trade in the GFDI, it helps us understand how much a country is integrating environmental concerns into its trade activities. This integration can have a meaningful impact on the growth of green financial markets.

In essence, green trade signifies a country's environmental policies and participation in the global green economy. Countries actively engaging in green trade often promote environmental standards and policies encouraging green investments. This, in turn, helps develop green financial tools and markets (Wei et al., 2023). By considering green trade as a variable, we can better capture the demand for green financial products and how the broader ecosystem, like green infrastructure and sustainable industries, supports green finance. The assessment of GFDi's performance in South Asia will be conducted utilising a relative ranking approach. The findings of this study will be helpful for researchers, policymakers, and financial institutions.

The rest of the paper is organised as follows: The South Asian green finance landscape is shown in Sect. 2, the literature review is covered in Sect. 3, the methodology and data sources are covered in Sect. 4, the empirical findings and discussion are in Sect. 5, and the conclusion and policy implications are covered in the final section.

14.1.1 Landscape of Green Finance in South Asia

The South Asian region is a very sensitive climatic zone. It suffers the most from frequent and intense extreme weather events, especially hydro-meteorological hazards like floods, droughts, hurricanes, and tornadoes, causing the most economic and human damage. At 2 °C global warming, rainfall in the area will rise by 10%, compared to 7% worldwide, causing more severe and frequent extreme events (Schleussner et al., 2016). Climate change is expected to increase drought over the twenty-first century, affecting food security in the subregion, which has the most food-insecure populations (IPCC, 2022). Climate change has caused massive social, economic, and environmental devastation in South Asia. Floods have harmed over one billion people in the subregion since 1990, killing over 75,000—the most significant number in Asia and the Pacific (UNESCAP 2021). The region's average yearly damage was 0.48% of GDP between 1990 and 2018, greater than the world average of 0.22% and the highest in South Asia. By 2030, climate-related economic losses will average $160 billion. More than 40 million South Asians may be climate migrants by 2050 as sea levels rise (International Development Finance Club, 2018). Climate change action must accelerate to cut emissions, increase resilience, and boost subregional economic development (Bronkhorst & Bhandari, 2021). All South Asian countries have accepted the Paris Agreement and submitted NDCS to reduce GHG emissions and adapt to climate change.

South Asia has plenty of renewable energy potential. In 2019, Climate Analytics reported that the International Energy Agency (IEA) forecasts a considerable shift to renewable energy sources in South Asia's electricity generation over the next few decades. Renewables will generate over 50% of the region's electricity by 2050. Decarbonisation boosts job development, innovation, energy security, and public health. For South Asian countries to move into greener economies, they must align their financial sector more closely with sustainable development. This will require switching investments from resource-intensive technologies or business models that emit high amounts of greenhouse gases to those using fewer such resources, thus highlighting the importance of banks and other financial institutions during this transformation (Diaz-Rainey et al., 2023).

It is observed from Fig. 14.1 that CO2 emissions by the developing South Asian countries show an upward trend over the years. Moreover, countries like Afghanistan, Maldives, India, and Sri Lanka are the most significant contributors to carbon emissions. In contrast, other countries have shown a slow decline in carbon emissions over the years.

South Asian climate investment prospects in 2018–2030 are \$283–\$464 billion annually (IFC, 2017; ADB, 2017). Due to its size and population, India has the most investment opportunities, while the

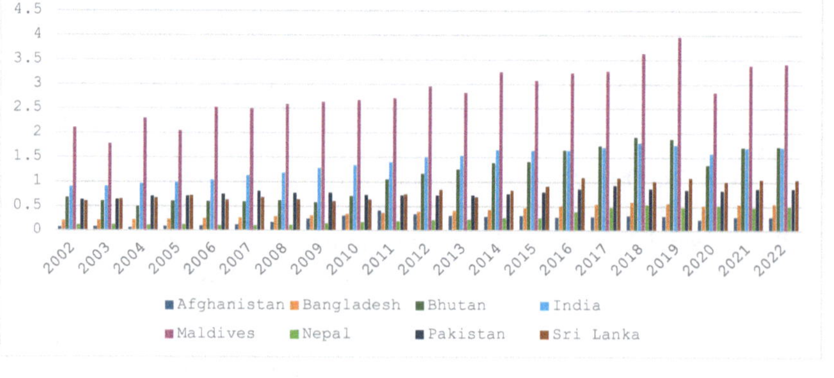

Fig. 14.1 Carbon emissions by selected South Asian countries. (*Source* Authors' calculation)

remainder of South Asia has significant development potential. Renewable energy, sustainable transportation, and green buildings may release billions in climate investments in all nations except Bhutan and Nepal between 2018 and 2030. South Asian building and infrastructure investments increased by 200% from $20.1 million in 2018 to $539 million in 2019, although financing remains low relative to investment demands, according to the Global Landscape (Barbara Buchner; Clark, 2019). In 2018–2030, the subregion needed $1.5 trillion (or $12.5 billion per year) in green construction investments, mainly for India and Bangladesh (ADB, 2014). Thus, 2018–2019 tracked financing fulfilled barely 0.5% of this sector's yearly investment requirements. To satisfy investment needs, South Asian green financing must grow tenfold in the next decade (ADB, 2023).

14.2 Literature Review

Given the ongoing progress in developing countries, policymakers encounter the challenge of achieving sustainable development in the face of climate change. Prior research on the measurement of green finance was analysed to identify voids in the literature and inspire further investigation.

Furthermore, it is crucial to acquire knowledge of the theoretical foundations of green finance to enhance comprehension. Before comprehending the green finance index, we must examine its structure and related concepts. In 1974 Germany established the first environmental protection bank with a policy orientation. The adoption of the "Rio Declaration" and "21st Century Agenda" in 1992 sparked global attention towards environmental protection, energy conservation, and emission reduction. Subsequently, the "United Nations Framework Convention on Climate Change" and "Convention on Biological Diversity" were established. These developments have so far driven the development of green finance. The 1997 Kyoto Protocol ratification increased green finance research (Dogan, 2022). ABN-AMRO BANK and the International Finance Corporation introduced the renowned "Equator Principles" in 2002. The 2015 Paris Agreement started an international transition towards a more environmentally friendly, carbon–neutral, and sustainable economy. By the end of 2017, 85% of global project funding had been allocated using Equator Principles, which were adopted by 92 financial institutions in 37 countries (Chen et al., 2018; Peng et al., 2018). In 2019, the International Seminar "Greening the Financial System in Central and South Asia" was convened in Kazakhstan. A gathering of more than 130 delegates from 19 countries was in attendance.

In Central and South Asia, the Green Finance Committee of CFA 2019 investigated and proposed solutions for a green financial system. The discourse surrounding green financing, meanwhile, persists. At the 2016 G20 meeting, the IFC expanded the definition of green finance to encompass all financing and investment activities that benefit the environment. This includes environmental finance and broader objectives of sustainable development, such as the preservation of biodiversity, reduction of pollution, and efficiency in the use of resources. Another component is environmental hazard management within the financial system (Green Finance Research Group 2016).

(Cowan, 1998) Introduced GF, which integrates sustainable development principles into financial decision-making and promotes sustainable production methods. It aims to protect the environment through financial innovation.

Labatt and White (2002) define GF as a blend of environmental preservation and financial innovation. However, Zadek and Flynn (2014) see it as a broader, harder-to-measure notion than merely green project investments. (Yang & Ni, 2022);(Berensmann & Lindenberg, 2016) emphasise the significance of government and private green investments, environmental legislation, and green financial institutions in promoting GF. Chen et al., 2018) and Jianliang (1998) emphasise the importance of green financing in supporting green firms and executing economic and environmental policies (Atta et al., 2023).

Developing GF is essential for attaining sustainable economic growth and resolving environmental concerns. South Asia's government backing, financial institution cooperation, and GF regulations may help overcome problems and restructure the economy.

After a thorough literature assessment, a theoretical framework was created to guide the investigation and provide a theoretical mechanism. Researchers have concentrated on the theoretical study of GF since there is no worldwide uniform assessment index system due to the late initiation of research. The present study aimed to create a measuring index of green financial development and examine the efficiency of green financial development in 8 countries of the South Asian region, which is not discussed in the existing literature.

14.3 Data and Methodology

The present study created a summary index of green financial development for eight emerging South Asian countries: Afghanistan, Bangladesh, Bhutan, India, Nepal, Maldives, Pakistan, and Sri Lanka. This study has utilised panel annual data for a time frame of 20 years from 2002 to 2022. The 2002 to 2022 timeframe was selected because this is when reliable, consistent annual data on green financial development became available for all eight South Asian countries in our study. Earlier years do not provide the same level of data quality. These two decades also saw significant changes: governments across the region began launching green finance policies, environmental awareness grew, and countries responded to global climate agreements like the Kyoto Protocol and the Paris Agreement. By focusing on this period, our analysis not only follows common research standards but also lets us track how these countries have progressed toward meeting international sustainability goals, such as the UN Sustainable Development Goals, during a crucial era for both policy and practice. The data for the same has been gathered from the secondary sources mentioned in Table 14.1

Further, for creating GFDi, the selection of variables was the first stage, across the different indicators, and the second step included the normalisation of the raw data. After that, using the PCA weights, we used arithmetic aggregation. Finally, the index values are used to see the present scenario of green finance in South Asian countries.

14.3.1 Indicators of Green Financial Development

Green investment refers to conventional investment vehicles whose underlying firms employ environmentally friendly operations, technology, and

Table 14.1 Variable description

Variables	*Time Frame*	*Data source*
Green Investment (GI)	2002–2022	IRENA
Green Trade (GT)		IRENA
Green Credit (GC)		World Bank
Carbon Finance (CF)		IRENA and the World Bank

Source: IRENA and World Bank Database

activities, focusing on climate change mitigation and adaptation (Inderst et al., 2012a, 2012b). This variable is often measured as the ratio of renewable energy investment to the sum of renewable and non-renewable energy investment.

Green trade focuses on the trade of environmentally sustainable commodities, services, and financial instruments that promote clean technologies and reduce the ecological impact of economic activity (Fahim & Mahadi, 2023). It is often measured as a percentage of low-carbon technology products in GDP.

Green Credit is a state financial mechanism wherein banks and financial organisations are encouraged to issue loans and aid to projects and businesses in ecological sustainability. Simply put, Green Credit is an incentive system for banks, where they can invest in environmentally friendly projects, prompting such activity on the part of financial organisations (He et al., 2019a, 2019b). The green credit facilities primarily address green financing and payments for SMES. The computation involves applying the sum of credit for listed firms to the green credit of registered firms for classification purposes.

Carbon finance focuses on the financial structures and resources that support projects and activities to produce measurable reductions in greenhouse gas (GHG) emissions. These reductions may be exchanged as carbon credits in carbon markets to promote sustainable development and attempt to mitigate climate change (Michaelowa et al., 2021). It is measured by the ratio of CO_2 emissions to GDP. The main contributors to CO_2 emissions are coal, oil, and natural gas. These emissions may be calculated using the formula: CO_2 emission = $\mu 1\beta 1$ coal + $\mu 2\beta 2$ natural gas + $\mu 3\beta 3$ petroleum. The International Panel on Environment Change (IPEC) is responsible for developing the CO_2 emission constant μ and the normal coal adaptation constant β (Nenavath & Mishra, 2023).

14.3.2 Methodology

In this study, significant indicators were identified and extracted before the application of PCA to generate a GFDi, thus minimising the complexity of the data (Dunteman, 1989). Although composite indexes are of the utmost importance in assessing green finance performance, their dependence on numerous variables poses difficulties that must be resolved by applying dimension-reduction analysis. To reduce the dimensionality of a dataset, PCA generates uncorrelated principal components.

Table 14.2 Descriptive statistics

	N	*Minimum*	*Maximum*	*Mean*	*Standard Deviation*
Green Investment	168	0.17	8502.45	2481.15	33.26
Green Trade	168	0.01	3.05	0.91	0.89
Carbon Finance	168	0.33	0.64	0.64	0.19
Green credit	168	0.01	1.30	2.31	2.03

Source: Author's calculation

By reducing variables, the representation of data is simplified without compromising essential information. According to Jolliffe (1990), data interpretation is enhanced when correlated indicators are merged into uncorrelated variables. Indices of GFD are frequently multicollinear as a result of their strong correlation. By generating uncorrelated principal components, PCA addresses this issue (Sarstedt et al., 2019; Wold & Geladi, 1987). Specific indicators are assigned greater weights during the index creation process. By calculating principal component weights to represent data, Santos (2019) accurately, PCA simplifies data representation to its most fundamental form. As stated by Shlens (2014) and Everitt et al. (2011), these components facilitate comprehension and communicate essential ideas.

The study's brief statistical summary is presented in Table 14.2 which shows the series mean, maximum, minimum, and standard deviation.

14.3.2.1 Normalisation of Data:
Due to the data being obtained from several sources and expressed in different units, it was impossible to compare the indicators' original values. Hence, data normalisation was conducted before the comparison. Normalisation is performed to prevent the combination of unlike or incomparable elements, as stated by Nardo et al., (2005, p. 27). The original data, which were not expressed as percentages, were standardised using the min–max method, which is often used in several research studies (Jemmali & Abu-ghunmi, 2016; Redhu & Jain, 2023).

After the process of normalisation, we can acquire values of indicators that can be readily compared.

Variables with a high value indicating a favourable scenario are normalised using Eq. (14.1), whereas variables with a high value indicating a deteriorating state are normalised using the approach described in Eq. (14.2).

$$Xnormalised = \frac{Xi - Xmin}{Xmax - Xmin} \tag{14.1}$$

$$Xnormalised = \frac{Xmax - Xi}{Xmax - Xmin} \tag{14.2}$$

The variable value of a single nation at the beginning is represented by xi, whereas the lowest and maximum variable values observed across all analysed countries are represented by xmin and xmax, respectively.

14.3.2.2 Weighting and Aggregation

The variables used in creating an index may correlate with each other, leading to a surplus of information that may perplex and misguide decision-makers. This could result in a situation where there is an excess of indicators but a lack of meaningful information (Nardo et al., 2005, p. 25). Hence, the statistical technique of PCA was used to create the GFDi and decrease the number of variables in the current investigation.

The Kaiser–Meyer–Olkin (KMO) test examines sample adequacy, and Bartlett's test of sphericity, a prerequisite for Principal Component Analysis (PCA), examines variable factorizability (Hair et al., 2006). Several factors at the component and sub-component levels may correlate.

Bartlett's test determines if the variables' correlation matrix is an identity matrix ($|D| = 0$) or an orthogonal matrix without correlations ($|D| = 1$). PCA is useless when variables are completely uncorrelated since each contains separate information. The null hypothesis in Bartlett's test is that all variables are orthogonal ($|D| = 1$).

Bartlett's test for the components of green financial development is statistically significant (p-value $= 0.00$). The KMO-MSA values for this are 0.550, indicating that PCA should be used for the GFD components (Table 14.3). Bartlett's test is unnecessary for the index's usage component since it only involves one variable, eliminating the need for multivariate analysis. Due to its sensitivity to the amount of data, Bartlett's sphericity test is complemented by KMO-MSA. The KMO-MSA test assesses the' variability level of variables' to determine whether factor analysis is necessary (Kaiser, 1974). PCA may be a beneficial strategy when the

KMO index value is close to one, but it should not be utilised when the KMO index value is below 0.5.

The principal component analysis was conducted using SPSS software, and the contribution rate of the primary factor is shown in Table 14.4. The top four key factors contribute 49.38%, 75.40%, 92.14% and 100% respectively in the final index. The concept of combining with eigenvalues larger than 1 selects four principal components and their distinctive values. Hence, the four primary components were chosen as the key elements to depict the whole of the green financial performance of the nations.

The Scree plot of Principal Component Analysis is a graphical illustration that displays the eigenvalues of each principal component in a decreasing order. It is used to decide which principal components to retain based on the variance explained by each. In PCA, the eigenvalues

Table 14.3 Factorability test

Statistics	*Green Financial Development*
Determinant of the correlation matrix	0.433
Kaiser–Meyer–Olkin measure of sampling adequacy KMO	0.550
Bartlett test of sphericity	
Chi-square	138.09
DF	6
P value	0.000

Source: Author's calculation

Table 14.4 Total Variance Explanation

Initial Eigenvalues				*Extraction Sums of Squared Loadings*			*Rotation Sums of Squared Loadings*		
Composition	*Total*	*% of Variance*	*Cumulative %*	*Total*	*% of Variance*	*Cumulative %*	*Total*	*% of Variance*	*Cumulative %*
1	1.98	49.38	49.38	1.98	49.38	49.38	1.95	48.68	48.68
2	1.045	26.03	75.40	1.04	26.02	75.40	1.07	26.72	75.40
3	0.67	16.73	92.14						
4	0.31	7.86	100.00						

Source: Author's calculation

are plotted against the number of principal components; for all the data points, they connect to form a line similar to a jagged rock's path. The Scree plot shows the "elbow of the rock when the values level off, as observed in Fig. 14.2". The Scree plot reveals a steady fall in eigenvalues, followed by a sudden decline, and then levelling out to create an elbow shape. Optimally, the number of components to maintain is chosen before this inflexion point. If more components are preserved, they will have little impact on explaining the overall variance in the data. The Scree plot of PCA ultimately informs us about the principal components that should be included in the investigation, depending on the explained variance.

As there are 4 components, the weights of the 4 components are given in Table 14.5 in 2 compositions. The calculation of the weighted linear average of the underlying series provides an aggregate. The weights used in this calculation are derived using PCA, which quantifies the contribution of each series to the variance of the subindex. The higher weights of the components are considered in the final index creation, which is indicated by Eq. 3.

$$\mathrm{GFDi} = (0.703 * \mathrm{GI} + 0.898 * \mathrm{GT} + 0.950 * \mathrm{CF} + 0.795 * \mathrm{GC})/(0.703 + 0.898 + 0.950 + 0.795) \tag{14.3}$$

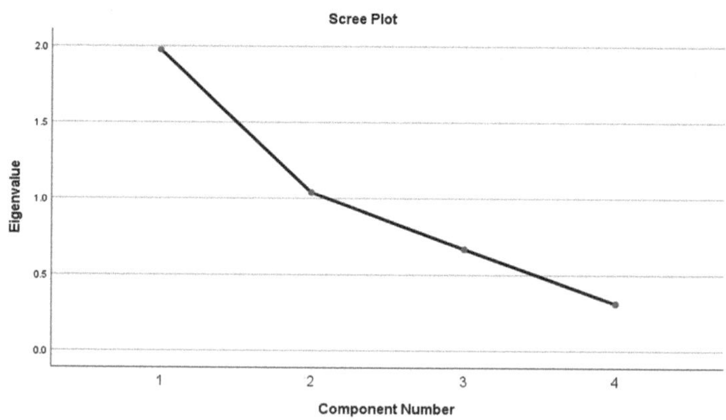

Fig. 14.2 Scree Plot. (*Source* Authors' calculation)

Table 14.5 Component Matrix

Composition		
	PC1	*PC2*
Green Investment	0.703	0.354
Green Trade	0.898	0.104
Carbon Finance	0.208	0.950
Green Credit	0.795	0.053

Source: Author's Calculation

14.4 Results and Discussion

The study period is from 2002 to 2022, and the index value is computed using PCA. The GFD ranks for 8 South Asian countries are computed at every 5-year interval and graphically shown in Fig. 14.3 for 2002 to 2022, respectively. This offers a comprehensive overview of the 8 South Asian countries' green financial development performance over the study period.

According to Fig. 14.3, India ranks first in green financial development since it issued green bonds, promoted green investments, and created green financial products. Additionally, these acts have raised funds for green causes. The nation has policies that encourage green business investment and sustainable growth policies, like the National Action Plan on Climate Change (NAPCC) in 2008, which laid the groundwork for sectoral missions in renewable energy and energy efficiency also the National Green Hydrogen Mission, PM-KUSUM for solar pumps

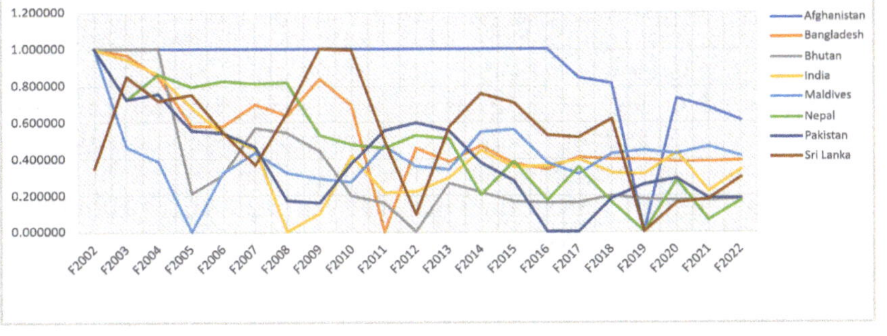

Fig. 14.3 GFDi from 2002 to 2022. (*Source* Author's Calculation)

and renewable energy in agriculture, and many more. The government's dedication to environmental conservation through finance has created an enabling climate for green finance initiatives. India also invested extensively in alternative energy, like solar and wind. These ventures sought to reduce carbon emissions and attract eco-investors. India has actively participated in international cooperation programs promoting sustainable practices, like financing environmental initiatives to boost global economic growth. Green ties between countries have been developed with the support of global organisations, drawing resources for building eco-friendly financing locally or overseas. India has introduced green banks and finance packages to help it become a green economy. Green banks in India, such as the Indian Renewable Energy Development Agency (IREDA) and the Small Industries Development Bank of India (SIDBI), make it much easier for businesses, especially small and medium enterprises, to access funding for clean energy and other sustainable projects. These institutions offer regular loans and special, lower-cost financing, share risks with other lenders, and create tailored products to help companies invest in solar panels, energy efficiency upgrades, and waste management (Almekinders et al., n.d.). These mechanisms have simplified funding for green projects. Green financing has succeeded in India due to its dedication to climate change and environmental sustainability. By taking financial measures to combat global warming, the nation has become a global leader in eco-friendly financing (Khanna et al., 2022). In general, between 2002 and 2022, India took proactive steps to green its financial sector, supported policies, invested in renewable energy sources like wind power generation plants across different states, and entered into international collaborations like joint development agreements. They all helped India rank #1 on green finance development according to annual reports from 2002 to the present, with every other country following closely behind (JAIN, 2020).

As reported in Fig. 14.3, Pakistan, Bangladesh, and Sri Lanka are ranked 2nd, 3rd, and 4th because Pakistan's economy is anticipated to grow, with business confidence improving. This has led to a forecasted growth rate of 2.3% in the Financial year 2024–2025. To mitigate the effect of devaluation on energy prices in Pakistan, the government is encouraging renewable energy and local fuel-based power projects (Turner, 2014). Despite having high inflation and constraints on trade and foreign exchange that limit economic activity, Bangladesh is expected to achieve a 5.7% increase in output during the Financial year 2024–2025.

The nation aims for sustainable economic expansion while expecting its output to rise over the next few years. Sri Lanka anticipates an output growth of 2.5% in 2025; such recovery would be supported by slight improvements in reserves recovery and remittances, as well as tourism improvement efforts made by governments towards strengthening economies and enhancing financial stability have helped them rank better among green financial development performers (Jha et al., 2018).

In the 5th, 6th, and 7th positions on the South Asian green financial strength are Afghanistan, Nepal, and the Maldives, respectively. There has been progress in implementing green projects, excessive green financing, promoting whimsicality alignment with financially dominated sustainable development goals, green investment, and green financial governance. Their strong commitment to environmental conservation and identification and implementation of green finance has placed them among the top performers in South Asian financial evolution (Volz, 2018; Zhang, 2023a, 2023b).

Despite being carbon-negative, Bhutan is a poor performer in South Asian green financial growth. The rationale behind Bhutan's poor performance in green financial growth is that Bhutan is above average in environmental sustainability but way below average in one of the key indicators of green financial growth and its economic and social components. Being carbon-negative and having a strong focus on conversation does not justify weak performance on its economic and social development. This means that while environmental sustainability was fully considered in the development efforts, these abilities were not linked with the economic and social development efforts. The balance in green financial development is impossible without economic growth and social fairness. As Turner (2014) shows, Bhutan needs to put much more effort into its economic growth and social justice performance to become a leader in green financial development in South Asia.

14.5 Conclusion and Policy Implications

This study aims to explore the green financial development of 8 emerging nations of South Asia from 2002 to 2022 using PCA on four indicators used to make the GFDi. This study shows India is leading the way in green financial development across South Asia. This success comes from India's active efforts to issue green bonds, boost green investments, and create innovative financial products supported by strong policies and international partnerships that have attracted global funding for eco-friendly projects. Hence, these activities have generated financial support for environmentally friendly initiatives from the rest of the world. The nation has enacted policies that promote sustainable growth and green business investment. Following India, Pakistan, Bangladesh, and Sri Lanka have made notable progress thanks to their economic growth and government backing for renewable energy. However, their financial systems are still mostly bank-focused and less developed, which limits green finance opportunities due to the anticipated growth of Pakistan's economy and the increasing confidence of businesses. The fiscal year 2024–2025 growth is anticipated to be 2.3%. The Pakistani government is actively supporting the development of renewable energy and domestic fuel power facilities to mitigate the depreciation of energy prices. Production in Bangladesh is projected to increase by 5.7% in 2024–2025, notwithstanding the country's trade and foreign currency restrictions and elevated inflation. The nation aspires to sustain economic expansion and augment output in the coming years. Sri Lanka anticipates a 2.5% increase in output in 2025, bolstered by a modest recovery in reserves, remittances, and tourism enhancements.

Government initiatives to strengthen economies and ensure financial stability have improved their standing in green financial development. Afghanistan, Nepal, and the Maldives are positioned 5th, 6th, and 7th, respectively, on the South Asian green financial strength list. There has been an improvement in the implementation of green projects, the allocation of excessive green funding, the promotion of arbitrary alignment with financially dominated sustainable development objectives, green investment, and green financial governance. They rank among South Asian's most successful financial institutions because of their commitment to GF and environmental preservation. Bhutan scores poorly in South Asian green financial growth despite being carbon negative. Bhutan has above-average environmental sustainability but below-average economic and social components, which explains its weak green financial growth record. Being carbon-negative and focused on conservation does not justify weak economic and social development, which means that while environmental sustainability was fully considered, these abilities were not linked to development. Overall, the findings emphasise the importance of creating common green finance standards, better aligning policies with market needs, and improving transparency to help South Asia close its large climate finance gap, a point also stressed by recent World Bank and IMF reports (Office et al., 2024).

South Asian nations anticipate a minimum of $68.1 billion in climate finance to meet their Nationally Determined Contributions (NDC) commitments, since present funding levels are inadequate (ADB, 2023). A large climate funding gap exists. Thus, governments should prioritise climate resilience in development strategies.

The subsequent policy recommendations are put forth in this article to promote GF in South Asia. Establishing a uniform method for assessing GF can go a long way. Due to the unclear categorisation of GF and the fluctuating criteria for assessing GF, it is necessary to establish green standards in South Asia. The second objective is to advocate for diverse ecological financial transmission mechanisms. To successfully implement GF, it is essential to integrate government policies with the market environment seamlessly.

Further, enhances the level of openness and provides comprehensive data analysis about green funding. GF encompasses many topics, including investments, trade, and green bonds. Agencies and websites often fail to offer uniform disclosure, highlighting the need to improve statistics and data presentation. Hence, broadens the use of GF indicators. Its application to ecological and regional economic growth should be expanded moderately to expedite the green finance index.

References

ADB. (2023). *Climate Finance Landscape of Asia and the Pacific (August 2023)—World|ReliefWeb* (Issue February 2021). https://reliefweb.int/report/world/climate-finance-landscape-asia-and-pacific-august-2023

Almekinders, G. J., Ahmed, F., & Ogawa, S. (n.d.). *Advancing Financial Development and Inclusion in South Asia.*

Asian Development Bank (ADB). 2014. Climate Change May Slash 9% from South Asia's Economy by 2100—Report. News release. 19 August.

Asian Development Bank (ADB). 2017. Southeast Asia Green Recovery Can Create More Than 30 Million Jobs by 2030—ADB.

Atta, F., Peter, S., George, S., Owusu, N., Agyeiwaa, E., Ahakwa, I., Blandful, B., Kalissa, C., & Kir, F. (2023). Green financial development efficiency : A catalyst for driving China's green transformation agenda towards sustainable development. *Environmental Science and Pollution Research, 30*(21), 60717–60745. https://doi.org/10.1007/s11356-023-26760-5

Barbara, B., & Clark, A. F. (2019). Global Landscape of Climate Finance 2019. *Climate Policy Initiative*, *November*, 15. https://www.climatepolicyinitiative.org/wp-content/uploads/2019/11/2019-Global-Landscape-of-Climate-Finance.pdf

Berensmann, K., & Lindenberg, N. (2016). Green finance: actors, challenges and policy recommendations. *German Development Institute/Deutsches Institut für Entwicklungspolitik (DIE) Briefing Paper, 23.*

Bronkhorst, B. Van, & Bhandari, P. (2021). Climate Risk Profile: Indonesia (2021). *World Bank*, 36. www.worldbank.org

Chen, N., Huang, H. H., & Lin, C. H. (2018). Equator principles and bank liquidity. *International Review of Economics & Finance, 55*, 185–202.

Cowan, E. (1998). Special Papers Topical Issues In Environmental Finance. *Cowan Research Inc* (pp. 1–20). http://www.eepsea.org/pub/sp/10536141350ACF346.pdf

Diaz-Rainey, I., Corfee-Morlot, J., Volz, U., & Caldecott, B. (2023). Green finance in Asia: Challenges, policies and avenues for research. *Climate Policy, 23*(1), 1–10. https://doi.org/10.1080/14693062.2023.2168359

Dogan, E., Chishti, M. Z., Alavijeh, N. K., & Tzeremes, P. (2022). The roles of technology and Kyoto Protocol in energy transition towards COP26 targets: Evidence from the novel GMM-PVAR approach for G-7 countries. *Technological Forecasting and Social Change, 181*, Article 121756.

Dunteman, G. H. (1989). *Principal components analysis* (Vol. 69). Sage.

Everitt, B., Hothorn, T., Everitt, B., & Hothorn, T. (2011). Principal components analysis. *An introduction to applied multivariate analysis with R* (pp. 61–103).

Fahim, F., & Mahadi, B. (2023). Green Trade Credit and Sustainable Firm Performances During COVID-19: A Conceptual Review. *Vision, 27*(5), 593–603. https://doi.org/10.1177/09722629221096050

Hair, J. F., Black, W. C., Babin, B. J., Anderson, R. E., & Tatham, R. L. (2006). *Multivariate data analysis* (pp. 1–816). Pearson prentice Hall.

He, L., Liu, R., Zhong, Z., Wang, D., & Xia, Y. (2019a). Can green financial development promote renewable energy investment efficiency? A consideration of bank credit. *Renewable Energy, 143*, 974–984.

He, L., Zhang, L., Zhong, Z., Wang, D., & Wang, F. (2019b). Green credit, renewable energy investment and green economy development: Empirical analysis based on 150 listed companies of China. *Journal of Cleaner Production, 208*, 363–372. https://doi.org/10.1016/j.jclepro.2018.10.119

Inderst, G., Kaminker, C., & Stewart, F. (2012). *Defining and measuring green investments.*

Inderst, G., Stewart, F., & Kaminker, C. (2012b). Defining and Measuring Green Investments: Implications for Institutional Investors' Asset Allocations. *OECD Publishing*. https://doi.org/10.1787/5k9312twnn44-en

Jain, S. (2020). Financing India's Green Transition. *Observer Research Foundation, 338*. https://www.orfonline.org/wp-content/uploads/2020/01/ORF_IssueBrief_338_FinancingGreenTransition_NEW27Jan.pdf

Jemmali, H., & Abu-Ghunmi, L. (2016). Multidimensional analysis of the water-poverty nexus using a modified Water Poverty Index: A case study from Jordan. *Water Policy, 18*(4), 826–843.

Jha, S., Sandhu, S. C., & Wachirapunyanont, R. (2018). Inclusive Green Growth Index: A New Benchmark for Quality of Growth. In *Asian Development Bank* (Issue October).https://www.adb.org/publications/inclusive-green-growth-index

Jianliang, G. (1998). Green finance and sustainable financial development. *Finance Theory Teach, 34*(4), 13–17.

Jolliffe, I. T. (1990). Principal component analysis: A beginner's guide—I Introduction and Application. *Weather, 45*(10), 375–382.

Kaiser, H. F. (1974). An Index of Factorial Simplicity. *Psychometrika, 39*(1), 31–36.

Khanna, N., Purkayastha, D., & Jain, S. (2022). Landscape of Green Finance in India 2022. *Climate Policy Initiative, August*. https://www.climatepolicyinitiative.org/publication/landscape-of-green-finance-in-india-2022/

Labatt, S., & White, R. R. (2002). *Environmental finance: A guide to environmental risk assessment and financial products* (Vol. 98). Wiley.

International Development Finance Club. (2018). *Lessons Learned from Three Years of Implementing the MDB-IDFC Common Principles for Climate Change Adaptation Finance Tracking*. 28. https://www.ebrd.com/news/2018/the-lessons-learned-from-tracking-climate-change-adaptation-finance.html

Michaelowa, A., Hoch, S., Weber, A. K., Kassaye, R., & Hailu, T. (2021). Mobilising private climate finance for sustainable energy access and climate change mitigation in Sub-Saharan Africa. *Climate Policy, 21*(1), 47–62.

Michaelowa, A. (n.d.). *Routledge Explorations in Environmental Economics Carbon Markets or Climate Finance?*

Nardo, M., Saisana, M., Saltelli, A., Tarantola, S., Hoffman, A., & Giovannini, E. (2005). *Handbook on constructing composite indicators: Methodology and user guide*.

Nenavath, S., & Mishra, S. (2023). Impact of green finance and fintech on sustainable economic growth: Empirical evidence from India. *Heliyon, 9*(5), Article e16301. https://doi.org/10.1016/j.heliyon.2023.e16301

Office, T., Economist, C., & Region, S. A. (2024). *South Asia Development Update Jobs for Resilience* (Issue April).

Olasehinde-Williams, G., & Folorunsho, A. (2023). Environmental policy, green trade and sustainable development in Europe: New perspective on the Porter hypothesis. *Energy & Environment*, 0958305X231193870.

International Finance Corporation (IFC). (2017). *Climate Investment Opportunities in South Asia—An IFC Analysis*.

Peng, H., Feng, T., & Zhou, C. (2018). International experiences in the development of green finance. *American Journal of Industrial and Business Management, 8*(2), 385–392.

Redhu, S., & Jain, P. (2024). Unveiling the nexus between water scarcity and socioeconomic development in the water-scarce countries. *Environment, Development and Sustainability, 26*(8), 19557–19577.

Santos, R. D. O., Gorgulho, B. M., Castro, M. A. D., Fisberg, R. M., Marchioni, D. M., & Baltar, V. T. (2019). Principal component analysis and factor analysis: Differences and similarities in nutritional epidemiology application. *Revista Brasileira De Epidemiologia, 22*, Article e190041.

Sarstedt, M., Mooi, E., Sarstedt, M., & Mooi, E. (2019). Principal component and factor analysis. *A Concise Guide to Market Research: The Process, Data, and Methods Using IBM SPSS Statistics* (pp. 257–299).

Schleussner, C. F., Lissner, T. K., Fischer, E. M., Wohland, J., Perrette, M., Golly, A., & Schaeffer, M. (2016). Differential climate impacts for policy-relevant limits to global warming: the case of 1.5 C and 2 C. *Earth System Dynamics, 7*(2), 327–351.

Shlens, J. (2014). *A tutorial on principal component analysis*. arXiv preprint arXiv: 1404.1100.

Turner, B. (2014). *Asian Development Bank Institute., 880*, 75–75. https://doi.org/10.1007/978-1-349-67278-3_116

Unescap, U. (2021). *Leveraging regional cooperation for achieving the SDGs in South Asia*.

Volz, U. (2018). Fostering Green Finance for Asian Development Bank Institute. *Ssrn, 814*, 1–30. https://www.adb.org/sites/default/files/publication/403926/adbi-wp814.pdf

Wei, S., Jiandong, W., & Saleem, H. (2023). The impact of renewable energy transition, green growth, green trade and green innovation on environmental quality: Evidence from top 10 green future countries. *Frontiers in Environmental Science, 10*, 1076859.

Wold, S., Esbensen, K., & Geladi, P. (1987). Principal component analysis. *Chemometrics and Intelligent Laboratory Systems, 2*(1–3), 37–52.

Yang, L., & Ni, M. (2022). Is financial development beneficial to improve the efficiency of green development? Evidence from the "Belt and Road" countries. *Energy Economics, 105*, Article 105734.

Zadek, S., & Flynn, C. (2014). *South-originating green finance: Exploring the potential*.

Zhang, C., & Liang, Q. (2023). Natural resources and sustainable financial development: Evidence from South Asian economies. *Resources Policy, 80*, Article 103282.

Zhang, Y. (2023a). Impact of green finance and environmental protection on green economic recovery in South Asian economies: Mediating role of FinTech. *Economic Change and Restructuring, 56*(3), 2069–2086.

Zhang, Y. Q. (2023b). Impact of green finance and environmental protection on green economic recovery in South Asian economies: Mediating role of FinTech. *Economic Change and Restructuring, 56*(3), 2069–2086. https://doi.org/10.1007/s10644-023-09500-0

CHAPTER 15

Exploring the Practical Relevance of Digital Currencies in Achieving Sustainable Development Goals (SDGs): Opportunities and Challenges

Madan Lal and Suzanee Malhotra

15.1 Introduction

The technological disruptions triggered by the onslaught of the 2019 pandemic have resulted in ripples of changes across the lives of people in varied sectors be it households, industry, education, service, or banking and finance (Tay et al., 2022). The governments across developed and developing economies have shifted their reliance on the evolving technologies to reach out to the people across different strata of people for developmental or welfare scheme programs.

M. Lal
Department of Commerce, Delhi School of Economics, University of Delhi, Delhi, India

S. Malhotra (✉)
Department of Commerce, Maitreyi College, University of Delhi, Delhi, India
e-mail: smalhotra23@maitreyi.du.ac.in

R. Aneja and R. Dygas (eds.), *Digital Currencies and the Green Economy*, https://doi.org/10.1007/978-981-95-2282-8_15

Accessibility of financial resources is much more critical and necessary for the bottom of the pyramid people for ensuring sustenance of their livelihoods (Aziz & Naima, 2021). Thus, achieving financial inclusion for the entire population has become a cornerstone for the government machinery across globe. The adoption of the latest technology has spurred the digitalized transfiguration of financial services globally (Tay et al., 2022). Several government and medical authorities globally have advocated for the non-cash and non-contact mode of payment mechanism coupled with other digital modes of financial transactions to save themselves from the hassles of varied administrative costs and cyber-attacks (Tay et al., 2022). The adoption of mobile payment services, digital banking, and rise of fintechs have all opened new sets of avenues for the digitalized financial inclusion of micro-businesses and bottom-of-pyramid families (Asongu et al., 2021).

Alongside the recent developments in the financial world, new developments have also evolved in the domain of environment and sustainability. The concept of doughnut economics has become an avantgarde notion for providing a vision to mankind to explore and foster its ways for correct and perfect living in the domain of the twenty-first century (Raworth, 2018). The credit to the word origin is given to the Oxfam report by Kate Raworth in the year 2012, and twelve years down the line this report has got international recognition from academicians, practitioners, policy makers, and organizations (Raworth, 2018).

The *"doughnut shape"* is the fundamental foundation of the notion of doughnut economics. The visual representation of a doughnut symbolizes two concentrical circles where in one circle is the representative of social footing signifying that no individual is deprived of the basic social amenities, and the second circle is the representative of ecological topline, stressing that the humans do not over-step their limit of utilizing earth's natural resources and nurturing the earth as well (Raworth, 2018). The space between these two concentric circles is what is representative of the blossoming precinct of life.

The conceptualization of doughnut economics lies in the time-tested concepts of trusteeship and sustainable development. However, the new dimension added to the notion is that people need to get into the space between the two circles, i.e. into the doughnut to meet their needs. The next comes the varied ways of getting into the doughnut to survive and prosper (Raworth, 2018).

In contrast to the age-old ways of policy and institutional framework guidelines to save the earth, doughnut economics focusses on the reformative ways of thinking and transformative ways of doing to bring actual impact from local to global level (Raworth, 2018). The five key triggers to actuate and accentuate things in achieving the paradigm of doughnut economics lie in the organizational purpose, inter-connected network, governance mechanism, ownership structure, and finance at hand (Raworth, 2018). The perfect blend of these five ingredients can enable people and organizations to make humanity thrive in the doughnut space prosperously. It would not be wrong to say that the concept of doughnut economics is a practical way to achieve the United Nations proposed Sustainable Development Goals (SDGs).

The timeline for the birth of the 17 Sustainable Development Goals (SDGs), traces back to 2015 where the United Nations 2030 Agenda for Sustainable Development aimed at the tranquility and security of both planet and people (United Nations, n.d.). The 17 SDGs, which took massive years of hard work and policy framing (from the years 1992 to 2015), are proposed directive actions the thrust of which lies on shoulders of both developed and developing world countries in cooperation and collaboration (United Nations, n.d.). With the zeal to improve the status of health facilities, education infrastructure, boosting economic development, and reduction of global poverty and other depriving inequalities, the goal directed strategies must be implemented (Ozili, 2023c). Alongside the proposed goals the proposed strategies must also be nurturing for the natural environment and climate change tracking. The SDGs are spread across broad themes like clean water and energy, ocean and water life, biodiversity and climate, urban infrastructure, science and development, partnerships for development, and international peace and prosperity (Tlemsani et al., 2023). The SDG progress report is an annual document that keeps a track record of the progress and development made in the areas of SDGs as per the global benchmarking indicators (United Nations, n.d.).

Thus, the present study tries to make an investigation into the existing literature in the domain area of Central Bank Digital Currencies (CBDCs) specifically categorizing the benefits, risks, and status quo relating to it. The purpose of this study is to provide an overview of how the evolving digital currency framework in the financial ecosystems can help in speeding up the progress towards the achievement of SDGs. The paper is directed to the goal of doing an intensive analysis of the available literature from the perspectives of law, technology, economy as well as the environment to understand the nuanced inter-linkages between the blockchain developments, digital currencies, and sustainability goals.

15.2 Literature Review

15.2.1 Concept of Digital Financial Inclusion

Financial inclusion as a concept "seeks to guarantee that formal financial services are accessible to all people" (Tay et al., 2022, p. 4). Financial inclusion is a means to enhance the ease of access and usefulness of the financial products and services offered by the formal sector among the common population (Tay et al., 2022). The regular utilization of the formal financial services and schemes by the common people is also a thrust area of financial inclusion (Demirguc-Kunt et al., 2018).

The onus of connecting and reaching out to the last mile of marginalized set of people is also a key function of financial inclusion (Aziz & Naima, 2021). One domain of defining financial inclusion is also described as people holding formal bank accounts from recognized banking institutes with wider access to facilities like credit, deposit, insurance etc. (Bruhn & Love, 2014; Rajan, 2009). Thus, a critical obligation of financial inclusion is to uplift the nation's economic barometer by aiding the bottom of the pyramid communities in their quest for income and job avenues (Ozili, 2023a).

The people involved at the helm of financial policy and decision-making gauged the latent influence of the digital financial inclusion as a "*game-changer*" in the year 2014 (Tay et al., 2022). Digital financial inclusion is a propellor to the achievement of an all-embracing financial world. Digital financial inclusion is an affordable approach to delivering formal banking and financial services to last mile people (Tay et al., 2022).

The digitalization of financial services and products marks the 4th stage of the financial progression after its predecessors—microcredit, microfinance, and financial inclusion (Wang & He, 2020). The fourth stage is characterized by the intensive use of technological advancements to widen the reach of financial services for all (Wang & He, 2020).

Globally over 80 countries have incorporated the application of mobile phones to deliver financial schemes and services (Pénicaud & Katakam, 2019). Such initiated actions are an indicator to bolster the faith and firm belief of the people in espousing digital financial services overall, rather than their partial dependency on cash transactions. The added cushion of customization in the provision of digitalized financial transactions furthers the advocacy of their use (Tay et al., 2022). The entire infrastructural set-up cost also makes it more appealing to be used for multiple service provisions (Nguyen, 2019).

15.2.2 Concept of Digital Financial Currency

Monetary policy is a policy measurement tool taken by the central bankers or public financial institutional authorities to assess the progression and impression of critical economic factors and decisions playing a key role in a nation's economic development (Prodan et al., 2024). The monetary policy decisions are often impacted by the interactional influences between the key global central banking players including the likes of the European Central Bank, the Bank of England, the Reserve Bank of Australia, the US Federal Bank, the Reserve Bank of India, or the Bank of Japan (Prodan et al., 2024). By way of implementation of monetary policies these central banking players also aim to uphold their own nation's currency, inflation targets, money supply, and exchange rates (Buckle, 2019; Cecchetti, 2000; Url, 2023).

Analogous to the creation of traditional tangible money, the central banking authorities are also responsible for the creation and supply of digital or virtual currencies (Prodan et al., 2024). Digital or virtual currency contrasting to the traditional tangible currency, do not exist physically but can be used for executing transactions seamlessly and are a part of the progressive financial journey from cash to cashless economy (Lee et al., 2021).

Many of the global central banking players are seriously thinking about the initiation of the digital currencies including the likes of the People's Bank of China (digital yuan), the Central Bank of Uruguay (e-peso), and the Sveriges Riksbank (e-krona), while those like the European Central Bank, the Federal Reserve, or the Bank of England have decided to analyze the practical implications before initiating any form of digital currencies (Dissaux, 2023; Fragkos et al., 2020; Nyagadza, 2022; Ozili, 2023b).

15.3 Material and Methods

The research method adopted for the present paper includes detailed literature review of the existing research studies touching across the themes of doughnut economy, 17 SDGs, the evolution and progress of CBDCs, the positive and negative aspects associated with CBDCs and how CBDCs can be successfully put to use to accomplish the SDGs. The identified research studies were scanned to see if they related with the stated themes of interest and were reviewed in depth to construct the theoretical framework of the present paper. They were probed for finding out the trajectory of CBDCs, their beneficial and problematic aspects and how the CBDCs can help in the fulfillment of the SDGs. The research studies for this paper were identified from the reputable database sources like Springer, Scopus, Science Direct, Emerald, ProQuest etc. The keywords like *"CBDCs"*, *"SDGs"*, *"digital money"*, *"digital financial inclusion"* etc. were used to identify the research papers.

15.4 Discussion

The accelerated need and demand for fintech products by governmental organizations, business organizations, and common population at large has opened an unanticipated domain of opportunities for digitalization of financial inclusion solutions. Thus, for the marginally isolated and disadvantaged group of families the digitized banking (particularly mobile money) has become a blessing in disguise for laying the stepping-stones of financial inclusion especially in the developing countries (Tram et al., 2023).

The research trajectory in the domain of digital currencies and their implications is on an upward curve (Cunha et al., 2021; Dissaux, 2023), spanning over topics like the evolution of Central Bank Digital Currencies (CBDCs), aligned risks and challenges in cybersecurity and privacy, precise utility of CBDCs, and public sentiment towards CBDCs.

The central bankers and policymakers at helm analyze the different dimensions CBDCs as an extensive arm of the advancement in the blockchain tech and AI-driven growth that keeps on surprising the banking and fintech industry also (Andronie et al., 2023; Barbu et al., 2021; Fragkos et al., 2020; Lăzăroiu et al., 2023; Prodan et al., 2024). The evolving financial landscape promises to achieve the Sustainable Development Goals (SDGs), for example SDG 8 (Ozili, 2023c). The creation of the Network of Central Banks and Supervisors for Greening the Financial System (NGFS) has been one cornerstone in the direction of achieving green finance, a blend of both sustainable development and economic growth (Breitenfellner et al., 2019).

Digital financial currency targets for the gradual elimination of the diverse hindrances for enthusiastic participation of people in the fintech services offered by financial institutions (Prodan et al., 2024). The contemporary technological progress curve, especially in the domains of mobile phones and social media (with intensive penetration rates), have too much to offer to the global countries to achieve their targeted economic development and financial steadiness much sooner than before (Nguyen, 2019).

The recent trends in digital currency, mobile phone adoption, and ever evolving fintech apps have all in a way re-engineered the formal financial services delivery system and ensuring equity in the access of financial products and services to reap economic gains (Aziz & Naima, 2021; Ghosh, 2021). A digitalized financial infrastructure is an enabler to attain 13 out of 17 SDGs (Tay et al., 2022). Thus, the core aim of the CBDCs is preservation of the environment by reducing carbon emissions (Ren et al., 2023) by consuming less energy than card-based transactions (Platt et al., 2021; Tiberi, 2021).

15.4.1 Positive Impacts of CBDCs Proliferation

The research interest in the domain of CBDC development has proliferated due to the positive benefits it brings to the accomplishment of the aim of financial inclusion. CBDCs have been cited as a positive propeller to the ease of payment, convenience, and access that they bring to the last mile people as well as the general public in large (Banerjee & Sinha, 2023; Banna & Alam, 2021; Cramarenco et al., 2023; Sommerhuber et al., 2022).

CBDCs have also been viewed as vehicles of financial innovation and seamless payment mechanisms in the existing literature. The inception of CBDCs is marked as one of the drastic revolutions, in the financial landscape of the global business environment. Their implementation calls for the adoption of new age technology and embracing the evolving fintech products and services (Adrian & Mancini-Griffoli, 2021; Daud, 2023; Kirillova et al., 2021; Kochergin & Yangirova, 2019; Zhou et al., 2023). In this way the CBDCs are earmarked as front-runners for financial innovation. They are also responsible for shortening the transaction cycle time coupled with lower costs, resulting in a seamlessly efficient payment system.

The role of CBDCs is also extendable to its application in the fulfilment of the monetary policy objectives. CBDCs can be used by the central banking bodies worldwide to discharge monetary policy responsibilities and maintain financial system stability. The distinct features of the CBDCs in bringing out monetary innovations in the credit system and management have been explored at length and width in the existing studies. CBDCs have a good share of advantageous benefits to their account for bringing in constructive financial influences at a macro level (Bojaj et al., 2022; Chen & Siklos, 2022; Wu et al., 2022; Xia et al., 2023). This advantageous side has also resulted in the exploration of adopting CBDCs at distinct regional or international levels (Ozili, 2022a).

For example, the Eurozone (Warren, 2023) has shown considerable interest in their adoption in nations like Germany (Tronnier et al., 2022) or Hungary (Terták & Kovács, 2022). Several studies have suggested efficient administration of the monetary policy goals in USA due to adoption of CBDCs (Bateman & Allen, 2022; Bordo & Levin, 2019). Past studies have also explored beneficial positive spillovers resulting due to the e-CNY project initiated by the Chinese central bank for a revolutionary introduction in terms of its CBDCs (Siu, 2023). There have been discussions also in countries like India (e-rupee digital currency) and Japan to assess the behavioral intentions and benefits due to the bringing in of CBDCs in their financial landscape (Fujiki, 2023; Kaur, 2023).

15.4.2 Negative Impacts of CBDCs Proliferation

The extensive review of the available literature also reflected the critical concerns and challenges related to the introduction and execution of the CBDCs. The first problem at hand is related to the varied legal limits and constitutional constraints. It has been brought to fore that the lack of transparency, trust deficit, and heavy dependence on the banks all question the long-term feasibility and continuance of CBDCs (Sheehy et al., 2023). Also, the current format in which global central banks are planning to progress on the path of CBDCs does not deem fit for a longer run (Sheehy et al., 2023).

The constitutional constraints like the Islamic law prohibiting the use of digital currencies (Albalawee & Al Fahoum, 2023), the problem of convergence among the laws of different individual countries of the EU, also the lawmakers from advanced nations like USA, UK, China may feel the brunt of such restrictions while implementing the CBDCs (Cheng & Torregrossa, 2021; Huang, 2021).

The other problems which could pose national as well as international threats include sovereignty of currency, threat to privacy, fear of potential cross-border attacks (Xu & Jin, 2022). Another potential negative concern is that the accumulated power in the hands of central banks in controlling the CBDCs framework, has been speculated to invade the personal privacy and individual freedom and a consequential erosion of public trust (Bodó & Janssen, 2022; Koziuk, 2021; Söilen & Benhayoun, 2021). However, another set of author group also disregards the potential threat to the privacy of public (Baronchelli et al., 2022).

Another potential area of challenge is the lop-sided spread of advanced technology and fintech products and services between developed and developing countries, which may delay or even derail the entire ambition of CBDCs implementation (Jain et al., 2023). Not only does the technological side need an advanced upgrade, but the upgraded infrastructure should also be coupled with safety, ease of usefulness, and bolstering speed of internet to counter the challenges well (Islam et al., 2019; Memon et al., 2020).

The entire mechanism of ensuring the digitalization of financial inclusion when evolved and conducted in methodical set-up following ethical and sustainable principles paves a way for accomplishing Sustainable Development Goals (SDGs). However, the greatest issue of consideration is that the progress and attainment of SDG for global poverty elimination, demand joint efforts on the parts of both developed and developing countries across the globe (Tay et al., 2022).

Being financially excluded is a big challenge for the most vulnerable group of people including people trapped in a bad-debts cycle, landless and impoverished migrants, female and senior citizens (Bede Uzoma et al., 2020). The reach of digital banking products and solutions across the youth populations of the developed countries is over 90% (OECD, 2020), contrasting to these are the set of marginalized and senior citizens who have shown a downward trajectory in terms of digital adoption of financial services. This reflects the slow-down in the pathway to attain the SDGs by 2030 (Tay et al., 2022).

15.4.3 CBDCs Proliferation and SDGs Accomplishment

The proliferation and utilization of CBDCs have been assessed in the existing studies for their relevance and practical application in the achievement of SDGs (Bede Uzoma et al., 2020; Chu, 2023; Foster et al., 2021; Hasan et al., 2023; Mahesh et al., 2024; Ozili, 2023a, 2023c; Tlemsani et al., 2023). There have been researchers who have studied the core theme under purview for developing, developed, underdeveloped, and also multi-perspective domains. Table 15.1 summarizes the prominent papers which were put under purview of the present study.

It has been found in the existing literature that the guided usage and application of CBDCs can help a pivotal role in the accomplishment of the SDGs. Table 15.2 has compiled the viewpoints from the existing literature to provide a snapshot view of CBDCs contribution in the accomplishment of the SDGS.

Table 15.1 Research papers under purview of present study

References	*Country/Region of Study*	*Development Status*
Bede Uzoma et al. (2020)	Sub-Saharan Africa	Developing
Chu (2023)	New Zealand	Developed
Foster et al. (2021)	Least Developed Countries (LDCs)	Underdeveloped
Hasan et al. (2023)	Gulf countries	Multi-perspective view
Mahesh et al. (2024)	India	Developing
Ozili (2023a) Ozili (2023c)	Diversified	Multi-perspective view
Tlemsani et al., (2023)	Emerging Islamic countries	Developing

Source The authors (compiled from existing literature)

Table 15.2 Summary of CBDCs contribution in accomplishment of SDGs

SDGs	*Authors*	*Contribution of CBDCs*
SDG 1 No poverty	Chu (2023), Hasan et al., (2023), Mahesh et al. (2024) and Ozili (2023a)	1. Affordable access to fintech services like digital credit transfers to beneficiary accounts 2. Financial access and ease can ameliorate the quality of life of the poor and marginalized 3. The quick and digital access to funds can also spur business growth
SDG 2 Zero hunger	Chu (2023), Hasan et al., (2023)	1. The provision of low-cost and subsidized loans to the marginalized poor, farmers, petty workers can kick-start their income generation cycle 2. Prompt safer and quicker money transfers 3. With the actuated production cycle and safe money transfers the problem of food crisis or hunger can be proactively countered
SDG 3 Good health and well-being	Chu (2023), Hasan et al., (2023) and Ozili (2023a)	1. With little transaction cost associated with CBDCs the cost of medical expenses or life insurance can become considerably lower for families and easily manageable 2. The access to insurance facility via the digital medium can reach far and wide connecting the last mile people also

(continued)

Table 15.2 (continued)

SDGs	*Authors*	*Contribution of CBDCs*
SDG 4 Quality education	Chu (2023), Hasan et al., (2023), Mahesh et al. (2024) and Ozili (2023a)	1. Efficiency and ease of transacting in CBDCs can enable financial institutes to better manage their funds for the implementation of different educational policies and programs 2. Also, digital transfer of scholarship funds can seamlessly help poor families in providing education for their children
SDG 5 Gender equality	Chu (2023), Hasan et al., (2023), Mahesh et al. (2024)	1. The application of CBDCs can help in bridging the gender gap, by giving more control and access to financial funds individually to the women 2. The added financial access to funds can help in women empowerment also
SDG 6 Clean water and sanitation	Chu (2023), Hasan et al., (2023)	1. The easy and efficient transfer of money via CBDCs can lead to speeding up of funds availability for large-scale developmental works 2. Also, the provision of digital money can automate the annual repair and maintenance work for such projects

(continued)

Table 15.2 (continued)

SDGs	*Authors*	*Contribution of CBDCs*
SDG 7 Affordable and clean energy	Chu (2023), Hasan et al., (2023), Ozili (2023a)	1. The financial viability offered by the CBDCs can enable the provision of low-cost budget-friendly and renewable energy facilities to the deprived people across the regions of Africa, Asia, and mid-income-group countries
SDG 8 Decent work and economic growth	Chu (2023), Hasan et al., (2023), Mahesh et al. (2024)	1. The application of CBDCs automates certain daily office tasks like digital salary transfer and payment to book debts 2. The digital money can fasten things up for the micro business units also
SDG 9 Industry, innovation, and infrastructure	Chu (2023), Hasan et al., (2023), Mahesh et al. (2024)	1. CBDCs are characteristically innovative in nature and a trigger for the industrial and infrastructural innovation boost
SDG 10 Reduced inequalities	Chu (2023), Hasan et al., (2023)	1. The basic provision of digital financial access and affordability at the same time can help in bridging the inequality gap between the rich and the marginalized poor people

(continued)

Table 15.2 (continued)

SDGs	*Authors*	*Contribution of CBDCs*
SDG 11 Sustainable cities and communities	Chu (2023), Hasan et al., (2023)	1. The use of cash is related to bureaucratic corruption and delays. But with CBDCs at fore the cost and efficiency of managing city expenses and community living can become sustainable enough
SDG 12 Responsible consumption and production	Chu (2023), Hasan et al., (2023), Mahesh et al. (2024)	1. CBDCs can direct funding towards the projects driven by responsible and sustainable consumption-production cycle 2. Use of CBDCs can also help in identifying, monitoring, and easily switching between projects
SDG 13 Climate action	Chu (2023), Hasan et al., (2023), Ozili (2023a)	1. The CBDCs financed funding can directly go to the avenues of climate action management and resolution which will be cost-effective, timely, and goal-directed also
SDG 14 Sustainable life below water	Chu (2023), Hasan et al., (2023)	1. CBDC directed funding can be used for sustainability-driven programs to converse the aquatic life sources of the earth
SDG 15 Sustainable life on land	Chu (2023), Hasan et al., (2023)	1. CBDC-based fundings will provide a new window of funding for sustainable land development projects

(continued)

Table 15.2 (continued)

SDGs	*Authors*	*Contribution of CBDCs*
SDG 16 Peace, justice, and strong institutions	Chu (2023), Hasan et al., (2023)	1. Transparency along with accountability establishment of CBDCs-based transactions make them the best candidate for initiating government, international, and peace transactions seamlessly
SDG 17 Partnership for the goals	Chu (2023), Hasan et al., (2023), Mahesh et al. (2024)	1. CBDCs can be used in a seamless manner to fund and encourage global environmental and sustainable projects

Source Compiled by the authors from Chu (2023), Hasan et al. (2023), Mahesh et al. (2024), Ozili (2023a)

15.5 Conclusion

The CBDCs are categorized as new money in evolutionary stage, complimentary to the traditional money which could be used at par as traditional money supply measures to achieve the fiscal and monetary policy goals (Hook, 2022, 2023). Existing literature has studied the web of articles ranging from the contemporary issues of green finance to carbon neutrality to digital economy and its impact in building sustainable global market.

The existing studies based on studying the relationship between the dimensions of carbon neutrality and proliferous extend of blockchain technology for Chinese landscape, have found that there exists both positive and negative relationship between the two (Qin et al., 2023). While the power of speed accelerates the transaction processing, at the same time it will seamlessly help in the achievement of carbon-neutrality goal. However, the process of transition to digital infrastructure and allied construction activities in the short to mid run could lead to a potential negative impact on the environment.

The existing studies on CBDCs have suggested that the adoption of CBDCs can help in the achievement of green finance objectives (Náñez Alonso et al., 2020). The correct benefit of green finance on the society and its contribution to the environment can be only experienced if the key policies are framed, and legalities are re-worked so that substantial efforts are taken by the people in tandem with the desired targets (Ozili, 2022b).

The target of reducing carbon emissions and energy efficiency in global scenario can be attained if a proper market-determined mechanism for carbon-tracking in terms of both origin of source and utilization can be done adequately. The CBDCs in question must have the desirable features for the fulfilment of the above-stated requirements, that is, CBDCs must be energy efficient, environmentally considerate, safe, and durable. If all this is done right, then the concept and meaning of CBDCs can be yielded and its benefits can be taken to people in its letter and spirit.

References

Adrian, T., & Mancini-Griffoli, T. (2021). The rise of digital money. *Annual Review of Financial Economics, 13*(1), 57–77. https://doi.org/10.1146/annurev-financial-101620-063859

Albalawee, N., & Al Fahoum, A. S. (2023). Islamic legal perspectives on digital currencies and how they apply to Jordanian legislation. *F1000Research, 12*, 97. https://doi.org/10.12688/f1000research.128767.1

Andronie, M., Iatagan, M., Uţă, C., Hurloiu, I., Dijmărescu, A., & Dijmărescu, I. (2023). Big data management algorithms in artificial Internet of Things-based fintech. *Oeconomia Copernicana, 14*(3), 769–793. https://doi.org/10.24136/oc.2023.022

Asongu, S. A., Biekpe, N., & Cassimon, D. (2021). On the diffusion of mobile phone innovations for financial inclusion. *Technology in Society, 65*, Article 101542. https://doi.org/10.1016/j.techsoc.2021.101542

Aziz, A., & Naima, U. (2021). Rethinking digital financial inclusion: Evidence from Bangladesh. *Technology in Society, 64*, Article 101509. https://doi.org/10.1016/j.techsoc.2020.101509

Banerjee, S., & Sinha, M. (2023). Promoting financial inclusion through Central Bank Digital currency: an evaluation of payment system viability in India. *Australasian Accounting, Business and Finance Journal, 17*(1), 176–204. https://doi.org/10.14453/aabfj.v17i1.14

Banna, H., & Alam, M. R. (2021). Impact of digital financial inclusion XE "digital financial inclusion" on ASEAN banking stability: Implications for the post-Covid-19 era. *Studies in Economics and Finance, 38*(2), 504–523. https://doi.org/10.1108/sef-09-2020-0388

Barbu, C. M., Florea, D. L., Dabija, D. C., & Barbu, M. C. R. (2021). Customer experience in fintech. *Journal of Theoretical and Applied Electronic Commerce Research, 16*(5), 1415–1433. https://doi.org/10.3390/jtaer16050080

Baronchelli, A., Halaburda, H., & Teytelboym, A. (2022). Central bank digital currencies risk becoming a digital Leviathan. *Nature Human Behaviour, 6*(7), 907–909. https://doi.org/10.1038/s41562-022-01404-9

Bateman, W., & Allen, J. (2022). The law of central bank reserve creation. *The Modern Law Review, 85*(2), 401–434. https://doi.org/10.1111/1468-2230.12688

Bede Uzoma, A., Omankhanlen, A. E., Obindah, G., Arewa, A., & Okoye, L. U. (2020). Digital finance as a mechanism for extending the boundaries of financial inclusion in sub-Saharan Africa: A general methods of moments approach. *Cogent Arts & Humanities, 7*(1), 1788293. https://doi.org/10.1080/23311983.2020.1788293

Bodó, B., & Janssen, H. (2022). Maintaining trust in a technologized public sector. *Policy and Society, 41*(3), 414–429. https://doi.org/10.1093/polsoc/puac019

Bojaj, M. M., Muhadinovic, M., Bracanovic, A., Mihailovic, A., Radulovic, M., Jolicic, I., & Milacic, V. (2022). Forecasting macroeconomic effects of stablecoin adoption: A Bayesian approach. *Economic Modelling, 109*, Article 105792. https://doi.org/10.1016/j.econmod.2022.105792

Bordo, M. D., & Levin, A. T. (2019). Improving the Monetary Regime: The Case for US Digital Cash. *Cato Journal, 39*(2), 383–405. Retrieved from https://www.proquest.com/scholarly-journals/improving-monetary-regime-case-u-s-digital-cash/docview/2253828363/se-2

Breitenfellner, A., Pointner, W., & Schuberth, H. (2019). The potential contribution of central banks to green finance. *Vierteljahrshefte Zur Wirtschaftsforschung, 2*, 55–71. https://doi.org/10.3790/vjh.88.2.55

Bruhn, M., & Love, I. (2014). The real impact of improved access to finance: Evidence from Mexico. *The Journal of Finance, 69*(3), 1347–1376. https://doi.org/10.1111/jofi.12091

Buckle, R. A. (2019). New Zealand's thirty-year experience with inflation targeting: The origins, evolution and impact of a monetary policy innovation. *History of Economics Review, 73*(1), 47–84. https://doi.org/10.1080/10370196.2019.1672614

Cecchetti, S. (2000). Making monetary policy: Objectives and rules. *Oxford Review of Economic Policy, 16*(4), 43–59. https://doi.org/10.1093/oxrep/16.4.43

Chen, H., & Siklos, P. L. (2022). Central bank digital currency: A review and some macro-financial implications. *Journal of Financial Stability, 60*, Article 100985. https://doi.org/10.1016/j.jfs.2022.100985

Cheng, J., & Torregrossa, J. (2021). What is Money? A Lawyer's Perspective on US Payment System Evolution and Dollars in the Digital Age. *A Lawyer's Perspective on US Payment System Evolution and Dollars in the Digital Age (July 12, 2021)*. https://doi.org/10.2139/ssrn.3885031

Chu, Q. (2023). Sustainable Development Goals (SDG): New Zealand's Outlook with Central Bank Digital Currency and SDG 8 Realization on the Horizon. *Nanyang Business School Research Paper*. https://doi.org/10.2139/ssrn.4465781

Cramarenco, R. E., Burcă-Voicu, M. I., & Dabija, D. C. (2023). Student perceptions of online education and digital technologies during the COVID-19 pandemic: A systematic review. *Electronics, 12*(2), 319. https://doi.org/10.3390/electronics12020319

Cunha, P. R., Melo, P., & Sebastião, H. (2021). From bitcoin to central bank digital currencies: Making sense of the digital money revolution. *Future Internet, 13*(7), 165. https://doi.org/10.3390/fi13070165

Daud, S. N. M. (2023). Financial inclusion, economic growth and the role of digital technology. *Finance Research Letters, 53*, Article 103602. https://doi.org/10.1016/j.frl.2022.103602

Demirguc-Kunt, A., Klapper, L., Singer, D., Ansar, S., & Hess, J. (2018). The Global Findex Database 2017: Measuring financial inclusion and the fintech revolution. *World Bank Publications*. https://doi.org/10.1596/978-1-4648-1259-0

Dissaux, T. (2023). A "digital euro", for what purpose?. *Political Economy, 1*, 92–103. https://shs.cairn.info/revue-l-economie-politique-2023-1-page-92?lang=fr

Foster, K., Blakstad, S., Gazi, S., & Bos, M. (2021). Digital currencies and CBDC impacts on least developed countries (LDCs). *The Dialogue on Global Digital Finance Governance Paper Series. SSRN 3871301*. https://doi.org/10.2139/ssrn.3871301

Fragkos, G., Minwalla, C., Plusquellic, J., & Tsiropoulou, E. E. (2020). Artificially intelligent electronic money. *IEEE Consumer Electronics Magazine, 10*(4), 81–89. https://doi.org/10.1109/mce.2020.3024512

Fujiki, H. (2023). Attributes needed for Japan's central bank digital currency. *The Japanese Economic Review, 74*(1), 117–175. https://doi.org/10.1007/s42973-021-00106-7

Ghosh, S. (2021). How important is trust in driving financial inclusion? *Journal of Behavioral and Experimental Finance, 30*, Article 100510. https://doi.org/10.1016/j.jbef.2021.100510

Hasan, R., Ashfaq, M., & Hassan, M. K. (2023). Central Bank Digital Currency (Cbdc) for Sustainable Development in the Gulf Region: A Closer Inspection of Project Aber. *SSRN*. https://doi.org/10.2139/ssrn.4581338

Hook, A. (2022). Examining modern money creation: An institution-centered explanation and visualization of the "credit theory" of money and some reflections on its significance. *The Journal of Economic educaTion, 53*(3), 210–231. https://doi.org/10.1080/00220485.2022.2075510

Hook, A. (2023). Towards an institutional "landscape" view of modern money creation mechanisms and some reflections on their ecological significance. *Sustainability Science, 18*(4), 1977–1993. https://doi.org/10.1007/s11625-023-01304-5

Huang, S. S. (2021). Crypto assets regulation in the UK: An assessment of the regulatory effectiveness and consistency. *Journal of Financial Regulation and Compliance, 29*(3), 336–351. https://doi.org/10.1108/JFRC-06-2020-0062

Islam, M. S., Hasan, M. F., Rahman, M. M., Baten, M. A., & Islam, M. Z. (2019). Promoting full-fledged electronic money in South Asia: Evidence from Bangladesh. *Banks and Bank Systems, 14*(4), 166–182. https://doi.org/10.21511/bbs.14(4).2019.16

Jain, R., Kumar, S., Sood, K., Grima, S., & Rupeika-Apoga, R. (2023). A systematic literature review of the risk landscape in fintech. *Risks, 11*(2), 36. https://doi.org/10.3390/risks11020036

Kaur, J. (2023, January 7). Central Bank Digital Currency - The 'digital rupee' in India. *Economic and Political Weekly, 58*(1). https://www.researchgate.net/publication/368817046_Central_Bank_Digital_Currency_-_The_'digital_rupee'_in_India

Koziuk, V. (2021). Confidence in digital money: Are central banks more trusted than age is matter. *Investment Management and Financial Innovations, 18*(1), 12–32. https://doi.org/10.21511/imfi.18(1).2021.02

Kirillova, E. A., Bogdan, V. V., Blinkova, E. V., Zulfugarzade, T., & Yunusova, K. V. (2021). The Main Features of the Use of Digital Technologies in the Financial and Banking Sector. Webology, 18(Special Issue on Computing Technology and Information Management), 1326–1341. https://doi.org/10.14704/WEB/V18SI04/WEB18201

Kochergin, D. A., & Yangirova, A. I. (2019). Central bank digital currencies: key characteristics and directions of influence on monetary and credit and payment systems. *Finance: Theory and Practice, 23*(4), 80–98. https://doi.org/10.26794/2587-5671-2019-23-4-80-98

Lăzăroiu, G., Bogdan, M., Geamănu, M., Hurloiu, L., Luminiţa, L., & Ştefănescu, R. (2023). Artificial intelligence algorithms and cloud computing technologies in blockchain-based fintech management. *Oeconomia Copernicana, 14*(3), 707-730. https://doi.org/10.24136/oc.2023.01

Lee, D. K. C., Yan, L., & Wang, Y. (2021). A global perspective on central bank digital currency. *China Economic Journal, 14*(1), 52–66. https://doi.org/10.1080/17538963.2020.1870279

Mahesh, K. M., Aithal, P. S., & Sharma, K. R. S. (2024). Impact of Centralized Blockchain Digital Currency (CBDC): For Financial Inclusion and Sustainability. *International Journal of Management, Technology and Social Sciences (IJMTS), 9*(2), 156–172. https://doi.org/10.47992/IJMTS.2581.6012.0351

Memon, R. A., Li, J. P., Ahmed, J., Nazeer, M. I., Ismail, M., & Ali, K. (2020). Cloud-based vs. blockchain-based IoT: A comparative survey and way forward. *Frontiers of Information Technology & Electronic Engineering, 21*(4), 563–586. https://doi.org/10.1631/FITEE.1800343

Náñez Alonso, S. L., Jorge-Vazquez, J., & Reier Forradellas, R. F. (2020). Detection of financial inclusion vulnerable rural areas through an access to cash index: solutions based on the pharmacy network and a CBDC. Evidence based on Ávila (Spain). *Sustainability, 12*(18), 7480. https://doi.org/10.3390/su12187480

Nyagadza, B. (2022). Sustainable digital transformation for ambidextrous digital firms: Systematic literature review, meta-analysis and agenda for future research directions. *Sustainable Technology and Entrepreneurship, 1*(3), Article 100020. https://doi.org/10.1016/j.stae.2022.100020

Nguyen, H. T. T. (2019). The interest rate sensitivity of output and prices with different levels of financial inclusion: Evidence from developing economies. *Journal of Economics and Development, 21*(2), 114–130. https://doi.org/10.1108/JED-07-2019-0018

OECD. (2020). Advancing the Digital Financial Inclusion of Youth. *OECD Publishing, Paris*. https://doi.org/10.1787/21b829d8-en

Ozili, P. K. (2022a). CBDC, Fintech and cryptocurrency for financial inclusion and financial stability. *Digital Policy, Regulation and Governance, 25*(1), 40–57. https://doi.org/10.1108/DPRG-04-2022-0033

Ozili, P. K. (2022b). Green finance research around the world: A review of literature. *International Journal of Green Economics, 16*(1), 56–75. https://doi.org/10.1504/IJGE.2022.125554

Ozili, P. K. (2023a). Central bank digital currency, poverty reduction and the United Nations sustainable development goals. In P.K. Tyagi, V. Nadda, V. Bharti, E. Kemer (Eds.), *Embracing Business Sustainability Through Innovation and Creativity in the Service Sector* (pp. 175–183). IGI Global. https://doi.org/10.2139/ssrn.4317557

Ozili, P. K. (2023b). Central bank digital currency research around the World: A review of literature. *Journal of Money Laundering Control, 26*(2), 215–226. https://doi.org/10.1108/JMLC-11-2021-0126

Ozili, P.K. (2023c). Using Central Bank Digital Currency to Achieve the Sustainable Development Goals. In K. Sood, B. Balusamy & S. Grima (Eds.), *Digital Transformation, Strategic Resilience, Cyber Security and Risk Management* (pp. 143–153). Emerald Publishing Limited. https://doi.org/10.2139/ssrn.4370181

Pénicaud, C., & Katakam, A. (2019). State of the industry 2013: Mobile financial services for the unbanked. *Gates Open Res, 3*(1429), 1429. https://doi.org/10.21955/gatesopenres.1116339.1

Platt, M., Sedlmeir, J., Platt, D., Xu, J., Tasca, P., Vadgama, N., & Ibañez, J. I. (2021, December). The energy footprint of blockchain consensus mechanisms beyond proof-of-work. In *2021 IEEE 21st International Conference on Software Quality, Reliability and Security Companion (QRS-C)* (pp. 1135–1144). IEEE. https://doi.org/10.1109/qrs-c55045.2021.00168

Prodan, S., Konhäusner, P., Dabija, D. C., Lazaroiu, G., & Marincean, L. (2024). The rise in popularity of central bank digital currencies. A Systematic Review. *Heliyon, 10*(9), Article e30561. https://doi.org/10.1016/j.heliyon.2024.e30561

Qin, M., Su, C. W., Lobonţ, O. R., & Umar, M. (2023). Blockchain: A carbon-neutral facilitator or an environmental destroyer? *International Review of Economics & Finance, 86*, 604–615. https://doi.org/10.1016/j.iref.2023.04.004

Rajan, R. G. (2009). The credit crisis and cycle-proof regulation. *Federal Reserve Bank of St Louis Review, 91*(5), 397–402.

Raworth, K. (2018). *Doughnut economics: Seven ways to think like a 21st century economist*. Chelsea Green Publishing.

Ren, D., Guo, H., & Jiang, T. (2023). Managed anonymity of CBDC, social welfare and taxation: A new monetarist perspective. *Applied Economics, 55*(42), 4990–5011. https://doi.org/10.1080/00036846.2022.2133896

Sheehy, B., Hawkins, J., & Diaz-Granados, J. (2023). Legal problems and solutions in stablecoins: A multi-disciplinary approach applied to euro stablecoins. *Review of Law & Economics, 19*(1), 85–98. https://doi.org/10.1515/rle-2022-0053

Siu, R. C. (2023). Social, political, and economic dimensions of the instituted process of Central Bank Digital currency: The case of the digital yuan. *Journal of Economic Issues, 57*(2), 458–465. https://doi.org/10.1080/00213624.2023.2201610

Söilen, K. S., & Benhayoun, L. (2021). Household acceptance of central bank digital currency: The role of institutional trust. *International Journal of Bank Marketing, 40*(1), 172–196. https://doi.org/10.1108/IJBM-04-2021-0156

Sommerhuber, M., Bobek, V., Strašek, R., & Horvat, T. (2022). Market potential of digital assets in developing countries: The case of Diem. *International Journal of Diplomacy and Economy, 8*(2), 133–168. https://doi.org/10.1504/ijdipe.2022.127044

Tay, L. Y., Tai, H. T., & Tan, G. S. (2022). Digital financial inclusion: A gateway to sustainable development. *Heliyon, 8*(6), Article e09766. https://doi.org/10.1016/j.heliyon.2022.e09766

Terták, E., & Kovács, L. (2022). The Motives for Issuing Central Bank Digital Currency and the Challenges of Introduction Thereof. *Public Finance Quarterly, 67*(4), 491–505. https://doi.org/10.35551/PFQ_2022_4_1

Tiberi, P. (2021). The carbon footprint of the Target Instant Payment Settlement (TIPS) system: A comparative analysis with Bitcoin and other infrastructures. *Bank of Italy Markets, Infrastructures, Payment Systems Working Paper*, (5). https://doi.org/10.2139/ssrn.3854995

Tlemsani, I., Zaman, A., Mohamed Hashim, M. A., & Matthews, R. (2023). Digitalization and sustainable development goals in emerging Islamic economies. *Journal of Islamic Accounting and Business Research. (in Press).* https://doi.org/10.1108/JIABR-03-2023-0092

Tram, T. X. H., Lai, T. D., & Nguyen, T. T. H. (2023). Constructing a composite financial inclusion index for developing economies. *The Quarterly Review of Economics and Finance, 87*, 257–265. https://doi.org/10.1016/j.qref.2021.01.003

Tronnier, F., Harborth, D., & Hamm, P. (2022). Investigating privacy concerns and trust in the digital Euro in Germany XE "Germany." *Electronic Commerce Research and Applications, 53*, Article 101158. https://doi.org/10.1016/j.elerap.2022.101158

United Nations (n.d.). *The 17 Goals. Sustainable Development*. https://sdgs.un.org/goals

Url, T. (2023). Highly Dispersed inflation rates challenge the ECB's monetary policy strategy. *SUERF Policy Brief No., 524.*

Wang, X., & He, G. (2020). Digital financial inclusion and farmers' vulnerability to poverty: Evidence from rural China. *Sustainability, 12*(4), 1668. https://doi.org/10.3390/su12041668

Warren, M. (2023). Let the Digital Euro Circulate: Introducing a Retail CBDC in the Eurozone with Unlimited Holdings by Users. *University of Bologna Law Review, 8*(1), 1–42. https://doi.org/10.6092/issn.2531-6133/16907

Wu, B., An, X., Wang, C., & Shin, H. Y. (2022). Extending UTAUT with national identity and fairness to understand user adoption of DCEP in China. *Scientific Reports, 12*(1), 6856. https://doi.org/10.1038/s41598-022-109 27-0

Xia, H., Gao, Y., & Zhang, J. Z. (2023). Understanding the adoption context of China's digital currency electronic payment. *Financial Innovation, 9*(1), 63. https://doi.org/10.1186/s40854-023-00467-5

Xu, C., & Jin, B. (2022). Digital currency in China: pilot implementations, legal challenges and prospects. *Juridical Tribune-Review of Comparative and International Law*, *12*(2), 177–194. https://EconPapers.repec.org/RePEc:asr:journl:v:12:y:2022:i:2:p:177-194

Zhou, C., Chen, Y., Wattenhofer, R., & Wang, Y. (2023, April). Print your money: cash-like experiences with digital money. In *Extended Abstracts of the 2023 CHI Conference on Human Factors in Computing Systems* (pp. 1–7). https://doi.org/10.1145/3544549.3585772

CHAPTER 16

Legal Challenges of Providing Urban Air Mobility Services in the Green Economy

Andrzej Krasuski

16.1 Introduction

Urban air mobility (UAM), electric and autonomous vehicles, are the three main pillars of disruptive technologies in transport (Garrow et al., 2021) that are pushing forward technological progress. These technologies relate to modes of transport. As such, they share similar characteristics and challenges, including in the area of law and regulation. Of course, there are also differences between these technologies.

Nowadays, UAM is not only a concept project reflected in the vehicle type 'Audi Pop. Up Next' (Pop.Up Next, 2018). It has already gained recognition from the authorities responsible for the certification of air transport equipment. A significant milestone in this field was reached when 'EHang's EH216-S' two-seat autonomous aircraft received the world's first type certificate from the Civil Aviation Administration of

A. Krasuski (✉)
Academic Department of Social Sciences, European Humanities University, Vilnius, Lithuania
e-mail: andrzej.krasuskia@ehu.lt

R. Aneja and R. Dygas (eds.), *Digital Currencies and the Green Economy*, https://doi.org/10.1007/978-981-95-2282-8_16

China on 13 October 2023. This certificate confirmed that the EH216-S meets safety and airworthiness standards, allowing it to be used commercially to carry passengers (Yan et al., 2024).

In the context of the current technological development of UAM, it is reasonable to identify the legal and regulatory challenges associated with implementing UAM vehicles. This analysis addresses concerns raised in the literature regarding the early stages of regulation in this area (Babetto et al., 2023).

The purpose of this paper is to analyse the regulatory framework applicable to the introduction of UAM vehicles into the market for transport services. A second objective is to identify legal and regulatory challenges related to the application of UAM and to formulate possible de lege ferenda recommendations. Based on this, it will be possible to assess the impact of law and regulation on the development of UAM vehicles.

16.2 Definition of UAM

The term 'Urban Air Mobility' (UAM) lacks a legal definition. It has emerged in literature and industry discussions to refer to the aviation sector focused on transporting people and cargo in urban and suburban areas. Some definitions indicate that it comprises a system that allows highly automated, on-demand air transport for passengers or cargo within and around metropolitan spaces (Lascara et al., 2018). Additionally, the literature defines UAM (Tojal et al., 2021) as a revolutionary mobility idea for urban settings, utilising various 'Unmanned Aircraft Systems' (UAS) to carry out diverse missions in 'Very Low-Level' (VLL) (EASA, 2018) airspace, to enhance the well-being of individuals and organisations. However, this definition is expected to evolve. As the UAM concept matures, its definition should adapt accordingly. Ultimately, broadening the understanding of UAM will foster its advancement, preventing limitations during research phases and promoting a unified operational concept.

The Federal Aviation Administration (FAA) in its report 'Concept of Operations' (FAA, 2023) distinguishes between two concepts, i.e. 'Urban Air Mobility' (UAM) and 'Advanced Air Mobility' (AAM). In the FAA's view, Urban Air Mobility (UAM) enables highly automated, cooperative, passenger or cargo-carrying air transportation services in and around urban areas. UAM is a subset of the Advanced Air Mobility

(AAM) concept under development by the Federal Aviation Administration (FAA), National Aeronautics and Space Administration (NASA), and industry. As a subset of AAM, UAM focuses on operations moving people and cargo in metropolitan and urban areas.

The European Union Aviation Safety Agency (EASA), in its Opinion No. 03/2023 (EASA, 2023), introduced the following concepts to standardise the communication on the matter at European Union level, and to be used for the development of future requirements (regulations and rules):

1. innovative aerial services (IAS): the set of operations and/or services that are of benefit to the citizens and the aviation market, and that are enabled by new airborne technologies; the operations and/or services include both the transportation of passengers and/or cargo and aerial operations (e.g. surveillance, inspections, mapping, telecommunications networking, etc.);
2. innovative air mobility (IAM): the safe, secure, and sustainable air mobility of passengers and cargo enabled by new-generation technologies integrated into a multimodal transportation system;
3. urban air mobility (UAM): the subset of IAM operations conducted in, within, or out of urban environments.

While the notion of UAS and electrical or hybrid engines may be immediately associated to 'innovative' aspects, the aircraft design or the propulsion systems do not necessarily play a role in the classification of an aircraft as 'innovative' (an example may be a conventionally propelled aeroplane or helicopter with a C2 link enabling the remote-piloting capability).

In EASA's view, while the term 'innovative' may seem to apply at some point, the regulatory framework remains operations oriented and performance based. Certification and operational requirements are proportionate to the type of operation and the environment in which it is performed. In the certification domain, more stringent requirements are imposed on aircraft carrying passengers or operating over congested areas. The same approach applies in the operational domain, where the driving factor remains the type of operation and the area in which the operation is performed (congested or uncongested areas). Passenger and/or cargo IAM operations will be able to be performed by aircraft with different design characteristics and different methods of generating lift during the cruise phase (e.g. using wings or thrust, or a combination of both) compared to aircraft and rotorcraft, with most expected to have VTOL capability to optimise and maximise their use in urban environments.

4. VTOL-capable aircraft (VCA): a power-driven, heavier-than-air aircraft, other than aeroplane or rotorcraft, capable of performing vertical take-off and landing using lift and thrust units used to provide lift during take-off and landing.

In performing the above assessment, EASA evaluated the possibility to adopt the existing International Civil Aviation Organisation's definition of 'powered-lift' (ICAO, 2018) as an alternative to VCA, but it was discarded as:—the definition does not include all potential aircraft configurations that would be categorised as VCA, and in particular those that do not depend 'on non-rotating airfoil(s) for lift during horizontal flight' (e.g. thrust vectoring and direct lift);—the ICAO framework for powered-lift aircraft is limited only to the requirements available in Annex 1 (applicable for flight crew licensing) while it lacks requirements for the remaining certification and operational domains.

The term UAM covers various areas of research and development, such as the application of drone technology (also known as remotely piloted aerial systems [RPAS]) in urban last-mile logistics, as well as future passenger transport in intra-urban and inter-urban environments (Pons-Prats et al., 2022).

The first realisation of this concept was made through the introduction by Glenn Curtin, in February 1917, of the Model 11 'Autoplane' at the New York Pan-American Aeronautical Exposition. It featured a fully enclosed aluminium body with plastic windows and could be driven on roads using power from the propeller. The three-seater had the driver/pilot in front and two passengers behind. A front-engine Curtiss motor powered the rear propeller with a driveshaft and pulleys, and the triplane's wings could be removed from the vehicle (Berg, 2012). Curtiss made the short flight with his winged vehicle, but the first patent for a flying car was awarded to rival inventor Felix Longobardi in 1918 (DeLuca, 2012).

In the twentieth century, the concept of building a flying car was further developed. In this respect, it is noteworthy to recall Waldo Dean Waterman's invention of 'Arrowbike'. In 1937 he received a patent for

'Arrowbile'. It featured a high-wing monoplane with detachable wings and was powered by a Studebaker engine. The concept was revolutionary; an automobile that could transform into an airplane, and vice versa (Corey, 2024). However, this car was never brought to market. Robert Fulton's 'Airphibian', built in 1945, was the first dual-use vehicle to be certified by the government for production. Following Fulton, a successful roadable aircraft was the 'Aerocar', built by Moult Taylor in 1949, certified by the FAA in 1956, considered by Ford Motor Co. in 1970, but never mass-produced (AOPA Pilot, 2007).

A groundbreaking solution in the development of transport means, that was presented at the late twentieth and early twenty-first century, was Paul Moller's powered lift 'Volantor' in 1991. This achievement paved the way for developing VTOLs and later eVTOLs (electric vertical take-off and landing). Apart from traditional aircraft, eVTOL uses electric power to take off, hover, and land vertically. The presentation of the Volantor is considered a shift from traditional 'flying cars' to VTOLs (Moller, 1998). In turn, eVTOLs are designed to revolutionise passenger transportation by serving as air taxis, emergency response vehicles, and leisure crafts while also offering increased capacity for freight transport compared to traditional drones. They differ significantly in terms of flight range and passenger capacity, providing the advantages of reduced noise, lower operating costs, and enhanced safety. The eVTOL sector is attracting a mix of startups and established companies (Yan et al., 2024).

The development of eVTOL vehicles, which promise to be quieter, safer, and cheaper, has revived the concept of UAM, utilising urban airspace for intracity passenger transport.

Today, eVTOL aircraft based on distributed electric propulsion (DEP), green new energy, new aviation materials, artificial intelligence, 5G network, and other technologies have gradually developed into the most promising and revolutionary unmanned aerial vehicles (UAV) (Xiang et al., 2024).

Amphibious flying vehicles, which are an evolution of eVTOLs, represent a pinnacle in automotive innovation driven by three critical factors: (1) technical feasibility, supported by advances in electrification and intelligent systems enabling autonomous aerial navigation; (2) demand, highlighting the need to address urban congestion by expanding transportation options from land to air; and (3) convenience, emphasizing the ability of these vehicles to seamlessly transition between land and air (Yan et al., 2024).

16.3 Reasons for the Development of UAM Paradigm

The reason for developing UAM is to provide efficient transport services in an urban environment with high population density in a small area, and to reduce the resulting traffic congestion. Istanbul in Turkey tops the list of the most congested urban areas in the INRIX 2024 Global Traffic Scorecard, with traffic delays increasing by 15% since 2023, beating the 102 hours lost to traffic jams in New York and Chicago (Pishue & Kidd, 2024).

As urbanisation continues to grow, road congestion in densely populated cities becomes a universal concern. The escalating environmental concerns and land use associated with intensive surface transportation further underline the importance of electric-based urban transport that takes advantage of vertical mobility (Yan et al., 2024).

The position set out in the literature in this context is correct that congestion in the ground transportation systems at the network level may improve as the air system provides additional capacity for transporting individuals and could reduce the number of long-distance ground vehicle trips. This is particularly relevant if UAM can replace single-occupancy ground transportation trips with shared-occupancy air trips, leading to improvements in energy use and reductions in greenhouse gas emissions (Brown & Dodder, 2019).

The proportion of a country's population living in urban areas is highly correlated with its level of income. According to the United Nations, in line with the urbanisation phenomenon, more than 70% of the European population and more than 80% of the North American population could live in urban areas by 2050, being nearly 80% of the inhabitants of the more developed areas (United Nations, 2018).

Urbanisation appears to have considerable potential to foster long-term economic development. This stems from the more intense interactions, resource efficiencies, learning, and enhanced productivity achieved by concentrated activity. However, this is not assured (Bloom et al., 2008).

Urbanisation also has a negative effect on the environment and health. It causes congestion and pollution. Therefore, it is misleading to say that urbanisation drives development as if it is an independent force for progress (Turok, 2017), exerting a damaging impact on the health of the people and the environment.

In 2019, the European Commission launched the Green Deal (European Commission and EASA, 2022) to call for the implementation of climate-neutral solutions by 2050. This target also applies to the aviation sector and therefore to UAM (Organisation for International Economic Relations, 2020). The literature on the subject rightly recognises that it is necessary to take into account not only the economic cost (including the cost of time) of traffic jams, but also the environmental cost concerning pollution, since a very large proportion of the population in urban areas breathes air that does not meet European standards, not to mention the World Health Organisation's health guidelines on air quality (Kelly & Fussell, 2015).

In this context, the application of eVTOL vehicles has received substantial attention and investment as an integral part of the UAM system. The eVTOLs aim to foster sustainability and are well-suited for urban environments as the capability for VTOL allows them to operate in densely populated areas, where space is limited (Babetto et al., 2023).

Uber, Airbus, and Boeing, among others, have made significant investments in creating UAM infrastructure and designing vehicles that succeed in all three dimensions of sustainability, namely environmental conservation, economic development, and social sustainability (Bauranov & Rakas, 2021).

16.4 Legal Aspects of the Application of UAM

In the literature (Yan et al., 2024), legal aspects of the application of UAM are presented as a group of three important layers, that is, next to the technological layer (which includes various aspects, such as battery technology and propulsion technology) and the infrastructural layer. Integrating flying vehicles into existing airspace requires the support of physical infrastructure and digital infrastructure. Nevertheless, these three layers are interdependent, since the legal framework impacts other layers, at least as regards compliance with the law. On the other hand, the technological layer and the infrastructural layer are important for the assessment of whether the legislator has responded appropriately to the issues raised under these two layers.

The third critical layer involves regulatory and policy considerations, taking into account societal and economic factors. The success of UAM relies on its perceived safety, reliability, and affordability. The three-layer classification is not the only classification of research areas. The literature also presents a broader classification of studies (Straubinger et al., 2020).

16.5 Development of the Regulatory Framework for UAM in Europe

In 2002, the European Parliament and the Council introduced a regulation as a legal basis to establish the EASA as a regulatory organisation and common rules of civil aviation (Regulation (EC) No 1592/2002). The agency was established on 15 July 2002 as the 'European Aviation Safety Agency', and reached full functionality in 2008, taking over the functions of the Joint Aviation Authorities. It was renamed the 'European Union Aviation Safety Agency' in 2018. EASA is an agency of the European Union. As an EU agency, EASA is a body governed by European public law; it is distinct from the Community Institutions and has its legal personality. EASA ('European Union Aviation Safety Agency') was established in 2018 (Regulation (EU) 2018/1139) and was given specific regulatory and executive tasks in the field of civil aviation safety and environmental protection (EASA, 2025a).

In 2012, the European Commission released their Commission Regulation on rules to attain an initial airworthiness and environmental certification of aircraft including products and parts as well as the certification of design and production organizations (Commission Regulation (EU) No 748/2012), replacing regulation, inter alia, on laying down implementing rules for the airworthiness and environmental certification (Commission Regulation (EC) No 1702/2003). The Commission Regulation (EU) No 748/2012 has been amended several times. The latest amendment dates to 2024 (Commission Implementing Regulation (EU) 2024/1110).

In 2019, several important milestones were achieved in the regulatory activity for UAM. The first concrete milestone for the regulation was done as a first step towards implementing a comprehensive framework for UAS operations across Europe. Remarkably, the 'Commission Delegated Regulation (EU) 2019/945 on unmanned aircraft systems' (Commission Delegated Regulation (EU) 2019/945) and the 'Commission Implementing Rules 2019/947' (Commission Implementing Regulation (EU) 2019/947) were published. Several risk factors must be taken into account when deploying UAVs, including challenges related to airspace management, safety protocols, public acceptance, and regulatory compliance with manned air traffic (Bauranov & Rakas, 2021). EASA's three categories of UAVs are based on their weight, size, and intended operation (Schuh et al., 2022).

In October 2020, EASA launched its Sustainable Aviation Programme in line with environmental protection regulations in alignment with the European Green Deal (EASA, 2025b). This initiative remains in the scope of obligations of EASA according to Article 87(2) of Regulation EU 2018/1139. According to this provision, the Commission, the Agency, other Union institutions, bodies, offices and agencies and the Member States shall, within their respective fields of competence, cooperate on environmental matters, including those addressed in the Directive on, inter alia, establishing a system for greenhouse gas emission allowance trading within the Union (Directive 2003/87/CE) and the Regulation on, inter alia, concerning the Registration, Evaluation, Authorisation and Restriction of Chemicals (Regulation (EC) No 1907/2006) to ensure that interdependencies between climate and environmental protection, human health and other, technical, domains of civil aviation are taken into account, giving due consideration to the international standards and recommended practices, environmental benefits, technological feasibility and economic impact. The goal is to develop new sustainable solutions for transportation, including the innovation represented by the UAM scenario by providing a low-emission mode of transportation with eVTOLs, which can contribute to the transition towards more low-carbon aviation. The concept of Standard Scenario (STS) is also introduced in both: Regulation on unmanned aircraft systems and on third-country operators of unmanned aircraft systems (Commission Delegated Regulation (EU) 2019/945) and Regulation on the rules and procedures for the operation of unmanned aircraft (Commission Implementing Regulation (EU) 2019/947). The STSs are collections of operational and technical requirements for UAV operations that are deemed low-risk and can be carried out without the need for a specific operational authorization (Babetto et al., 2023).

16.6 EU's New Regulatory Package 2024

16.6.1 General Overview

The adoption of the Commission Implementing Regulation (EU) 2024/1110 constitutes an element of the European Commission's new package of secondary legislation on drones and vertical take-off and landing (VTOL) capable aircraft, which puts the final rules in place for the launch of Innovative Air Mobility (IAM), including air taxi services.

The package is based on regulatory proposals from EASA, published in EASA's opinion in August 2023 (Opinion No 03/2023). The European Union Aviation Safety Agency has submitted to the Commission Opinion No 03/2023 in accordance with Article 75(2), points (b) and (c), of Regulation (EU) 2018/1139 and with Article 76(1) of that Regulation.

The legislation introduces a comprehensive set of requirements for piloted electric air taxis, spanning the domains of Air Operations (Air OPS), Flight Crew Licensing (FCL), Standardised European Rules of the Air (SERA), and Air Traffic Management (ATM). It also establishes criteria and processes for the certification and maintenance of drones. (EASA, 2024).

The package is the last legislative element required for the launch of air taxi services, complementing other existing legislation. Air taxis will additionally require certification from EASA before such services can become operational in Europe.

The regulatory package encompasses the following secondary regulations:

1. Regulation supplementing Regulation (EU) 2018/1139 of the European Parliament and of the Council by laying down detailed rules for the continuing airworthiness of certified unmanned aircraft systems and their components, and on the approval of organisations and personnel involved in these tasks (Commission Delegated Regulation (EU) 2024/1107);
2. Regulation amending Regulation (EU) No 748/2012 as regards the initial airworthiness of unmanned aircraft systems subject to certification and Delegated Regulation (EU) 2019/945 as regards unmanned aircraft systems and third-country operators of unmanned aircraft systems (Commission Delegated Regulation (EU) 2024/1108);

3. Regulation laying down rules for the application of Regulation (EU) 2018/1139 of the European Parliament and of the Council as regards competent authority requirements and administrative procedures for the certification, oversight and enforcement of the continuing airworthiness of certified unmanned aircraft systems, and amending Implementing Regulation (EU) 2023/203 (Commission Implementing Regulation (EU) 2024/1109);
4. Regulation amending Regulation (EU) No 748/2012 as regards the initial airworthiness of unmanned aircraft systems subject to certification and Implementing Regulation (EU) 2019/947 as regards the rules and procedures for the operation of unmanned aircraft (Commission Implementing Regulation (EU) 2024/1110);
5. Commission Implementing Regulation (EU) 2024/1111 of 10 April 2024 amending Regulation (EU) No 1178/2011, Implementing Regulation (EU) No 923/2012, Regulation (EU) No 965/2012 and Implementing Regulation (EU) 2017/373, as regards the establishment of requirements for the operation of manned aircraft with a vertical take-off and landing capability, C/2024/2268 (Commission Implementing Regulation (EU) 2024/1111).

In order to provide stakeholders with sufficient time to ensure compliance with the new framework, in principle the secondary regulations forming the regulatory package of 2024 apply as of 1 May 2025 and are entirely and directly applicable in all Member States.

The objectives and scope of each of secondary regulations forming this EU regulatory package on UAM are set out below.

16.6.2 Commission Delegated Regulation (EU) 2024/1107

Commission Delegated Regulation (EU) 2024/1107 was adopted based on the authorisation vested according to Article 58(1) of the Regulation (EU) 2018/1139. The objective of this regulation is to supplement Regulation (EU) 2018/1139 of the European Parliament and of the Council by laying down detailed rules for the continuing airworthiness of certified unmanned aircraft systems and their components, and on the approval of organisations and personnel involved in these tasks C/2024/1569. The supplementation is justified with the following arguments.

Annex IX to Regulation (EU) 2018/1139 sets out essential requirements for the maintenance of unmanned aircraft, in particular those which may be subject to certification referred to in Article 56(1) of that Regulation.

Article 40 of Commission Delegated Regulation on unmanned aircraft systems and on third-country operators of unmanned aircraft systems (Commission Delegated Regulation (EU) 2019/945) provides that UAS intended to be operated in the 'specific' category referred to in Article 5 of Commission Implementing Regulation on the rules and procedures for the operation of unmanned aircraft (Commission Implementing Regulation (EU) 2019/947) for which the risk of the operation cannot be adequately mitigated, are to be certified and comply with detailed requirements in respect of their continuing airworthiness.

Considering the specific nature of UAS it is necessary to establish detailed, dedicated continuing airworthiness requirements for those UAS, their components, and for organisations and personnel involved in continuing airworthiness tasks.

In accordance with Article 4(2) of Regulation (EU) 2018/1139, the detailed requirements for UAS should be proportionate to the risk of the particular operation or type of operation required by Implementing Regulation (EU) 2019/947 for high-risk operations in the 'specific' category.

Those detailed requirements for the UAS continuing airworthiness should be based on and harmonised with the detailed requirements laid down in Regulation on the continuing airworthiness of aircraft and aeronautical products, parts and appliances, and on the approval of organisations and personnel involved in these tasks (Commission Regulation (EU) No 1321/2014) applicable to light aircraft in manned aviation, however, those detailed requirements for the UAS should be adapted and adjusted to ensure that they are appropriate for the specific nature of UAS and are proportionate to the risks posed by their operation.

Where a valid certificate of airworthiness is not available and a permit to fly is issued to an UAS, those detailed requirements should not apply, and instead the continuing airworthiness requirements established in the flight conditions approved in accordance with Regulation laying down implementing rules for the airworthiness and environmental certification of aircraft and related products, parts and appliances, as well as for the certification of design and production organisations (Commission Regulation (EU) No 748/2012) should apply.

It was necessary to provide for a smooth transition to the new regulatory framework established by this Regulation. Therefore, it was necessary to provide stakeholders and Member State administrations with sufficient time to adapt to and ensure compliance with the new regulatory framework 2024.

The requirements for the protection of information and communication systems and data established for the continuing airworthiness organisations should be deferred until Regulation laying down rules for the application of Regulation as regards requirements for the management of information security risks with a potential impact on aviation safety for organisations (Commission Implementing Regulation (EU) 2023/203) becomes applicable.

16.6.3 Commission Delegated Regulation (EU) 2024/1108

The Commission Delegated Regulation (EU) 2024/1108 was adopted based on the authorisation vested according to Article 58(1) and Article 72(5) of the Regulation (EU) 2018/1139. The objective of this regulation was to amend Regulation (EU) No 748/2012 as regards the initial airworthiness of unmanned aircraft systems subject to certification and Delegated Regulation (EU) 2019/945 as regards unmanned aircraft systems and third-country operators of unmanned aircraft systems. These amendments were necessary for the following reasons.

Article 56 of Regulation (EU) 2018/1139 on the compliance of unmanned aircraft, considering the nature of and risk entailed by unmanned aircraft operations, establishes that, depending on such risk and nature, a certificate may be required for the design, production and maintenance of unmanned aircraft and their engines, propellers, parts, non-installed equipment, and equipment to control them remotely.

In accordance with Article 56 of Regulation (EU) 2018/1139, Article 40 of Regulation (EU) 2019/945 lays down the requirements for the certification of unmanned aircraft systems.

Point (b) of Article 58(1) of Regulation (EU) 2018/1139 provides that the conditions and procedures for issuing the certificate required under Article 55 of that Regulation may be based on, or consist of, the essential requirements for the design as set out in Annex IX of Regulation (EU) 2018/1139 and environmental performance requirements set out in Annex III of the same regulation.

Commission Regulation (EU) No 748/2012 laying down requirements for the design and production of civil aircraft, as well as of engines, propellers, and parts to be installed therein, should be adapted to address the specificities of unmanned aircraft systems.

Such specificities include the equipment to control unmanned aircraft remotely, as defined by Article 3 of Regulation (EU) 2018/1139. That equipment is defined as a 'control and monitoring unit' by Commission Implementing Regulation (EU) 2024/1110.

The safe operations of unmanned aircraft that are subject to certification require the control and monitoring unit to be subject to the same procedures under which certificates are issued for unmanned aircraft, determining that the same certification process applies to unmanned aircraft systems since they are composed of the unmanned aircraft and its control and monitoring unit.

Lighter-than-air unmanned aircraft systems pose an intrinsic risk to third parties, albeit lower than other unmanned aircraft configurations, and therefore may be operated without the need to issue a certificate for the design.

The verification of the design of unmanned aircraft systems specifically designed or modified for research, experimental, or scientific purposes may be conducted without the need to issue a type certificate because they are typically operated in a lower-risk environment.

The continuing airworthiness of unmanned aircraft systems for which a type certificate is required should comply with Commission Delegated Regulation (EU) 2024/1107, while compliance is not required for those unmanned aircraft systems that are intended to be used in operations for which a type certificate is not mandated under point (d) of Article 40(1) of Regulation (EU) 2019/945, even if the manufacturer has elected to apply for it.

16.6.4 Commission Implementing Regulation (EU) 2024/1109

The Commission Implementing Regulation (EU) 2024/1109 was adopted based on the authorisation vested according to Article 62(14) and (15), points (a), (b), and (c) and Article 72(5) of the Regulation (EU) 2018/1139.

The adoption of the Commission Implementing Regulation (EU) 2024/1109 was based upon three objectives. Firstly, to ensure the uniform application of the detailed continuing airworthiness requirements, rules, and procedures for the assessment of compliance laid down in Commission Delegated Regulation (EU) 2024/1107. Secondly, to ensure the uniform application of those detailed continuing airworthiness requirements, rules and procedures for the assessment of compliance with those requirements to be applied by the competent authorities. Those rules and procedures reflect the requirements for the competent authorities responsible for the continuing airworthiness of manned aircraft laid down in Commission Regulation (EU) No 1321/2014, but at the same time adapted to the specific unmanned aircraft systems (UAS) framework. Thirdly, in order to manage safety risks deriving from information security threats it is necessary that the competent authorities responsible for the continuing airworthiness of certified unmanned aircraft and their components apply the requirements for the management of information security risks with a potential impact on aviation safety laid down in Commission Implementing Regulation (EU) 2023/203. Therefore, the Implementing Regulation (EU) 2023/20 had to be amended to include in its scope also those competent authorities.

The Commission Implementing Regulation (EU) 2024/1109 obliges each Member State to designate one or more entities as the competent authority with the necessary powers and allocated responsibilities for the performance of certification, oversight, and enforcement tasks in accordance with this regulation and with Delegated Regulation (EU) 2024/1107. Specific requirements regarding organisation and management systems of the competent authority have been set out in an annex to this regulation (i.e. UAS Continuing Airworthiness—Authority Requirements), obliging the competent authority to comply with.

The Commission Implementing Regulation (EU) 2024/1109 set out the terms on the basis of which more than one competent authority should cooperate, should a Member State decide to designate several entities to perform this task. In addition, this regulation covers the scope of competence of the competent authority when it is necessary to perform certification, oversight, or enforcement tasks. These powers have to be exercised in compliance with the applicable legal provisions of the relevant Member State.

16.6.5 *Commission Implementing Regulation (EU) 2024/1110*

The Commission Implementing Regulation (EU) 2024/1110 was adopted on the basis of the authorisation vested according to Article 57 and Article 62(14), point (a) of the Regulation (EU) 2018/1139. The purpose of this Regulation was to ensure harmonisation of the rules when an unmanned aircraft (UA) whose design is certified does not meet or has not been shown to meet the applicable airworthiness requirements. This can be achieved by amending Regulation (EU) No 748/2012 and Implementing Regulation (EU) 2019/947.

An unmanned aircraft system (UAS) includes the control and monitoring unit (CMU) and its components which should be addressed by the safety information analysis system implemented by the EASA in order for the relevant authority of the Member States and the Commission to be provided with information (including recommendations or corrective actions to be taken), to react to a safety problem and to an information security incident or vulnerability with a potential impact on aviation safety.

For the purposes of granting the required operational authorisation in accordance Article 12 of Commission Implementing Regulation (EU) 2019/947, the competent authority has to consider the terms and conditions laid down in the flight conditions established and approved in accordance with Commission Regulation (EU) No 748/2012 where an unmanned aircraft (UA) which design is certified, does not meet, or has not been shown to meet, the applicable airworthiness requirements.

In order to ensure a uniform implementation of the airworthiness requirements for the operations of an UAS, and compliance with such requirements, where the risk of operation with an UAS in the 'specific' category, as set out in Article 5 of Implementing Regulation (EU) 2019/947, can only be mitigated by using an UAS that has been issued with a type certificate or a restricted type certificate for the design, then a certificate of airworthiness or restricted certificate of airworthiness for the UA should be required. In addition, a noise certificate should also be required in cases where environmental protection requirements were established by EASA.

For the purposes of exchanging safety information in accordance with Article 19 of Implementing Regulation (EU) 2019/947, the UAS operator of an UA which design is certified should report to the design approval holder of the UAS or of the component any safety-related event or condition of the UAS or of the component identified by the organisation in accordance with Regulation on the reporting, analysis and follow-up of occurrences in civil aviation, amending Regulation (EU) No 996/2010 of the European Parliament and of the Council and repealing Directive 2003/42/EC of the European Parliament and of the Council and Commission Regulations (EC) No 1321/2007 and (EC) No 1330/2007 (Regulation (EU) No 376/2014).

In order to contribute towards the improvement of safety, the UAS operator of an UA which design is certified or that uses a certified UAS component should implement any safety measures mandated by the competent authority or relevant mandatory safety information issued by EASA, including airworthiness directives in accordance with the UAS continuing airworthiness requirements set out in Commission Delegated Regulation (EU) 2024/1107.

16.6.6 *Commission Implementing Regulation (EU) 2024/1111*

The objective for the adoption of the Commission Implementing Regulation (EU) 2024/1111 was the future integration of manned aircraft with a vertical take-off and landing capability into the transportation systems of the Member States. It is appropriate to apply the same regulatory framework available for operations with aeroplanes and helicopters, with the necessary amendments considering the new air mobility concepts of operations with manned aircraft with a vertical take-off and landing capability, performance and operating limitations, and specific risks. Given this objective, the European Commission decided to amend the following regulations to meet this main objective (point 6 of the recitals of Commission Implementing Regulation (EU) 2024/1111):

1. Regulation laying down common requirements for providers of air traffic management/air navigation services and other air traffic management network functions and their oversight, repealing Regulation (EC) No 482/2008, Implementing Regulations (EU) No 1034/2011, (EU) No 1035/2011 and (EU) 2016/1377 and amending Regulation (EU) No 677/2011 (Commission Implementing Regulation (EU) 2017/373);
2. Regulation laying down technical requirements and administrative procedures related to civil aviation aircrew pursuant to Regulation

(EC) No 216/2008 of the European Parliament and of the Council (Commission Regulation (EU) No 1178/2011);

3. Commission Regulation (EU) No 965/2012 of 5 October 2012 laying down technical requirements and administrative procedures related to air operations pursuant to Regulation (EC) No 216/2008 of the European Parliament and of the Council (Commission Regulation (EU) No 965/2012);
4. Commission Implementing Regulation (EU) No 923/2012 of 26 September 2012 laying down the common rules of the air and operational provisions regarding services and procedures in air navigation and amending Implementing Regulation (EU) No 1035/2011 and Regulations (EC) No 1265/2007, (EC) No 1794/2006, (EC) No 730/2006, (EC) No 1033/2006 and (EU) No 255/2010 (Commission Implementing Regulation (EU) No 923/2012).

The specific purpose for amending Commission Regulation (EU) No 1178/2011 was to ensure the availability of appropriately qualified pilots during the initial phase of operations with aircraft with a vertical take-off and landing capability, holders of commercial pilot licences for aeroplanes or helicopters. These pilots were given the possibility to add to their licence a type rating for manned aircraft with a vertical take-off and landing capability, including privileges to operate that aircraft under instrument flight rules, where necessary. Where such pilots also hold instructor or examiner certificates for aeroplanes or helicopters, they were also given the possibility to obtain additional instructor or examiner privileges for that aircraft. The amendment of the Regulation (EU) No 1178/2011, by Commission Implementing Regulation (EU) 2024/1111, encompasses also the introduction of the definitions of 'rotocraft' (Article 2(8a)) and 'vertical take-off and landing (VTOL)-capable aircraft (VCA)' (Article 2(8b)). According to first definition, a 'rotorcraft' means a power-driven, heavier-than-air aircraft that depends principally for its support in flight on the lift generated by up to two rotors. A 'vertical take-off and landing (VTOL)-capable aircraft (VCA)' means a power-driven, heavier-than-air aircraft, other than aeroplane or rotorcraft, capable of performing vertical take-off and landing by means of lift and thrust units used to provide lift during take-off and landing. These definitions were introduced to other secondary regulations subject to amendments based on the Commission Implementing Regulation (EU) 2024/1111.

The specific purpose for amending Regulation (EU) No 923/2012 was to provide for a safe, orderly, and efficient air traffic management of manned aircraft with a vertical take-off and landing capability and avoid mid-air collisions.

The specific purpose for amending Regulation (EU) No 965/2012 was to provide, inter alia, for a new Annex with detailed requirements to address the operations of manned aircraft with vertical take-off and landing capability. Annex I to Regulation (EU) No 965/2012 was amended to include a new aircraft category, while precising existing definitions. Annex II and Annex III were amended to enlarge the scope of existing certification requirements for commercial air transport and Annex V includes new provisions enabling emergency medical services and rescue operations with manned aircraft with vertical take-off and landing capability.

The Implementing Regulation (EU) No 2017/373 was also amended in point ATS.TR.305 of Annex IV, regarding the Scope of flight information service, by inserting point (7a) extending the set of information by information on unmanned aircraft.

16.7 Replacing a Human Pilot with an Artificial Agent

Subject to infrastructure challenges, there is technical capacity to construct an autonomous flying vehicle suitable for providing air taxi services. In the UAM BluePrint (Airbus, 2025; Zart, 2019), Airbus stated that UAM covers passenger and cargo flights operated in densely populated areas, including air taxis, delivery drones, remotely piloted, and autonomous operations (Tojal et al., 2021). This statement refers to the design suited for the air taxi services of wingless Airbus—CityAirbus. The CityAirbus is a multi-passenger, fully electric quadrotor that utilises autonomous flight control (Ross, 2018). The UAM concept proposed in recent years is based on a new type of electric aircraft that can take off and land vertically, known as eVTOLs. This new type of aircraft, at its mature stage, integrates advanced autonomous and distributed electric propulsion technologies and can provide safer, quieter, and more efficient air transportation service in low-altitude space (Wu & Zhang, 2021).

The literature was initially sceptical about the possibility of using an artificial agent instead of a human to perform air taxi services. It was argued that aviation is a highly regulated industry with inherent scepticism about the potential of autonomy for replacing pilots in the near future. This viewpoint has led to research in simplified vehicle operations (SVO) focused on enabling piloted aircraft with increasingly automated but not autonomous systems for flight control and navigation (Goodrich & Moore, 2015).

Over time, the advantages of artificial intelligence have been acknowledged, including in economic terms, as exemplified by automated passenger drones (Yan et al., 2024), including in economic terms. After the fuel cost, expenses associated with the manpower constitute the second-largest cost component in the air transportation industry. Although air taxi services are not projected to function with flight attendants, the vehicles are required to be operated by pilots; nevertheless, in the long run, they are expected to be fully autonomous. Pilot training and scheduling is a challenging workforce planning problem faced by the commercial aviation sector (Rajendran & Srinivas, 2020).

So far, studies have been conducted on the acceptance of air taxi services implemented by an artificial agent instead of a human pilot. For example, in the literature (Fu et al., 2019) a mode-choice analysis in the UAM environment based in Munich, Germany was performed. The study included data collection from an online stated-preference survey and the creation of several discrete choice models. The study found that for commuting, public transit is the most desirable choice, followed by auto, whereas UAM selection is the least likely. Their model estimates suggest a relative increase in acceptance for autonomous modes in the higher-Value-Of-Time (VOT) group. Since this study is based on a stated-preference survey, it is possible that results could differ from actual, revealed-preference behaviour.

In this context, reference should be made to the definitional grid contained in the regulatory framework. The definition of the notion 'command unit', as given in Article 2(26) of Commission Implementing Regulation (EU) 2019/947 and Article 3(38) of Commission Delegated Regulation (EU) 2019/945, refers to the functions of 'control or monitoring of the unmanned aircraft during any phase of flight'.

Such a definition relates two concepts that are rather complementary to each other. The EASA's opinion 03/2023 distinguishes the concept of 'command' and 'control' as they are defined as follows. The notion 'command' is the authority vested in an individual for the direction, coordination, and control of functions and tasks required for a flight operation; such authority may be exercised either directly by executing the flight operation, or by directing other individuals/organisations involved in the flight operation. The notion 'control' is the management and execution of functions and tasks required for a flight operation consistent with a command authority.

The operational assumptions underpinning the regulatory framework for UAS proposed in EASA's opinion 03/2023 state that:

1. a human is always in command as autonomous operations are excluded;
2. the remote pilot may control one unmanned aircraft (UA) at a time, or control simultaneously several UA, also of different types and from different operators;
3. the handover of command is not considered; however, the handover of control of a UA between different command units, hence between different remote pilots, is possible.

Given EASA shared Opinion 03/2023 and the above assumptions and notional concepts, there is a need to coherently identify the system that provides the functions to control and monitor the UA's flight operation and through which the command authority may be exercised. Depending on the specific operational concepts, the command and control of a UA's flight operation may be exercised by the same person or by different members of the UAS operator's organisation. Accordingly, duties and responsibilities for the safe conduct of the flight may be allocated to different persons within the organisation.

The replacement of the 'command unit' with the newly proposed concept of 'control and monitoring unit' re-establishes coherence with the functions that can be exercised through that specific system. The definition accommodates a variety of operational concepts ranging from those where the system can actively control and monitor the flight trajectory of the UA to those where the system is limited to a monitoring function and where the UA flies under increased levels of automation up to complete autonomy.

The Commission Delegated Regulation (EU) 2024/1107 introduces in art. 2(2) the definition of the notion 'control and monitoring unit', which means the equipment to control unmanned aircraft remotely, as defined in Article 3, point (32), of Regulation (EU) 2018/1139. The notion 'equipment to control unmanned aircraft remotely' means any instrument, equipment, mechanism, apparatus, appurtenance, software, or accessory that is necessary for the safe operation of an unmanned aircraft, which is not a part, and which is not carried on board that unmanned aircraft. In addition to the definition of the notion 'control and monitoring unit', the Commission Delegated Regulation (EU) 2024/1107 also lays down in Article 2(11) the definition of the notion 'control and monitoring unit installation'. It means the process to integrate the control and monitoring unit's elements in a physical environment that is eligible for that purpose, according to a set of installation and testing instructions, such that the installed control and monitoring unit may be used to operate an unmanned aircraft. According to Annex 1 Subpart C (Continuing Airworthiness) ML.UAS.305 point (a) of the Commission Delegated Regulation (EU) 2024/1107, for each UAS, as identified by the UA registration and control and monitoring unit ('CMU') type and serial number, a system shall be established to record continuing airworthiness information of the UAS. That system shall be used by the remote pilot and the person(s) involved in the continuing airworthiness of the UAS.

16.8 Privacy Protection Challenges

Privacy as a legal right is a relatively new concept. The idea was first put forward by Warren and Brandeis in 1890 in their seminal article 'The Right to Privacy as a right to be let alone' (Warren, 1890). Since then, the definition has evolved to include ideas such as privacy of data, privacy of communication, privacy of location, and other related concepts (Solove, 2002). The legal protection of privacy on a European level dates back to 1950, when the Council of Europe drafted their European Convention on Human Rights (ECHR, 1950), thereby protecting a person's (personal) freedom (Pons-Prats et al., 2022).

The specific privacy type associated with UAM is difficult to define, given drones' diverse capabilities and applications. For example, aircraft equipped with cameras can capture images that can provide information about people's location, behaviour, and activity patterns (Bauranov & Rakas, 2021). This can be the case when VTOL is in the phase of descending or climbing in the vicinity of private property (Pons-Prats et al., 2022), irrespective of the designation of the aerial vehicles, i.e. autonomous air taxi, ambulance, and airport shuttle (Serrao et al., 2018).

As a result of a study of social acceptance of UAM conducted in 2021 in Europe (EASA, 2021), EASA found that society may be concerned about privacy, as UAM aircraft like air taxis and drones may fly above or close to places of residence. In this regard, harassment was mentioned as a potential concern from drones operated by private users (e.g. stalking), particularly if more flights take place in densely populated areas. These privacy threats were also emphasised in EASA's opinion 03/2023. Given EASA's privacy concerns, it is expected that the first type of operations of manned VTOL-capable aircraft in urban environments will follow a limited set of predefined routes or areas/corridors for which the relevant competent authorities have been assured that the air and ground risks, including the privacy risk, are properly mitigated.

This approach will be necessary until experience is gained on how to validate operations in urban environments from a safety, environmental, security, and privacy point of view. In addition, there will be a limited number of vertiports and operating sites in each city, and safety and efficiency must be ensured for air traffic that takes off from and lands at those areas, together with other air traffic in urban environments and current air operations. Additionally, when operating within urban airspace, parts of the airspace need to be predefined to enable dynamic airspace reconfiguration. If, during the development process, it can be demonstrated and validated that safety, environmental protection and compatibility, security, and privacy can be guaranteed without the need for predefined routes or areas/corridors for manned VTOL-capable aircraft, then this potential limitation would be removed.

Similar findings also emerge from the 2018 NASA UAM report (NASA, 2018), which recognises that civil liberties groups have privacy concerns about the widespread adoption of UAM, but may misunderstand how cameras are used in sensing system technology.

If the air taxi services are to be provided in Europe, their provision could require compliance with the General Data Protection Regulation (GDPR, 2018). This prerequisite will be met if, during its provision, personal data is processed. The notion 'personal data' is defined in the GDPR (Article 4(1) GDPR). Once the subject of the processing of personal data has been established, it is necessary to determine the purpose(s) for which the personal data are processed. Based on the known purpose and means of processing of personal data, it is possible to determine which of the actors involved in the processing determines the purpose and means of such processing. Such an entity alone bears the status of a controller within the meaning of Article 4(7) of the GDPR. If both entities decide about the means and purposes of processing personal data, they a jointly considered as joint controllers. These entities shall in a transparent manner determine their respective responsibilities for compliance with the obligations under the GDPR, in particular as regards the exercising of the rights of the data subject and their respective duties to provide the information on the processing of data (Articles 13 or 14 of the GDPR), by means of an arrangement between them unless, and in so far as, the respective responsibilities of the controllers are determined by Union or Member State law to which the controllers are subject (Article 26(1) GDPR). A controller (or joint controllers) are, inter alia, obliged to fulfil the obligation of data protection by design (Art. 25(1) of the GDPR) and by default (Art. 25(2) of the GDPR). In line with Article 25(1) of the GDPR the controller shall implement appropriate technical and organisational measures which are designed to implement the data protection principles (Article 5(2) and (2) of the GDPR) and to integrate the necessary safeguards into the processing to meet the requirements and protect the rights and freedoms of data subjects. Both appropriate measures and necessary safeguards are meant to serve the same purpose of protecting the rights of data subjects and ensuring that the protection of their personal data is built into the processing. When determining the appropriate technical and organisational measures, each controller should take into account the current progress in technology that is available in the market. The requirement is for controllers to have knowledge of and stay up to date on technological advances.

The literature already presents concepts on the mode of ensuring privacy by design. For example, one of the concepts (Martin et al., 2016) is based on a two-stage approach. It is developed for privacy assurance. First, a privacy-aware flight planner for UAV mission planning and second, a target-based video masking algorithm.

Additionally, controllers must take into consideration the nature, scope, context, and purpose of processing when determining needed measures. When performing the risk analysis for compliance with Article 25, the controller has to identify the risks to the rights of data subjects that a violation of the principles presents, and determine their likelihood and severity to implement measures to effectively mitigate the identified risks. Data protection by design shall be implemented 'at the time of determination of the means for processing'. The 'time of determination of the means for processing' refers to the period of time when the controller is deciding how the processing will be conducted and how the processing will occur and the mechanisms which will be used to conduct such processing. It's in the process of making such decisions that the controller must assess the appropriate measures and safeguards to effectively implement the principles and rights of data subjects into the processing, and take into account elements such as the state of the art, cost of implementation, nature, scope, context, and purpose, and risks. This includes the time of procuring and implementing data processing software, hardware, and services (EDPB, 2020).

16.9 Conclusions

UAM is a paradigm relating to disruptive urban mobility technology, presenting it as the ultimate solution to the pervasive problem of congestion in urban areas. The implementation of this paradigm will also lead to environmental protection, especially as a result of the electric propulsion of aerial vehicles.

The implementation of UAM is complex in nature. The literature (Straubinger et al., 2020) identifies eight areas of research in this area, including vehicles, regulation, infrastructure, operations, market actors, integration, acceptance, and modelling. This paper focused on the legal and regulatory aspects associated with the introduction of UAM.

To conduct deliberations on the definition of the legal framework for the UAM paradigm, to assess the sufficiency of these provisions and, at the same time, to identify possible gaps in the law, it is necessary to establish the meaning of the term UAM. Currently, there is no single unified legal definition. One legal definition of UAM could be introduced in an international agreement, as the paradigm of extending modes of transport in urban agglomerations to include air transport is considered worldwide in different legal systems. Existing international agreements, including the Convention on International Civil Aviation, signed at Chicago on 7 December 1944 (Chicago Convention, 1944), are limited in their scope of application. Different concepts in understanding this paradigm have been put forward by air traffic safety agencies, including EASA and FAA. EASA provided an in-depth analysis in this regard in its Opinion 03/2023. In the EU legal framework, there is a need for a legal definition of the term 'Urban Air Mobility'. A legal definition of 'vertical take-off and landing (VTOL)-capable aircraft (VCA)' has been introduced based on Commission Implementing Regulation (EU) 2024/1111.

The reasons described in this paper for the development of UAM, as a paradigm, demonstrate the lack of alternatives to UAM in the context of the increasing urbanisation of cities and the fact that road congestion in densely populated cities has become a universal concern. This makes it necessary for the legislator to focus on the need for an appropriate legal framework in this respect. It is important to point out the regulatory progress being made by the European Commission and EASA, including the 2024 regulatory package, which applies as of 1 May 2025. The regulatory package introduces a comprehensive set of requirements for piloted electric air taxis, spanning the domains of Air Operations (Air OPS), Flight Crew Licensing (FCL), Standardised European Rules of the Air (SERA), and Air Traffic Management (ATM). It also establishes criteria and processes for the certification and maintenance of drones.

The introduction of the 2024 regulatory package is an important step towards a regulatory framework in Europe for the application of UAM. However, it does not cover all legal issues. Among other things, the attention of the legislator should be focused on the legal issues concerning the infrastructure necessary for UAM services (including vertiport deployment and the creation of an adept air traffic control [ATC] system) as well as integration with urban infrastructure. Privacy and data protection concerns must also be considered. In the context of the obligation to provide data protection by design described in this paper, it would be recommended that the European Data Protection Board develop detailed guidance on the application of Article 25(1) of the GDPR on the use of aerial vehicles for the provision of air taxi services.

References

Airbus. (2025). https://acubed.airbus.com/blueprint/. Accessed 10 February 2025.

Annex 1 to the Convention on International Civil Aviation, 12th edition, July 2018. https://www.icao.int/APAC/Meetings/2019%20COSCAP%20SEAEASA%20PEL/AN01_cons.2019_compressed.pdf. Accessed 12 February 2025.

AOPA PILOT. (2007, January 5). *A Flying Car...Seriously Why can't my airplane be more like a car — or vice versa?* https://www.aopa.org/news-and-media/all-news/2007/january/pilot/a-flying-car-seriously#baby. Accessed 8 February 2025.

Babetto, L., Kirste, A., Deng, J., Husemann, M., & Stumpf, E. (2023, June). Adoption of the Urban Air Mobility System: Analysis of technical, legal and social aspects from a European perspective. *Journal of the Air Transport Research Society, 1*(1), 152–174. https://doi.org/10.59521/C97BE694514DD2F. Accessed 10 February 2025.

Bauranov, A., & Rakas, J. (2021). Designing airspace for urban air mobility: A review of concepts and approaches. *Progress in Aerospace Sciences, 125*(100726), 0376–0421. https://doi.org/10.1016/j.paerosci.2021.100726

Berg, P. (2012, March 28). Top 10 attempts to build a flying car. *Popular Mechanics*. https://www.popularmechanics.com/flight/how-to/g803/top-10-attempts-to-build-a-flying-car/. Accessed 9 February 2025.

Bloom, D. E., Canning, D., & Fink, G. (2008). Urbanization and the wealth of nations. *Science, 319*(5864), 772–775. https://doi.org/10.1126/science.1153057

Brown, K. E., & Dodder, R. (2019). Energy and emissions implications of automated vehicles in the U.S. energy system. *Transportation Research Part D: Transport and Environment, 77*, 132–147. https://doi.org/10.1016/j.trd.2019.09.003. Accessed 10 February 2025.

Chicago Convention. (1944). https://www.icao.int/publications/Documents/chicago.pdf. Accessed 12 February 2025.

Commission Delegated Regulation (EU) 2019/945 of 12 March 2019 on unmanned aircraft systems and on third-country operators of unmanned aircraft systems, C/2019/1821, OJ L 152, 11.6.2019, p. 1–40.

Commission Delegated Regulation (EU) 2019/945 of 12 March 2019 on unmanned aircraft systems and on third-country operators of unmanned aircraft systems C/2019/1821, OJ L 152, 11.6.2019, p. 1–40.

Commission Delegated Regulation (EU) 2024/1107 of 13 March 2024 supplementing Regulation (EU) 2018/1139 of the European Parliament and of the Council by laying down detailed rules for the continuing airworthiness of certified unmanned aircraft systems and their components, and on the approval of organisations and personnel involved in these tasks C/2024/1569, OJ L, 2024/1107, 23.5.2024, ELI: http://data.europa.eu/eli/reg_del/2024/1107. Accessed 10 February 2025.

Commission Delegated Regulation (EU) 2024/1108 of 13 March 2024 amending Regulation (EU) No 748/2012 as regards the initial airworthiness of unmanned aircraft systems subject to certification and Delegated Regulation (EU) 2019/945 as regards unmanned aircraft systems and third-country operators of unmanned aircraft systems, C/2024/1570, OJ L, 2024/1108, 23.5.2024, ELI: http://data.europa.eu/eli/reg_del/2024/1108/oj. Accessed 10 February 2025.

Commission Implementing Regulation (EU) No 923/2012 of 26 September 2012 laying down the common rules of the air and operational provisions regarding services and procedures in air navigation and amending Implementing Regulation (EU) No 1035/2011 and Regulations (EC) No 1265/2007, (EC) No 1794/2006, (EC) No 730/2006, (EC) No 1033/2006 and (EU) No 255/2010 OJ L 281, 13.10.2012, p. 1, ELI: http://data.europa.eu/eli/reg_impl/2012/923/oj. Accessed 10 February 2025.

Commission Implementing Regulation (EU) 2017/373 of 1 March 2017 laying down common requirements for providers of air traffic management/air navigation services and other air traffic management network functions and their oversight, repealing Regulation (EC) No 482/2008, Implementing Regulations (EU) No 1034/2011, (EU) No 1035/2011 and (EU) 2016/1377 and amending Regulation (EU) No 677/2011, OJ L 62, 8.3.2017, p. 1, ELI: http://data.europa.eu/eli/reg_impl/2017/373/oj. Accessed 10 February 2025.

Commission Implementing Regulation (EU) 2019/947 of 24 May 2019 on the rules and procedures for the operation of unmanned aircraft (Text with EEA relevance), C/2019/3824, OJ L 152, 11.6.2019, p. 45–71.

Commission Implementing Regulation (EU) 2023/203 of 27 October 2022 laying down rules for the application of Regulation (EU) 2018/1139 of the European Parliament and of the Council, as regards requirements for the management of information security risks with a potential impact on aviation safety for organisations covered by Commission Regulations (EU) No 1321/2014, (EU) No 965/2012, (EU) No 1178/2011, (EU) 2015/340, Commission Implementing Regulations (EU) 2017/373 and (EU) 2021/664, and for competent authorities covered by Commission Regulations (EU) No 748/2012, (EU) No 1321/2014, (EU) No 965/2012, (EU) No 1178/2011, (EU) 2015/340 and (EU) No 139/2014, Commission Implementing Regulations (EU) 2017/373 and (EU) 2021/664 and amending Commission Regulations (EU) No 1178/2011, (EU) No 748/2012, (EU) No 965/2012, (EU) No 139/2014, (EU) No 1321/2014, (EU) 2015/340, and Commission Implementing Regulations (EU) 2017/373 and (EU) 2021/664, OJ L 31, 2.2.2023, p. 1, ELI: http://data.europa.eu/eli/reg_impl/2023/203/oj. Accessed 12 February 2025.

Commission Implementing Regulation (EU) 2024/1109 of 10 April 2024 laying down rules for the application of Regulation (EU) 2018/1139 of the European Parliament and of the Council as regards competent authority requirements and administrative procedures for the certification, oversight and enforcement of the continuing airworthiness of certified unmanned aircraft systems, and amending Implementing Regulation (EU) 2023/203 C/2024/2000, OJ L, 2024/1109, 23.5.2024, ELI: http://data.europa.eu/eli/reg_impl/2024/1109/oj. Accessed 10 February 2025.

Commission Implementing Regulation (EU) 2024/1110 of 10 April 2024 amending Regulation (EU) No 748/2012 as regards the initial airworthiness of unmanned aircraft systems subject to certification and Implementing Regulation (EU) 2019/947 as regards the rules and procedures for the operation of unmanned aircraft C/2024/2001, OJ L, 2024/1110, 23.5.2024, ELI: http://data.europa.eu/eli/reg_impl/2024/1110/oj. Accessed 10 February 2025.

Commission Implementing Regulation (EU) 2024/1111 of 10 April 2024 amending Regulation (EU) No 1178/2011, Implementing Regulation (EU) No 923/2012, Regulation (EU) No 965/2012 and Implementing Regulation (EU) 2017/373, as regards the establishment of requirements for the operation of manned aircraft with a vertical take-off and landing capability, C/2024/2268, OJ L, 2024/1111, 23.5.2024.

Commission Regulation (EC) No 1702/2003 of 24 September 2003 laying down implementing rules for the airworthiness and environmental certification of aircraft and related products, parts and appliances, as well as for the certification of design and production organisations (Text with EEA relevance), OJ L 243, 27.9.2003, p. 6–79.

Commission Regulation (EU) No 1178/2011 of 3 November 2011 laying down technical requirements and administrative procedures related to civil aviation aircrew pursuant to Regulation (EC) No 216/2008 of the European Parliament and of the Council, OJ L 311, 25.11.2011, p. 1, ELI: http://data.europa.eu/eli/reg/2011/1178/oj. Accessed 10 February 2025.

Commission Regulation (EU) No 965/2012 of 5 October 2012 laying down technical requirements and administrative procedures related to air operations pursuant to Regulation (EC) No 216/2008 of the European Parliament and of the Council, OJ L 296, 25.10.2012, p. 1, ELI: http://data.europa.eu/eli/reg/2012/965/oj. Accessed 10 February 2025.

Commission Regulation (EU) No 1321/2014 of 26 November 2014 on the continuing airworthiness of aircraft and aeronautical products, parts and appliances, and on the approval of organisations and personnel involved in these tasks, OJ L 362, 17.12.2014, p. 1, ELI: http://data.europa.eu/eli/reg/2014/1321/oj. Accessed 12 February 2025.

Corey, B. (2024, September 11). *November 9, 1937 – Patent issued for flying car dubbed the 'Arrowbile'*. This day in automotive history. https://automotivehistory.org/arrowbile-history/#:~:text=Waterman%E2%80%99s%20destiny%20reached%20a%20turning%20point%20in%201937,of%20engineering%2C%20based%20on%20the%20earlier%20Arrowplane%20design. Accessed 8 February 2025.

DeLuca, M. (2012, August). *17 flying cars: A mostly factual history of airborne autos*. https://www.thedailybeast.com/17-flying-cars-a-mostly-factual-history-of-airborne-autos/. Accessed 8 February 2025.

Directive 2003/87/EC of the European Parliament and of the Council of 13 October 2003 establishing a system for greenhouse gas emission allowance trading within the Union and amending Council Directive 96/61/EC, OJ L 275, 25.10.2003, p. 32–46.

EASA. (2018, November 27). *Altitudes below 500 feet are referred to as very low level (VLL) airspace: See: EASA, UAS ATM Integration, Operational concept.* https://www.eurocontrol.int/sites/default/files/publication/files/uas-atm-integration-operational-concept-v1.0-release%2020181128.pdf. Accessed 12 February 2025.

EASA. (2021). *Study of social acceptance of UAM in Europe.* Technical report. https://www.easa.europa.eu/sites/default/files/dfu/uam-full-report.pdf. Accessed 10 February 2025.

EASA. (2023). *European Union Aviation Safety Agency's Opinion No 03/2023. Introduction of a regulatory framework for the operation of drones.* https://www.easa.europa.eu/en/document-library/opinions/opinion-no-032023. Accessed 10 February 2025.

EASA. (2024). *European Commission adopts regulatory package, giving go-ahead for VTOL operations and air taxis.* https://www.easa.europa.eu/en/newsroom-and-events/news/european-commission-adopts-regulatory-package-giving-go-ahead-vtol. Accessed 12 February 2025.

EASA. (2025a). *About EASA.* https://www.easa.europa.eu/en/the-agency/faqs/about-easa. Accessed: 10 February 2025.

EASA. (2025b). *EASA's Sustainable Aviation Programme.* https://www.easa.europa.eu/en/light/topics/easas-sustainable-aviation-programme. Accessed 2 February 2025.

European Convention on Human Rights (ECHR).(1950). https://eur-lex.europa.eu/legal-content/EN/TXT/?uri=LEGISSUM:eu_human_rights_convention. Accessed 12 February 2025.

European Data Protection Board Guidelines 4/2019 on Article 25, Data Protection by Design and by Default Version 2.0, adopted on 20 October 2020. https://www.edpb.europa.eu/sites/default/files/files/file1/edpb_guidelines_201904_dataprotection_by_design_and_by_default_v2.0_en.pdf. Accessed 10 February 2025.

European Union and EASA. (2022). *Guidelines on noise measurement of unmanned aircraft systems lighter than 600 kg operating in the specific category (low and medium risk).* Technical report. https://www.easa.europa.eu/en/document-library/product-certification-consultations/guidelines-noise-measurement-unmanned-aircraft. Accessed 8 February 2025.

Federal Aviation Administration. (2023, April 26). *Urban Air Mobility (UAM) Concept of Operations, v 2.0.* https://www.faa.gov/sites/faa.gov/files/Urban%20Air%20Mobility%20%28UAM%29%20Concept%20of%20Operations%202.0_0.pdf. Accessed 10 February 2025.

Fu, M., Rothfeld, R., & Antoniou, C. (2019). Exploring preferences for transportation modes in an urban air mobility environment: Munich case study.

Transportation Research Record Journal of the Transportation Research Board, 2673(10), 036119811984385, 427–442. https://doi.org/10.1177/0361198119843858

Garrow, L. A., German, B. J., & Leonard, C.E. (2021). Urban air mobility: A comprehensive review and comparative analysis with autonomous and electric ground transportation for informing future research. *Transportation Research Part C, 132*, 103377. https://doi.org/10.1016/j.trc.2021.103377. Accessed 10 February 2025.

GDPR. (2018). Regulation (EU) 2016/679 of the European Parliament and of the Council of 27 April 2016 on the protection of natural persons with regard to the processing of personal data and on the free movement of such data, and repealing Directive 95/46/EC (General Data Protection Regulation), OJ L 119, 4.5.2016, pp. 1–88.

Goodrich, K., & Moore, M. (2015, July 22). *Simplified vehicle operations roadmap*. Presentation at: On-Demand Mobility Forum, Oshkosh, WI. http://www.nianet.org/ODM/odm/docs/Industry%20forum%20OSH%20Ease%20of%20Use%20and%20Safety%20Pathway%202015.pdf. Accessed 10 February 2025.

Kelly, F. J., & Fussell, J. C. (2015). Air pollution and public health: Emerging hazards and improved understanding of risk. *Environmental Geochemistry and Health, 37*(4), 631–649.

Lascara, B., Spencer, T., DeGarmo, M., Lacher, A., Maroney, D., & Guterres, M. (2018, April). *Urban air mobility landscape report initial examination of a new air transportation system*. The MITRE Corporation. https://www.mitre.org/sites/default/files/2021-11/pr-18-0154-4-urban-air-mobility-landscape-report.pdf. Accessed 08 February 2025.

Martin, R. A., Hall, A., Brinton, C., Franke, K., & Hedengren, J. D. (2016). *Privacy aware mission planning and video masking for UAV systems*. AIAA Infotech @ Aerospace. https://doi.org/10.2514/6.2016-0250. Accessed 10 February 2025.

Moller, P. (1998). Airborne personalized travel using 'powered lift. Airborne personalized travel using "powered lift aircraft.' In: AIAA and SAE, 1998 World Aviation Conference. Anaheim, CA.U.S.A.: American Institute of Aeronautics and Astronautics aircraft In: AIAA and SAE, 1998 World Aviation Conference. Anaheim, CA. U.S.A.: American Institute of Aeronautics and Astronautics.

NASA. (2018). *Urban air mobility (UAM) – market study*. Technical report. https://ntrs.nasa.gov/citations/20190002046. Accessed 10 February 2025.

Opinion No 03/2023, Introduction of a regulatory framework for the operation of drones — Enabling innovative air mobility with MVCA, the initial airworthiness of UAS subject to certification, and the continuing airworthiness of those UAS operated in the 'specific' category. https://www.easa.europa.eu/en/document-library/opinions/opinion-no-032023. Accessed 12 February 2025.

Organization for International Economic Relations. (2020). *Urban air mobility: Policy recommendations for the next 5 years*. https://www.oier.pro/ic-orig/LdDmrXrEQIMl/Inhalte/AB-20102-Headway-Whitepaper-3-31-20.pdf. Accessed 8 February 2025.

Pishue, B., & Kidd, J. (2024). *INRIX Global Traffic Scorecard, 1/2025*. https://ftnnews.com/wp-content/uploads/2025/01/INRIX_2024_Global_Traffic_Scorecard.pdf#:~:text=The%202024%20INRIX%20Global%20Traffic%20Scorecard%20includes%20transportation,monitor%20and%20measure%20traffic%20in%20their%20respective%20areas. Accessed 2 February 2025.

Pons-Prats, J., Živojinović, T., & Kuljanin, J. (2022). On the understanding of the current status of urban air mobility development and its future prospects: Commuting in a flying vehicle as a new paradigm. *Transportation Research Part E, 166*(102868), 1366–5545. https://doi.org/10.1016/j.tre.2022.102868. Accessed 10 February 2025.

Pop.Up Next. (2018, November 27). *Flying taxi concept of Audi, Airbus and Italdesign*. https://www.audi-mediacenter.com/en/videos/video/pop-up-next-flying-taxi-concept-of-audi-airbus-and-italdesign-4424. Accessed 6 February 2025.

Rajendran, S., & Srinivas, S. (2020). Air taxi service for urban mobility: A critical review of recent developments, future challenges, and opportunities. *Transportation Research Part E, 143*(102090), 1–33. https://doi.org/10.48550/arXiv.2103.01768

Regulation (EC) No 1592/2002 of the European Parliament and of the Council of 15 July 2002 on common rules in the field of civil aviation and establishing a European Aviation Safety Agency (Text with EEA relevance), OJ L 240, 7.9.2002, p. 1–21. Date of end of validity: 07.04.2012. Repealed by Regulation (EC) No 216/2008 of the European Parliament and of the Council of 20 February 2008 on common rules in the field of civil aviation and establishing a European Aviation Safety Agency, and repealing Council Directive 91/670/EEC, Regulation (EC) No 1592/2002 and Directive 2004/36/EC (Text with EEA relevance). Date of end of validity: 10.09.2018. Repealed by Regulation (EU) 2018/1139 of the European Parliament and of the Council of 4 July 2018 on common rules in the field of civil aviation and establishing a European Union Aviation Safety Agency, and amending Regulations (EC) No 2111/2005, (EC) No 1008/2008, (EU) No 996/2010, (EU) No 376/2014 and Directives 2014/30/EU and 2014/53/EU of the European

Parliament and of the Council, and repealing Regulations (EC) No 552/2004 and (EC) No 216/2008 of the European Parliament and of the Council and Council Regulation (EEC) No 3922/91 (Text with EEA relevance.), PE/2/2018/REV/1, OJ L 212, 22/08/2018, p. 1–122.

Regulation (EC) No 1907/2006 of the European Parliament and of the Council of 18 December 2006 concerning the Registration, Evaluation, Authorisation and Restriction of Chemicals (REACH), establishing a European Chemicals Agency, amending Directive 1999/45/EC and repealing Council Regulation (EEC) No 793/93 and Commission Regulation (EC) No 1488/94 as well as Council Directive 76/769/EEC and Commission Directives 91/155/EEC, 93/67/EEC, 93/105/EC and 2000/21/EC, OJ L 396, 30.12.2006, p. 1–849.

Regulation (EU) No 376/2014 of the European Parliament and of the Council of 3 April 2014 on the reporting, analysis and follow-up of occurrences in civil aviation, amending Regulation (EU) No 996/2010 of the European Parliament and of the Council and repealing Directive 2003/42/EC of the European Parliament and of the Council and Commission Regulations (EC) No 1321/2007 and (EC) No 1330/2007 (Text with EEA relevance). http://data.europa.eu/eli/reg/2014/376/2018-09-11. Accessed 12 February 2025.

Regulation (EU) 2016/679 of the European Parliament and of the Council of 27 April 2016 on the protection of natural persons with regard to the processing of personal data and on the free movement of such data, and repealing Directive 95/46/EC, OJ L 119, 4.5.2016, p. 1–88.

Regulation (EU) 2018/1139, Regulation (EU) 2018/1139 of the European Parliament and of the Council of 4 July 2018 on common rules in the field of civil aviation and establishing a European Union Aviation Safety Agency, and amending Regulations (EC) No 2111/2005, (EC) No 1008/2008, (EU) No 996/2010, (EU) No 376/2014 and Directives 2014/30/EU and 2014/53/EU of the European Parliament and of the Council, and repealing Regulations (EC) No 552/2004 and (EC) No 216/2008 of the European Parliament and of the Council and Council Regulation (EEC) No 3922/91 (Text with EEA relevance), PE/2/2018/REV/1, OJ L 212, 22.8.2018, p. 1–122.

Ross, P. E. (2018). The prius of the sky [Blueprints for a Miracle]. *IEEE Spectrum, 55*(6).

Schuh, G., Krebs, L., Babetto, L., Kniebel, B., Spangenberg, M., & Stumpf, E. (2022). *Technical and legal boundary conditions for the extension of the air cargo logistics chain by UAVs into the city centre*. Deutscher Luft- und Raumfahrtkongress 2021. https://doi.org/10.25967/550082

Serrao, J., Nilsson, S., & Kimmel, S. (2018). *A legal and regulatory assessment for the potential of urban air mobility (UAM)*. Final Report, NASA,

Booz-Allen-Hamilton. https://doi.org/10.7922/G24M92RV. https://escholarship.org/uc/item/49b8b9w0. Accessed 10 February 2025.

Solove, D. J. (2002). Conceptualizing privacy. *California Law Review, 90*(4), 1087–1155.

Straubinger, A., Rothfield, R., Shamiyeh, M., Büchter, K.-D., Kaiser, J., & Plotner, K. O. (2020). An overview of current research and developments in urban air mobility – Setting the scene for UAM introduction. *Journal of Air Transport Management, 87*, 101852. https://doi.org/10.1016/j.jairtraman.2020. Accessed 10 February 2025.

The Commission Regulation (EU) No 748/2012 of 3 August 2012 laying down implementing rules for the airworthiness and environmental certification of aircraft and related products, parts and appliances, as well as for the certification of design and production organisations (recast) Text with EEA relevance, OJ L 224, 21.8.2012, p. 1–85.

Tojal, M., Hesselink, H., Fransoy, A., Ventas, E., Gordo, V., & Xu, Y. (2021). Analysis of the definition of Urban Air Mobility—How its attributes impact on the development of the concept. *Transportation Research Procedia, 59*, 3–13.

Turok, I. (2017). Urbanisation and development. In *The Routledge companion to planning in the global south* (pp. 93–103). Routledge.

United Nations. (2018). *World urbanization prospects*. https://population.un.org/wup/Download/. Accessed 10 February 2025.

Warren, S. D., & Brandeis, L. D. (1890, December 15). The right to privacy. *Harvard Law Review, 4*(5), 193–220. https://doi.org/10.2307/1321160. Accessed 10 February 2025.

Wu, Z., & Zhang, Y. (2021). Integrated network design and demand forecast for on-demand urban air mobility. *Engineering, 7*, 473–487. Electric VTOL-News.

Xiang, S., Xie, A., Ye, M., Yan, X., Han, X., Niu, H., Li, Q., & Huan, H. (2024). Autonomous eVTOL: A summary of researches and challenges. *Green Energy and Intelligent Transportation, 3*, 2773–1537. https://doi.org/10.1016/j.geits.2023.100140. Accessed 10 February 2025.

Yan, Y., Wang, K., & Qu, X. (2024). Urban air mobility (UAM) and ground transportation integration: A survey. *Frontiers of Engineering Management, 11*(4), 734–758. https://doi.org/10.1007/s42524-024-0298-0. Accessed 10 February 2025.

Zart, N. (2019, February 24). *Airbus Reveals UTM Blueprint and UAM Perceptions*. Electric VTOL-News. https://evtol.news/news/airbus-reveals-utm-blueprint-and-uam-perceptions. Accessed 10 February 2025.

CHAPTER 17

Digital Currencies and the Green Economy: Opportunities and Challenges in Achieving Sustainable Development Goals

Jesty Mariam Philip, Naived George Eapen, and Shine Raju Kappil

17.1 Introduction

The Sustainable Development Goals (SDGs) emphasize economic growth, innovation, reduced inequalities, and climate action. A green economy framework that prioritizes low-carbon, resource-efficient, and accessibility can aid the attainment of SDGs in various aspects. Digital

J. M. Philip (✉) · S. R. Kappil
School of Business and Management, Christ University, Bengaluru, India
e-mail: jesty.philip@christuniversity.in

S. R. Kappil
e-mail: shine.kappil@christuniversity.in

N. G. Eapen
Department of Computer Science, Christ University, Bengaluru, India
e-mail: naived.eapen@christuniversity.in

R. Aneja and R. Dygas (eds.), *Digital Currencies and the Green Economy*, https://doi.org/10.1007/978-981-95-2282-8_17

currencies play a vital role in efficient and fast transactions with the disadvantage of a high carbon footprint. A balance of innovation and sustainability is required through energy-efficient mechanisms, carbon-neutral initiatives, and regulatory frameworks.

This chapter provides an overview and a structured analysis of digital currencies within the context of the green economy and the sustainable development goals. Development of modern finance and financial technologies, various forms of digital currencies, environmental impact, and the path towards attaining sustainable financial practices are illustrated through an outline of DeFi, examination of policy frameworks, and emerging green finance trends.

Background and Significance of Digital Currencies

The history of money and the development of digital currencies had different phases. The first transaction was based on the exchange of commodities, known as the barter system where goods and services were exchanged directly. The use of shells or grain as commodity money emerged around 2000 BCE. Metal coins were introduced around 600 BCE. By the eleventh century, China introduced paper money. Later it was adopted by the European economy. The paper currency was backed by central authority, it helped to develop the modern banking system. Fiat currency—government issued money not backed by any physical commodity had a growth in the twentieth century.

The emergence of digital systems, primarily electronic computers and the internet, led to financial transactions being digitized and recorded. The introduction of systems such as Automated Teller Machines (ATMs), credit cards, online banking, and electronic payment platforms such as PayPal made use of technology to record and transfer money in digital formats. The emergence of mobile and digital payment systems further made steps towards popularizing transactions that did not necessitate paper currency. The emergence of the first Cryptocurrency, *Bitcoin*, aimed at providing a secure and independent means to hold value and make transactions, followed the financial crisis of 2008. The development of the blockchain system on which decentralized forms of data can be stored led to the rapid development of digital currencies. Blockchain networks further led to inventions of volatile digital currencies, non-volatile digital currencies (stablecoins such as USDT and USDC), and smart contracts. The early 2020s witnessed the rise of Central Bank Digital Currencies

(CDBCs) and various Proof-of-Work to the development of frameworks that can help in sustainable innovations in the FinTech field.

The adoption of digital currencies provides significant opportunities for economic growth, and some of the perspectives are enumerated below:

- Enhanced transaction efficiency that can stimulate economic growth
- Lower transaction costs compared to traditional banking methods
- Enhanced cross-border trade for better economic integration; improved global trade
- Bridges gaps in access to financial services
- Reduce the environmental impact in terms of physical cash production, distribution, and monitoring
- Improved payment systems
- Increased transparency and global regulatory frameworks
- Support for circular economy, and boosting economic digitalization

Digital currencies reduce reliance on physical currency production and distribution, thus making a transformative shift in financial systems. Digital currencies align with broader sustainability objectives as it minimizes transactional barriers. The tokenization of real-world assets and commodities has increased liquidity and accessibility. Governments are actively developing CBDCs, it will help to improve transparency in transactions and reduce financial fraud. As economic growth remains central to achieving the SDGs, it is imperative to examine its intricate relationship with sustainability, equity, and technological advancements in the evolving financial landscape.

17.2 Economic Growth and Sustainable Development Goals

Global economy is widely integrating digital finance, it incorporates sustainable practices within this sector. Sustainable digital finance involves including environmental, social, and governance (ESG) considerations into financial services through digital platforms (OECD, n.d.). By including sustainability within digital finance, the economy can have long-term growth at the same time reducing the footprint and promoting financial sustainability. The increased adoption of digital currencies requires sustainable approaches to assure long-term economic stability.

Optimizing blockchain for carbon credit trading and increasing financial inclusivity through decentralized applications are crucial strategies in implementing eco-friendly mechanisms. Sustainable finance helps to reduce the carbon footprints related to traditional banking systems. Digital transactions, conducted through blockchain technology, require few physical resources and generate lower emissions compared to traditional operations. CBDCs are a sustainable alternative to private cryptocurrencies. Countries such as China and Sweden have started pilot programs to develop energy efficient CBDCs that reduce risk associated with traditional cryptocurrency (Auer et al., 2021). Integrating sustainable finance and digital currency frameworks ensures flexibility against economic and environmental challenges.

Green Digital Finance

Green Finance refers to structured financial operations aimed to support climate actions and environmental sustainability while generating financial returns. By integrating ESG into financial decision-making, it creates a link between traditional financial systems and sustainability goals.

Green Finance includes various financial products and services. It includes green bonds, sustainable investment funds, and climate risk insurance (see Fig. 17.1). The fund raised through these investments will channel capital towards projects that create positive environmental impact such as sustainable transportation systems, renewable energy infrastructure etc. The sector has grown notably with the emergence of sophisticated risk assessment methodologies that will analyze both financial and environmental benefits.

Green Finance has developed drastically as governments and organizations strive to achieve net-zero emission and implement sustainable development goals. Financial institutions identify that environmental risks are business risks and it will lead to development of more green financial products. Technological developments that make it possible to measure the environmental impacts and legal frameworks that support sustainable finance practices are further accelerating this change.

Digital Currencies: Concepts, Types, and Current Adoption

Digital currencies do not have physical existence and they are available only in digital form. They are also known as digital money, electronic money, or cybercash. Type of digital Currencies:

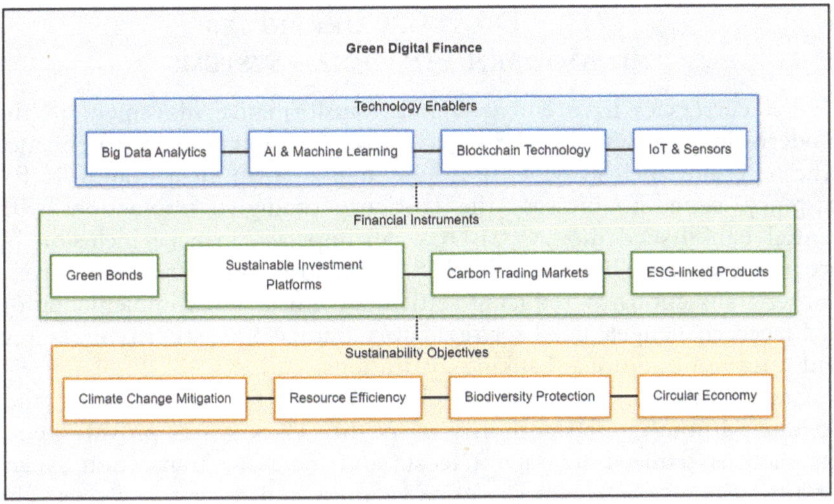

Fig. 17.1 Overview of Green Digital Finance. (*Source* Created by the authors)

1. Cryptocurrencies: Digital currencies that use cryptographic techniques to secure the transactions. The trade of cryptocurrency may or may not be regulated based on the jurisdiction. First cryptocurrency is bitcoin that was introduced in 2009.
2. Central Bank Digital Currencies (CBDCs): Regulated digital currency issued by the central bank of the country. CBDC can be a replacement of traditional currency. It aims to provide the efficiency of digital transactions with the trust and confidence of traditional fiat currency.
3. Virtual Currencies: It is unregulated digital money, issued and controlled by its developers. Virtual currency is used by the members of a specific virtual community.

The adoption of digital currency based on various factors including technological infrastructure, regulatory environment, and societal trust.

17.3 Digital Currencies and Modern Financial Systems

Digital currencies have emerged as a transformative movement in the modern financial system. The objective of this integration is to enhance efficiency and inclusivity. CBDC is a digital form of a country's fiat currency, aimed to increase the efficiency of digital transactions with central bank-issued money. CBDCs can improve financial inclusion by providing accessibility to unbanked population and streamline cross-border transactions by reducing settlement times. Their implementation had faced challenges, need for regulatory frameworks, security measures, and future of traditional banking institutions.

Cryptocurrencies introduced decentralized financial systems that operate without central authority oversight. These assets provide benefits such as reduced transaction costs and increased transaction speed. Crypto also has challenges like price volatility and regulatory issues. The growth of cryptocurrency has created a discussion among policymakers and institutions regarding their impact on financial stability and monetary policy. Stablecoins have gained attention for their potential to combine the advantage of cryptocurrencies with the stability of traditional money. They can provide real time, low-cost international payments.

Evolution of Digital Currencies

The concept of digital currencies started from the 1990s when David Chaum introduced the concept of e-cash. It aims to replicate the features of physical currencies in the digital form, providing secure transactions through the internet. The widespread use of e-cash faced challenges because of its scalability and centralization. As the internet gained popularity, online payment systems became an alternative to traditional banking systems. The platform, like Paypal, acted as intermediaries between traditional banks and users for transactions.

In 2009 bitcoin was introduced by an anonymous individual known as Satoshi Nakamoto. The blockchain provides secure and transparent transactions without the intervention of intermediaries. Multiple cryptocurrencies were developed after this. Altcoins such as Litecoin, Ripple, etc introduced. These cryptocurrencies aimed to rectify some limitations of Bitcoin, such as energy consumption and transaction speed. Smart contract concept was introduced by Ethereum. Smart contract automated the complex processes and eliminated the need of intermediaries.

Importance of Sustainable Practices in Digital Finance

Global economy is widely integrating digital finance, it incorporates sustainable practices within this sector. Sustainable digital finance involves including ESG considerations into financial services through digital platforms (OECD, n.d.). By including sustainability within digital finance, the economy can have long-term growth at the same time reducing the footprint and promoting financial sustainability. The increased adoption of digital currencies requires sustainable approaches to assure long-term economic stability. Optimizing blockchain for carbon credit trading and increasing financial inclusivity through decentralized applications are crucial strategies in implementing eco-friendly mechanisms. Sustainable finance helps to reduce the carbon footprints related to traditional banking systems. Digital transactions, conducted through blockchain technology, require few physical resources and generate lower emissions compared to traditional operations. CBDCs are a sustainable alternative to private cryptocurrencies. Countries such as China and Sweden have started pilot programs to develop energy efficient CBDCs that reduce the risk associated with traditional cryptocurrency. Integrating sustainable finance and digital currency frameworks ensures flexibility against economic and environmental challenges.

Digital Currencies in Green Economy: Recent Trends

Digital currencies have developed as an innovative financial tool with the potential to support the green economy. The green economy prioritizes reduction in carbon emissions, resource efficiency, and sustainability (United Nations, 2022). Cryptocurrencies and blockchain technology are transparent and decentralized mechanisms that support these goals. It reduces the reliance on traditional banking systems, which are energy-intensive (Truby, 2018). Green bonds can be tokenized and it will allow for easier tracking of proceeds and ensuring that they are directed towards environmental projects.

It is important to note the market dynamics of Green Finance. Certain observations from the recent past are as follows:

1. As per the global green bond market reached $500 Billion issuance in 2023. It represents growth from its beginning in 2007 when the first green bond was issued by the European Investment Bank. By the end of 2023, world bank being one of the largest issues, raised over $150 billion through green bonds.
2. The global benchmark for defining green investments is the European Union's taxonomy for sustainable activities implemented in 2020. Chinese green credit market grew up approximately 10% of total bank credit, it shows the increasing demand of emerging markets in sustainable finance.
3. Since large pension funds are committing to green finance, the institutional investors have changed. The world's largest sovereign wealth fund has set aside over $10 billion for environmental requirements. UN Principles for Responsible Investment have been signed by asset managers controlling more than $100 trillion, it shows the shift in investment priorities.
4. Beyond bonds the development of green finance instruments includes green mortgages, insurance for renewable energy initiatives, and sustainability-linked loans. 75% of institutional investors include climate risk analysis into their investment decisions.
5. Blockchain-based platform provides transparent carbon credit trading and AI powered tools improving the environmental impact assessment competencies. These advancement in technology approximately reduced 30% cost of monitoring and validating green investments.

The environmental impact of digital currencies used for Proof-of-Work mechanisms raises concerns. Bitcoin consumes a significant amount of electricity, causing a substantial carbon footprint. Consensus efforts are taking to mitigate these effects, changing to more energy efficient consensus mechanisms like Proof-of-Stake (PoS) and integrating renewable energy sources into mining operations. Bitcoin mining consumes 146 terawatt-hours of electricity yearly, exceeding the energy consumption of small nations like Sweden. The integration of digital currencies will have opportunities and challenges. Digital currencies can support investments in sustainable projects by aiding transparent and efficient transactions. The integration of green finance, carbon-neutral blockchain initiatives, is vital for aligning digital currencies with sustainability objectives.

Digital Currencies, Green Economy in Attaining SDGs

- Financial Inclusion: Financial inclusion is essential for eradicating poverty and for enhancing sustained economic growth. Digital currencies eliminate the need of traditional banking infrastructure, it provides access to financial services for unbanked and underbanked populations. By using decentralized platforms, individuals can engage in financial activities, it leads to the growth of economic equity. Green digital finance enhances financial inclusion and contributes to sustainable developments (Xiao et al., 2024).
- Reduced Fraud and Improved Transaction Efficiency: Blockchain technology helps digital currencies to enhance efficiency, reduce fraud, and to streamline transactions. Blockchain's ledger ensures transparent and verifiable records of transactions and promotes accountability. The decentralized nature of blockchain technology minimizes transaction cost, intermediaries' intervention, and reduces settlement time.
- Tokenization for Better Accessibility: Tokenization involves converting assets into digital tokens, it improves liquidity and accessibility. In the renewable energy market, tokenization allows for fractional ownership of assets like wind turbines, solar panels etc. quill enable more investors to involve in funding clean projects. Green bonds can be tokenized, it will help to attract investors, and facilitate capital flow into sustainable initiatives (Kalaiarasi & Kirubahari, 2023).

17.4 Digital Currencies and Sustainable Economic Growth

Sustainable economic growth refers to economic development that satisfies the present needs without compromising the future generation's ability to meet their needs. Sustainability in digital finance involves creating economic opportunities by reducing environmental harm. The change towards the digital currency aligns with United Nations SDGs, specifically in increasing financial inclusion, reducing transaction costs, and supporting sustainable investments.

Role of CBDCs in Financial Stability

CBDCs help to reduce the systematic risks, prevent banking crises, and improve the financial system (Kosanović, 2025). The impact of CBDC on financial stability:

1. Reducing the Risk Bank Runs
   Traditional banking institutions face an issue of bank runs, where investors/ customers withdraw huge amounts of money and it leads to liquidity crises. During financial crises, by using CBDC wallets individuals and businesses can deposit the fund, reducing the panic withdrawals from commercial banks.
2. Increase the Monetary policy effectiveness
   CBDC provides direct control over the money supply to the central bank, it helps to enable more efficient monetary policy. It can allow the central bank to directly influence saving and spending behavior by controlling interest rates on CBDC holding. This feature helps to reduce the economic downturns by an increase in spending or controlling inflation by encouraging savings.
3. Balancing Privacy and Regulatory Oversight
   Balance between transaction privacy and regulatory transparency is an opportunity provided by CBDCs. Cryptocurrency raises concerns about illegal activity due to anonymous transactions, CBDC allows for controlled anonymity ensuring user privacy by enabling regulatory oversight to control money laundering, tax evasion, and fraud transactions (Fernández-Villaverde, 2024). It can increase financial stability by implementing tiered privacy models, it will help to prevent illegal financial activities.
4. Improving payment systems efficiency
   Traditional payment system depends on intermediaries like commercial banks and payment processors. CBDCs operate in a blockchain secured network, it provides faster, secure, and cost-efficient transactions. Real-time settlement reduces the risk and delays, it provides greater financial stability during economic crises (Fernández-Villaverde, 2024). CBDC can be involved in cross-border transactions; it reduces the foreign exchange risks and increases global financial stability.

Risks of Economic Instability and Market Volatility

Digital currencies have risks, including volatility in price, regulatory uncertainties, and cybersecurity risks (Panigrahi, 2023). Bitcoins price fluctuations demonstrate the uncertain nature of digital assets, which will cause the adoption of stable economic instruments (Eng-Tuck Cheah, 2015). Regulatory instability across the jurisdictions raises challenges to creating a standardized ecosystem in digital finance. To reduce the risk governments and financial institutions must establish regulatory frameworks that improve stability while nurturing innovation.

Sustainable FinTech Solutions and Smart Contracts

Sustainable Financial technology is moving the financial industry towards an environmentally responsible future. It aims to reduce the environmental footprints of financial activities by promoting transparency and efficiency. As climate change concerns are growing globally, the need for sustainable economic growth is increasing. FinTech innovations like blockchain, decentralized finance (DeFi) are transforming financial services into sustainable systems (Kwong et al., 2023).

Smart contracts automate financial transactions in a decentralized manner. It is built on blockchain technology and enables transparency, cost reduction, and sustainability (Ren et al., 2023). Smart contracts will help to ensure that funds allotted for green initiatives are used efficiently for the intended purpose and prevent fraud from the misuse of resources. Blockchain technology helps green finance by tracking carbon credits and creating tamper-proof records of sustainable investments. AI-driven platforms analyse the ESG risk in investment portfolio, insights from this will help the institutions to align their investments with the sustainability goals (Khan & Ahmad, 2022).

Environmental Impact of Digital Currencies

The increasing analysis on the environmental impact of digital currencies is leading way for a transition towards carbon-neutral solutions. Figure 17.2 (University of Cambridge, 2025) shows the percentage of contribution of global hash rate, country wise, as on January 2022. The United States holds the highest share with 37.84% and China, the second highest country, holds 21.11%. It gives an idea of how these two economies would be depending on various energy sources for generating electricity required for these operations.

Adoption of carbon-neutral digital currencies is dependent on the type of energy sources, optimization of the resources and technology used in the transactions (such as blockchains), and implementation of carbon offset mechanisms. The predominant recommendation in this regard is the utilization of renewable energy in cryptocurrency mining. Initiatives such as CryptoClimate Accord aim to transition blockchain networks towards 100% renewable energy utilization by 2030. Movements have been initiated by forums to increase the usage of green energy, thereby significantly reducing the reliance on fossil fuels.

Carbon Footprint of Cryptocurrency Mining

Cryptocurrency mining through Proof-of-Work (PoW) mechanism has raised environmental concerns due to energy consumption and carbon emissions. The process requires solving complex mathematical problems to validate the transactions which require computational power and large

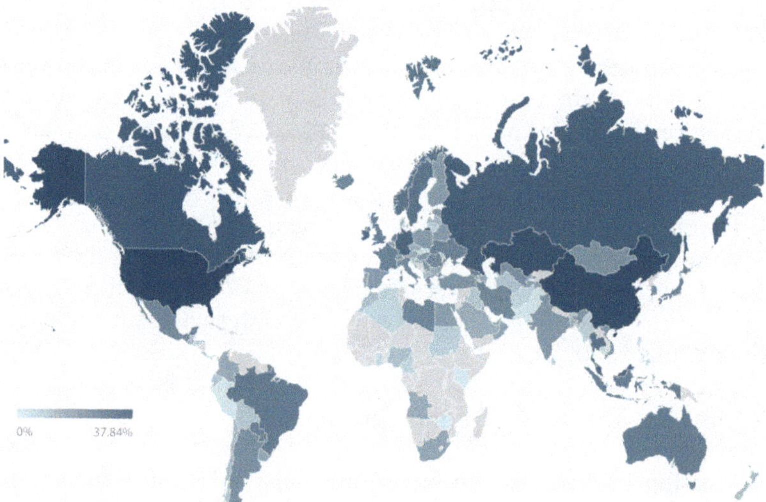

Fig. 17.2 Bitcoin Electricity Consumption. (*Source* University of Cambridge [2025])

amounts of electricity. From 2016 to 2021, each U.S. dollars' worth of mined Bitcoin caused 35 cents worth of climate change, it shows the issue of PoW mining (Jones et al., 2022; Kwong et al., 2023).

Geographical location of mining operations influences the carbon footprints of cryptocurrencies. Before 2021, a major portion of bitcoin mining happened in China, miners used a mix of coal and hydropower energy sources for mining. In June 2021 China banned cryptocurrency mining, then operations shifted to the United States, Russia, and Kazakhstan.

The increasing electricity consumption associated with Bitcoin mining, as depicted in the graph, highlights the rising energy demands of the Proof-of-Work (PoW) consensus mechanism. Cambridge Bitcoin Electricity Consumption Index continuously tracks the usage of selected cryptocurrency coins, and their actual and estimated power usage. As observed in Fig. 17.3 (Cambridge Center for Alternative Finance, 2025), from 2018 to 2023, Bitcoin's energy consumption has exhibited a consistent upward trajectory, growing from approximately 40 TWh in 2018 to over 120 TWh in 2023. This escalation is driven by the increasing computational complexity of Bitcoin mining, the expansion of mining operations, and the growing adoption of cryptocurrencies.

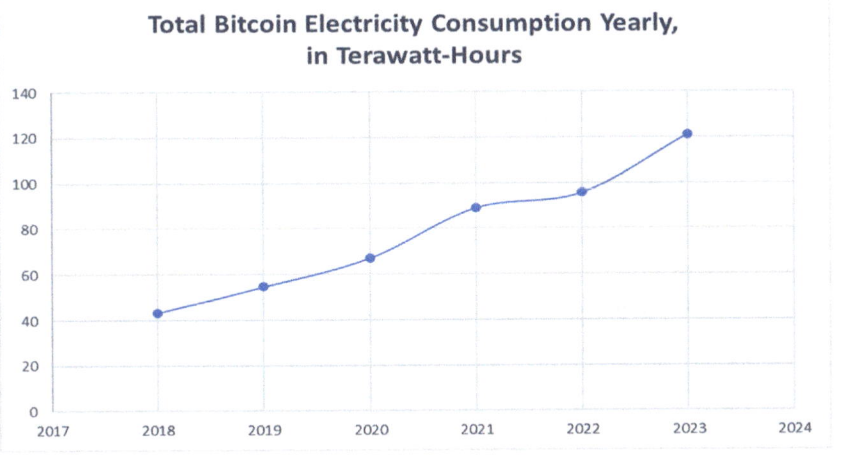

Fig. 17.3 Bitcoin Electricity Consumption. (*Source* University of Cambridge [2025])

Efforts were taken to reduce the environmental impacts, including change to less energy intensive mechanisms such as Proof-of-Stake (PoS) and incorporation of renewable energy sources into mining operations. These strategies aim to reduce carbon footprints related to mining activities. Addressing these challenges requires technology and policies.

Energy Efficient Blockchain Technologies

Proof-of-Stake (PoS) consensus mechanism, replaces the energy intensive mining process of Proof-of-Work with a system, where validators are chosen based on the number of tokens they take as collateral. Blockchain-based platforms have emerged as facilitators of carbon credit trading, enabling transparent and verifiable transactions for offsetting emissions. Projects such as KlimaDAO tokenize carbon credits, allowing individuals and businesses to invest in environmentally sustainable initiatives. Similarly, initiatives towards optimizing the process of transactions have already exhibited significant reduction in energy usage. For instance, the transition from Ethereum transitions to Ethereum 2.0 has led to 99.9% reduction in energy consumption (De Vries, 2023).

Carbon-Neutral Digital Currencies: Perspectives

The rise of sustainable cryptocurrencies further highlights the possibility of carbon-neutral digital finance. Currencies like Chia Network use a revolutionary Proof-of-Space-and-Time mechanism that is far less energy-intensive than the processes used to mine most cryptocurrencies. Other sustainable digital currencies, like SolarCoin (SLR), Nano (XNO), and Worldcoin (WLD), operate on efficient models that practically eliminate the use of fossil fuels. These upstart currencies are helping to create a carbon-neutral ecosystem that very much includes comprehensive climate action in its sights.

The following recent developments are observed as steps towards achieving carbon-neutral digital currencies, thereby attempting for economic transformations, supporting SDGs (Table 17.1).

The pursuit towards carbon-neutral digital currencies or tokens marks important milestones in the modern financial sectors and FinTech systems, where sustainability and technological innovation intersect to redefine economic models. As blockchain technology is looked at optimization, the impact extends beyond environmental benefits, opening

Table 17.1 Carbon-Neutral digital currencies—Recent developments in economic transformations

Development	*Contribution to economic transformations & SDGs*
Transition from Proof-of-Work (PoW) to Proof-of-Stake (PoS)	Reduces energy consumption by over 99% (e.g., Ethereum 2.0), promoting sustainable blockchain operations and lowering carbon emissions
Blockchain-Based Carbon Credit Markets (e.g., KlimaDAO, Toucan)	Enhances transparency in carbon offset training, as it incentivizes business to adopt financial practices that are sustainable, and that support green investments
Renewable Energy Integration in Mining	Enables low-carbon digital currency production, reducing reliance on fossil fuels while fostering sustainable economic growth
Tokenization of Sustainable Assets	Improves capital allocation; encourages green infrastructure developments and expands access to environmentally conscious investments
Emergence of Eco-Friendly Cryptocurrencies (Chia, Nano, SolarCoin)	Eliminates reliance on energy-intensive mining, ensuring transactions leave a minimal carbon footprint, unlike the older cryptocurrencies
Smart Contracts; CBDCs with ESG Integration	Allows programmable money for low-carbon spending; Ensures monetary systems support climate-aligned economic activities

Source Created by the authors

up opportunities to grow broader financial ecosystems. These advancements set the stage for deeper exploration of how the systems contribute to economic transformations, shaping financial accessibility, green finance practices, and sustainable development objectives.

17.5 Digital Currency Economic Transformations for SDGs

Many of the practices in the modern financial sectors (or FinTech systems) are redefining credit markets, financial inclusion, and economic resilience. As economies are showing tendencies to shift towards digital finance models, the operations related to those streamline financial operations that align with SDGs. Digital finance systems, in particular, digital currency systems must be looked up through the lens of environmentally conscious economic growth. Advantages such as transparency available in the blockchain systems can ensure secure and low-cost transactions while driving capital flows toward sustainable investments.

The intersection of digital finance and environmental sustainability is impacting global finance transformation. Instead of merely transferring value, digital currencies are now being used for impact measurement and the tokenization of environmental benefits. The programmability of digital assets is creating new paths of economic reformations. Carbon-tracking technologies now use digital currencies to provide direct correlation with environmental benefits whenever a financial transaction takes place. Aspects of ESG investment frameworks suffer from a lack of comprehensive data and diverse stakeholder input, which has impeded their evolution and efficacy. The ESG investing framework is a relatively new construct for investors seeking to analyze climate-related risks within their portfolios. In this situation, AI could, in theory, provide some much-needed clarity (Harvey et al., 2021; Kwong et al., 2023).

Economic transformations, in alignment with the SDGs, are possible through effective implementation of digital currencies as it promotes financial inclusion, efficient systems, transparency, decentralized finance, and tokenization of sustainable assets. Digital financial services, CBDCs, green bonds, carbon credits, etc. are investments that are, in practice, enhancing liquidity and accessibility.

The seamless integration of decentralized finance, tokenized assets, and programmable digital transactions is fostering new economic opportunities while addressing traditional barriers to financial accessibility. It obviously comes with several benefits, such as:

- Lower Transaction costs: Digital currency can reduce the transaction costs by eliminating the intermediaries. In the traditional banking system banks and payment processors have become the intermediary between the sender and the receiver. Lower transaction costs will be beneficial for cross-border transactions, which includes high fees and lengthy processes. Digital currency can streamline the process and provide faster payments.

- Transparency and Security: Blockchain technology used behind the digital currency will provide transparency and security. Each transaction will be recorded in public ledger. This can reduce fraud in the financial system.
- Financial Inclusion: The unbanked population can avail these facilities digitally. Digital Currency provides access to the people without the need for a bank account, individuals can contribute to the global economy.
- Investment and Speculations: Digital currency attracts institutional and retail investors; it becomes a popular investment asset. The volatility has led to speculation, the prices are fluctuating dramatically. It creates an opportunity for investors to contribute to market instability.

Decentralized Finance (DeFi)

One of the most important economic reformations is how financial institutions are offering decentralized services for the access and operations. Decentralized Finance (DeFi) eliminates the intermediaries in financial transactions, without a centralized control. Very similar to how the crypto systems are built with *Mutual Distrust*, it is interesting to see how the platforms that have come up in the last decade offer services such as lending, borrowing, and asset trading through decentralized networks. DeFi enables users to earn interest on cryptocurrency holdings, and facilitate peer-to-peer trading of digital assets. DeFi platforms are accessible globally, offering financial services to unbanked populations, where the only barrier is the connection to the network.

DeFi has reshaped financial accessibility by offering decentralized exchanges, peer-to-peer lending, and financial transactions based on smart contracts. Traditional finance relies on centralized authorities, DeFi platforms operate transparently. DeFi insurance platforms offer coverage against smart contract failures and hacks. Ethereum-based DeFi protocols have enabled millions in developing countries to access credit, savings, and investment tools without intermediaries (Kwong et al., 2023). DeFi's rapid growth has attracted attention from regulators concerned about consumer protection and financial stability, though it follows community-driven protocols. The shortcomings of the DeFi systems revolve around difficulty in transaction reversal, lack of KYC processes, impermanent loss, and dependence on the market.

The Financial Action Task Force (FATF) updated its guidance to include DeFi within certain regular frameworks, urging various countries to assess and determine whether the entities in their partial control quality as VASPs (Virtual Asset Service Providers) are subject to the standards. This development shows the evolving nature of digital finance, and the increasing emphasis on regulatory frameworks to ensure compliance and mitigate risks (Bodó, 2023).

Regulatory Frameworks and Policy Interventions

Digital finance is becoming prominent with regulations centered on sustainability. Governments and financial regulators advocate for carbon disclosures in not just cryptocurrency operations, but also in those for various forms of digital assets-like Decentralized Autonomous Organizations (DAOs) or NFTs, so that they might assist in gauging the impact of these activities on the climate. Some regulatory bodies have taken to proposing initiatives that would offset any negative impact the previously mentioned asset operations might have.

International bodies such as FATF are collaborating to establish unified standards for digital asset regulations. There are also regulations being developed by institutions and countries, especially focusing on consumer protection measures. Taxation frameworks, economic regulation methods, data privacy standards, laws or regulations related to trades, cross-border payment policies, environmental impact reporting, public-private partnerships, transparency and compliance requirements, audit-related aspects, etc. are need to be thoughtfully addressed for the better implementation of sustainable economic frameworks.

17.6 Conclusion

The adoption of digital currencies, including cryptocurrencies and CBDCs, is reshaping the financial ecosystems and markets. The advancements of financial inclusion, transparency, and several other factors in the domain align support economic growth, innovation, and equitable financial access that contribute to attainment of SDGs. The Green Economy highlights the environmental footprint of digital currencies and FinTech systems, necessitating energy-efficient technologies, and carbon-neutral sustainable innovations. Regulatory interventions are progressively integrating sustainability focused policies and economic governance. Though Governments and international organizations are actively developing regulatory frameworks to ensure financial stability while addressing AML compliance, there is a need for collaboration between policymakers, technology leaders, and financial institutions to align digital currencies with sustainable practices.

Digital currencies have the potential to drive economic transformation while contributing to sustainability, whereas, on the other hand, the requirement of regulatory oversight and environmental responsibility remains an important challenge. The integration of decentralized, efficient, and sustainable digital currency ecosystems will be essential for achieving a resilient and inclusive global economy, and can reshape financial systems for better progression and development.

References

Auer, R. A., et al. (2021). Central bank digital currencies: Motives, economic implications and the research frontier. *Social Science Research Network* [Preprint]. https://papers.ssrn.com/sol3/papers.cfm?abstract_id=3922836. Accessed 11 February 2025.

Bodó, T. B. A. (2023). Beyond financial regulation of crypto-asset wallet software: In search of secondary liability. *Computer Law & Security Review, 49*, 105829. https://doi.org/10.1016/j.clsr.2023.105829

Cambridge Centre for Alternative Finance. (2025). *Cambridge Bitcoin Electricity Consumption Index (CBECI)*. University of Cambridge. https://ccaf.io/cbnsi/cbeci. Accessed 13 February 2025.

De Vries, A. (2023). Cryptocurrencies on the road to sustainability: Ethereum paving the way for Bitcoin. *Patterns, 4*(1), 100633. https://doi.org/10.1016/j.patter.2022.100633

Eng-Tuck Cheah, J. F. (2015). Speculative bubbles in Bitcoin markets? An empirical investigation into the fundamental value of Bitcoin. *Economics Letters, 130*, 32–36. https://doi.org/10.1016/j.econlet.2015.02.029

Fernández-Villaverde, U. L. S. (2024). Central bank digital currency: When price and bank stability collide. *Journal of Monetary Economics, 145*, 103554. https://doi.org/10.1016/j.jmoneco.2024.01.007

Harvey, C. R., Ramachandran, A., & Santoro, J. (2021). *DeFi and the Future of Finance*. https://doi.org/10.2139/ssrn.3711777

Jones, B. A., Goodkind, A. L., & Berrens, R. P. (2022). Economic estimation of Bitcoin mining's climate damages demonstrates closer resemblance to digital crude than digital gold. *Scientific Reports, 12*(1), 14512. https://doi.org/10.1038/s41598-022-18686-8

Kalaiarasi, H., & Kirubahari, S. (2023). Green finance for sustainable development using blockchain technology. In *Green blockchain technology for sustainable smart cities* (pp. 167–185). Elsevier. https://doi.org/10.1016/B978-0-323-95407-5.00003-7

Khan, N., & Ahmad, T. (2022). DCarbonX decentralised application: Carbon market case study. *arXiv [cs.CE]*. https://doi.org/10.48550/ARXIV.2203.09508

Kosanović, N. (2025). Central Bank Digital Currencies: Financial stability perspective. *Journal of Central Banking Theory and Practice, 14*(1), 145–162. https://doi.org/10.2478/jcbtp-2025-0008

Kwong, R., Kwok, M. L. J., & Wong, H. S. M. (2023). Green FinTech innovation as a future research direction: A bibliometric analysis on green finance and FinTech. *Sustainability, 15*(20), 14683. https://doi.org/10.3390/su152014683

OECD. (n.d.). *ESG investing: Practices, progress and challenges (Report)*. https://www.oecd.org/en/publications/esg-investing-practices-progress-and-challenges_b4f71091-en.html; https://doi.org/10.1787/b4f71091-en

Panigrahi, S. (2023). Are cryptocurrencies a threat to financial stability and economic growth of India? Evidence from the cointegration approach. *Investment Management and Financial Innovations, 20*(2), 307–320. https://doi.org/10.21511/imfi.20(2).2023.26

Ren, Y.-S., Ma, C.-Q., Chen, X.-Q., Lei, Y.-T., & Wang, Y.-R. (2023). Sustainable finance and blockchain: A systematic review and research agenda. *Research in International Business and Finance, 64*, 101871. https://doi.org/10.1016/j.ribaf.2022.101871

Truby, J. (2018). Decarbonizing Bitcoin: Law and policy choices for reducing the energy consumption of Blockchain technologies and digital currencies. *Energy Research & Social Science, 44*, 399–410. https://doi.org/10.1016/j.erss.2018.06.009

United Nations. (2022). *Green economy: A path towards sustainable development and poverty eradication, United Nations Western Europe*. United Nations. https://unric.org/en/green-economy-a-path-towards-sustainable-development-and-poverty-eradication/. Accessed 2 February 2025.

University of Cambridge. (2025). *Cambridge Bitcoin Electricity Consumption Index: Mining Map*. https://ccaf.io/cbnsi/cbeci/mining_map. Accessed 13 February 2025.

Xiao, Y., Lin, M., & Wang, L. (2024). Impact of green digital finance on sustainable development: Evidence from China's pilot zones. *Financial Innovation, 10*(1), 1–32. https://doi.org/10.1186/s40854-023-00552-9

CHAPTER 18

Green Innovation in Digital Payments: Opportunities for a Low-Carbon Economy

Gabriel A. Ogunmola

18.1 Introduction

Digital payment systems have revolutionized financial systems around the world, facilitating speedier, more efficient, and more inclusive financial transactions (Hu et al., 2025; Kou et al., 2021). From mobile wallets to blockchain-powered platforms, digital payments have replaced traditional cash-based means of transacting and are fundamentally changing how economies function. This has been critical in facilitating financial inclusions, innovations, and access to those who are underbanked. For example, mobile payment systems, such as M-Pesa in Kenya, have formed the lifeline of financial transactions in some rural settings (Maiti, 2022; Ogunmola et al., 2024). For all the rapid proliferation, however, the spread of digital payment systems has brought environmentally related issues along that can no longer be ignored-things that, though

G. A. Ogunmola (✉)
Department of Economic Theory, Tashkent State University of Economics, Tashkent, Uzbekistan
e-mail: Gabriel00lead@yahoo.com

R. Aneja and R. Dygas (eds.), *Digital Currencies and the Green Economy*, https://doi.org/10.1007/978-981-95-2282-8_18

reducing the environmental impacts of physical cash production, transport, and disposal, they bring along different types of unsustainability issues, particularly through their voracious appetite for energy-dependent infrastructures (Bansal et al., 2025; Zhang et al., 2023). From data centers to communication networks and even the production and disposal of electronic payment devices, there are contributions to greenhouse gas emissions and e-waste. Since digital payment will increasingly be the pivot on which most modern financial systems function, there is an urgent need to revisit and discuss its environmental implications. Unfortunately, most of the existing literature predicates arguments on the efficiencies, conveniences, and financial inclusions facilitated by digital payments (Kou et al., 2021; Maiti, 2022). Quantitative studies on the environmental footprint of digital payment systems are a rare occurrence. While conceptual discussions surround the potential of green innovations in the financial sector, empirical evidence remains scant on how effective they are in lowering the carbon footprint of digital payments. Additionally, only a few studies have explored the interaction between regulatory frameworks and the adoption of green innovations within the digital payment system. While there are studies that suggest policy can encourage greener practices within industries like energy and transport, the applicability to financial technologies remains an understudied area. These fallacies need to be overcome for a rapid development regarding how digital payment systems can help achieve a low-carbon economy to meet overall sustainable development goals.

The environmental impact of digital payment systems, including carbon footprint, has hardly been examined empirically, as the interest in digital payment systems spreads. Most of the current studies focus either on operational efficiencies or the benefits derived from digital payments in terms of financial inclusion and do not estimate the environmental cost associated with the life cycle (Dai et al., 2025; Guo et al., 2025). One of the major barriers to understanding the sustainability challenges related to this sector is a lack of reliable data on carbon emission from the digital payment system. While green innovations around the integration of renewable energy and energy-efficient technologies have not been explored well in digital payment infrastructures, their contribution to making digital payment systems greener is not well examined. It is also worth noting that the role of policies and regulatory frameworks in shaping financial institutions' greening practice has not been analyzed well. This study addresses these gaps through: first, a quantitative examination of the carbon footprint related to digital payment systems; second, an examination of the role of green innovation in reducing carbon footprint from digital payment systems; and lastly, how policy and regulatory measures may support the integration of sustainability in Fintech. In sum, and in relation to the research problem at hand, the present study sets out to address the following questions: What is the carbon footprint related to digital payment systems, and how does it compare with the carbon footprint of traditional means of paying? How do green innovations, which include the integration of renewable energy and energy-efficient protocols, lower carbon emissions from the operation of digital payment systems? Precisely, what are the major drivers and barriers to the adoption of green practices in digital payments, and how does policy and regulation support such implementation? Specific key objectives of the study would include the following:

1. To analyze digital payment systems carbon footprint across their lifecycle, from energy consumption to data processing, and device usage.
2. To evaluate the impact of green innovations such as renewable energy adoption, energy-efficient technologies, and carbon offset initiatives on reducing the environmental footprint of digital payment systems.
3. To determine the role of policy and regulatory frameworks concerning green innovations and their influence on the adoption of sustainable practices within digital payment infrastructures.

The study addresses academic discourses and practical policymaking because it fills a gap that exists in the environmental analysis of digital payment systems. The study will address the call of global efforts toward the attainment of the United Nations' SDGs, particularly Goal 9 on building resilient infrastructure and Goal 13 on climate action, by quantifying the carbon footprint of digital payments and exploring the role of green innovations. From these bases, policymakers will have evidence-based recommendations on how to design and implement regulations to fast-track the adoption of green innovation in digital payments. The study gives insight to financial institutions and technology providers on sustainable best practices that can be adopted to improve operational efficiency while reducing adverse environmental impacts. Most of all, this research sends an important message pertaining to the multi-stakeholder approach that will drive the financial sector toward sustainability and eco-friendliness.

18.2 Literature Review

The transition from traditional cash-based payment systems to digital payment methods has profoundly transformed financial transactions, marking a pivotal shift in global financial systems. It has changed the way people make financial transactions, and the effect is enormous on global financial systems. Previously economies depended so much on hard cash for transactions, and this meant the production, circulation, and storage of paper cash and coins. However, the introduction of electronic payment methods, such as credit cards, mobile systems, and blockchain-related technologies, has broken this monopoly with more speed, security, and convenience for the trading communities (Kou et al., 2021; Kumar & Ayodeji, 2022). Third-party online payment providers such as PayPal, Alipay, and M-Pesa are facilitating financial transactions even in regions where access to the formal banking network is not well developed. For instance, M-Pesa in Kenya has provided the facility to millions of users for executing financial transactions in electronic form, thereby increasing financial inclusion on a pan-country basis in a big way (Maiti, 2022). Besides, blockchain, being decentralized in nature, has also introduced some innovations in mechanisms for secure and transparent transactions, thus furthering the cause of digital payments (Zhang et al., 2023).

The digitization of payments has increased dramatically worldwide, wherein regional differences in adoption are driven by infrastructure, regulatory frameworks, and consumer preferences. For instance, the early and wide usage of credit and debit cards in developed economies like the United States and Europe has, in turn, seen a spur of mobile payments in countries such as India, as efforts put forth by the government have shown enthusiasm for digital transactions (Ogunmola & Kumar, 2024a; Suri & Jack, 2016). According to Anitha et al. (2025) it stated that digitization of payment methods also has sustainability potential in decreasing the overall ecological footprint of traditional means of payment. An example is the production of paper-based banknotes and metal coins, which, in general, is extremely resource-intensive in terms of energy and natural resources. Furthermore, their transport further enhances greenhouse gas emissions. This dependency on physical cash could decrease when digital payment systems replace older forms of payment, thereby aligning with sustainable transitions within financial systems in general (Kou et al., 2021). However, if digital payments are truly sustainable, then it needs to take into account its environmental impact, which is more glaring nowadays because of its increasing adoption.

18.2.1 Environmental Impacts of Payment Systems

In spite of the possible sustainability gains from digital payment systems, they do not come without environmental cost. Traditional means of payment systems, like producing cash and coins, involve energy-intensive operations which add to carbon emissions. Similarly, manufacturing, transporting, and operating ATMs for supplying cash also require huge amounts of energy and result in massive emissions. For instance, the energy consumption in transporting cash alone accounts for a major share of the environmental impact of traditional systems (Maiti, 2022). Digital payment systems, however, do not include the manufacture and transportation of cash. However, all digital payment systems are based on data centers, network infrastructures, and electronic devices, adding another dimension to the environmental impact. Data centers, which form the backbone for digital transaction processing, are power-hungry and usually fed with fossil fuels. Besides this, the network infrastructures, like cellular networks and broadband connections, further contribute to carbon emissions. All these put together make the carbon footprint of digital payment systems a critical area of concern (Zhang et al., 2023).

There are various steps in the whole lifecycle of digital payments, resulting in considerable environmental impacts. The most critical challenge is energy consumption due to processing, storing information, and verifying transactions. For instance, blockchain-based systems, such as Bitcoin, though innovative, have been known for their vast energy consumption because of the computational intensity of their processes used in verifying transactions (Kou et al., 2021). Another major challenge entails electronic wastes generated within an economy. Many hardware components in digital payment systems, including payment terminals, smartphones, and point-of-sale devices, contribute to electronic wastes. Their manufacture, use, and eventual disposal result in e-waste, whose improper disposal poses considerable environmental risks. The rapidity of technological changes reduces the life of devices and aggravates the problem (Maiti, 2022). Such life cycle challenges need to be responded to with broad-based efforts toward adopting energy-efficient technologies, incorporating renewable sources of energy, and creating robust e-waste management systems. These measures will be important to ensure that no negative environmental externalities arise from digital payment systems.

18.2.2 Green Innovation and Opportunities in Digital Payments

Green innovation refers to technologies and practices contributing to enhancing operational efficiency along with reducing environmental impact (Rennings, 2000). In the context of digital payment systems, it refers to a reduction in energy consumption, enhancement of transaction protocols, and thus using renewable sources for sustainability (Maiti, 2022). The ability of green innovation in digital payment systems to address two most crucial challenges simultaneously, environmental sustainability, and financial inclusion, is its prime essence. United Nations SDGs, especially Goal 13, emphasize the need for incorporating environmentally feasible practices into every sector, also extending to financial technologies (United Nations, 2023). Digital payment systems are among the most integral parts of modern economies and hence provide a perfect area where such global causes can be combined along with the cause of technological advancement (Zhang et al., 2023). Green innovations have shown the potential for transformation from lessons in other industries. For example, manufacturing industries have started using renewable sources of energy, like wind and solar energy, to decrease dependency on fossil fuels, whereas in the case of cloud computing, considerable energy consumption reduction has been achieved by developing highly efficient ways of data processing (GeSI, 2015). The above two examples demonstrate that it is very well possible to incorporate sustainable practices into energy-intensive industries and therefore contain a lesson or two for digital payment providers.

18.2.2.1 Renewable Energy Adoption

The use of renewable energy sources is considered one of the most promising avenues for reducing the environmental footprints of digital payment systems. The data centers, which account for the lion's share of the carbon emissions associated with digital payment systems today, process and store billions of digital transactions every year. Renewable energy sources will go a long way in reducing this carbon footprint. A number of technology companies have proven the possibility of using renewable energy sources. For instance, Apple announced that, by 2022, all its facilities worldwide, including data centers, were powered by 100% renewable energy, setting the pace for other sectors to emulate (Apple, 2022). The adoption of sustainability by the company culture through tapping into renewable energy sources in operations has been implemented by several payment service providers such as Visa to cushion their carbon footprint (Visa, 2021).

18.2.2.2 Energy-Efficient Technologies and Protocols

Energy-efficient technologies and protocols are another critical pathway toward environmental sustainability in digital payments. Blockchain one of the growing segments within the digital payment landscape has been criticized because of the energy-intensive nature emanating from computational resources needed by PoW consensus mechanisms (Hasanin et al., 2021; Kou et al., 2021). However, alternative consensus algorithms have been developed that could reduce energy usage without compromising security and transparency, such as PoS and PoA consensus algorithms among others (Lu et al., 2021; Zhang et al., 2023). Corresponding to this move, edge computing and lightweight cryptographic protocols will further improve energy efficiency across the payment networks. Edge computing reduces the need for centralized data processing; hence, computing happens closer to the source, reducing energy needs accordingly (GeSI, 2015). These technologies have obviously improved not only sustainability considerations but also the velocity and reliability of digital payment transactions.

18.2.2.3 Carbon Offset Initiatives

Carbon offsetting initiatives are among the latest ways in which digital payment providers can offset their carbon footprint. These schemes invest in projects that reduce or remove carbon dioxide from the atmosphere for example, afforestation, the development of renewable energy sources, and methane capture (Maiti, 2022). For instance, Mastercard's Priceless Planet Coalition has pledged to plant 100 million trees by 2025 as part of its broader ambitions in sustainability, thereby offsetting emissions that may have been created from its operations (Mastercard, 2021). The collaboration of financial institutions with organizations oriented toward sustainability can amplify the positive impacts of carbon offset schemes.

Payment providers can also make consumers more engaged with green practices by creating options for them to take part in the offsetting of emissions; for example, rounding up transaction amounts for use in environmental projects (Kou et al., 2021).

18.2.3 Digital Payments and Environmental Sustainability

Digital payment systems provide more impetus to global financial transactions in terms of efficiency and financial inclusiveness but are greater contributors to environmental degradation. According to a recent study by Utami et al. (2021), some of the major environmental efficiencies of digital payment systems are related to a reduction in the demand for cash production and circulation. Traditional processes in this respect are very resource-consuming; for instance, energy and raw materials are needed in the minting and printing of money, logistics and maintenance of ATMs are energy-consuming, and so on. The replacement of these by digital payments means lower GHG emissions. However, digital payment systems themselves are not bereft of environmental costs. According to Ayodeji and kumar (2025), since every transaction is processed and stored through data centers, they are one of the most energy-intensive components. Very often, these data centers operate with renewable sources of energy. Consequently, the carbon emissions they give rise to are considerable. Similarly, infrastructure accompanying digital payments consists of network servers and payment terminals which generate appreciable e-waste due to their rapid rates of technological obsolescence.

Recent studies have discussed how such environmental degradation can be outweighed through some greening alternatives. For instance, edge computing, or transmitting the data closer to where it is created, reduces energy consumption by limiting the demand for data transfer. Besides, machine learning and AI can predict the maintenance needs of all the payment gateways and reduce unnecessary expenses and wastage of resources (Nithyanantham et al., 2021). The case study evidence also depicts empirical evidence as to how green innovation has been embraced by the major players of the financial industry. For instance, PayPal has vowed to achieve carbon neutrality by integrating renewable energy into its operations and making its platforms energy-efficient in every transaction cycle. By this shift in operating mode, the firm has succeeded in shrinking its carbon footprint without losing its leading edge in financial markets. Similarly, Paytm, a major Indian digital payment platform, has developed green data centres powered by renewable energy sources and has cut its operation-related emissions by 40% in three years. Besides, the platform does not stop here but further motivates users to integrate environmentally-friendly habitations by giving them incentives for paperless billing and ecologically friendly consumptions. Another related case is Ant Group's operation of Alipay, which also introduced blockchain technology with energy-efficient protocols for processing micro-transactions. According to a company report, this effort cut its energy use by 25% while increasing speed and security in transactions. These case studies thus illustrate how digital payment systems can embody the principles of sustainability without necessarily affecting their functional efficiency or profitability, hence setting benchmarks for the wider financial industry.

18.2.4 Theoretical Foundations

Green innovation is defined as the process of developing and implementing products, processes, or services that result in a marked reduction in environmental impact without jeopardizing or improving economic viability (Wang et al., 2022). In the field of financial technologies, green innovation is all about adopting practices that reduce the ecological footprint of financial transactions. Such practices include moving from energy-intensive processes to renewable energy, optimizing blockchain protocols, and carbon offset programs. For instance, the application of green innovation can be seen in blockchain-based digital payment systems. Conventional blockchain systems, such as those that apply proof-of-work consensus mechanisms, are notoriously energy-intensive. Innovations like the proof-of-stake mechanism, however, have drastically reduced energy consumption by removing computationally intensive mining processes from the system (Ogunmola & Kumar, 2024b). Green innovation in financial technologies also covers the hardware aspect of payment systems. For instance, lightweight and energy-efficient payment terminals have been developed that use less power and offer more enhanced processing capabilities. Additionally, innovations in cloud computing have enabled financial institutions to avoid physical data centers and transition into virtualized and energy-optimized environments.

Low-carbon economy frameworks stand out as the indispensable drivers in reducing GHG emissions in all industries, including financial, and putting into action the quest for global sustainability. The frameworks of the low-carbon economy involve changing from carbon-intensive practices to low-carbon options, with regulatory mechanisms, financial incentives, and industry standards. The largest among them is the Paris Agreement, which is an internationally legally binding treaty adopted by 196 countries under UNFCCC in 2015. It aspires to limit global warming to well below 2 °C above the pre-industrial level and, if possible, pursue the nighttime target of not exceeding 1.5 °C increase. The framework challenges states to cause no climate harm, with their climate resilience and low-carbon growth enabling financial institutions to align investment portfolios with climate objectives while fostering green finance in the process. The European Green Deal aims at making sure that Europe is the first climate-neutral continent by 2050 and proposes different legislative proposals and financial mechanisms that will foster clean energy, energy efficiency, sustainable agriculture, and reductions of pollution. This Deal requires financial institutions to disclose carbon risks and integrate sustainability criteria into their financial decision-making processes, promoting green bonds and investments in low-carbon technologies (European Commission, 2020). Similarly, the U.S. Green New Deal calls for massive investments in renewable energy, energy efficiency, and green jobs, with a focus on climate change mitigation and promotion of economic equity. Financial institutions are expected to mobilize capital for renewable energy projects, thereby supporting the transition to a low-carbon economy (AOC, 2019).

The UK Climate Change Act is the world's first legally binding climate change legislation, setting a target to reduce GHG emissions by at least 80% by 2050. The Act provides a framework for transitioning to a low-carbon economy by using carbon budgets to limit emissions over five-year periods. This has driven investments in low-carbon technologies and sustainable infrastructure, creating opportunities for financial institutions to invest in carbon-reducing initiatives (UK Government, 2008). Meanwhile, the Task Force on Climate-related Financial Disclosures (TCFD) established by the Financial Stability Board makes recommendations for both companies and financial institutions to disclose financial risks involved with climate change. Following its recommendations, it helps financial institutions manage climate-related risks and investment aligned with low-carbon transition globally (TCFD, 2017). The Kyoto Protocol's Clean Development Mechanism (CDM) provides developed countries the opportunity to invest in developing countries on projects that reduce GHG emissions in exchange for certified emission reduction units. This promotes development in a sustainable way and helps developed nations meet their emission reduction targets according to the specified protocol (UNFCCC, 1997). Similarly, the International Finance Corporation (IFC) had been a firm advocate of issuance of green bonds to raise finance for environmentally sustainable projects, notably renewable energy and energy efficiency initiatives (IFC, 2020). This is also part of the overall effort by institutions like the CDP, a global disclosure system in which investors and companies engage in disclosing environmental risk, encouraging every financial institution and organization to measure the carbon footprint and integrate these into their business and investment strategies (CDP, 2000).

The Global Green Bond Initiative and the UN Principles for Responsible Banking further encourage the application of green finance through the call on financial institutions to invest in sustainable infrastructure and to align their approaches with the UN SDGs and the Paris Agreement. These further elucidate the vital role of the financial sectors in contributing or catalyzing a low-carbon economy through financing clean energy projects, creating carbon offset schemes, and furthering world climate goals. According to the UN, 2020, all these frameworks provide an overall approach to cutting carbon emission and furthering sustainable practices. They show the significant role those financial institutions can play in supporting a low-carbon future by facilitating investments in renewable energy, energy-efficient technologies, and sustainable development projects.

18.2.5 Research Model & Hypothesis

The model conceptualizes the relationship between green innovations and carbon footprint from digital payment systems, emphasizing their impact on environmental sustainability and financial inclusions; see Fig. 18.1. It identifies three independent variables, namely, renewable energy, energy-efficient technologies, and policy and regulatory support, which influence the carbon footprint directly. Green innovations are the mediating variable, representing the implementation of sustainable technologies and practices in an endeavor for further improving their environmental performance. The dependent variable, which is carbon footprint, is expressed by the environmental impacts from digital payments, usually measured by the amount of CO2 emitted. The model states that a reduction of

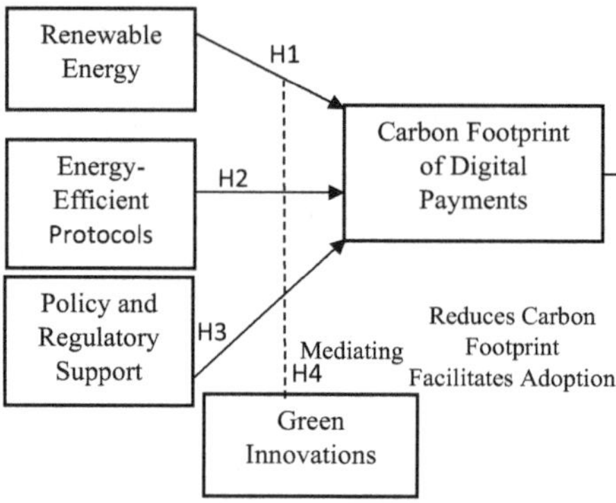

Fig. 18.1 Research model. (*Source* Compiled by researcher)

carbon footprint will positively impact improving environmental sustainability. This framework reveals the importance of technological and regulatory interventional approaches toward the attainment of sustainable development within the digital payment ecosystem.

To be able to answer the research questions and objectives the study has hypothesis of the following;

> *H1: The adoption of renewable energy in digital payment systems significantly reduces the carbon footprint of digital payments.*
> *H2: The implementation of energy-efficient technologies significantly reduces the carbon footprint of digital payments.*
> *H3: Supportive policy and regulatory frameworks have a significant negative impact on the carbon footprint of digital payments.*
> *H4: Green innovations mediate the relationship between (a) renewable energy, (b) energy-efficient technologies, and (c) policy and regulatory support, and the carbon footprint of digital payments.*
> *H5: A lower carbon footprint of digital payment systems leads to greater environmental sustainability.*

18.3 Research Methodology

The study employed a quantitative research design to quantify the environmental impacts of digital payment systems and establish the effectiveness level of green innovations in mitigating them. This design enabled numeric data collection that analyzed critical dependencies of green innovations, such as the adoption of renewable energy and energy-efficient protocols, on the carbon footprint of digital payments. In this light, a quantitative design was selected because it allows the findings to be reported in an objective, measurable way that is generalizable across sectors and geographical regions (Creswell, 2014; Gopal & Pitts, 2025).

18.3.1 Sample and Sampling Techniques

This target population included financial institutions, digital payment providers, regulators, and consumers in a select number of countries. Stratified random sampling ensured that representative samples for both developed and developing economies were included. This means that large differences in respect to the level of economic development, its regulatory framework, and the existing technological infrastructure are well taken care of by the countries that included the survey population (Flick, 2018). The sample size utilized, 501, was the threshold for the minimum sample size required for statistical power and, therefore, reliable analysis of the collected data (Field, 2013).

18.3.2 Data Collection Instrument

For the quantitative data, this study adopted a web-based survey instrument. The key stakeholders that the instrument targeted for digital payment include financial institutions, technology providers, and policy makers. The reason behind the adoption of this instrument is its efficiency, considering that the population being surveyed is geographically spread, making the study cost-effective. The survey is segmented into four parts, each focused on a particular theme of interest to correspond to the respective specific objectives of the study. The first section was designed to capture demographic and organizational data from respondents, including the type of institution (for example, financial institutions, a regulatory body, a digital payment service provider), region of operation, and whether or not the firm was involved in sustainability initiatives. This instrument, therefore, provides context for the subsequent data and helps ensure that the sample is representative. This section seeks to establish the extent of adoption of green innovation in digital payments. Accordingly, respondents were asked to indicate whether their organizations had adopted renewable sources of energy, integrated energy-efficient technologies, and implemented carbon offset programs, thus capturing both presence and extent of green practices. This section evaluates the effectiveness of policies and regulatory frameworks in supporting sustainability in the digital payment sector. In this case, a Likert scale was used in which respondents indicated the degree to which they agree with statements on the role of policies in enabling low-carbon practices in the financial sector. This final section solicited data on carbon footprints for digital payment systems and, hence, requested estimates of the emissions associated with activities such as energy use by data centers, transaction verification, and infrastructure.

18.3.3 Variables and Measurements

The dependent variable for this research was the carbon footprint resulting from digital payment systems, expressed in CO2-equivalent emissions. This represents the internationally accepted measure of greenhouse gas emitted during any operation in various sectors, including those involving digital payment systems. Basically, this measuring criterion was presented by Stern (2007). Thus, the independent variables are: Adoption of Renewable Energy: This was measured as a binary variable Yes/No to indicate whether renewable energy sources such as solar, wind, and hydropower had been adopted by each of the considered digital payment systems to power their operations. Utilization of Energy-Efficient Protocols: Extent to which energy-efficient technologies were adopted in digital payment systems, including blockchain optimization and cloud computing assessed through a yes/no type of variable to represent the presence of these technologies. Policy and Regulatory Support: It was based on the Likert scale: "Strongly Disagree" to "Strongly Agree," where the respondents rated the effectiveness of government and institutional policies in encouraging green practices in digital payments.

18.3.4 Data Analysis Techniques

The first step in analyzing data was running descriptive statistics to summarize the data. The description provided an overview of the rates of adoption of green innovations and the environmental impact triggered by digital payments. Descriptive analysis gave a good insight into the trend, for example, on how renewable energy adoption has been distributed across regions and how energy-efficient protocols have been integrated.

Then regression analysis was performed to analyze the influence of green innovations on digital payments' carbon footprint. From the regressions, it was observed that there existed a meaningful relationship between the independent variables such as adoption of renewable energy and the adoption of energy-efficient technologies and the carbon emission reduction in digital payment systems. The regression analysis helped to establish which of the factors was the best to ensure the carbon footprint is reduced in this sector, argued by Tabachnick and Fidell (2013). Finally, SEM was utilized in exploring the causal link that exists between policy support for green innovations, its adoption, and the sustainability consequences of the adoption. SEM gave a full conceptual framework from which to understand the causality of these variables, which the study used to model how policy frameworks influence green innovation adoption and, in turn, the carbon footprint of digital payment systems. This is as shown by Kline (2015).

18.4 Results

As shown in Table 18.1, the descriptive analysis highlights the diversity of the respondents and their respective perceptions concerning green innovation in digital payments. Accordingly, the majority represented financial institutions 34.93% and technology providers 27.95%, while contributors such as policymakers stood out at 19.96% and others at 17.16%. A majority 55.89% of respondents operate in developed economies, but developing economies represented a good portion at 44.11%. Almost 59.88% had adopted green practices, and there was some good progress in the adoption of renewable energy use at 57.88% and energy-efficient protocols at 52.89%. This means that 40.12% and 47.11%, respectively, did not adopt these measures, showing some existing challenges. There are varying perceptions of the support from policy and regulatory frameworks, as close to half 49.90% agree or strongly agree that it is effective, while 25.15% disagree or strongly disagree, indicating some mixed perception on the adequacy of regulatory frameworks. Male-dominated, 59.88%, and the age category of 31–45 years was the highest represented, 39.92%, indicating active mid-career-level professionals in driving green innovation.

Table 18.1 Descriptive analysis

Variable	*Category*	*Frequency (n)*	*Percentage (%)*
Type of institution	Financial institution	175	34.93
	Technology provider	140	27.95
	Policymaker	100	19.96
	Others	86	17.16
Region of operation	Developed economies	280	55.89
	Developing economies	221	44.11
Adoption of green practices	Adopted green innovations	300	59.88
	Not adopted green innovations	201	40.12
Use of renewable energy	Yes	290	57.88
	No	211	42.12
Energy-efficient protocols	Implemented	265	52.89
	Not Implemented	236	47.11
Policy and regulatory support	Strongly agree	100	19.96
	Agree	150	29.94
	Neutral	125	24.95
	Disagree	76	15.17
	Strongly disagree	50	9.98
Gender of respondents	Male	300	59.88
	Female	200	39.92
	Prefer not to say	1	0.20
Age group	18–30 years	150	29.94
	31–45 years	200	39.92
	46–60 years	100	19.96
	Above 60 years	51	10.18

Source Compiled by researcher

18.4.1 Reliability Test

The performance of the items was put to a test, and the results of the evaluation showed that all the constructs achieved an acceptable reliability or a good one as a metric by Cronbach's Alpha. The third construct, "Policy and Regulatory Support," ranked first with a reliability of 0.88 which means that the internal consistency of the items measuring this construct was very high (see Table 18.2). Other constructs, including Adoption of Green Practices (0.82), Energy-Efficient Protocols (0.85), Environmental Sustainability (0.81) also showed good reliability. Use of Renewable Energy (0.78) demonstrated acceptable reliability, suggesting

Table 18.2 Reliability test

Construct	*Number of items*	*Cronbach's alpha*	*Interpretation*
Adoption of green practices	3	0.82	Good reliability
Use of renewable energy	3	0.78	Acceptable reliability
Energy-efficient protocols	4	0.85	Good reliability
Policy and regulatory support	5	0.88	Good reliability
Environmental sustainability	4	0.81	Good reliability

Source Compiled by researcher

that the items did provide a consistent measure of their concepts. These findings also imply that the instruments for the different constructs can be relied on to sufficiently measure the objectives of the study.

18.4.2 Variance Inflation Factors (VIF)

The VIF values for all variables remain well below the threshold of 5, confirming the absence of multicollinearity issues. The corresponding tolerance values, which are calculated as the reciprocal of VIF, are above 0.2 for all variables, further supporting the conclusion of low multicollinearity. Among the variables, "Policy and Regulatory Support" shows the highest VIF (2.50) and lowest tolerance (0.40), but these values are still within acceptable limits (see Table 18.3). Therefore, the independent variables are suitable for inclusion in the regression model, as they do not pose any multicollinearity concerns.

18.4.3 Heterotrait-Monotrait Ratio

As shown in Table 18.4 the HTMT values for all construct pairs are below the commonly accepted threshold of 0.85, indicating strong discriminant validity. This suggests that each construct in the model is distinct and measures a unique concept. The highest HTMT value is 0.78 (between "Use of Renewable Energy" and "Environmental Sustainability"), but it remains within acceptable limits, further confirming that the constructs

Table 18.3 Analysis of variance inflation factors (VIF)

Variable	*VIF value*	*Tolerance value*	*Interpretation*
Adoption of green practices	1.85	0.54	Low multicollinearity
Use of renewable energy	2.10	0.48	Low multicollinearity
Energy-efficient protocols	2.25	0.44	Low multicollinearity
Policy and regulatory support	2.50	0.40	Low multicollinearity
Environmental sustainability	1.95	0.51	Low multicollinearity

Source Compiled by researcher

Table 18.4 Heterotrait-Monotrait ratio

Constructs	*Adoption of green practices*	*Use of renewable energy*	*Energy-efficient protocols*	*Policy and regulatory support*	*Environmental sustainability*
Adoption of green practices	1.00	0.75	0.68	0.60	0.72
Use of renewable energy	0.75	1.00	0.70	0.62	0.78
Energy-efficient protocols	0.68	0.70	1.00	0.65	0.73
Policy and regulatory support	0.60	0.62	0.65	1.00	0.69
Environmental sustainability	0.72	0.78	0.73	0.69	1.00

Source Compiled by researcher

are not excessively correlated. These results validate the theoretical model, ensuring that the constructs can be reliably used for hypothesis testing and interpretation.

18.4.4 Hypothesis Path Analysis

The hypothesis path analysis reveals that all proposed hypotheses are statistically significant ($p < 0.05$), confirming the relationships within the model. Renewable energy ($\beta = 0.45$), energy-efficient protocols ($\beta =$

0.38), and policy support ($\beta = 0.30$) significantly reduce the carbon footprint, while also driving green innovation adoption. Green innovation acts as a mediating factor ($\beta = 0.48$) in reducing the carbon footprint (see Table 18.5). The reduction in carbon footprint has the strongest positive impact on environmental sustainability ($\beta = 0.60$). These findings underscore the importance of integrating renewable energy, energy-efficient protocols, and supportive policies to drive green innovation and enhance sustainability in digital payment systems.

18.4.5 Model Fit Test

The model fit test results indicate that the structural model achieves an excellent fit to the data. The Chi-Square test shows an acceptable model fit ($p > 0.05$), and the Comparative Fit Index (CFI = 0.96) and Tucker-Lewis Index (TLI = 0.94) exceed the threshold of 0.90, confirming a well-fitting model. Additionally, the Root Mean Square Error of Approximation (RMSEA = 0.04) and Standardized Root Mean Square Residual (SRMR = 0.03) fall well below their respective thresholds, indicating minimal discrepancies between the observed and predicted data (see Table 18.6). These results validate the robustness of the hypothesized model, supporting its reliability for explaining the relationships among constructs.

18.5 Discussion

The results of this study confirm the significant impact of renewable energy, energy-efficient protocols, and policy support on reducing the carbon footprint of digital payment systems. For example, renewable energy adoption and energy-efficient protocols were found to be significant predictors of carbon footprint reduction. These findings align with theoretical assumptions that transitioning to renewable energy sources and optimizing digital payment protocols can directly mitigate environmental impacts. Additionally, policy support facilitates both carbon footprint reduction and the adoption of green innovations, consistent with Zhang et al. (2023), who emphasized the role of regulatory frameworks in driving sustainable practices. The mediating role of green innovation highlights its importance in amplifying the positive effects of renewable energy and energy-efficient protocols on sustainability. The findings of this study are consistent with existing literature, particularly in

Table 18.5 Analysis of model hypothesis path analysis

Hypothesis	*Path coefficient (β)*	t-*value*	p-*value*	*Significance*	*Interpretation*
H1: Renewable energy → Carbon footprint reduction	0.45	6.78	0.000	Significant	Renewable energy significantly reduces the carbon footprint
H2: Energy-efficient protocols → Carbon footprint reduction	0.38	5.62	0.000	Significant	Energy-efficient protocols significantly reduce the carbon footprint
H3: Policy support → Carbon footprint reduction	0.30	4.20	0.000	Significant	Policy and regulatory frameworks significantly impact carbon footprint reduction
H4a: Renewable energy → Green innovation	0.50	7.12	0.000	Significant	Renewable energy significantly drives green innovation adoption
H4b: Energy-efficient protocols → Green innovation	0.42	6.05	0.000	Significant	Energy-efficient protocols significantly drive green innovation adoption
H4c: Policy support → Green innovation	0.35	5.00	0.000	Significant	Policy support significantly facilitates green innovation adoption

(continued)

Table 18.5 (continued)

Hypothesis	*Path coefficient (β)*	*t-value*	*p-value*	*Significance*	*Interpretation*
H5: Green innovation → Carbon footprint reduction	0.48	6.85	0.000	Significant	Green innovation mediates the relationship, significantly reducing carbon footprint
H6: Carbon footprint reduction → Environmental sustainability	0.60	8.45	0.000	Significant	Reduced carbon footprint strongly enhances environmental sustainability

Source Compiled by researcher

Table 18.6 Model fit test analysis

Fit index	*Value*	*Threshold*	*Interpretation*
Chi-square (χ^2)	245.30	$p > 0.05$	Acceptable model fit (non-significant p-value)
Comparative Fit Index (CFI)	0.96	≥ 0.90	Excellent fit
Tucker-Lewis Index (TLI)	0.94	≥ 0.90	Excellent fit
Root mean square error of approximation (RMSEA)	0.04	≤ 0.06	Excellent fit
Standardized root mean square residual (SRMR)	0.03	≤ 0.08	Excellent fit

Source Compiled by researcher

highlighting the environmental benefits of green innovations in digital payments. For instance, Maiti (2022) emphasized the role of energy-efficient protocols in reducing carbon footprints, similar to this study's findings. However, this research extends prior work by quantifying the mediation effect of green innovation, which has been less explored in previous studies. Furthermore, the strong influence of policy support observed here contrasts with earlier studies, such as Kou et al. (2021), where policy effects were deemed less significant. This discrepancy may be attributed to regional differences in regulatory enforcement or the maturity of green innovation frameworks in different economies. The higher impact of renewable energy adoption observed in this study also supports findings by Zhang et al. (2023), who reported similar results in the context of blockchain systems.

The results are highly credible, given the robustness of the model's fit indices and the statistical significance of all paths. However, certain limitations should be acknowledged. Regional disparities in policy effectiveness and varying levels of technological maturity may have influenced the strength of the observed relationships. For example, developing economies may face barriers such as high initial costs and limited access to renewable energy infrastructure, which could explain variations in the adoption rates of green practices. Despite these limitations, the results provide a comprehensive and reliable framework for understanding the interplay between green innovations and environmental sustainability in digital payments. The analysis reveals that all relationships in the model were significant and positive. For instance, renewable energy's strong effect on green innovation indicates its foundational role in sustainability efforts, consistent with findings by Kou et al. (2021). However, the relatively lower impact of policy suggests that while policies are crucial, their effectiveness may depend on factors such as enforcement and stakeholder engagement. These nuanced insights emphasize the need for a multifaceted approach, integrating both technological and regulatory measures.

18.5.1 Theoretical Implication

This study makes several key contributions to the literature on green innovation and digital payments. First, it addresses the gap in empirical evidence regarding the mediating role of green innovation in reducing carbon footprints. Second, it advances understanding of the interplay between renewable energy, energy-efficient protocols, and policy support, providing a holistic perspective on sustainability in the financial sector. Third, the study offers comparative insights across different regions, highlighting the variability in adoption rates and the effectiveness of regulatory frameworks. By bridging these gaps, the research enriches the discourse on sustainable financial technologies and aligns with global sustainability goals.

18.5.2 Practical Implications

Green innovation holds immense potential for driving financial inclusion in developing economies. By integrating renewable energy into digital payment infrastructures, operational costs can be reduced, enabling service providers to expand into underbanked and rural areas. Additionally, energy-efficient protocols lower technological barriers, making digital payment systems more accessible to smaller financial institutions and low-income populations. Sustainable digital payment systems offer dual advantages. Economically, they enhance efficiency, reduce costs, and foster financial inclusion. Environmentally, they contribute to significant reductions in greenhouse gas emissions and e-waste. These benefits collectively support the transition to a low-carbon economy while driving equitable economic development. Governments and institutions are instrumental in fostering eco-friendly financial practices. By implementing supportive policies and offering incentives, such as subsidies for renewable energy projects and tax breaks for green innovations, they can accelerate the adoption of sustainable practices. Furthermore, public–private partnerships can facilitate the development of infrastructure necessary for widespread adoption.

18.6 Conclusion

The primary objective of this study was to investigate how green innovations, including renewable energy, energy-efficient protocols, and policy support, contribute to reducing the carbon footprint of digital payment systems and enhancing environmental sustainability. Furthermore, the study establishes a strong link between carbon footprint reduction and environmental sustainability. These results highlight the critical role of integrating green innovations into digital payment systems to align with global sustainability objectives, particularly the Sustainable Development Goals (SDGs). By addressing research gaps related to the mediating role of green innovation and the interplay between policy, technology, and sustainability, this study contributes to advancing the discourse on sustainable financial technologies. The findings underscore the importance of a multi-stakeholder approach to green innovation in digital payments. Governments, financial institutions, technology providers, and consumers must collaborate to achieve sustainability goals. Governments play a crucial role in implementing supportive policies and offering incentives, while financial institutions and technology providers drive technological innovation and operational efficiency. Consumers, in turn, can support sustainability through behavioral changes, such as opting for eco-friendly payment methods. Such collaboration ensures that green innovations are not only adopted but also scaled effectively to maximize their environmental and economic benefits. While this study provides significant insights, certain limitations must be acknowledged. First, the sample, though diverse, may not fully capture the regional nuances and disparities in green innovation adoption, particularly in low-income or technologically underdeveloped regions. Second, the study focuses on a quantitative approach, which, while robust, may not fully explore the qualitative aspects of stakeholder perceptions and behavioral motivations. Third, the reliance on self-reported data introduces the possibility of response bias, which may affect the accuracy of the findings. Lastly, the study primarily examines direct and mediated relationships but does not account for potential moderating factors, such as organizational culture or economic conditions, which could influence the adoption of green innovations. Future research should address the limitations identified in this study by: Examining the role of emerging technologies, such as artificial intelligence and the Internet of Things, in enhancing the efficiency and sustainability of digital payment infrastructures. Furthermore, study may investigate how variables such as organizational culture, economic stability, or consumer awareness influence the effectiveness of green innovations and policy support.

References

Anitha, K., Ghosal, I., Amala, J. and Hossain, I., 2025. Future Trends and Innovations in Environmental Governance for Sustainable Development. In *Intersecting Environmental Governance with Technological Advancements* (pp. 381–412). IGI Global Scientific Publishing.

AOC (2019) *The Green New Deal*. Available at: https://ocasio-cortez.house.gov (Accessed: 13 January 2025).

Apple (2022) *Environmental Progress Report 2022*. Available at: https://www.apple.com/environment/pdf (Accessed: 12 January 2025).

Ayodeji Ogunmola, G., & Kumar, V. (2025). Policy regulations and global standards: A perspective on sustainable computing. *EDPACS*, 1–16.

Bansal, D., Bhattacharya, N., & Ghosal, I. (2025). Encouraging public private collaborations for low carbon green infrastructure in India: The impact of

government policies. In *Intersecting environmental governance with technological advancements* (pp. 149–180). IGI Global Scientific Publishing.
Bryman, A. (2016). *Social research methods* (5th ed.). Oxford University Press.
CDP. (2000). *Carbon disclosure project*. https://www.cdp.net. Accessed 13 January 2025.
Creswell, J. W. (2014). *Research design: Qualitative, quantitative, and mixed methods approach* (4th ed.). Sage.
Dai, B., Zhang, J., & Hussain, N. (2025). Policy pathways through FinTech and green finance for low-carbon energy transition in BRICS nations. *Energy Strategy Reviews, 57*, Article 101603.
European Commission. (2020). *A European green deal*. https://ec.europa.eu/green-deal. Accessed 13 January 2025.
Field, A. (2013). *Discovering statistics using IBM SPSS statistics* (4th ed.). Sage.
Flick, U. (2018). *An introduction to qualitative research* (6th ed.). Sage.
GeSI. (2015). *SMARTer2030: ICT solutions for 21st century challenges*. Global e-Sustainability Initiative.
Gopal, S., & Pitts, J. (2025). The intersection of carbon pricing, fintech, and blockchain technology. In *The FinTech revolution: Bridging geospatial data science, AI, and sustainability* (pp. 317–343). Springer Nature Switzerland.
Guo, J., Zhao, X., & Fu, Y. (2025). Green finance, technological innovation, and low-carbon development in logistics industry: Mechanisms and threshold effects. In *Environment, Development and Sustainability* (pp. 1–39).
Hasanin, T., Alsobhi, A., Khadidos, A., Qahmash, A., Khadidos, A., & Ogunmola, G. A. (2021). Efficient multiuser computation for mobile-edge computing in IoT Application using optimization algorithm. *Applied Bionics and Biomechanics, 2021*(1), 9014559.
Hu, H., Jia, Z., & Yang, S. (2025). Exploring FinTech, green finance, and ESG performance across corporate life-cycles. *International Review of Financial Analysis, 97*, Article 103871.
IFC. (2020). *Green bonds*. https://www.ifc.org/en/green-bonds. Accessed 13 January 2025.
Kline, R. B. (2015). *Principles and practice of structural equation modeling* (4th ed.). Guilford Press.
Kou, G., Xu, Y., Peng, Y., & Shen, F. (2021). Blockchain technology and its applications in the financial sector. *Technological Forecasting and Social Change, 164*, Article 120543.
Kumar, V., & Ayodeji, O. G. (2022). Web analytics applications, opportunities and challenges to online retail in India. *International Journal of Services and Operations Management, 41*(4), 463–485.
Lu, J., Guo, W., Ogunmola, G. A., & Shibly, F. H. A. (2021). Digital learning for students and its impact on the present system of education. *Journal of Multiple-Valued Logic & Soft Computing, 36*.

Maiti, M. (2022). Digital payments and environmental sustainability: Opportunities and challenges. *Journal of Sustainable Finance & Investment, 12*(4), 872–891.

Mastercard. (2021). *Priceless planet coalition report 2021.* https://www.mastercard.com/sustainability. Accessed 12 January 2025.

Nithyanantham, V., Ogunmola, G. A., Venkateswaran, P. S., Rajest, S. S., & Regin, R. (2021). The impact of gender diversity on organizational performance in banks. *Turkish Journal of Physiotherapy and Rehabilitation, 32*(3), 45453–45489.

Ogunmola, G. A., & Kumar, V. (2024a). Harmonizing digital currencies with industry 5.0: A transformative nexus for economic evolution. *EDPACS, 69*(7), 30–50.

Ogunmola, G. A., & Kumar, V. (2024b). A strategic model for attracting and retaining environmentally conscious customers in E-retail. *International Journal of Information Management Data Insights, 4*(2), Article 100274.

Ogunmola, G. A., Zia, A., & Kumar, V. (2024). Digital currencies: The technology adoption vs. policy implications. *International Journal of Technology, Policy and Management, 24*(4), 375–391.

Rennings, K. (2000). Redefining innovation eco-innovation research and the contribution from ecological economics. *Ecological Economics, 32*(2), 319–332.

Stern, N. (2007). *The economics of climate change: The Stern review.* Cambridge University Press.

Suri, T., & Jack, W. (2016). The long-run poverty and gender impacts of mobile money. *Science, 354*(6317), 1288–1292.

Tabachnick, B. G., & Fidell, L. S. (2013). *Using multivariate statistics* (6th ed.). Pearson.

TCFD. (2017). *Final report: Recommendations of the task force on climate-related financial disclosures*. https://www.fsb-tcfd.org/publications/. Accessed 13 January 2025.

UK Government. (2008). *Climate Change Act 2008.* https://www.gov.uk/government/collections/climate-change-act-2008. Accessed 13 January 2025.

UN. (2020). *Principles for responsible banking*. https://www.unepfi.org/banking/. Accessed 13 January 2025.

UNFCCC. (1997). *Kyoto protocol.* https://unfccc.int/kyoto_protocol. Accessed 13 January 2025.

UNFCCC. (2015). *Paris agreement*. https://unfccc.int/paris-agreement. Accessed 13 January 2025.

United Nations. (2023). *Sustainable development goals: Climate action.* https://www.un.org/sustainabledevelopment/climate-action. Accessed 12 January 2025.

Utami, A. F., Ekaputra, I. A., & Japutra, A. (2021). Adoption of FinTech products: A systematic literature review. *Journal of Creative Communications, 16*(3), 233–248.

Visa. (2021). *Visa's commitment to sustainability*. https://www.visa.com/sustainability. Accessed 12 January 2025.

Wang, C., Gao, Y., Aziz, A., & Ogunmola, G. A. (2022). Agricultural disaster risk management and capability assessment using big data analytics. *Big Data, 10*(3), 246–261.

Zhang, X., Li, J., & Zhao, Y. (2023). Energy efficiency in digital payment systems: A pathway to green financial innovation. *Renewable and Sustainable Energy Reviews, 168*, Article 112934.

CHAPTER 19

The Environmental Paradox of Digital Currency Mining: Innovation at Nature's Expense

Amisha Sherawat and Ranjan Aneja

19.1 Introduction

The development of money is closely related to the history of human civilization and the establishment of the modern monetary system. Over centuries, money has transformed from simple commodities to inventive digital forms that reflect changes in economic structures, technological advancements, and societal demands. In the late twentieth and early twenty-first century, the monetary system witnessed transformation with the rise of digital currency involving cryptocurrencies, stable-coins and CBDCs, offering a new paradigm in the monetary system. Digital currency and sustainability goals:

A. Sherawat (✉) · R. Aneja
Department of Economics, Central University of Haryana, Mahendergarh, India
e-mail: amisha230051@cuh.ac.in

R. Aneja
e-mail: ranjananeja@cuh.ac.in

R. Aneja and R. Dygas (eds.), *Digital Currencies and the Green Economy*, https://doi.org/10.1007/978-981-95-2282-8_19

Digitalization of money has been revolutionizing the global financial system and promoting resource efficiency and environmental balance. As nations adopt green, circular and doughnut economic models, the utilization of digital currencies offers possibilities to match economic growth with social and environmental goals, thus directly supporting the Sustainable Development Goals.

By removing barriers associated with traditional banking systems, digital currencies enable millions of individuals to access financial services, thereby promoting fair economic participation and reducing inequality (SDG10). Digital currency contributes to the UNSDG by preventing the spread of communicable diseases that are acquired through contact with bank paper and plastic notes (SDG3). The environmental impact of digital currency mining highlights the alignment with SDG7 and SDG13. Greener mining practices are being made possible by innovations like Proof-of-Stake and the incorporation of renewable energy sources into mining operations, even though energy intensive practices like Proof-of-Work are still an issue. Therefore, to reap the full potential of sustainable development of digital currencies, nations should enhance necessary infrastructure and foster innovation in digital currency industries (United Nations ESCAP, n.d.).

19.1.1 Digital Currency Mining

In the early phase of digital currency mining, things were simple in a way that seems almost unimaginable now. Initially, mining made use of CPUs, the standard processors found in computers. With the growth of decentralized digital currency networks, mining became increasingly difficult and demanded more sophisticated hardware. This need led to the utilization of Graphics Processing Units (GPUs), which are usually used for gaming and applications that demand extensive graphics processing. Because of their ability to process in parallel, GPUs have shown significant improvement in efficiency regarding the computational demand of mining.

This transition began to alter the mining landscape because an activity that had once welcomed the enthusiasts began to transform into a more competitive arena, favouring those who could afford to invest in superior equipment. During this time, currency mining was evolving into a professional and commercial venture, setting the stage for future advancements.

In the ever-evolving ecosystem of digital currencies, mining is essential for ensuring blockchain networks operate securely, transparently, and in a decentralized manner. Mining serves the dual purpose of verifying the transactions and generating new digital tokens. The mechanism allows cryptocurrencies such as Bitcoin, Litecoin, and Ethereum classic to operate smoothly without depending on a central authority. Thus, to keep a record of transactions and monitor coin ownership, decentralized ledger technology, typically a blockchain is employed. Each block in the blockchain holds transaction details and a timestamp from a designated time frame, as well as summary information from the preceding block, preserving the chain's overall integrity. Linking these blocks together in the chain ensures that any modification made to a block would result in a breakage of the chain, safeguarding its information and ownership for upcoming generations. By this means each block can authenticate the others to maintain the integrity and non-repudiation of transaction data (Zhang, 2022). A peer-to-peer network of computers known as nodes is in charge of managing this blockchain. They validate transactions and maintain a copy of the blockchain. When a voting model is employed to the blockchain, it requires that the majority of nodes responsible with preserving the blockchain agree to any block being added to the chain. The block is considered official only after the peers confirm or validate the precision of the addition (Read, 2022). This process of confirming transactions is referred to as mining and the participants are called miners (Capponi et al., 2021).

19.2 What Makes Digital Currencies Truly Decentralized: The Blockchain Itself or the Rules?

Unlike the conventional currency system, decentralized digital currencies rely on cryptographic security to establish trust and operate on blockchain technology. Nonetheless, blockchain technology by itself is unable to provide security or stop fraudulent transactions. It is here that consensus mechanisms come into play. This system establishes rules for verifying transactions, determining who has the authority to add new blocks to the chain, and forbidding unethical behaviour such as double spending. Currency mining, generating new coins and validating transactions, is directly impacted by the choice of consensus process.

Different blockchains, each with different levels of security, decentralization and energy efficiency, employ distinct techniques to reach consensus. Nonetheless, not all consensus processes involve conventional mining.

The diversity of consensus methods shows that mining is just one way to secure a blockchain network. The move toward more scalable, cost-effective and environmentally friendly solutions has led to the development of a number of non-mining consensus approaches that safeguard robust blockchain network security coexisting with operational efficiency. The shift from mining to staking and validation is being replaced with more sustainable and efficient procedures.

The sustainability of mining-based processes versus non-mining-based approaches such as proof of stake and delegated proof of stake varies substantially. Wendl et al. (2023) assert that the PoS technique used in staking lowers the energy needed for blockchain upkeep, making it a more sustainable practice as it is less damaging than mining. Unlike operations that do not involve staking, mining-based systems rely on larger carbon footprint, higher energy consumption and intricate computations to verify transactions, which often results in environmental strain.

19.2.1 Energy Consumption in Digital Currency Mining

Digital currency mining, particularly for cryptocurrency, is an energy-intensive operation that depends on figuring out complex mathematical riddles to validate transactions and protect the blockchain network. The most well-known cryptocurrency, bitcoin, relies on computation-heavy cryptographic operations that require an enormous amount of electricity to mine. People worldwide are encouraged to mine bitcoin by the ongoing mining cycle. People are prepared to use power-hungry devices to get rewards from mining since it can generate a steady flow of income (Digiconomist, 2025). As the price of the cryptocurrency continued to surge to all-time highs, the network's overall energy consumption exploded. Bitcoin is responsible for two-thirds of the energy consumption while understudied cryptocurrencies account for the remaining one-third (Gilbert & Bazilian, 2020). While bitcoin uses up most of the global crypto-asset electricity acquiring the share between 60 and 77%, Ethereum uses 20–39% share, both being the main culprits in the cryptocurrency world ("Implication of Crypto Mining," 2024). Figure 19.1 depicted below shows the Bitcoin energy consumption worldwide from January 2018 to February 2025.

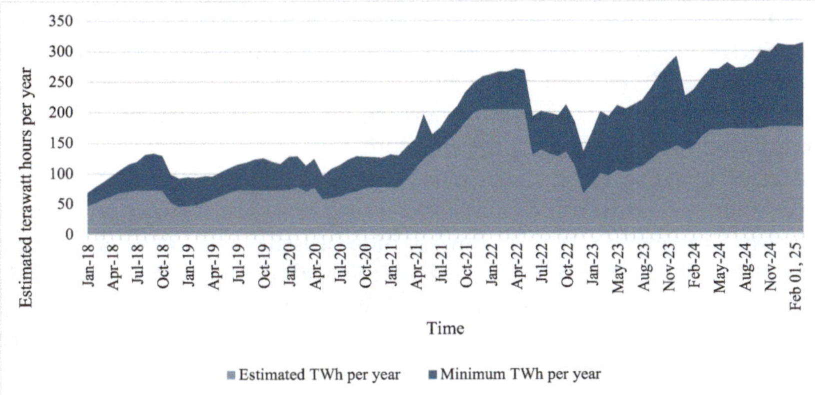

Fig. 19.1 Worldwide Energy Consumption of Bitcoin (January 2018–February 2025). (*Source* Statista, 2025)

It is evident from the figure that Bitcoin's annualized electricity consumption reached a record level in early 2022 which reportedly broke Finland's present power consumption and by 2025, BTC energy consumption was on par with that of Australia and the Netherlands. The total amount of electricity required for a single transaction of bitcoin depends on a various factor, including the data centres where bitcoin users and holders reside, the computational load, the number of machines used, the network's current difficulty, and the server's performance (Li et al., 2019; Masanet et al., 2019; Narayanan et al., 2016; Onat et al., 2024; Stoll et al., 2019). The Cambridge Blockchain Network Sustainability Index (CBNSI) estimated that the annualized electricity consumption of Bitcoin for the year 2024 was between 135 and 174 terawatt-hours (TWh). For instance, this level has surpassed the domestic electricity consumption of nations such as Argentina, Belgium and Netherlands, as of 2023 (Enerdata, 2024).

Bitcoin, the biggest cryptocurrency by market capitalization and the pioneer of blockchain technology, dominates the energy consumption landscape due to its reliance on the Proof-of-Work (PoW) consensus process. Proof of Work (PoW) fulfils two functions of rewarding miners and validating the transactions. Since bitcoin puzzles are so vital and popular, their complexity is growing. The process of documenting and verifying transactions involves numerous computer calculations, consequently the need for electricity and powerful computer processing rises (Mora et al., 2018). But other PoW-based cryptocurrencies particularly Litecoin, Ethereum cash and Monero contribute to global energy usage, though at a far lesser extent than bitcoin.

Many different mining consensus techniques have been devised to lower energy consumption while preserving network security and decentralization in response to the environmental issue of PoW energy usage. Mining method of Proof of Space (PoSpace) protects the network by using storage space instead of computing power, because of this it eliminates the need for energy-intensive calculations. However, it still requires a large amount of storage space, which could have an impact on the environment. Chia, a well-known cryptocurrency that uses the PoSpace mechanism for mining, uses a lot less energy than Bitcoin, it has come under criticism for depending too much on storage technology, which might result in more electronic waste. Unlike PoW, energy consumption of remaining mining mechanisms such as PoB, PoC, and PoSpace are incredibly energy efficient, but carry other environmental challenges.

19.2.2 Energy Usage of Traditional Financial System

The conventional system of physical and digital infrastructure such as payment networks, data centres, ATMs, and bank branches differ greatly from decentralized digital currencies in terms of scale and infrastructure. The traditional banking system and decentralized digital currency system are not precisely the same. While commercial and retail financial institutions require several settlement processes, decentralized currency offers final settlement. Bank branches, ATMs, bank data centres, and data centres for card networks are the main areas of electricity consumption in the larger banking system.

Both decentralized digital currency and traditional banking systems have significant shortcomings due to their complex counterparty and intermediate settlement structures and statistics about electricity in the banking sector are scarce. Based on publicly accessible data, Galaxy Digital Research has estimated that the banking industry uses 263.72 TWh of energy annually. The estimates suggest the financial system uses more energy overall but it serves a purpose of handling a larger number of transactions and caters to a far wider customer base. The financial system requires greater infrastructure as transaction volume rises. Meanwhile,

Bitcoin's energy consumption is determined by network economies rather than transaction volume (Galaxy Digital Research, 2021).

19.2.3 Factors Contributing to High Energy Demand

19.2.3.1 Computational Intensity of PoW Algorithms

Proof-of-Work (PoW) needs significant computing power which is provided by the specialized hardware such as Application-Specific Integrated Circuits (ASICs). Because these devices are designed to perform billions of calculations each second, they require a significant amount of electricity. This computational intensity is one of the primary reasons why mining digital currencies requires so much energy. According to the investigation into devices' history, the initial mining procedure was conducted using CPUs (hash rate < 0.1TH/s), GPUs (<3TH/s) and FPGAs (<6TH/s) were in use at that time (Akbarnavasi et al., 2023). Since GPU mining became less economical and cost ineffective as PoW algorithms improved, ASICs emerged. When the first ASIC device with a 130-nanometre chip was introduced to the market in 2013, the mining business experienced a transformation (Taylor, 2017). Since then, ASICs have come a long way. Currently the S21 + Hyd is the most potent and modern ASIC for bitcoin mining in the market, with hashing power of 319 TH/s and efficiency of 0.02 J/Gh (CBECI, 2025). While this technology is far more efficient than earlier generations, energy consumption is still rather substantial because of the sheer size of mining operations.

19.2.3.2 Increased Mining Difficulty Over Time

As more miners join the network, cryptographic problems make it harder to maintain a constant rate of block generation. However, in order to stay competitive, miners need to use more powerful technology and work harder at increasing difficulty levels. For instance, the Bitcoin system automatically modifies the mining difficulty every 2,0.16 blocks, or around every two weeks (graniteshares, 2025). Because miners have more computational power, it becomes harder to slow them down if they solve blocks too quickly. If blocks are being found too slowly, the difficulty is reduced to speed up mining. This self-regulating system maintains network stability and avoids significant swings in the rate of bitcoin production. Therefore, this never-ending loop of increasing energy usage and complexity demonstrates how unsustainable contemporary mining practices are.

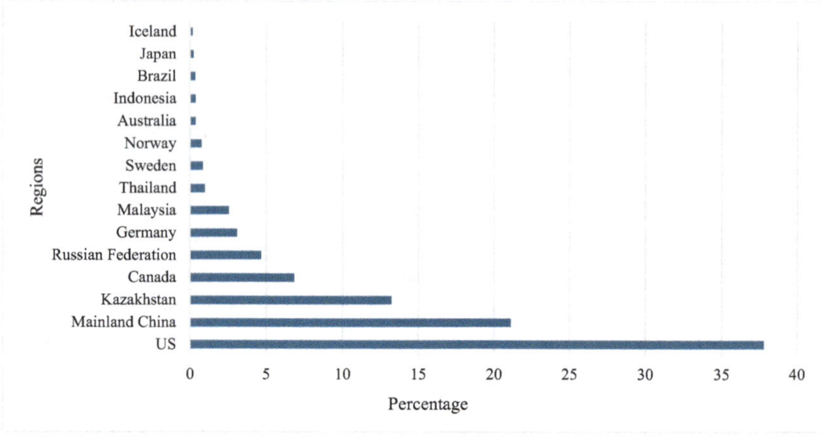

Fig. 19.2 Top 15 regions worldwide in BTC mining. (*Source* Cambridge Centre for Alternative Finance)

19.2.3.3 Geographic Concentrations of Mining Operations

Mining activities are often located in sites with cheap electricity, quick internet access, cool temperatures, and supportive regulatory frameworks to boost profits. Before a crackdown in summer 2021, up to 75% of the world's bitcoin mining power was in China (Cambridge Judge Business School, 2021). However, within a few months, their share completely disappeared. Cheap power, loose regulations and a stable political climate drew miners to neighbouring Kazakhstan, while others decided to relocate to the US and Canada. Figure 19.2 depicted below shows the average monthly hash rate share of the top 15 regions in the world, based on the geolocational mining pool data published by Cambridge Centre for Alternative Finance for January 2022. This spatial concentration brought on by rising energy demand is made worse by an excessive dependence on non-renewable energy sources and stress on local energy infrastructures.

19.2.3.4 Reliance on Non-Renewable Energy Sources

Despite growing awareness of the detrimental effects on the environment, a significant portion of mining operations still rely on non-renewable energy sources like coal and natural gas. This dependence rises from the need for affordable and adequate energy to maintain profitability. For instance, Fig. 19.3 illustrates that bitcoin electricity consumption

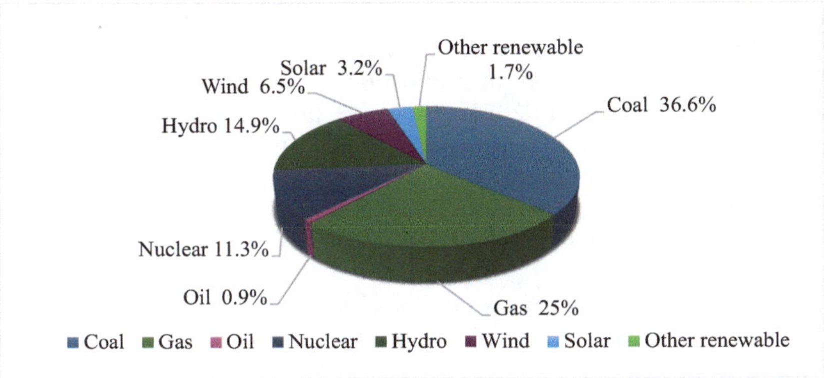

Fig. 19.3 Bitcoin electricity consumption by source (September 2021–January 2022). (*Source* Cambridge Centre for Alternative Finance)

is majorly powered by non-renewable energy sources and BTC mining activities have relied heavily on coal-fired power plants for their electricity which is more than 1/3 of the total sources.

The data shows that approximately 25 percent of electricity consumption is powered by renewable energy sources and 2/3 electricity is sourced by non-renewable sources, highlighting the critical need for more attention toward the environment.

19.2.4 Lack of Energy-Efficient Replacements

Bitcoin, Litecoin, and other well-known cryptocurrencies still use PoW algorithm, while some, like, Ethereum have shifted from PoW to PoS with the aim of PoS outperforming in few ways, counting efficiency of energy, expansion, cost and privacy (Cao et al., 2020). Depending on how many cryptocurrencies tokens a user has and how long they have owned them, the Proof-of-Stake technique chooses which users will add a new block to the network. Under this, individuals must prove that they are the owners of a specific quantity of tokens. The Proof-of-Stake technique requires users to demonstrate that they are the owners of a certain number of cryptocurrency tokens, depending on that users are selected to add a new block to the network based on the number of tokens they possess and the length of the time they have owned them, termed as staking (Asif & Hassan, 2023). This method makes it more likely that someone will be selected to contribute a new block by raising their weight in the network in proportion to the quantity of tokens they own (Lashkari & Musilek, 2021). However, problems with centralization, wealth concentration, complexity and lack of incentives and fairness still keep these alternatives from being popular (Asif & Hassan, 2023). Until more energy-efficient mechanisms are widely adopted, the massive energy consumption associated with digital currency mining is likely to persist.

19.2.4.1 Carbon Footprint and Greenhouse Gas Emissions

The world's annual CO_2 emissions have skyrocketed from about 2 billion metric tons at the beginning of the twentieth century to over 36 billion metric tons in 2019, being the primary GHG emitted through human activities (Sullivan, 2022). Despite a flurry of climate agreements, global greenhouse gas emissions reached a highest amount which was equivalent to 53 billion metric tons of carbon dioxide ($GtCO_2e$) in 2023 (Tiseo, 2025). The World Energy Outlook, 2021 stated that in 2020, the electricity sector released more CO_2 than any other sector, accounting for 36% of all energy-related emissions and coal remains the world's largest source of emissions from the electricity sector by emitting nearly three-quarters of CO_2.

While the sheer scale of energy consumption in digital currency mining is alarming, the carbon emissions it generates worsens this energy's detrimental environmental effects. The "carbon footprint" of an individual, event, or product is the total amount of greenhouse gases produced into the atmosphere as a direct or indirect result of their activities over a specific time period (Otero, n.d.). The staggering amount of energy used to power mining operations have a direct effect on their carbon footprint. This energy can be produced from both renewable and non-renewable resources. Since each source has a distinct emission intensity per kWh of power generated, it is crucial to ascertain the resources a nation employs to measure their carbon emissions from electricity generation (Onat et al., 2024). Mining-related carbon emissions are substantially higher in areas where fossil fuels, like coal or natural gas, are the main source of electricity generation than in areas that depend on renewable energy sources, like solar, wind, or hydropower. As Fossil fuels remain the dominant source of electricity in many mining regions, it results as the main contributor to the greenhouse gas emissions, which drives climate change (Onat et al., 2024).

The cryptocurrency business is becoming a major polluting business in the world and is challenging sustainability as a result of bitcoin mining. (Hebous & Vernon, 2023) estimated that the mining cryptocurrencies contributed to 0.33% of the global emissions in 2021, with bitcoin, Ethereum, and other cryptocurrencies emitting 60, 17, and 47 mtCOe each. Due to the growing popularity of bitcoin there is a high demand of electricity due to the continuous operation of bitcoin mining equipment, increasing carbon emissions from the mining sector (De Vries, 2019). According to a University of Cambridge study, the BTC network uses more than 121 TWh of electricity annually, which is comparable to the energy usage of whole nations like Argentina and Netherlands (Enerdata, 2024); (CBECI, 2023). If coal has been used to produce this electricity, significant carbon emissions may arise. Additionally, the estimates Cambridge Centre for Alternative Finance released showed that during 2021–2022, use of coal for BTC electricity consumption has been reduced by 1.5% whereas use of gas increased by 2%. By 2024, bitcoin mining has used over 16 gigawatts of electricity and produced about 80 megatons of annual carbon emissions. Figure 19.4 displayed below illustrates yearly bitcoin greenhouse gas emissions expressed with the unit of metric tons of carbon dioxide equivalent ($MtCO_2e$). Bitcoin greenhouse gas emissions soared from 2010 to 2024 before falling sharply in 2025. The recent spike in the emissions during 2023–2024 was triggered by the record breaking prices in cryptocurrency, causing sudden boom in the energy demand, threatening power grid capacity and releasing significant volumes of CO_2 into the atmosphere (Tang, 2024).

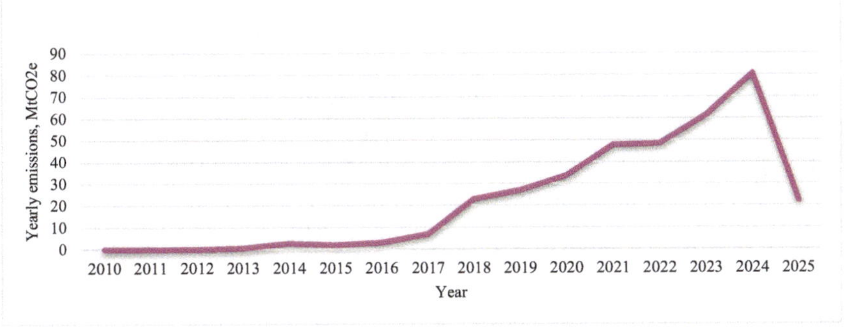

Fig. 19.4 Total bitcoin greenhouse gas emissions. (*Source* CCAF)

According to a press release article of UNU in 2023 the greenhouse emissions from BTC mining alone could surpass the Paris Agreement's goal of limiting anthropogenic climate change to less than 2 degrees Celsius. The annualized total carbon footprint from bitcoin mining is 98.10Mt CO_2 which is comparable to the carbon footprint of Qatar. The digiconomist's Bitcoin Energy consumption Index estimates that a single BTC transaction is responsible for causing 622.53 $kgCO_2$ which is comparable to the carbon footprint of 1,379,733 VISA transactions or 103,754 hours of watching YouTube. This depicts that a single BTC transaction has an outsized environmental impact compared to an average non-cash representative of the traditional financial system highlighting the inefficiency of PoW-based algorithm of bitcoin. The key reason for BTC's extreme carbon footprint lies in its limited transaction capacity of processing only around 220 million transactions annually due to its 1 MB block size constraint, less than the global financial system's 700 billion digital payments per year (digiconomist, 2025).

19.2.4.2 Bitcoin Emission Intensity and Carbon Footprint

Bitcoin's carbon footprint and emission intensity are strongly correlated as they are primarily dictated by the energy sources that fuel its Proof of Work (PoW) mining mechanism. Bitcoin mining emission intensity calculates the network's expected emissions for every kilowatt-hour of power used.

Emission Intensity (g/KWh) = Annual emissions (tonnes CO_2e/year) / Annual energy consumption (GWh/year)

Bitcoin mining's carbon footprint rises sharply if it depends on energy from fossil fuels with high coal or natural gas. However, mining operations that employ renewable energy sources such as solar, wind, or hydro, have lower emission intensities and a smaller carbon footprint. Due to the energy intensive nature of bitcoin mining, even a slight variation in emission intensity can have a significant impact on the total carbon footprint of the cryptocurrency. Figure 19.5 displays the greenhouse gas emission intensity of BTC ranging from 2010 to 2024. The unit is specified in terms of greenhouse gases emitted per kilowatt-hour (gCO_2e/kWh). It displays that between 2010 and 2020, the emission intensity stayed relatively constant at 500–600 gCO_2e/kWh indicating the carbon footprint per unit of power used did not change significantly.

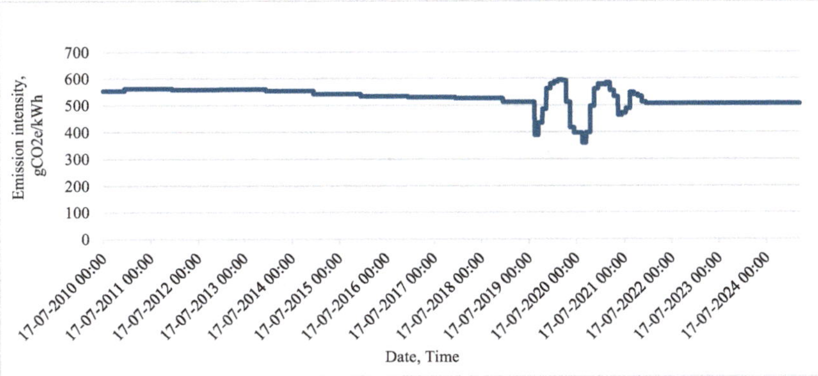

Fig. 19.5 Bitcoin emission intensity. (*Source* Cambridge Centre for Alternative Finance)

After that the noticeable fluctuations between 2021 and 2022 indicate significant changes in mining sites and power resources, primarily due to China's ban on bitcoin mining in 2021 and the energy consumption shift away from coal and toward gas. Following 2022, the emission intensity returned to a more stable level.

19.2.4.3 Global Inequities in Carbon Footprint of BTC

Regardless of the precise location to which the cryptocurrencies are transported, bitcoin transactions result in worldwide greenhouse gas emissions (Onat et al., 2024). Because bitcoin mining is decentralized, its carbon impact is distributed throughout the world rather than in a single location, reflecting the diverse energy conditions of the participating nations. As mining's worldwide distribution has changed over time, its effects on the environment have grown more complicated. Initially concentrated in regions with cheap coal-based power, the business was upended when big centres enforced strict regulations and outright bans. Many mining companies relocated to other nations as a result; some of these nations still rely on fossil fuels, while others have superior energy profiles. Instead of reducing emissions, the adjustment moved them, often to areas with weaker energy infrastructure or looser environmental regulations. Prior to miners moving to Kazakhstan and the United States following China's mining ban in June, studies indicate that two-thirds of the network was in

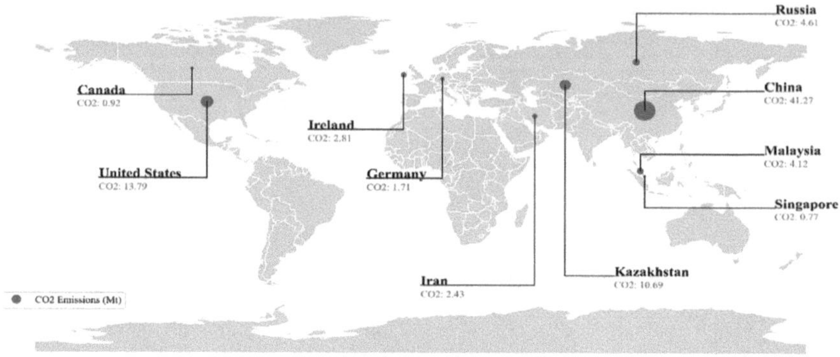

Fig. 19.6 Carbon footprint of BTC mining across the world (2020–2021). (*Source* The Hidden Environmental Cost of Cryptocurrency, UNU-INWEH (2023)

Asia, with the still ongoing trend of miners moving to the US (Stoll et al., 2025). Figure 19.6 displayed below shows the global carbon footprint of BTC mining from 2020–2021 which is before the Chinese mining crackdown.

According to Chamanara and Madani (2023), China being the biggest GHG emitter, followed by US, Kazakhstan, Russia, and Malaysia, needed to offset their emissions by planting some 2 billion trees between 2020–2021. This would encompass 45,000 times the area of central park in NY city, or an area equivalent to the combined size of Portugal and Ireland. However, after Beijing's severe crackdown on the mining practice, the US has overtaken it with heavy reliance on fossil fuels, making the situation worse ("Bitcoin mining consumes more," 2023).

19.3 Environmental Costs Beyond Carbon

19.3.1 Land Footprint of Digital Currency Mining

Digital currency mining has far more detrimental effects on environmental sustainability than just its well-known carbon footprint. Even though greenhouse gas emissions are in the headlines, the ecological damage goes much beyond carbon. The land footprint, which results from both direct infrastructure sprawl and indirect land degradation connected to energy sources, is one of the most important but little studied effects of mining activities. As demand increases, digital currencies particularly Bitcoin and other PoW cryptocurrencies' spatial impact expands as well, uprooting ecosystems, resource competition, and industrial encroachment in ways that jeopardize environmental stability and local livelihood.

19.3.2 *Direct Land Use: The Physical Expansion of Mining Infrastructure*

Cryptocurrency mining is an industrial scale operation requiring a large number of high-performance computer rigs in large data centres. These facilities need a large amount of area to store electrical infrastructure, cooling equipment, and computers. According to a UNU study, the worldwide land footprint of the BTC mining operations was more than 1,870 square kilometres in 2020–2021, which is 1.4 times the area of Los Angeles. The majority of this direct land footprint is found in places with cheap electricity, such as Kazakhstan, Russia, and the US, where mining farms repurpose old warehouses, industries, and even farmland. Out of eight largest bitcoin farms in the world, four are situated in the US, with others located in Canada, Russia, Switzerland, Netherlands, and Iceland (Tashev, 2024).

Figure 19.7 displayed below illustrates the land footprint (km^2) of BTC mining regions across the world from 2020 to 2021. The map displays that prior to the 2021 prohibition, 913 km^2 of this land footprint was controlled by China, mostly through coal-powered facilities in Inner Mongolia and Xinjiang (Samford & Domingo, 2019). This mining boom accelerated the extraction of illegal coal leading to unchecked deforestation and soil degradation. The US became the new mining hotspot after China's crackdown with mining farms expanding in states like Texas and New York frequently clashing with residential and agricultural land uses. Germany ranked below China and the US being the significant contributor of land footprint due to mixed energy grid and industrial capacity as ASIC miners are housed in industrial sites, usually converted warehouses or data centres. After Germany, Canada, Kazakhstan, Malaysia holds the spot followed by Thailand, Russia, UK, and Sweden.

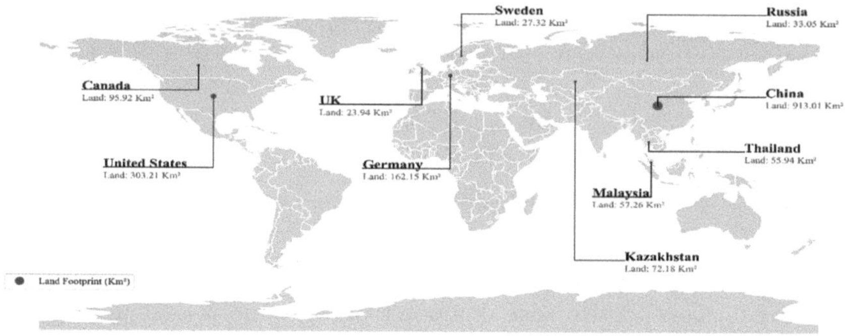

Fig. 19.7 Land footprint of BTC mining countries across the world (2020–2021). (*Source* The Hidden Environmental Cost of Cryptocurrency, UNU-INWEH (2023)

19.3.3 Indirect Land Degradation: The Hidden Cost of Energy Sourcing

Beyond the actual physical footprint of mining farms, the most notable terrestrial effects of cryptocurrencies are brought by their dependence on fossil fuels, particularly coal. About 37% of BTC energy comes from coal, and another 25% accounts from natural gas. Even if the data centres are located on land that is physically occupied by mining operations, their reliance on fossil fuels damages the environment through extraction activities. For instance, in Appalachia, the practice of mountaintop removal coal mining up to 2010 has buried nearly 2000 miles of headwater streams, some of the most biologically diverse streams in the nation (Appalachian Heartbreak, 2007).

When land use is altered to create space for energy infrastructure, the cascading effects of extracting fossil fuels worsens. The mining renaissance has resulted in the reactivation of abandoned coal operations, which has led to the maintenance of land-intensive extraction methods in the US. The mining boom in Texas, for example, has increased grid demands, postponing renewable energy projects and extending the usage of fossil fuels, both of which indirectly contribute to the degradation of land related to fuel supply. The studies show that the previously estimated portion of Texas' total bitcoin mining activity increased from just over 4% in 2021 to more than 15% in 2022 (Stoll et al., 2025). As evidenced in Canada and Scandinavia, where river ecosystems are altered to meet mining's energy needs, hydropower, despite being marketed as a greener alternative, disrupts land through reservoir flooding and dam construction.

19.3.4 The Blue Cost of Digital Gold

In addition to the massive carbon and land footprints, mining digital currencies has substantial and sometimes overlooked water impacts that contribute to ecological stress and global water scarcity. As global usage of bitcoin exceeds domestic demands for millions of people and worsens water scarcity in vulnerable locations, the water footprint of mining these currencies has become significant. Bitcoin miners require water in two ways depending on the type of cooling system and local climate conditions. First, for on-site (direct) water use for air humidification and cooling systems and second for the indirect water consumption associated with generating the electricity required to power their devices (Vries, 2023). Since mining devices are operating 24/7, cooling systems are required to keep mining equipment at ideal temperatures. Hence, water is required for cooling purposes in thermoelectric power generation in addition to the fact that water evaporates from hydroelectric reservoirs (Singh, 2023).

As per the recent estimates of Digiconomist, the annual total bitcoin fresh water consumption footprint has reached to 2,772 gigalitres which is comparable to the total water use of Switzerland. Moreover, a single bitcoin transaction consumed 18,684 litres of which is equivalent to the amount of water in a backyard swimming pool. Figure 19.8 presents the water footprint (MCM) of BTC mining of leading nations during 2020–2021. Although the total water footprint of mining has continued to rise till the date, the estimates of regional water footprint are available until 2022.

This represents that before the government's restrictions, the total water footprint of China contributed to a significant water footprint, especially in provinces like Sichuan. Following that, the water footprint of US miners is 205.73 MCM, which could be equal to yearly water consumption of 300,000 US households, equivalent to a city like Washington, DC (de Vries, 2024). Further the availability of cooler climate conditions especially in places like Canada and northern US helps in reducing cooling costs but substantially requires water use in the mining operations. After China's mining exodus, Kazakhstan became the hotspot for mining due

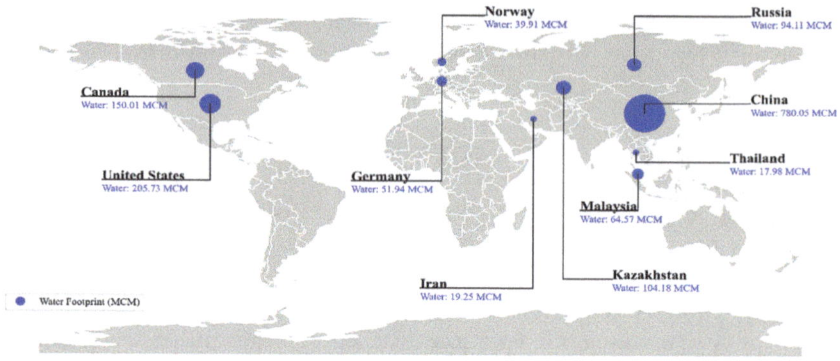

Fig. 19.8 Water footprint of BTC mining across the world (2020–2021). (*Source* The Hidden Environmental Cost of Cryptocurrency, UNU-INWEH (2023)

to cheap electricity and lax regulations making hydropower a common option for miners seeking cheap electricity. In response, as climate change calls for us to reduce the energy demand curve, bitcoin miners are using city-sized electricity supplies and the water used to generate them. The biggest environmental footprints for bitcoin are found in China (pre-ban) and the US, however, the rankings of the top bitcoin miners slightly change over time when countries are ranked based on their carbon, land, and water footprints rather than how much electricity they use for mining (Chamanara et al., 2023).

19.4 E-Waste: The Afterlife of Mining Hardware

In the competitive computational race of bitcoin mining, miners compete for block rewards based on their share of the network's total processing power. As newer, more efficient mining equipment emerges, older ones become obsolete and turn into electronic trash due to their inability to compete economically. Since specialized mining equipment has a limited lifespan, cryptocurrency mining generates massive amounts of electronic garbage directly adding to the mass of landfills. The most popular kind of Bitcoin mining equipment, Application-Specific Integrated Circuits (ASICs), only lasts 1.29 years before being replaced by more modern and effective models. This bitcoin mining equipment has a 1.29-year lifespan and the total BTC network's yearly equipment consumption is 30.7 metric kilotons (de Vries & Stoll, 2021). This e-trash is similar to the 30 metric kilotons of garbage generated by small IT and telecom equipment in the Netherlands in 2018 (Balde et al., n.d.).

Apart from the mining equipment, miners may produce additional e-waste from the use of cooling devices, computers, cables, and lights (de Vries & Stoll, 2021). The air-based cooling devices in mining sites and data centres require fans to move air throughout the building, causing lots of noise during the operation (Akbarnavasi et al., 2023). The e-waste generated by mining activities contains metals and toxic chemicals such as lead and mercury that might pollute the air, water, and land if not recycled properly. In 2019, 53.6 million metric tons of electronic waste were generated globally, and just 17.4% of the total waste was collected and recycled and this waste is predicted to double by 2050 (Wiwoho et al., 2024). According to the estimates of Digiconomist, the annual total e-waste in 2025 has reached 44.49 kt, where average e-waste per transaction generated is 303.30 grams, which is equivalent to the weight of 1.85 iPhone 12, as depicted in Fig. 19.9. Additionally, it shows a very sharp decline in e-waste during 2023–2024 and after bottoming out, the e-waste generation begins to climb again, although not yet back to peak levels.

19.4.1 *The Neighbourhood Effects of Cryptocurrency Mining*

Despite the fact that digital currency mining has a global impact on the environment, local communities are disproportionately impacted by the mining operations. To meet the mining industry's massive energy demands, local air pollution is exacerbated which are mostly met by fossil fuel power plants that emit sulphur dioxide, nitrogen oxides and particulate matter. These contaminants worsen the local population's cardiovascular and respiratory conditions. Along with air pollution, the water used to cool the mining operations, flows to the city's wastewater treatment plant, which requires $30 million for long term and $3 million for emergency repairs, will be borne by the local residents (Deroche, 2022). This thermal pollution can endanger health, wildlife biodiversity, local microclimates and stress ecosystems when waste heat from mining operations is released into the environment.

While all fossil fuel plants damage the air and water, bitcoin mining invites a new local hazard of noise pollution to constantly disturb nearby

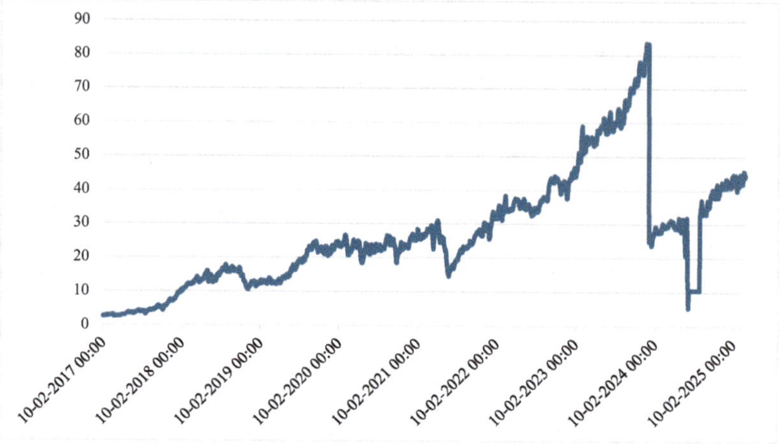

Fig. 19.9 Bitcoin electronic waste generation (kt) per year. (*Source* The data has been obtained from Digiconomist at https://digiconomist.net/bitcoin-electronic-waste-monitor/)

towns. The 24/7 operation of mining equipment produces noise pollution. Since bitcoin mining involves the use of ASICs and typically an ASIC's noise levels range from 50 to 75 dB, it is comparable to the noise levels of running vacuum cleaner or food blender ("The Basics of Mining", 2021). Additionally, constant operations of mining devices, enclosed spaces, and high-density electrical equipment produce tremendous amounts of heat, contributing to mining facility fires around the world. The industry's rapid expansion usually surpasses governmental oversight and safety regulations, with many plants establishing in the old warehouses and buildings which are not designed for high-intensity computing, causing fire explosions. For instance, a mining substation in Niagara Falls had been destroyed by an explosion and subsequent fire along with the power outage at one of their factories in North Tonawanda due to faulty equipment owned by the power utility (Wright, 2022). Due to these cumulative effects of mining operations, local residents face serious quality of life problems, including unsafe living circumstances due to fire hazards, poor health effects and noise-induced sleep issues.

19.5 Conclusion

Mining digital currencies is energy-intensive and has a detrimental effect on the environment since it degrades land, depletes water supplies and produces e-waste. Despite the carbon footprint taking centre stage in discussions, the industry's impact on water and land resources points to a larger ecological problem. Mining accelerates deforestation, reuses industrial land, and uses a lot of water, particularly in places where there is already a water shortage. The dangerous e-waste from the mining equipment that soon becomes outdated contributes to pollution and land degradation. Stricter regulations, shift to renewable energy sources, use of non-fresh water for cooling systems, and more efficient consensus mechanisms such as Proof-of-Stake are needed to mitigate these effects. Without systemic changes, the environmental costs of digital currency mining will continue to increase, compromising global sustainability goals.

Data Availability All the data used are publicly accessible. The data related to BTC emission intensity, total bitcoin greenhouse gas emissions, bitcoin electricity consumption by source and top 15 regions worldwide in BTC mining have been estimated by the Cambridge Centre for Alternative Finance and can be accessed at www.cbeci.org. The environmental footprint data for carbon, land, and water were extracted from https://digiconomist.net/bitcoin-energy-consumption and https://doi.org/https://doi.org/10.53328/INR23ASC02. Data for bitcoin electronic waste generation per year is available via Digiconomist at https://digiconomist.net/bitcoin-electronic-waste-monitor/.

References

Akbarnavasi, H., Ledari, M. B., & Ghadertootoonchi, A. (2023). An optimization strategy for enhancing energy consumption performance in digital currency miner's building. *Energy Conversion and Economics, 4*(2), 137–157. https://doi.org/10.1049/enc2.12085

Asif, R., & Hassan, S. R. (2023). Shaping the future of Ethereum: Exploring energy consumption in Proof-of-Work and Proof-of-Stake consensus. In *Frontiers in Blockchain* (Vol. 6). Frontiers Media SA. https://doi.org/10.3389/fbloc.2023.1151724

Baldé, C. P., & Van Den Brink, S. (n.d.). Monitoring exports of used Electrical and Electronic Equipment (EEE) from the Netherlands. Retrieved October 23, 2025, from https://www.nvmp.nl/uploads/pdf/nieuws/2012/raportfuture/Report%20The%20Dutch%20WEEE%20Flows.pdf

Bitcoin Energy Consumption Index - Digiconomist. (n.d.). Retrieved October 23, 2025, from https://digiconomist.net/bitcoin-energy-consumption

Bitcoin mining consumes more electricity than most countries, study suggests | Science, Climate & Tech News | Sky News. (n.d.). Retrieved October 23, 2025, from https://news.sky.com/story/bitcoin-mining-consumes-more-electricity-than-most-countries-study-suggests-12991456

Capponi, A., Olafsson, S., & Alsabah, H. (2021). *Proof-of-work cryptocurrencies: Does mining technology undermine decentralization?* http://arxiv.org/abs/2106.09783

Cambridge Centre for Alternative Finance. (n.d.). *Bitcoin GHG emissions*. University of Cambridge Judge Business School. Retrieved April 7, 2025, from https://ccaf.io/cbnsi/cbeci/ghg

Cambridge Centre for Alternative Finance. (n.d.). *Bitcoin mining map*. University of Cambridge Judge Business School. Retrieved April 7, 2025, from https://ccaf.io/cbnsi/cbeci/mining_map

Cambridge Blockchain Network Sustainability Index: CBECI: Change Log. (n.d.). Retrieved October 24, 2025, from https://ccaf.io/cbnsi/cbeci/change_log

Cambridge Blockchain Network Sustainability Index: CBECI. (n.d.). Retrieved October 23, 2025, from https://ccaf.io/cbnsi/cbeci

Cao, B., Zhang, Z., Feng, D., Zhang, S., Zhang, L., Peng, M., et al. (2020). Performance analysis and comparison of pow, pos and dag based blockchains. *Digital Communication and Networking, 6*, 480–485. https://doi.org/10.1016/j.dcan.2019.12.001

Chamanara, S., & Madani K. (2023). The hidden environmental cost of cryptocurrency: How bitcoin mining impacts climate, water and land. *United Nations University, Institute for Water, Environment and Health*. https://doi.org/10.53328/INR23ASC02

Chamanara, S., Ghaffarizadeh, S. A., & Madani, K. (2023). The environmental footprint of bitcoin mining across the globe: Call for urgent action. In *Earth's future* (Vol. 11, Issue 10). John Wiley and Sons Inc. https://doi.org/10.1029/202EF003871

Compass Mining. (2021, August 20). *The basics of mining bitcoin at home*. Compass Mining. https://compassmining.io/education/how-to-mine-bitcoin-at-home-basics/

de Vries, A. (2019). Renewable energy will not solve Bitcoin's sustainability problem. *Joule, 3*, 893–898. https://doi.org/10.1016/j.joule.2019.02.007

de Vries, A. (2024). Bitcoin's growing water footprint. *Cell Reports Sustainability, 1*(1), Article 100004. https://doi.org/10.1016/j.crsus.2023.100004

de Vries, A., & Stoll, C. (2021). Bitcoin's growing e-waste problem. *Resources, Conservation and Recycling, 175*. https://doi.org/10.1016/j.resconrec.2021.105901

Deroche, M. (2022). *The energy bomb: How proof-of-work cryptocurrency mining worsens the climate crisis and harms communities now.*

Earth Justice. https://earthjustice.org/wp-content/uploads/energy_bomb_bitcoin_white_paper_101322.pdf

Digiconomist. (2024, February 27). *A deep dive into cryptocurrency decentralization*. Digiconomist. https://digiconomist.net/a-deep-dive-into-cryptocurrency-decentralization/

Digiconomist. (2024). *Bitcoin energy consumption index*. Digiconomist. https://digiconomist.net/bitcoin-energy-consumption

Digiconomist. (2023). *Bitcoin electronic waste monitor*. https://digiconomist.net/bitcoin-electronic-waste-monitor/

Digital and virtual currencies for sustainable development | ESCAP. (n.d.). Retrieved October 23, 2025, from https://www.unescap.org/resources/digital-and-virtual-currencies-sustainable-development

Enerdata. (2024). *Electricity domestic consumption: World energy statistics*. Enerdata. https://yearbook.enerdata.net/electricity/electricity-domestic-consumption-data.html

Gilbert, A. Q., & Bazilian, M. D. (2020). Can Distributed nuclear power address energy resilience and energy poverty? In *Joule* (Vol. 4, Issue 9, pp. 1839–1843). Cell Press. https://doi.org/10.1016/j.joule.2020.08.005

GraniteShares. (n.d.). *Understanding mining difficulty and hash rate*. GraniteShares. Retrieved April 2025, from https://graniteshares.com/institutional/us/en-us/research/understanding-mining-difficulty-and-hash-rate/

Hebous, S., & Vernon, N. (2023, September). *Cryptocarbon: How much is the corrective tax?* WP/23/194.

International Energy Agency. (2021). *World energy outlook 2021*. IEA. https://www.iea.org/reports/world-energy-outlook-2021

Implication Of Crypto Mining In The Environment (2018–2024) | The Luxury Playbook. (n.d.). https://theluxuryplaybook.com/implication-of-crypto-mining-in-the-environment2018-2024

Lashkari, B., & Musilek, P. (2021). A comprehensive review of blockchain consensus mechanisms. In *IEEE Access* (Vol. 9, pp. 43620–43652). Institute of Electrical and Electronics Engineers Inc. https://doi.org/10.1109/ACCESS.2021.3065880

Li, J., Li, N., Peng, J., Cui, H., & Wu, Z. (2019). Energy consumption of cryptocurrency mining: A study of electricity consumption in mining cryptocurrencies. *Energy, 168*, 160–168.

Masanet, E., Shehabi, A., Lei, N., Vranken, H., Koomey, J., & Malmodin, J. (2019). Implausible projections overestimate near-term Bitcoin CO_2 emissions. *Nature Climate Change, 9*(9), 653–654.

Mora, C., Rollins, R. L., Taladay, K., Kantar, M. B., Chock, M. K., Shimada, M., & Franklin, E. C. (2018). Bitcoin emissions alone could push global warming above 2 C. *Nature Climate Change, 8*(11), 931–933. https://doi.org/10.1038/s41558-018-0321-8

Narayanan, A., Bonneau, J., Felten, E., Miller, A., & Goldfeder, S. (2016). *Bitcoin and cryptocurrency technologies: A comprehensive introduction*. Princeton University Press.

New data reveals timeline of China's bitcoin mining exodus—News & insight—Cambridge Judge Business School. (n.d.). Retrieved October 23, 2025, from https://www.jbs.cam.ac.uk/2021/new-data-reveals-timeline-of-chinas-bitcoin-mining-exodus/

On Bitcoin Energy Consumption A Quantitative Approach to a Subjective Question. (2021). www.galaxydigital.io/research.

Onat, N. C., Jabbar, R., Kucukvar, M., Wakjira, T., Kutty, A. A., & Fetais, N. (2024). Carbon footprint of global Bitcoin mining: Emissions beyond borders. *Sustainability Science*. https://doi.org/10.1007/s11625-024-01576-5

Otero, P. (n.d.). Carbon footprint: What it is and how to calculate it. Manglai. https://www.manglai.io/en/blog/carbon-footprint-what-it-is-how-to-calculate

Read, C. L. (2022). *Weighing the Economic and Environmental Costs and Benefits THE BITCOIN DILEMMA*. https://doi.org/10.1007/978-3-031-09138-4

Samford, H., & Domingo, F. (2019, July 10). *The political geography and environmental impacts of cryptocurrency mining*. Henry M. Jackson School of International Studies. https://jsis.washington.edu/news/the-political-geography-and-environmental-impacts-of-cryptocurrency-mining/

Singh, G. (2023, December 6). *Unveiling Bitcoin's water consumption with Alex de Vries*. Greenpeace. https://www.greenpeace.org/usa/unveiling-bitcoins-water-consumption-with-alex-devries/

Statista. (2024). *Global Bitcoin energy consumption from 2017 to 2023*. Statista. https://www.statista.com/statistics/881472/worldwide-bitcoin-energy-consumption/

Stoll, C., Klaaßen, L., & Gallersdörfer, U. (2019). The carbon footprint of Bitcoin. *Joule, 3*(7), 1647–1661. https://doi.org/10.1016/j.joule.2019.05.012

Stoll, C., Klaaßen, L., Gallersdörfer, U., & Neumüller, A. (2025). *Climate impacts of bitcoin mining in the US*. https://www.jstor.org/stable/resrep51839

Sullivan. (2022, October 25). Renewable energy is slowing the rise of carbon emissions. *Smithsonian Magazine*. https://www.smithsonianmag.com/smart-news/renewable-energy-is-slowing-the-rise-of-carbon-emissions-180980988/

Tang. (2024, November 19). *Cryptocurrency's carbon catastrophe: The clash between climate goals and energy-intensive mining*. http://www.cpreview.org/articles/2024/11/cryptocurrencys-carbon-catastrophe-the-clash-between-climate-goals-and-energy-intensive-mining-1

Tashev. (2024, December 16). *8 largest bitcoin farms globally*. Webopedia. https://www.webopedia.com/crypto/learn/bitcoin-mining-farms/

Taylor, M. B. (2017). The Evolution of Bitcoin Hardware. *Computer, 50*(09), 58–66. https://doi.org/10.1109/MC.2017.3571056

Tiseo. (2025, January 15). *Greenhouse gas emissions worldwide-statistics & facts*. Statista. https://www.statista.com/topics/5770/global-greenhouse-gas-emissions/#topicOverview

The Source Magazine. (2018, September 3). How Bitcoin's footprint is impacting water use. https://thesourcemagazine.org/how-bitcoins-footprint-is-impacting-water-use/

United Nations University. (2023, October 24). *UN study reveals hidden environmental impacts of Bitcoin: Carbon is not the only harmful product*. https://unu.edu/press-release/un-study-reveals-hidden-environmental-impacts-bitcoin-carbon-not-only-harmful-product

Wendl, M., Doan, M. H., & Sassen, R. (2023). The environmental impact of cryptocurrencies using proof of work and proof of stake consensus algorithms: A systematic review. *Journal of Environmental Management, 326*, 116530. https://doi.org/10.1016/J.JENVMAN.2022.116530

Wiwoho, J., Trinugroho, I., Kharisma, D. B., & Suwadi, P. (2024). Cryptocurrency mining policy to protect the environment. *Cogent Social Sciences, 10*(1). https://doi.org/10.1080/23311886.2024.2323755

Wright, T. (2022, May 20). *3K Bit Digital hosting partner's crypto miners go offline after explosion and fire*. Cointelegraph. https://cointelegraph.com/news/3k-bit-digital-hosting-partner-s-crypto-miners-go-offline-after-explosion-and-fire

Zhang, W. (2022). The current situation and trend of blockchain technology in the financial field. *Mobile Information Systems, 2022*. https://doi.org/10.1155/2022/7908625

Index

R. Aneja and R. Dygas (eds.), *Digital Currencies and the Green Economy*, https://doi.org/10.1007/978-981-95-2282-8

Kolibri 360 GmbH
Ferdinand-Jühlke-Straße 7
99095 Erfurt, Deutschland
produktsicherheit@kolibri360.de